REVELATION

DR. SIEGBERT W. BECKER
1914-1984

REVELATION
The Distant Triumph Song

Siegbert W. Becker

NORTHWESTERN PUBLISHING HOUSE
Milwaukee, Wisconsin

Fourth printing, 2013
Third printing, 2008
Second printing, 1988

Library of Congress Card 84-60230
Northwestern Publishing House
1250 N. 113th St., Milwaukee, WI 53226-3284
www.nph.net

Published 1985
Printed in the United States of America
ISBN 978-0-8100-0190-9

CONTENTS

Acknowledgements

The author owes a debt of deep gratitude to Professors David Kuske and Armin Panning, co-workers in the New Testament Department of the faculty of Wisconsin Lutheran Seminary, who have read the manuscript and have made many valuable suggestions for improvement, almost all of which were adopted. Special thanks are due to Mrs. Robert (Cornelia) Rude for her faithful and diligent labors in transcribing a manuscript that should probably have been rewritten and to Dr. Robert G. Hoerber for his critical review and careful reading of the galleys. Thanks are due also to the Aid Association for Lutherans of Appleton, Wisconsin, for a grant that underwrote the cost of the preparation of the manuscript.

May the Lord of the church use this commentary for the edification of his people and the glory of his name.

S.W.B.

FOREWORD

Perhaps no other book of the Bible has been so grossly misinterpreted as the book of Revelation. Already in the early church false teachers used this book to introduce millennialistic views into the theology of the church. Though these views were not incorporated into any of the three ecumenical creeds, the Apostles', the Nicene and the Athanasian, yet they continued to trouble the church. Today the majority of Protestant churches, even many Lutherans, teach a full-blown doctrine of a final great tribulation, a rapture, and a thousand-year (millennial) reign of Christ here on earth at the end of time. Even bumper stickers have been used to spread the message.

But is the millennial error really that serious? Yes, it is. Since according to millennialistic doctrine the millennium will take place before judgment day, the implication is that we really need not worry about the judgment day at all. We'll have plenty of warning — at least a thousand years! This, however, totally violates what our Lord Jesus says in Luke 12 and 21: "Be ready, because the Son of Man will come at an hour when you do not expect him. . . . Be careful, or your hearts will be weighed down with dissipation, drunkenness and the anxieties of life, and that day will close on you unexpectedly like a trap. For it will come upon all those who live on the face of the whole earth. Be always on the watch, and pray that you may be able to escape all that is about to happen, and that you may be able to stand before the Son of Man." This is the underlying concern of the author of this commentary, Dr. Siegbert W. Becker, who served as chairman of the New Testament Department at Wisconsin Lutheran Seminary in Mequon, Wisconsin until 1984.

Dr. Becker bases his commentary on the original Greek text. Yet he writes in a style anyone can follow and understand. This commentary is not meant only for scholars and pastors. In his book Dr. Becker addresses himself to many of the questions put to him by students in his classroom and laymen in his Bible lecture courses.

Dr. Becker's introductory words are especially noteworthy. The last two centuries have witnessed the rise of the historical-critical method of Bible interpretation, a method which sounds very scholarly and scientific but rejects everything the Bible says about itself. Unfortunately, this method of interpretation is accepted today by the majority of theologians. But not by Dr. Becker. He makes a point of exposing the fallacies of this method and himself uses the scripturally correct method of looking at the words of Scripture from the grammatical-historical point of view. As we follow his exposition, we come face to face with the Spirit of God, as Jesus tells us in John 16, "But when he, the Spirit of truth, comes, he will guide you into all truth. He will not speak on his own; he will speak only what he hears, and he will tell you what is yet to come. He will bring glory to me by taking from what is mine and making it known to you. All that belongs to the Father is mine. That is why I said the Spirit will take from what is mine and make it known to you." The author of this commentary succeeds marvelously well in bringing the reader and student face to face with what the Spirit has to say.

Anyone who reads this commentary will profit personally from it. And he will also be the better prepared to bring others face to face with the Redeemer so that they too will be ready to stand before the Son of Man on the last and great day. In spirit we join the Apostle John and the author of this commentary in listening to our Lord as he closes the final book of the New Testament with the words, "He who testifies to these things says, 'Yes, I am coming soon,' " and then the saints, past and present, in praying, "Amen. Come, Lord Jesus."

Harold E. Wicke

REVELATION
The Distant Triumph Song

The Revelation of St. John

THE MESSAGE OF THE BOOK

The prophecies of John in Revelation exhibit an interesting parallelism to the predictions of the Old Testament prophets. When those ancient spokesmen for God portrayed the coming Messiah they often seemed to contradict one another or even themselves. On the one hand, they spoke of the promised Savior as a conquering king who would destroy his enemies and rule over all the nations of the earth. On the other, they saw him as the suffering servant, who would be wounded, bruised, spit upon, and rejected by men.

In a similar way John speaks of the followers of the Messiah as kings and priests. They will "reign on the earth" (5:10). When they die, their departed souls will "reign with him (Christ) for a thousand years" (20:6). After the resurrection in the new heaven and the new earth "they will reign for ever and ever" (22:5).

But just as Christ came to glory and exaltation by way of humiliation and death (Php 2:6-11), just as he was made "perfect through suffering" (He 2:10), so the royal priesthood of believers must also expect to come to the crown of life by way of the cross.

When the Old Testament believers contemplated the seemingly contradictory prophecies concerning a Messiah who was both a conquering king and a suffering servant, they often must have been puzzled as to how both prophetic portrayals could be true. As believing children of God they certainly believed that both sets of statements were true and gave the Holy Ghost credit for being more learned than they were. But that the Jews did find the prophecies perplexing is evident in their ancient theological development. Some of the ancient Jews tried to solve the problem by teaching that there would be two Messiahs, one a priest from the tribe of Levi who would be a great sufferer, the other a king from the tribe of Judah who would be a great conqueror. If they had paid careful attention to the words of the prophets they would have known that such a solution was inconsistent with the clear statements of the Old Testament. The words of Zechariah, "He shall be a priest upon his throne," should have been enough to avert such an erroneous solution. The suffering priest and the victorious ruler were evidently one and the same.

Other Jews, we might even say the majority of them, escaped the dilemma by ignoring the prophecies that spoke of the sufferings of the Messiah. Instead, they emphasized the passages that spoke of his glory and victorious might. As a result, the Jews became more and more millennial in their hopes. More and more they failed to see that the redemption of the world would come through the suffering of the Messiah, on whom the Lord would lay "the iniquity of us all." Instead they began to envision a Messianic victory, not over sin and death and Satan, but over earthly enemies. They basked in dreams of an earthly king who would come to glory through a military conquest by the application of his almighty power.

How firmly this carnal concept of the Messiah's mission was fixed in the minds of the Jews is apparent even in the reaction of the disciples when the Savior first announced his suffering and death. It is significant that Jesus withheld this announcement until about six months before Good Friday. It came only after the disciples had come to the firm conviction which Peter expressed, "You are the Christ, the Son of the living God" (Mt 16:16). For two and a half years they had seen his power at work in the miracles, healing the sick, bringing hearing to the deaf and sight to the blind, cleansing lepers, commanding water to become wine, feeding multitudes with a handful of food, ordering the stormy sea to obey and devils to depart from those whom they had possessed. They had seen the conquering king in action, doing what the Old Testament prophets said he would do. And they were convinced that the Messiah had come.

But then "Jesus began to explain to his disciples that he must go to Jerusalem and suffer many things . . . and that he must be killed" (Mt 16:21). To that announcement Peter's response was, "Never, Lord! This shall never happen to you." Even at that late stage in their training the apostles still found it difficult to understand how the conquering king could be the suffering servant.

In the following months Jesus spoke to them often about his impending suffering and death, and after each report of such an announcement at least one of the evangelists tells us that they did not understand what the Savior was talking about. It perplexed them until after they saw the risen Savior ascend to the right hand of God and were instructed by the Holy Ghost on Pentecost. Then they understood how the Messiah had become the king of the universe through suffering and death, by conquering sin, death and the devil.

A similar problem faced the church of the New Testament. Peter had taught the early Christians that they were a "royal priesthood" (1 Pe 2:9). From the Apostle Paul they had learned that the universe was theirs (1 Cor 3:21-23). On the night before he died, the Savior had told his first followers, "I confer on you a kingdom" (Lk 22:29), and how they understood those words becomes clear from the question they asked on the day of the ascension, "Lord, are you at this time going to restore the kingdom to Israel?" (Ac 1:6). They were still infected with the disease of millennialism.

We can sympathize with them in their ignorance, even though we cannot excuse it. Members of the struggling young church were suffering exile and the confiscation of their property, and even the loss of life itself, because of their loyalty to the gospel. We can hardly blame them if sometimes they found it difficult to see the truth of Paul's words, "All things are yours, whether Paul or Apollos or Cephas or the world or life or death or the present or the future — all are yours" (1 Cor 3:21f).

In such a time of testing the book of Revelation was written. The Roman authorities were making a concerted effort to wipe out the infant church. John was in exile, and the church was undergoing great tribulation. In such a time of danger and temptation the Savior once more rephrased the lesson his church should have learned from his victory. Like the Savior himself, they too were kings and priests. But the manifestation of their kingship and their priesthood was to come only after suffering and death. "We live by faith, not by sight" (2 Cor 5:7).

It is a lesson we all need to learn. Reason fairly concludes that the sons of millionaires should live in mansions and drive expensive cars. We are the sons and daughters of the great King who created and possesses the earth and everything in it. Knowing this, we are tempted to dream about a millennial kingdom. To combat this temptation the Apostle John wrote his Revelation, which happens to be the most anti-millennial book in the whole Bible. In it John teaches us not to look for victories in this world and in this life. Instead, Revelation reminds us of the words of the Savior, "In this world you will have trouble. But take heart! I have overcome the world" (Jn 16:33). Christ's victory belongs to us indeed — for all eternity!

> And when the fight is fierce, the warfare long,
> Steals on the ear the distant triumph song;
> And hearts are brave again, and arms are strong.
> Alleluia! Alleluia! Amen.

THE CANONICITY OF THE BOOK

Eusebius, the father of church history, who was active in the beginning of the fourth century, divided the books of the New Testament into two classes, the "homologoumena" and the "antilegomena." He also identified another group of books, which he did not consider part of the inspired Word of God. These he called the "spurious" books. The homologoumena were those books which all Christians agreed were inspired and part of the canon. The antilegomena were those books of the New Testament which the great majority of Christians accepted but concerning whose canonical authority some early church fathers expressed doubt. The spurious books were those the great majority of Christians rejected from the canon.

The antilegomena, according to Eusebius, were Hebrews, James, 2 Peter, 2 and 3 John and Jude. Usually the book of Revelation also is called an antilegomenon. Eusebius, however, did not classify it as such. His remarks about Revelation are rather strange. He includes it first in the homologoumena, but then later in the same context he suggests that it might also be grouped with the "spurious" books. But why the appearance of this contradiction?

On the one hand, it seems that Eusebius could find little, if any, objection to the canonicity of Revelation in the writings of the early church fathers, whom he used as sources in the writing of his history. But on the other hand, at the time of Eusebius false teachers were using the book of Revelation to introduce Jewish millennialistic views into the theology of the Christian church. During the intertestamental period the concept of the coming Messiah had grown more and more secularized, and the idea of a thousand years of peace during which the Messiah would set up his kingdom here on earth had become rather common. Salvation was pictured in terms that grew more and more carnal. The reign of the Messiah was portrayed as a time when every grape vine would put out a thousand branches, and every branch would bear a thousand bunches of grapes, and every bunch would contain a thousand grapes, and every grape would produce a thousand gallons of wine.

The only similarity between these Jewish views and the book of Revelation is found in Revelation 20, where John speaks of a thousand years during which the souls of those who were beheaded for their faith would live and reign with Christ. It seems that instead of engaging in careful exegesis and showing the impossibility of reconciling the views of Jewish millennialism with Revelation 20, the later church fathers, such as Eusebius, simply began to suspect that the book might contain false doctrine and therefore could not be canonical. As a result, the book of Revelation came to be classified as an antilegomenon.

It is against this background that Luther's attitude toward this book must be viewed. When he translated the Bible into German, he added prefaces to all the books. In these prefaces he discussed such questions as the authorship, date and contents of the individual books. In the earliest prefaces to Revelation he expresses the opinion that the book could not be the work of an apostle. His reasoning sounds rather strange. He says, first of all, that it is the very nature of an apostle to write clearly. This book, he says, is not written in clear language and therefore cannot be the work of an apostle.

Luther's second reason is just as strange. He says that the author praises himself too highly. Luther does not give examples of what he has in mind, but he must, in part, have reference to the benefits that the book promises to those who read it. But if we accept the claims to inspiration which are made in the book, such benefits are promised not in the human author's name but in the name of Christ, whose word it is. Luther can hardly have objected to the claims of inspiration in principle, because he accepts such claims when they are made in other books of the Bible.

Luther's third reason is the strangest of all. He says that Christ is neither known nor taught in the book. Yet we can say that from the first verse of the book, where it is called the Revelation "of Jesus Christ," to the last prayer in which the apostle prays, "Even so, come, Lord Jesus," the Savior occupies a central position in the book.

To understand how it was possible for Luther to speak in this way about a book from which the Lutheran Church later chose the epistle lesson for Reformation Day (Rev. 14:6,7), it is necessary to review the situation as it obtained at that time.

Luther's first acquaintance with the Bible came through the

Vulgate, the Latin translation of the Bible. In this Bible, the Old Testament apocrypha were printed together with the canonical books. Luther became convinced that the apocrypha were not part of the inspired Scriptures. It might be mentioned in this connection that it was not until after Luther's death that the Roman Church at the Council of Trent for the first time officially declared the apocrypha to be canonical. St. Jerome, the translator of the Vulgate, denied the canonicity of at least some of the apocryphal books. Luther therefore held a view of the apocrypha which at that time was not heretical even in Roman eyes. When he published his German Bible, he moved the apocrypha out of the place they occupied in the Vulgate. Instead, he published them as an appendix to the Old Testament which was preceded by a note that these books were not inspired by God, yet good and useful to read. Luther especially appreciated the common sense displayed in the Wisdom of Sirach, and he believed that Judith and Tobit were edifying literature.

In the New Testament Luther was aware of a situation that was in some ways similar. There were no New Testament apocryphal books that had ever been a part of the Greek New Testament, just as the Old Testament apocrypha had never been a part of the Hebrew Bible. But there were some books about which the early church had not been in unanimous agreement. For that reason Luther, too, had some doubts about their canonicity. Yet he never treated the New Testament antilegomena as he had treated the Old Testament apocrypha. They were not treated as an appendix to the New Testament with a separate heading that unequivocally denied their inspiration. He did rearrange the order of the New Testament books so that Hebrews, James, Jude, and Revelation were printed at the end. He did not change the position of 2 Peter and 2 and 3 John.

It is true that in his early prefaces Luther denies the apostolic origin of these books. His severest remarks are made about James and Revelation. Of James he says in his first edition of the New Testament, "I do not want him in my Bible." This is perhaps as close as he ever came to giving any of the antilegomena the same treatment he accorded to the Old Testament apocrypha, but this remark disappears from the later prefaces to James. However, it would seem that to the end of his life he had his doubts about the canonicity of James.

Luther's attitude toward Revelation also changed noticeably

through the years. The last edition of Luther's German Bible, which was published in the year before his death, shows that he had modifed his position rather significantly. By that time, his early remark, "My spirit cannot accommodate itself to this book," as well as his severest strictures against the book had disappeared from the preface completely. After citing the doubts of some of the fathers about the Johannine authorship, Luther writes, "For our part, we still share this doubt. By that, however, no one should be prevented from regarding this as the work of John the apostle."

Lutherans have often taken their cue from Luther's early preface and treated this last book of the New Testament with neglect. However, if, instead of leaving the interpretation of this book to the millennialists, Lutheran scholars would have paid more attention to it, the folly of the millennialistic interpretation of the book would have been made clear. Even if the book contains many exegetical conundrums and even if there is much in the book that we do not fully understand, yet it is still true that some of the most beautiful and comforting passages in the New Testament are found in this book. It is surely not difficult to see why Luther in later years no longer said that Christ is neither known nor taught in the book. Where will you find a more beautiful doxology in praise of the Savior than that found in the first chapter, "To him who loves us and has freed us from our sins by his blood, and has made us to be a kingdom and priests to serve his God and Father — to him be glory and power for ever and ever" (1:5f). Where is the evangelical Christian who does not with a happy heart join in the song sung to the Lamb in chapter five, "You are worthy to take the scroll and to open its seals, because you were slain and with your blood you purchased men for God from every tribe and language and people and nation. You made them to be a kingdom and priests to serve our God, and they will reign on the earth" (5:9f). And what Christian does not long for the day when we shall stand before the throne and before the Lamb with that great host arrayed in white, of whom it is said, "These are they who have come out of the great tribulation; they have washed their robes and made them white in the blood of the Lamb. Therefore they are before the throne of God, and serve him day and night in his temple; and he who sits on the throne will spread his tent over them. Never again will they hunger; never again will they thirst. The sun will not beat upon them, nor any scorching heat.

For the Lamb at the center of the throne will be their shepherd; he will lead them to springs of living water. And God will wipe away every tear from their eyes" (7:14-17).

The present writer's view is that there is really no good reason for doubting the canonicity of the Revelation of John, and that the book has special value and significance just for our time when Christians are again being persecuted and when the visible church to such a large degree has drifted into apostasy and away from simple childlike faith in the promises of the gospel.

THE AUTHOR

As we have already seen, Luther, taking his cue from Eusebius, whom he specifically cites in this connection, expressed his doubts about the Johannine authorship. But a closer look reveals that Eusebius misread his sources. As evidence for his position that the Apostle John did not write the Revelation Eusebius quotes from the writings of Papias. He says that Papias speaks of two men called John, one of whom he mentions "with Peter and James and Matthew, and the other apostles" and another John, who together with a man named Aristion is not included in the number of the apostles and is distinguished from them "plainly by the name of presbyter." Eusebius seems to have overlooked, or did not want to see, that in this particular context Papias does not call Peter and James and Matthew "apostles," as Eusebius says, but he calls all of them "elders," or "presbyters." Therefore the title "presbyter" does not necessarily mean that this John is "another" John. In fact, Papias does not apply the title "presbyter" to Aristion. Therefore it would seem that he singles John out as a "presbyter" to make it clear that, unlike Aristion, he is in the same class with Matthew, Peter, James, etc.

Moreover, there is a clear explanation in the text itself for the double mention of John. The point is lost in the English translation of Eusebius which is commonly used. There Papias is quoted as saying, "If I met with anyone who had been a follower of the elders (presbyters) anywhere, I made it a point to inquire what were the declarations of the elders (presbyters), what was said by Andrew, Peter, or Philip. What by Thomas, James, John, Matthew, or any other of the disciples of our Lord. What was said by Aristion, and the presbyter John, disciples of the Lord" (HE, III, 39). According to the original Greek text of

Eusebius, however, the last sentence should read, not "What *was said* by Aristion and the presbyter John," but rather, "What *is being said* by Aristion and the presbyter John," for the Greek verb is in the present tense, and the double mention of John is explained by the fact that the Apostle John was still living at the time of which Papias is speaking. It might be pointed out also that in his second and third epistles the Apostle John gives himself the title "elder," or "presbyter."

Eusebius also quotes Dionysius of Alexandria as another of the early fathers who had his doubts about the Johannine authorship. Dionysius gives several reasons for his doubt. It is significant that he does not quote any earlier church fathers but limits himself to questions of literary style. He says that although this John mentions himself several times as the author of Revelation, the Apostle John does not do this in his Gospel nor in any of his three letters. He mentions also that there were two monuments to John in Ephesus, and from this he concludes that there must have been two men by the name of John who were prominent there and that the second must be the author of the Revelation. He cites also many similarities between the Gospel and the First Epistle of John and says that the Revelation has "not even a syllable in common with them" (HE VII, 25). His final reason for rejecting the authorship of John he finds in the "poor Greek style" of the Revelation.

Thanks to the weakness of such arguments, we have little reason to doubt the apostolic origin of this book. The author calls himself John in both the first and last chapter, and the authority he claims for his writing in both of those chapters would ill befit anyone who does not speak at the commission of Christ. If the author is not the Apostle John, then Luther is right when he says that he praises his own work too highly. Moreover, in this book we have one of the strongest claims to inspiration found anywhere in the New Testament. He hears and writes the words and the revelation of Jesus Christ. When he calls himself the "servant" or "slave" of Jesus Christ, he speaks in the same terms Paul, Peter, James and Jude used to introduce themselves in their letters.

Besides this, contrary to the opinion expressed by Dionysius of Alexandria, there are many points of similarity between Revelation, on the one hand, and the fourth Gospel and the First Epistle of John, on the other. We will mention only a few. In the First Epistle John speaks of the blood of Christ that cleanses us from all sin (1:7); the book of Revelation speaks of those who have washed their robes and made them white in the blood of the Lamb (7:14). Besides, John's Gospel, his First Epistle and the book of Revelation are the only books of the New Testament that call the second person of the Holy Trinity the "Word" of God. John's Gospel speaks of a twofold resurrection (5:25-29) and the Revelation in chapter 20 also speaks of two resurrections.

The author of Revelation is either the Apostle John or someone who is trying very hard to give the impression that he speaks with apostolic authority. The only real choice open to us if we take the words of the book at face value is either to reject it outright or else to accept it as part of the canon. This much already appears to be clear from the strange classification of this book in the *History* of Eusebius. Either it is canonical or it is spurious.

It is true that the Greek style in which Revelation is written is significantly different from that found in the other writings of John, as Dionysius of Alexandria points out. There may be several explanations for the difference. First of all, we know that the apostles, as well as the prophets, often used secretaries in reducing their preaching to writing. There is nothing in the doctrine of verbal inspiration that would keep the Holy Ghost from using suggestions as to wording and style from these secretaries, who were also sometimes permitted to add remarks of their own (*e.g.*, Rm 16:22). John very likely had such help in writing his Gospel, for otherwise it is difficult to explain the plural pronoun in the second last verse of that book. But on Patmos, where the visions of the Apocalypse were seen and written down, John had no such help.

It seems very clear also that some of the grammatical irregularities found in the book are deliberate and significant. There is no question that the apostle knew that the Greek preposition ἀπό takes the genitive case. He uses it with the genitive in the same sentence in which he writes, ἀπὸ ὁ ὢν καὶ ὁ ἦν καὶ ὁ ἐρχόμενος (from him who is and who was and who is to come). So when he here uses ἀπὸ with the nominative case, contrary to the rules of Greek grammar, it seems rather obvious that the phrase is being used as an indeclinable proper name for the immutable God, who has called himself "Jahweh," "I AM THAT I AM," in the Old Testament.

A third reason for the difference in style is to be found in the radically different type of material treated in the book. Because of this we should hesitate to deny the apostolic authorship of the book on the basis of what we perceive as a few irregularities in the grammar.

Those who speak a foreign language may find it relatively easy to converse and to write the language so long as they are dealing with the language of their profession. Yet, at the same time, they may have difficulty as soon as they begin to deal with subjects that are less familiar. For example, Lutheran pastors in America who still use German perhaps have little difficulty with the language when they use it to present the teachings of Scripture, but when they seek to employ an illustration taken from an area other than the Bible, they have difficulty rendering that illustration in German, and the difficulty in groping for the proper German words often carries over into the German grammar. For those who are experienced in such things the language of Revelation should present no special problem.

And the "problem" takes on even less signficance when one remembers that a mistake in grammar does not constitute a mistake in fact. "He stopped by our place on his way home," may make an editor cringe, but not because the author's message is unclear.

THE DATE OF WRITING

When John wrote Revelation, he was in exile for his faith and the church was undergoing persecution. There were two periods of widespread persecution in the first century, one during the last years of Nero in the mid-sixties and the other during the reign of Domitian in the early nineties. There are some who believe that the book was produced during the reign of Nero, but most scholars agree that it was written during the later persecution.

THE PLACE OF WRITING

The Revelation is one of the few books of the New Testament which leaves no room for argument about the place where it was written. John tells us that at the time of his vision he was in exile on the island of Patmos, off the coast of Asia Minor, not far from Ephesus, the city in which John, according to the tradition of the church, served as pastor of the congregation during the last years of his life (1:9).

THE OCCASION AND PURPOSE

We have already noted that the book was written during a time of persecution. John himself was on Patmos "because of the Word of God and the testimony of Jesus Christ" (1:9). Christians could expect to be cast into prison (2:10). A Christian by the name of Antipas had suffered a martyr's death (2:13). Others were being beheaded for their faith (6:9-11; 20:4).

Efforts were thus being made to destroy the Christian faith and to wipe out the Christian church. Under the inspiration of God, John wrote to comfort the infant church, to remind God's people that they could expect to experience such things and to assure the church of final victory. The book of Revelation might be viewed as a commentary on two Bible passages, namely, "We must through much tribulation enter into the kingdom of God" (Ac 14:22), and "The gates of hell shall not prevail against" the church (Mt 16:18).

THE INTERPRETATION OF THE BOOK

The Greek word for Revelation is Ἀποκάλυψις, and this book is often called also in English by the Anglicized form of the Greek name, the Apocalypse. It has also given its name to a type or form of literature that is found already in the Old Testament, which became popular during the intertestamental period and did not die out even in early New Testament times. In the Old Testament especially the books of Daniel and Ezekiel contain much apocalyptic writing. In a very general way, apocalyptic writing may be defined as an effort to portray the future by means of strange and even fantastic symbolism.

Unbelieving, critical scholars usually hold that, since prophecy in the sense of long-range prediction is impossible, the authors of apocalyptic works usually portray events of their own time or the recent past with perhaps a few shrewd guesses about the future. These scholars usually view apocalyptic books as attacks on the authorities of the day. Therefore, according to them, the writers had to veil their messages in strange symbols which the intended readers would understand, but which would remain a mystery to the persecuting government officials. The authors of apocalyptic literature, they contend, usually wrote pseudonymously, commonly letting their productions claim authorship by one of the great figures of past ecclesiastical history. Apocalyptic literature, so the critical theory goes, is usually written during times of persecution or suffering and always holds out the hope for a better day to come.

On the basis of such a definition of apocalyptic, the book of Daniel, for example, is said to be written, not by the Prophet Daniel, but by some unknown author who lived during the reign of Antiochus Epiphanes. This unknown author pretended to be the Prophet Daniel and, in Daniel's name, described events of his own time in terms of prophecies supposedly written by Daniel.

Such false views are so wedded to the term "apocalyptic" in the historical-critical method of Bible interpretation and its literature that we perhaps ought to hesitate to describe this last book of the New Testament in such terms without further explanation.

One hermeneutical view of the Revelation is based on such modern denigrations of all apocalyptic literature. It is the so-called "preterist" view, which holds that the events portrayed in the book in symbolic terms had already taken place or were taking place when the book was written or that they were clearly foreseeable at the time of writing. This view must be rejected by anyone who takes the book at face value and considers it to be the inspired and inerrant Word of God in the normal meaning of that term.

A second view, which must also be rejected, is the "futuristic" interpretation. This approach to the message of the book holds that the events described here still lie in the future and will be fulfilled in the final period of the history of this present world. It is said that the visions in the book foretell a literal seven years of "great tribulation," the "rapture," and the "millennial reign" of Christ. The refutation of this view shall not detain us here, even though it is one of the tragedies of modern conservative Protestantism and even though more and more people are being exposed to such views and have their morbid curiosity about the future tickled by them.

A Bible-believing Lutheran, who, together with the Augsburg Confession, rejects the "Jewish opinions" read into Revelation by many fundamentalistic Protestants, is left with a choice between two views concerning the interpretation of Revelation. Probably the most popular view among Lutherans of earlier times was what might be called the "church-historical" interpretation. This was the view held by Martin Luther and most orthodox Lutheran commentators until recent times. This method may be illustrated by pointing out that Luther says that in the vision of the seven trumpets which begins in chapter eight, the first angel is Tatian, the second Marcion, the third Origen, the fourth Novatian, the fifth Arius, and the sixth Mohammed. Another example of this approach to the book is found in the later Lutheran interpretation which held that the angel "flying in the midst of heaven having the everlasting gospel to preach" (Rv 14:6) was a clear prediction concerning Martin Luther and the Lutheran Reformation. Lutheran churches use this passage as the historic Epistle for Reformation Day.

The proponents of this method of interpreting Revelation, which seeks a specific personage or event in each symbolic detail in the book, generally have their heart in the right place and understand the basic message of the book very well. Luther, for example, comments that the vision of the seven trumpets assures us that "even under heretics, Christendom will have good angels and the pure word," a remark which is very much in place.

Nevertheless, this method of reading the book has perhaps contributed a great deal to the hesitation with which the book is often approached. Many things that are said by Lutheran commentators who use this method must be labeled as pure guesswork that always leaves the hearer in doubt unless he is willing to accept human opinion as authoritative. Luther may be right when he says that the third angel is Origen, and the interpreter may sometimes be inclined to believe that the Reformer is very close to being right when he says that the sixth angel is Mohammed, but no matter how hard one tries, one cannot become absolutely certain about such a specific interpretation. We are always inclined to ask such commentators, "How do you know that?" Moreover, what is to prevent a commentator from saying that the angel flying in the midst of heaven having the everlasting gospel to preach is C. F. W. Walther or Adolph Hoenecke?

Luther himself gives us the clue to the proper reading of the book in his general observations. At the conclusion of his remarks on the vision of the seven trumpets he writes, "The scholars who know history will be able to figure this out, for it would take too long to relate and prove everything here." Yet it is also clear that Luther himself did not hold strictly to a church-historical interpretation. That is evident when he says, "The second (angel) is Marcion, with his Cataphrygians, Manichaeans, Montanists, etc., who extol their own spirituality above all the Scriptures, and who move, like the burning mountain, between heaven and earth, as, for example, Muenzer, and the fanatics in our day." Luther, thus, is not nearly as specific as may appear at first glance. He realizes that the symbols are drawn in broad outline and have their application in every age and to a variety of circumstances.

In this way Luther foreshadows what may be called, for want of a better name, the "idealistic" interpretation. In this view the red horse of chapter six is not a symbol for any specific war, but a symbolic portrayal of every war that has brought great tribulation to men; the black horse symbolizes not any specific famine in the end times but every famine that has raised the price of food out of reach. The smoke from the bottomless pit which obscures the sun in chapter nine is not one specific heresy, but every false doctrine that obscures the light of the gospel. In this interpretation the flying angel with the everlasting gospel to preach is not specifically Martin Luther and the Lutheran Reformation but every movement in the church carrying the clear gospel to the ends of the earth. That does not mean that the symbols may not fit some of these movements better than others. The idealistic interpretation does not prevent us from using Revelation 14:6 as a Reformation text, but it refuses to limit the interpretation to one specific time and one specific event. I would not hesitate to suggest that the angel is flying more or less vigorously in the Wisconsin Synod today and that apostate Protestantism, also, is a part of Babylon. Luther was very likely not far from the truth when he said that the sixth angel with his hordes of horsemen from the east is a symbol for the armies of Mohammedanism.

The idealistic intepretation enables us to read the book of Revelation as a clear book. The broad outlines of this book and its basic teachings are generally very clear. But just as we create difficulties for ourselves when we try to interpret every detail of a parable and in so doing often make the interpretation uncertain and the parable unclear, so we must guard against interpreting the Apocalypse in every detail. Symbolic and figurative language must never be pressed beyond the point of comparison. That does not mean that the symbols are arbitrary and can be interpreted any way at all. There is a reason why the Savior is described as a lamb and the devil is pictured as a great red dragon. Those who remember that the Savior told his disciples to let their light shine will know why the seven golden candlesticks are used as symbols for the seven churches. *We will have learned how to deal with this book when we have learned to read the Apocalypse the way we read the parables.* And when we have familiarized ourselves, not only with those sections of the Old Testament which are commonly classified as "apocalyptic" but with the rich symbolism which is so prevalent in the Old Testament and by no means missing in the New, we will find this prophetic book not nearly so formidable as it appears to be at first glance.

What we have in the seven distinct sections of Revelation might be compared to seven grand paintings depicting in broad outline the whole history of the church in this present evil world during the whole period of the New Testament. In each of the seven portraits we see the everlasting gospel being preached in the midst of great tribulation. And over and over again we see the church victorious in spite of all the trials that she must suffer at the hands of ecclesiastical and political anti-Christian forces that seek to silence the witness of the messengers of God. The whole message of the book may be summed up in the words of the apostles, "We must through much tribulation enter into the kingdom of God," and enter it we shall by the grace of God and the blood of the Lamb.

This "idealistic" interpretation is really only a variation of the "church-historical" interpretation of Revelation. The use of such terminology may suggest that we use a different method of interpreting Revelation from the one we use in reading most of the rest of Scripture. Our opponents in modern Lutheranism may well ask us why we object so strongly to *Formgeschichte* when we recognize so clearly that Revelation must be read as a different type of literature from that found in the Gospels or in the Epistles. We can only answer that there are elements of truth in *Formgeschichte*, just as there were many elements of truth in the words of Satan spoken in the garden of Eden.

There are different forms of literature in the Bible. However, what type of literature we are dealing with must be determined by the grammatical-historial method, which lets the text speak for itself, and not by the whims of the historical-critical method, which imposes itself on the text. The text itself tells us that the "stars" in the first chapter are not luminous objects in the sky, but the seven angels of the seven churches. We may not be able to decide beyond the shadow of a doubt whether these angels are guardian angels assigned to the churches (such a notion is not altogether out of harmony with the teaching of Scripture, although there would be little to substantiate it) or whether these angels of the seven churches are the pastors of those congregations. The latter view not only has the literal meaning of the Greek word to commend it, but also fits much more neatly into the whole of Christian doctrine, or, as we sometimes call it, the analogy of faith.

A variation of the same argument is employed by those who ask us why we will not permit them to read Genesis the way we ourselves read Revelation. Why is it not possible for *them* to read Genesis as "*Rueckschauende Prophetie*" (prophecy concerning things past), if *we* insist on reading Revelation as what I suppose they would call "*Vorwaertschauende Prophetie*" (prophecy looking to the future). One can only wonder whether such questions are honest and honorable or whether they are intended to sow confusion among the simple.

The fact of the matter is that we read Genesis and Revelation in exactly the same way. When John says that he was on the island of Patmos we read that as a historical statement just as we read the account of creation and the fall. When Genesis 15 tells us that Abraham had a vision, we read that exactly the same way we read the words of John when he tells us of the visions he saw on Patmos. And when we read the description of the vision in Genesis 15 we read that part of the chapter in exactly the same way we read John's account of his vision. The only difference is that the vision of John was considerably longer than that of Abraham. It might also be remarked in passing that the vision of Abraham contains figures which are in a sense just as fantastic as some of those we find in the vision of John. Moreover, it might also be said that the lesson taught by both visions is the same. Abraham's vision, too, clearly signifies that the descendants of Abraham would through much tribulation enter the kingdom by the grace of God, who will have his way and keep his covenant in spite of all opposition.

The "idealistic" or "church-historical" interpretations are really the grammatical-historical method of interpretation applied to this particular form of literature. And it ought to be stressed again and again that the words of the text itself tell us that we are dealing with symbols that stand for something else.

Sometimes we are told exactly what the symbols mean. This is done, for example, in the case of the seven candlesticks and the seven stars.

Sometimes the immediate context makes the symbol clear. No one needs to tell us that the majestic figure with the two-edged sword coming out of his mouth is the Lord Jesus. In fact, after reading the first chapter I suppose that most of us are unaware of the fact that the Savior has not once in the vision been identified by name.

Sometimes the whole context of Revelation makes the symbolism clear. After we read in chapter 12 that the great dragon has been overcome by the blood of the Lamb and by the word of the testimony of God's people, it is surely clear that the chain that binds Satan in chapter 20 is the preaching of the everlasting gospel concerning the cleansing blood of Christ.

Sometimes other books of the Bible leave no doubt about the meaning of the symbols used by John in the Apocalypse. Why the sword comes out of the mouth of the Savior instead of being held in his hand, as we might expect, is no mystery to anyone who has read in the book of Hebrews that the word of God is quick and powerful and sharper than any two-edged sword. The significance of the Savior standing in the midst of the seven candlesticks is not unclear to anyone who knows that he promised, "Lo, I am with you always," and "Where two or three are gathered together in my name, there I am in the midst of them."

The "idealistic" interpretation is also the literal interpretation. We Lutherans are often accused of not reading Revelation literally enough because we will not let the thousand years of chapter 20 be a thousand literal years. And yet those who accuse us of this read the book much less literally than we do. A literal interpretation is one which allows the context to govern the meaning of the letters and the words of the text. Just a few moments of reflection ought to make clear how unliteral those people are who accuse us of ignoring the literal meaning of the text. Anyone who says, for example, that the seven letters to the seven churches are not real letters but representations of the seven ages of church history, should not accuse us of failure to use a literal interpretation. And the same thing can be said of anyone who can read the universal conversion of the Jews into the words directed to the congregation in Philadelphia: "I will make those who are of the synagogue of Satan, who claim to be Jews though they are not, but are liars — I will make them to come and fall down at your feet and acknowledge that I have loved you." Anyone who sees in those words the conversion of even one Jew has already forsaken the literal meaning of the text.

Likewise, it is totally foreign to the literal meaning of Revelation 20 to say that Christ will reign on this earth with his resurrected believers for exactly a thousand years. This is clear to anyone who pays close attention to the rest of the words and letters of that chapter. John says that the *souls* of the believers live and reign with Christ for a thousand years. Everyone who pays attention to what John says in the first chapter, namely, that the Savior has made us kings, knows that our souls began to reign with Christ on the day of our conversion. This is also the "first resurrection," as anyone will know who has read literally what the Savior had to say about a double resurrection in John 5:28,29, where he speaks of one resurrection that takes place in time when spiritually dead men hear the voice of the Son of God, and a second resurrection that takes place at the end of time, when the bodies of believers and unbelievers shall come out of the graves where they lie buried. And what the thousand years must be is also clear from the text. It is the period during which our *souls* live and reign with Christ. For the individual believer it is the period between his conversion and the day when his body, too, is raised to share in the freedom that his soul has known by faith during all that time. For the church as a whole it is the whole period from the conversion of the first member of the New Testament church until that day when all believers will receive their glorified bodies from him who will change our vile bodies into ones that will be fashioned like his glorious body, according to the working by which he is able to subdue all things.

The millennialists further demonstrate how far they themselves have wandered from the literal meaning of the text when they find the rapture in 4:1. John there tells us that a door was opened in heaven and he heard a voice that said to him, "Come up here, and I will show you what must take place after this." Anyone who has read the preceding context knows that this is something unique that happened to the Apostle John on a Sunday on the island of Patmos and not something that will happen to all believers seven years before the beginning of a millennium. Yet I once heard a millennialist say that this *must* be the rapture, because if it is not the rapture, then the rapture is not mentioned in Revelation, which, according to him, is impossible to imagine.

Lutherans are often accustomed to saying that we must not read Revelation literally. This is a bad habit we have gotten into, which makes it a little difficult for us to answer the charge brought against us by the chiliasts. We read Revelation just as literally as we read Genesis, and much more literally than millennialistic misinterpreters of this book. The literal truth is that Revelation is a vision, and it is literally true that John saw the things he described here, and that the things he saw were symbols which pictured the future history of the church. This is the literal meaning of the plain words of the text.

What we do not do is read the book literalistically. The very fact that the Savior is in one verse (5:5) called the Lion of the tribe of Judah and in the very next verse is described as a Lamb having seven horns and seven eyes ought to make clear to us that we are to be as free in our interpretation of the symbols as the writer is in the use of them. One of the beauties of figurative language is that a man can be a snake in the grass and a wolf in sheep's clothing at the same time. So the devil can be a great red dragon in one verse, an old serpent in another verse, and the angel of the bottomless pit in still another place, without doing violence to the proper use of figurative language. So also it is distinctly possible that in symbolic description the time of the New Testament could be a thousand years in one passage and 42 months in another place. A wooden, literalistic interpretation of symbolism is an offense against literal interpretation. Some months ago a famous radio preacher pontificated for all the world to hear that the rider on the white horse in chapter 6 and the rider on the white horse in chapter 19 could not be the same person because the rider in chapter 6 wears only one crown and the rider in chapter 19 wears many crowns. (Obviously he never considered the fact that in chapter 6 the rider "rides forth to conquer" and that long before chapter 19 we read, "The kingdoms of this world have become the kingdoms of our Lord and of his Christ" [11:15].) This is the kind of wooden, literalistic interpretation which displays ignorance of the fundamental nature of human language. It would have been just as sensible for him to say that the rider on the white horse in chapter 6 cannot be the Lord Jesus because in chapter 5 he is called a lamb and a lion, and lambs don't ride on horses and horses are afraid of lions.

THE OUTLINE OF THE BOOK

Introduction: John's Vision of Jesus on the Island of Patmos 1:1-20

I. The Seven Letters to the Seven Churches 2:1 — 3:22
II. The Vision of the Seven Seals 4:1 — 8:6
III. The Vision of the Seven Trumpets 8:7 — 11:19
IV. The Seven Visions 12:1 — 15:8
V. The Vision of the Seven Vials 16:1-21
VI. The Victory over Antichrist 17:1 —19:21
VII. The Victory over Satan 20:1 — 22:7.

Conclusion: 22:8-21

The Seven Letters (ch. 2-3)							
Congregation	The Command to Write	Description of the Speaker	The Word of Praise	The Word of Rebuke	The Admonition	The Call to Hear	The Promise
Ephesus	1	2	3	4	5	6	7
Smyrna	1	2	3	X	5	6	7
Pergamos	1	2	3	4	5	6	7
Thyatira	1	2	3	4	5	6	7
Sardis	1	2	5	3	4	7	6
Philadelphia	1	2	3	X	5	7	6
Laodicea	1	2	X	4	5	7	6

<table>
<tr><th colspan="2">The Seven Seals (6 — 7)</th><th colspan="2">The Seven Trumpets (8 — 11)</th></tr>
<tr><td colspan="2">The Church in the World</td><td colspan="2">The Church in the "Church"</td></tr>
<tr><td rowspan="2">The Gospel preached in the midst of great tribulation. The man on the white horse rides in the midst of great calamities, all of which are signs of the end
6:1-17</td><td rowspan="2">The destruction of the present world delayed while the elect are gathered in. The elect (the church) are safe in the midst of tribulation
7:1-9</td><td rowspan="2">The danger and damage of false doctrine. False doctrine is at the same time a punishment from God (cp 2 Th 2:11, 12) and has its origin in hell (cp 1 Tm 4:1)
8:1 — 9:21</td><td>The church's assignment to witness. The church is to proclaim God's Word
10:1-11</td></tr>
<tr><td>But even in the "church" God's true church is not without opposition
11:1-14</td></tr>
<tr><td colspan="2">The church's victory in the great tribulation
7:10-17</td><td colspan="2">The kingdoms of the world have become the kingdom of our Lord and of his Christ
11:15-19</td></tr>
<tr><th colspan="4">The Seven Visions (12 — 14)</th></tr>
<tr><td colspan="2">The enemies who seek to destroy the church: the devil (12:1-17), persecuting governments (the beast from the sea) (13:1-10), and the Antichrist (13:11-18)</td><td colspan="2">The victory of the elect (14:1-5) and the continued preaching of both law and gospel (14:6-13)</td></tr>
<tr><td colspan="4">The Last Judgment and the harvest of the world (14:14-20)</td></tr>
<tr><th colspan="4">The Seven Vials (15 — 16)</th></tr>
<tr><td colspan="2">The victorious saints in the presence of God. (15:1-4)</td><td colspan="2">The judgment of God on an unbelieving world which gave its worship to a false object (15:5 — 16:3), persecuted God's people (16:4-7), blasphemed the name of God (16:8-12), and opposed his rule (16:13-16)</td></tr>
<tr><td colspan="4">The final judgment (16:17-21)</td></tr>
<tr><th colspan="4">Christ and Antichrist (17 — 19)</th></tr>
<tr><td colspan="2">The anti-Christian forces that seek to destroy the church (17:1-18) destroyed (18:1-24)</td><td colspan="2">The victory of Christ and his people (19:1-18)</td></tr>
<tr><td colspan="4">The final destruction of the anti-Christian forces (19:19-21)</td></tr>
<tr><th colspan="4">Christ and Satan (20 — 22)</th></tr>
<tr><td colspan="2">The binding of Satan and his final destruction (20:1-15)</td><td colspan="2">The glory of the heavenly Jerusalem and the final victory of God's people (21:1 — 22:21)</td></tr>
</table>

	I The Seven Letters	II The Seven Seals	III The Seven Trumpets	IV The Seven Visions	V The Seven Vials	VI Christ and Antichrist	VII Christ and Satan	
INTRODUCTION Rev. 1:1-20	Ephesus 2:1-7	*1st Seal:* The white horse 6:1,2	*1st Trumpet:* Hail and fire 8:7	*1st Vision:* The woman clothed with the sun 12:1-17	*1st Vial:* Sore (Ulcer) 16:1,2	The Power (17:1-18) and Destruction (18:1-24) of Antichrist and the Final Victory of Christ (19:1-21) (The Destruction of Satan's earthly agents)	The Victory over Satan, the Last Judgment, and the Triumph of Christ and his Church (20:1 — 22:7) (The Destruction of Satan)	CONCLUSION 22: 8-21
	Smyrna 2:8-11	*2nd Seal:* The red horse 6:3,4	*2nd Trumpet:* Blood 8:8,9	*2nd Vision:* The beast from the sea 13:1-10	*2nd Vial:* Bloody seas 16:3			
	Pergamos 2:12-17	*3rd Seal:* The black horse 6:5,6	*3rd Trumpet:* Bitter waters 8:10,11	*3rd Vision:* The beast from the earth 13:11-18	*3rd Vial:* Bloody rivers and fountains 16:4-7			
	Thyatira 2:18-29	*4th Seal:* The pale horse 6:7,8	*4th Trumpet:* Darkness 8:12,13	*4th Vision:* The 144,000 in heaven 14:1-5	*4th Vial:* Burning heat 16:8,9			
	Sardis 3:1-6	*5th Seal:* The souls under the altar 6:9-11	*5th Trumpet:* Smoke obscuring the sun-locusts 9:1-12	*5th Vision:* The flying angels 14:6-13	*5th Vial:* Darkness 16:10,11			
	Philadelphia 3:7-13	*6th Seal:* The last judgment 6:12-19	*6th Trumpet:* The army from the east 9:13-21	*6th Vision:* The last judgment 14:14-20	*6th Vial:* The army from the east 16:12-16			
	Laodicea 3:14-22	*Interlude:* The church on earth 7:1-8 The church in heaven 7:9-17	*Interlude:* The witnessing church in its sufferings 10:1 — 11:14	*7th Vision:* The seven angels with the seven vials 15:1-8	*7th Vial:* The end of the world 16:17-21			
	Interlude: Prelude to the seven seals 4:1 — 5:14	*7th Seal:* The vision of the seven trumpets introduced 8:1-6	*7th Trumpet:* The end of the world 11:15-19					

The Introduction
1:1-20

THE "TITLE PAGE" (1:1-3)

**1) ΑΠΟΚΑΛΥΨΙΣ Ἰησοῦ Χριστοῦ, ἣν ἔδωκεν αὐτῷ ὁ Θεός,
δεῖξαι τοῖς δούλοις αὐτοῦ ἃ δεῖ γενέσθαι ἐν τάχει, καὶ ἐσήμανεν
ἀποστείλας διὰ τοῦ ἀγγέλου αὐτοῦ, τῷ δούλῳ αὐτοῦ Ιωάννῃ, 2) ὅς
ἐμαρτύρησεν τὸν λόγον τοῦ Θεοῦ καὶ τὴν μαρτυρίαν Ἰησοῦ Χριστοῦ, ὅσα εἶδεν. 3) Μακάριος ὁ ἀναγινώσκων καὶ οἱ ἀκούοντες
τοὺς λόγους τῆς προφητείας καί τηροῦντες τὰ ἐν αὐτῇ γεγραμμέ-
να· ὁ γὰρ καιρὸς ἐγγύς.**

1) *The Revelation of Jesus Christ, which God gave to him, to show his servants the things which must soon take place.*

He made these things known by sending them through his angel to his servant John 2) *who, as a witness, spoke the word of God and the testimony of Jesus Christ, things which he saw.*

3) *Blessed is the one who reads and those who hear the words of this prophecy and keep the things which are written in it. The time is near.*

The first three verses of the book might be called its "title page." It gives us the name of the book and the name of the author.

In the original language, the name of the book is Ἀποκάλυψις, the Apocalypse. Ἀποκάλυψις is an "unveiling," a "making known" of things that have heretofore been hidden. We are told why the message of the book is such a revelation. John says that the book will deal with "things which must shortly come to pass." Ordinarily the future is hidden from men. It can definitely be known only by a revelation from the all-knowing God. From the very beginning, therefore, anyone who believes that the Bible is the true Word of God must reject the view which holds that Revelation describes events that already had happened or that were happening at the time of writing.

The real author of the book is designated as Jesus Christ, viewed especially according to his human nature, for Jesus, in turn, is said to have received this revelation from God. We might therefore also very correctly say that God is the author of this book.

During his earthly ministry Jesus often emphasized this same thought, that the message he proclaimed was given to him by his Father (cp Jn 5:36-38; 8:38; 12:49,50; 14:10; 17:8). It should be noted that this is a favorite theme of John's Gospel, and its repetition here is an indication of the Johannine authorship of Revelation. By saying here that he received his message from Jesus, the human author of the book of Revelation claims divine inspiration for himself. It is also said that Jesus used an angel as his messenger to make known the revelation to his servant John. The message thus comes from God to Jesus, from Jesus to the angel, and from the angel to John:

God ⟶ Jesus ⟶ angel ⟶ John

John claims inspiration for himself also in verse 2. There he says that he spoke the word of God as a witness. Twice in verse 2 he points out that he is a witness: first, in the verb μαρτυρεῖν, which we have translated "spoke as a witness," and which is in the AV translated "bear record"; secondly, in the description of his message as "the *testimony* of Jesus Christ," namely the testimony which Jesus gives, or that comes from Jesus Christ. By emphasizing this point John very likely had in mind that last evening in the upper room when Jesus had told his disciples it would be their task to bear witness to him (Jn 16:26,27). But here John has in mind especially the things which Jesus revealed to him and which he was about to write in this book. The verb μαρτυρεῖν is a favorite word in John's writings. He uses it more often than all the rest of the New Testament authors together, and its use here is another indication of Johannine authorship.

He describes the revelation of Jesus as something that he *saw* (v. 2). In that description John speaks in terms that the Old Testament prophets regularly used. They often spoke of their prophecies as "visions" (cp, *e.g.,* Is 1:1; Eze 1:1; Dn 7:1; 8:1; Ob 1:1; Na 1:1), and they often referred to their message as something they had *seen.* Prophets therefore were also called "seers" or "see-ers" (cp 1 Sa 9:9). This note will sound again and again throughout the course of the following chapters. And it implies the inspired nature of the message. John saw these things (v. 2), because Jesus was pointing them out to him and was showing them to him through the ministration of his angel (v. 1).

The clear claim to inspiration repeats itself in many ways in the first two verses and the promise in verse 3 reinforces it. There John promises a blessing to the one who reads the message (the pastor) and to those who hear and keep it. This promise echoes the words of Jesus, "Blessed are those who hear the word of God and keep it" (Lk 11:28). The words, as they fall, imply that John expects this book to be read in the public services of the church. In the original text the participles "those hearing" and "those keeping" are preceded by a single article, which indicates that the blessing belongs only to those who keep, as well as hear, the words. All of these claims are characteristic of God's Word. Thus they also imply the inspiration of the book.

THE GREETING (1:4,5a)

4) Ἰωάννης ταῖς ἑπτὰ ἐκκλησίαις ταῖς ἐν τῇ Ἀσίᾳ· χάρις ὑμῖν καὶ εἰρήνη ἀπὸ ὁ ὢν καὶ ὁ ἦν καὶ ὁ ἐρχόμενος, καὶ ἀπὸ τῶν ἑπτὰ Πνευμάτων ἃ ἐνώπιον τοῦ θρόνου αὐτοῦ, 5) καὶ ἀπὸ Ἰησοῦ Χριστοῦ, ὁ μάρτυς ὁ πιστός, ὁ πρωτότοκος τῶν νεκρῶν καὶ ὁ ἄρχων τῶν βασιλέων τῆς γῆς.

4) *John to the seven churches which are in Asia:*

Grace be to you and peace from He *(sic)-Who-Is, and the He-Was, and He-Who-Will-Be, and from the seven Spirits which are before his throne,* 5) *and from Jesus Christ, the faithful witness, the firstborn of the dead, and the ruler of the kings of the earth.*

The whole book has the form of a letter, with these verses forming the standard epistolary greeting. John at the very beginning names himself again as the author of the letter. The letter is addressed to the seven churches in Asia. Asia here denotes the Roman province of Asia which was composed of the western quarter of Asia Minor. "Grace" and "peace" are the standard words of greeting in most of the New Testament letters. The word "grace" (χάρις) is a variation of the standard Greek greeting, often used in letters (χαῖρε, or χαίρετε). The word "peace" (*shalom*) is the standard Hebrew greeting. "Grace" summarizes all the gifts of God's love that come to us through Jesus Christ and "peace" sums up all the blessings that are ours as a result of God's grace, peace with God, peace for our troubled consciences and peace for our hearts and souls.

This grace and peace come to us from the triune God. It is interesting to note the triadic arrangement of the phrases in which John speaks of the God who bestows all these blessings. We may make this arrangement clear by arranging the words in the following way:

Grace and peace from

1) the one
   a) who is
   b) who was
   c) who is to come
2) The seven Spirits which are before the throne
3) Jesus Christ
   a) the faithful witness
   b) the first-begotten of the dead
   c) the ruler of the kings of the earth

The person most clearly identified is the second person of the Holy Trinity, who is spoken of here in the third place. A comparison with the greetings found at the beginning of the other letters in the New Testament will make clear immediately that the first three phrases describe God the Father. It will then also occur to the reader that "the seven Spirits which are before the throne" must be a reference to the Holy Spirit. Why John uses the term "seven Spirits" is never clearly spelled out anywhere in the book, but it may be that John has in mind the seven-fold description of the Holy Spirit found in the Old Testament book of Isaiah (11:2):

1) the Spirit of the Lord
2) the Spirit of wisdom
3) and understanding
4) the Spirit of counsel
5) and might
6) the Spirit of knowledge
7) and of the fear of the Lord.

In the description of God the Father we meet the first of many so-called "grammatical errors" in the Revelation. The Greek preposition ἀπό normally governs the genitive case, but here we find it followed by three phrases in the nominative case. The first and last phrases consist of an article with a participle, which is a normal phrase in Greek. The second phrase, however, consists of an article and the finite verb "he was" (ἦν), which is not normal Greek.

It is, however, obvious from the context that John knows he is not using normal or "correct" Greek grammar, since in the next two phrases, where he mentions the Holy Ghost and Jesus, he uses the same preposition, ἀπό, with the genitive case. John knows this preposition governs the genitive. Therefore he had a reason for not using the genitive in the first phrase. The thought that he undoubtedly wants to emphasize by using abnormal grammar is the unchangeable eternity of God. The description of God as the one who is and was and is coming (who is to be) reminds us of the name God gave himself at the burning bush, "I AM THAT I AM," a name which is reflected in the word Jehovah, or Jahweh, "The One Who Is." The words themselves point to God's eternality, and the unchanged grammatical forms reflect the complete immutability of God. The phrases are treated as proper names, and proper names are sometimes not declined or have the same form often in two or more cases.

The description of Jesus Christ as "the faithful witness" reminds us of Jesus' function as our divine prophet who has brought to us the true knowledge of God. The words, "the first-begotten of the dead," point to his priestly office in his death and resurrection. The phrase, "the ruler of the kings of the earth," designates Jesus as our king, who governs all other rulers and uses them to carry out his divine purposes. Again the phrases referring to Jesus are in the nominative case, instead of the genitive, indicating that his office is unchanging. His is an unchangeable prophetic office (He 1:1,2), an unchangeable priesthood (He 7:24), and an unchangeable kingship (Rv 11:15).

A FURTHER DESCRIPTION OF JESUS (1:5b-8)

Τῷ ἀγαπῶντι ἡμᾶς καὶ λύσαντι ἡμᾶς ἐκ τῶν ἁμαρτιῶν ἡμῶν ἐν τῷ αἵματι αὐτοῦ, 6) καὶ ἐποίησεν ἡμᾶς βασιλείαν, ἱερεῖς τῷ Θεῷ καὶ Πατρὶ αὐτοῦ, αὐτῷ ἡ δόξα καὶ τὸ κράτος εἰς τοὺς αἰῶνας τῶν αἰώνων· αμην.

7) Ἰδοὺ ἔρχεται μετὰ τῶν νεφελῶν, καὶ ὄψεται αὐτὸν πᾶς ὀφθαλμὸς καὶ οἵτινες αὐτὸν ἐξεκέντησαν, καὶ κόψονται ἐπ' αὐτὸν πᾶσαι αἱ φυλαὶ τῆς γῆς. ναί, αμην.

8) Ἐγώ εἰμι τὸ Ἄλφα καὶ τὸ Ω, λέγει Κύριος ὁ Θεός, ὁ ὢν καὶ ὁ ἦν καὶ ὁ ἐρχόμενος, ὁ Παντοκράτωρ.

To the one who loves us and freed us from our sins by his own blood — 6) *and he made us a kingdom, priests to his God and Father — to him belong the glory and the power forever. Amen.*

7) *Behold, he is coming with clouds,*
And every eye shall see him,
Also those who pierced him,
And because of him all the tribes of earth shall mourn.

Yes, so it will be.

8) *"I am the Alpha and the Omega," says the* LORD *God, the one who is, and the one who was, and the one who is to be, the Almighty.*

Again Jesus is praised in a three-fold doxology. He is described as 1) the one who loves us, 2) the one who freed us from our sins, and 3) the one who made us kings and priests.

The first description is in the present tense. He is the one who loves us. The present tense points to the ongoing, eternal nature of his love for us, which never wavers from one day to the next. The second descriptive phrase is in the past tense. He freed us from our sins by means of his blood. This is a work that was completed in the past when he shed his blood and gave up his life to pay the wages of our sins and thus to set us free from our sins and from the punishment they deserve. Many manuscripts read, "He washed us from our sins in his blood." The difference in the original Greek is one letter (λύσαντι and λούσαντι). There is little real difference in meaning between the two readings.

Once more the grammatical construction is broken, which we have tried to indicate by the dashes in our translation. John unexpectedly changes the construction. After using two participles in the dative case, he continues with a finite past tense verb. We might try to reproduce the effect of the broken construction by translating as follows: "To him who loves us and freed us from our sins by means of his blood — yes, he even made us a kingdom, priests to his God and Father — to him belong the glory and the power forever."

It would already have been a tremendous gift of love if the Lord Jesus had only set us free from the punishment of our sins. The punishment of hell is so terrible that just the cancellationof that punishment would have provided us at least with the hope that our future would be without pain and torment, even if it would have been nothing more than untroubled sleep. But Jesus has not only set us free from punishment; he has given us an exalted position. John says that he has made us into a kingdom, a royal house of kings. This opening description of God's people as a kingdom even now, in this present world, is something we need to keep in mind when we read the later chapters.

Not only has Jesus made us to be a kingdom, but we are also priests, who have the right to approach God directly in our own behalf and in behalf of other men. In speaking of God as "his God and Father," John points to the twofold nature of Christ. In his human nature the Father is his God, and in his divine nature God is his Father.

The designation of God's people as a "kingdom" (βασιλεία) and "priests" (ἱερεῖς) is an Old Testament theme which is repeated several times in Revelation. In the song of praise addressed to the Lamb by the elders around the throne it is said that the Savior by his atoning death had made his redeemed "a kingdom and priests" (5:10) and in one of John's last visions (20:6) the same combination of thoughts is expressed in the words "They will be priests (ἱερεῖς) . . . and reign (βασιλεύσουσιν)."

There is only one other passage in the New Testament that speaks of Christians in those express terms. Peter (1 Pe 2:9) calls them a "royal priesthood" (βασίλειον ἱεράτευμα). The Greek words he uses are a direct quotation from the Septuagint version of Exodus 19:6. In that passage God spoke of the children of Israel as a "kingdom of priests." To apply these same words now to Christian believers is another way of teaching that in New Testament times the church is the "Israel of God."

The closing words of the doxology may express a wish, "May glory and power be ascribed to him!" or a statement of fact, "The glory and the power belong to him forever."

Verse 7 contains the first prophecy of the book. "Behold he comes with clouds." The Old Testament Prophet Daniel had spoken of the coming Savior in the same terms (Dn 7:13), and Jesus himself in his eschatological discourses (Mt 24:30; Mk 13:26; Lk 21:27) and in his trial before the Sanhedrin (Mt 26:64; Mk 14:62) had predicted that he would come again in this way. As he had disappeared in a cloud at his ascension (Ac 1:9), so he will reappear again in the clouds in a visible second coming. Then "every eye will see him," and his enemies will quail at the sight. As the book opens, so it also closes (22:20) with a reference to the second coming of Christ.

The first direct message coming from Jesus in this "Revelation" is found in verse 8: "I am the Alpha and the Omega." That it is Jesus speaking these words is clear from the whole context of the book, but it is established most directly and beyond question in the last chapter. There Jesus is identified by name and makes the same claim for himself (22:12,16,20). The thought expressed is the same as that found in the words, "I am the first and the last" (1:17) and "I am the beginning and the end" (22:13).

Jesus then specifically identifies himself as "the LORD God." The Greek phrase κύριος ὁ θεός is the standard translation for the Old Testament phrase *JHVH ELOHIM* (the LORD God). Jesus thus identifies himself as Jehovah, or Jahweh, the I AM, the God who had revealed himself to Moses at Mt. Sinai. He further refers to himself as the one who "is and was and is to be," the same terms of eternality which described God the Father in verse 4. He adds also the title "the Almighty," thus claiming for himself still another divine attribute. It might be mentioned in this connection that the Greek word for "Almighty," παντοκράτωρ, is the word regularly used in the Septuagint to translate the Old Testament name "Lord *of hosts*."

THE VISION OF CHRIST (1:9-20)

John Hears the Voice of Christ (1:9-11)

9) Ἐγὼ Ἰωάννης, ὁ ἀδελφὸς ὑμῶν καὶ συνκοινωνὸς ἐν τῇ θλίψει καὶ βασιλείᾳ καὶ ὑπομονῇ ἐν Ἰησοῦ, ἐγενόμην ἐν τῇ νήσῳ τῇ καλουμένῃ Πάτμῳ διὰ τὸν λόγον τοῦ Θεοῦ καὶ τὴν μαρτυρίαν Ἰησοῦ.
10) ἐγενόμην ἐν πνεύματι ἐν τῇ κυριακῇ ἡμέρᾳ, καὶ ἤκουσα ὀπίσω μου φωνὴν μεγάλην ὡς σάλπιγγος
11) λεγούσης, Ὃ βλέπεις γράψον εἰς βιβλίον καὶ πέμψον ταῖς ἑπτὰ ἐκκλησίαις, εἰς Ἔφεσον καὶ εἰς Σμύρναν καὶ εἰς Πέργαμον καὶ εἰς Θυάτειρα καὶ εἰς Σάρδεις καὶ εἰς Φιλαδελφίαν καὶ εἰς Λαοδικίαν.

9) *I, John, your brother and companion in tribulation and kingship and patience in Jesus, was on the island called Patmos because of the word of God and the testimony about Jesus.* 10) *I was in spirit on the Lord's day, and I heard behind me a loud voice, like a trumpet,* 11) *saying, "What you see write in a book and send it to the seven churches, to Ephesus and to Smyrna and to Pergamos and to Thyatira and to Sardis and to Philadephia and to Laodicea."*

For the third time John identifies himself as the author. He tells us also where the visions he saw had come to him. He was on the island of Patmos, a small island off the coast of Asia Minor, southwest of the city of Ephesus, and almost directly west of Miletus. It is a barren island about ten miles long and six miles wide at its widest point. Patmos was used as a place of exile by the Roman government, and when John says that he was on Patmos "because of the word of God and the testimony about Jesus" he undoubtedly means to say that he had been exiled there as a punishment for preaching the gospel. An old tradition preserved in the writings of Irenaeus and the church history of Eusebius says that John was sent into exile on Patmos by the Roman government in the fourteenth year of Domitian, or 95 A.D., and that he was released in 96 A.D. after Domitian's death. We know that there was sharp persecution of the Christian church during the reign of Domitian. But, whether the tradition is correct or not, the words of John still make it clear that he is writing in a time of persecution.

John says that he is to his readers a brother and companion (literally, one who shares in something with someone else) in tribulation and kingship (or, ruling activity) and patience in Jesus. Thus he sounds the theme that will unfold in this book. The church must suffer much tribulation, often open persecution, in this present world. But the church should remember that this tribulation is "in Jesus" — because of the church's connection with Jesus. Therefore it is no cause for despair. For while we must experience much tribulation together, yet we are also partners in kingship, or ruling activity, which is also "in Jesus."

Already in verse 6 John had said that Jesus has made us into a kingdom, a royal house. The word βασιλείᾳ, which we have translated here with "kingship," is usually translated with "kingdom." In Scripture, however, this word often refers to a king's activity, the process of ruling. The risen Jesus, enthroned at the right hand of God, rules over all things in heaven and on earth. The suffering Christians, persecuted by the kings of the earth who rule over them, are, in spite of this, people who share with Jesus in his ruling activity. By their prayers for those in authority (1 Tm 2:1f), by their petition that God's will may be done, by their proclamation of the gospel, and in countless other ways, they are participating with Jesus in the process by which he carries out the good pleasure of his will. Christians therefore are not to judge by appearance. In spite of the suffering they must endure at the hands of earthly rulers, they are in reality the actual rulers of this world, for whose benefit all things in this world are governed (Rm 8:28).

"In Jesus" the members of the church can also endure in patience all the evils that an ungodly world and a pagan government can inflict on them. In the following chapters John will depict the tribulations that the church will experience until the end of time. And he will constantly remind his readers that the victory will finally be theirs. Therefore they ought to endure patiently to the end. And so the Christians in the seven churches are, in Christ, partners with John in suffering, ruling and enduring.

On a certain Sunday, John was "in spirit." This phrase "in spirit" denotes a spiritual state in which he was able to see and hear things that ordinarily are not seen and heard, the state in which visions are perceived. Many translators render this phrase, ἐν πνεύματι, "in the Spirit." This is a possible translation. However, the absence of the article in Greek and the fact that there is no other indication in the context that the word is a proper name seems to make the translation "in spirit" preferable — here and every other time it is so used in the book (cp. 4:2; 17:3; 21:10).

The phrase "the Lord's day" is used only here in the New Testament. In modern Greek this term denotes Sunday and there is no reason to doubt that it has this meaning here.

In the spiritual state in which John found himself he heard a voice behind him commanding him to write in a book the visions he would receive and to send what he had written to the seven churches. The order in which the churches are mentioned is the order in which they would be visited by someone traveling in circuit from one to the other. Ephesus is near the sea coast in central Asia, Smyrna is about 35 miles almost directly north of Ephesus and Pergamos about 50 miles north of Smyrna. Thyatira is about 40 miles southeast of Pergamos and Sardis 35 miles south and a little east of Thyatira. Philadelphia lies to the east and south of Sardis and Laodicea about 50 miles southeast of Philadelphia.

It is evident that here we are dealing with real cities. Any notion that the letters to the seven cities are not intended to be understood as real letters but as symbolic representations of various states of church history must be viewed as something read into the text. The cities are real cities and the letters are real letters.

The Appearance of Jesus (1:12-18)

12) Καὶ ἐπέστρεψα βλέπειν τὴν φωνὴν ἥτις ἐλάλει μετ᾽ ἐμοῦ· καὶ ἐπιστρέψας εἶδον ἑπτὰ λυχνίας χρυσᾶς, 13) καὶ ἐν μέσῳ τῶν

λυχνιῶν ὅμοιον υἱὸν ἀνθρώπου, ἐνδεδυμένον ποδήρη καὶ περιεζωσμένον πρὸς τοῖς μαστοῖς ζώνην χρυσᾶν· 14) ἡ δὲ κεφαλὴ αὐτοῦ καὶ αἱ τρίχες λευκαὶ ὡς ἔριον λευκὸν ὡς χιών, καὶ οἱ ὀφθαλμοὶ αὐτοῦ ὡς φλὸξ πυρός, 15) καὶ οἱ πόδες αὐτοῦ ὅμοιοι χαλκολιβάνῳ ὡς ἐν καμίνῳ πεπυρωμένης, καὶ ἡ φωνὴ αὐτοῦ ὡς φωνὴ ὑδάτων πολλῶν, 16) καὶ ἔχων ἐν τῇ δεξιᾷ χειρὶ αὐτοῦ ἀστέρας ἑπτά, καὶ ἐκ τοῦ στόματος αὐτοῦ ῥομφαία δίστομος ὀξεῖα ἐκπορευομένη, καὶ ἡ ὄψις αὐτοῦ ὡς ὁ ἥλιος φαίνει ἐν τῇ δυνάμει αὐτοῦ. 17) Καὶ ὅτε εἶδον αὐτόν, ἔπεσα πρὸς τοὺς πόδας αὐτοῦ ὡς νεκρός· καὶ ἔθηκεν τὴν δεξιὰν αὐτοῦ ἐπ' ἐμὲ λέγων,

Μὴ φοβοῦ· ἐγώ εἰμι ὁ πρῶτος καὶ ὁ ἔσχατος 18) καὶ ὁ Ζῶν, καὶ ἐγενόμην νεκρὸς καὶ ἰδοὺ ζῶν εἰμι εἰς τοὺς αἰῶνας τῶν αἰώνων, καὶ ἔχω τὰς κλεῖς τοῦ θανάτου καὶ τοῦ Ἅιδου.

12) *And I turned to see the voice which was speaking with me. And when I turned, I saw seven lampstands of gold,* 13) *and among the lampstands one like a son of man, clothed with a garment that reached to his feet, and around his chest he wore a belt of gold.* 14) *His head and his hair were white, like white wool, like snow. And his eyes were like fiery flames.* 15) *And his feet were like Lebanese brass, glowing in a furnace, and his voice was like the sound of much water.* 16) *And he held in his right hand seven stars, and out of his mouth proceeded a sharp two-edged sword, and his face shone as the sun shines at its brightest.* 17) *And when I saw him, I fell at his feet as a dead man. And he laid his right hand on me and said, "Stop being afraid. I am the first and the last* 18) *and the living one. I was dead and, behold, I am alive forevermore, and I have the keys of death and of hell."*

"I turned to *see* the voice" is obviously a figure of speech, meaning "I turned to see who was speaking." When John turned he saw "one like a son of man." Many translators and commentators have seen in the phrase "son of man" (υἱὸν ἀνθρώπου) a reference to Daniel's prophecy concerning the everlasting king (Dn 7:13) and have therefore translated "the Son of Man." Now, there is no doubt that this is possible, and one is reluctant to adopt the translation "a son of man," since it is clear from the context that this indeed refers to the Lord Jesus.

There is also no doubt that in the Gospels the Savior often called himself "the Son of Man" in obvious reference to the Messianic prophecy in Daniel. (*e.g.*, Mt 24:30; 26:64; Mk 13:26; 14:62). The mention of his appearing "in the clouds of heaven" precludes any other interpretation.

On the other hand, there are many passages in which the term "son of man" is a synonym for "human being." Ezekiel, for example, uses it in that way almost a hundred times, and there are at least a dozen other passages in the Old Testament which use it in this way. The question whether the term is used in this way in the New Testament depends on the interpretation of two passages in Revelation (1:8; 14:14) and one in Hebrews (2:6). In the Hebrews passage, the parallelism shows clearly that it designates a "man" — in this case, the man named Jesus, in whom the psalm is ultimately fulfilled. The Revelation passages could conceivably be understood in either way.

The name "Son of Man" as a name for Jesus is used eighty times in the four Gospels and once in Acts. In every case except one (Jn 5:27) both nouns have the definite article (ὁ υἱός τοῦ ἀνθρώπου). The second article is not translated in English because it is generic. In John 5:27 the phrase is obviously a name of Jesus, but there neither noun has the article, as is also the case in the two passages in Revelation. There is, however, a clear reason why the articles are missing in John 5:27. The name there precedes the copula. In that case Greek grammar demands, or at least allows, the articles to be dropped. There is no such reason that justifies the dropping of the articles in the two passages from Revelation. Another significant fact is that in the Gospels this name occurs only in passages in which Jesus himself is speaking or where he is directly quoted by his enemies. The Gospel writers themselves never use it when speaking of Jesus. For these reasons it is possible reluctantly to conclude that the NIV and the NASB have adopted the correct translation. The NIV is also very likely correct when it translates the Hebrew phrase in Daniel 7:13 with "a son of man," and the article in the New Testament allusions to that passage is an article of previous reference.

Thus John turned and saw someone who looked like a human being. This heavenly visitor had hair, eyes, hands and feet like a human being. Yet he was also remarkably different from other human beings.

John saw him standing among the seven lampstands, wearing a long robe and a golden belt. Neither the immediate nor the wider context enables us to determine if anything in particular is signified by the long robe and the golden belt, but a later verse tells us that the seven lampstands are symbols of the seven churches. The use of this symbolism is not at all unusual. Jesus had spoken of his disciples as the light of the world and had compared their conversion to the lighting of a candle (Mt

5:14-16). The fact that Jesus was standing among or "in the midst of" the seven lampstands is a symbolic way of setting forth the truth that the ascended Christ, who is now at the right hand of God, is at the same time still with his people here on earth. Many years before this John himself had heard him promise, "Where two or three are gathered together in my name there am I *in the midst* of them," and "Lo, I am with you always even unto the end of the world."

"His head and his hair were white." The whiteness of his head and hair is symbolic of the sinlessness and purity of Jesus. White is the standard symbol of holiness and righteousness.

"His eyes were like fiery flames." In the anthropomorphic language of the Old Testament the eyes of God always have some connection with God's knowledge or with his concern for his people. The ability of the eyes of Jesus to see into the darkest recesses of men's hearts may very well have been in the mind of John when he described the eyes of Jesus as fiery flames.

Whether there is any special significance in the description of Jesus' feet is hard to determine. We can say that the feet of Jesus in biblical symbolism have something to do with his authority and the exercise of his power over his enemies, who must serve as his footstool (cp. 1 Cor 15:27; He 2:8; Ps 8:6). The sound of his voice, which John compares to the sound of a thundering waterfall, surely points to the power of Jesus' word. It is also an indication of his deity, for in the Old Testament the voice of God is compared to the "noise of many waters" (Eze 43:2, KJV).

There is no question about the significance of the seven stars in his right hand. In the last verse of this chapter they are identified as the seven angels of the seven churches. Neither can there be any doubt about the two-edged sword that comes out of his mouth. What comes out of Jesus' mouth is his word. St. Paul speaks of God's words as a sword (Eph 6:17) and the book of Hebrews calls it a two-edged sword (He 4:12). Fantastic and strange as the vision is, the symbolism is appropriate, and it creates no problems for the interpreter.

This vision of Jesus in his glorious majesty closes with the words, "And his face shone as the sun shines at its brightest." Once before, many years earlier, on the Mount of Transfiguration, John had seen Jesus demonstrate his glory in the same way, and even if we cannot be sure whether there is any special significance in all the details of the vision, one thing can definitely be said about the vision as a whole. We have here a clear assertion that the same Jesus who had suffered humiliation and death on the cross, and who had experienced the same kind of persecution that his followers were enduring, now occupies an exalted position as the ruler of the whole earth. What had happened to Jesus would someday also happen to them. They, too, would be glorified (Rm 8:18; Php 3:21).

John was so overwhelmed by the majesty of Jesus that he fell down at his feet in a dead faint. But Jesus roused him and told him to "stop being afraid." The present imperative in Greek in the negative form usually denotes a command to stop doing something. "Stop being afraid!" becomes in the New Testament a prelude to the preaching of the gospel (cp. Lk 1:13,30; 2:10). The fall into sin destroyed man's knowledge of God and brought fear into the world. Before the fall into sin, man knew God as the holy judge who will not tolerate any disobedience to his commands, but man had no reason to be afraid of this God for he had not transgressed any of his laws. Man also knew God as the loving source of all good. After the fall, man no longer knows God's grace and love, for there is no way for him to discover a real solution to the difficulty involved in the thought that God is both gracious and holy, that he is, as he himself says, a God who forgives sins and does not forgive sins (Ex 34:6,7). Because of that, the natural man's thoughts about God can be nothing else than a certain "fearful expectation of judgment" (He 10:27). That is why Adam hides from God in the bushes of the garden (Gn 3:10). That is why the words "Fear not!" or better, "Stop being afraid!" are a fitting introduction to the message of the gospel, which is the only antidote to man's fear. With those same words, Gabriel greeted Zacharias and Mary when he came to announce the coming birth of John and of Jesus. With those same words the angel of Bethlehem introduced the message of the Savior's birth when he announced the Savior's coming to the shepherds. It is significant that while man's first words after the fall contain the statement "I was afraid," the first spoken words in the earliest historical account in the New Testament are "Fear not!" Likewise, the first message to John in the last historical account in the New Testament (Rv 1:17) contains the same liberating call to put away all fear.

Then Jesus once more describes himself as the eternal one by saying, "I am the first and the last" — the same words with which God described his eternality in the book of Isaiah (44:6).

Therefore Jesus is God.

He continues with a reference to his death and resurrection: "I am the living one. I was dead, and, behold, I am alive forevermore." Because of his death and resurrection, he claims for himself the keys of death and hell. He has the power to release men from death, as he promised his disciples, "Because I live, you also shall live." This is a word of great comfort to Christians in the day of persecution. Even the executioner's sword cannot place a believing child of God beyond Jesus' power to help.

The word which is translated "hell" is the Greek word "Hades," which, in turn, is often used as a translation of the Hebrew word "*Sheol.*" The Greek word very likely means a place which is unseen or where men exist in an invisible state. There is not complete agreement even among conservative scholars as to the exact meaning of the word. There can be no doubt that it often, perhaps even most generally, means what we understand by the word "hell." It is possible, though doubtful, that at times it means nothing more than "grave." In some contexts it simply means the place where men go when they die, the "next world," the "great beyond," the "unseen country from whose bourne no traveler returns," as Shakespeare called it. Hades, therefore, is a word that can include both heaven and hell. It would be possible here to understand Hades as the grave. Then the assertion that Jesus has the key to Hades would mean that he has the power to release from the grave. This would then imply the resurrection of those who had died for their faith as well as the rising again of all men, believers and unbelievers alike. If Hades, however, is a reference to the next world in general, or to hell in particular, the "keys" signify that Jesus' power extends beyond the boundaries of this present life. This, too, is a special word of comfort to a persecuted church. More will be said about the meaning of Hades in the comments on chapter 20.

The Repeated Command To Write (1:19,20)

19) γράψον οὖν ἃ εἶδες καὶ ἅ εἰσὶν καὶ ἃ μέλλει γενέσθαι μετὰ ταῦτα. 20) τὸ μυστήριον τῶν ἑπτὰ ἀστέρων οὓς εἶδες ἐπὶ τῆς δεξιᾶς μου, καὶ τὰς ἑπτὰ λυχνίας τὰς χρυσᾶς· οἱ ἑπτὰ ἀστέρες ἄγγελοι τῶν ἑπτὰ ἐκκλησιῶν εἰσιν, καὶ αἱ λυχνίαι αἱ ἑπτὰ ἑπτὰ ἐκκλησίαι εἰσίν.

19) *Therefore, write what you saw, both those things which are and those which will take place after these things.* 20) *The mystery of the seven stars which you saw in my right hand, and the seven golden lampstands: the seven stars are the angels of the seven churches, and the seven lampstands are the seven churches.*

The command to "write" emphasizes both the inspiration of this book and the related concept of revelation. The words "which are and which will take place" refer either to the visions John was about to see or to the events they symbolized.

After the command to write, there follows an explanation of two of the symbols in the first vision, the seven stars and the seven lampstands. Thus from the beginning it becomes clear that in this book we will be dealing with two types of material, which we may call historical and symbolical. For example, the seven churches are real, historical churches. Nowhere are we told that they represent anything, nor is there any indication anywhere that they are symbols. The golden candlesticks, however, are not real candlesticks, but they exist only for the sake and the duration of the vision. They have historical reality only in the sense that on a certain day and at a certain place the Apostle John actually had a vision in which he saw seven golden candlesticks.

On the other hand, not everything that is seen or heard in the visions is without direct historical existence. The son of man, who appears in the vision, is a real historical personage who, according to the text, once lived and died at a certain place and at a certain time in history. The sword that comes out of his mouth, however, has no independent historical and material existence, but it again is a symbol that represents a historical reality. There are therefore some visionary descriptions in which we have a mixture of historical and symbolical features.

"The seven stars are the seven angels of the seven churches." Lutheran commentators have not been agreed on what is meant by the seven *angels*. The word "angel" in Greek (ἄγγελος) means "messenger." In modern English the word refers exclusively to a heavenly or spiritual messenger, but the Greek word is much less specific. In verse 1, which speaks of Jesus sending his angel or messenger it is obvious that the messenger is a spirit. But in the light of verse 1 of the next chapter, where John is directed to send a letter to the angel of the church at Ephesus, it seems certain that we are dealing here with an earthly messenger. The messenger of the church is the man who delivers the Lord's message to the church. He is the pastor of the congregation. While the idea of an angel being assigned to the care of a specific congregation is without support anywhere else in the Bible, it is not an impossible interpretation. If, however, we understand the angel of the church to be the pastor of the congregation, then we can in a very natural way look upon the pastor of each of the seven congregations as the messenger through whom the message intended for each congregation is conveyed from Jesus to the people of God.

EXCURSUS: The Numbers in Revelation

The number seven is the most common of the numbers used in the Revelation. The first chapter speaks of seven churches, the seven spirits of God, the seven stars and the seven candlesticks. The next two chapters contain the seven letters to the seven churches.

Already in the Old Testament this number has special significance. The seventh day of the week was a holy day. There were seven great annual festivals: Passover, the feast of unleavened bread, Pentecost, the feast of trumpets, the great day of atonement, the feast of tabernacles and the eighth day of Tabernacles. Four of these festivals fell in the seventh month, which made this month especially holy. Every seventh year was a Sabbatical year, and after seven cycles of seven years a special year of jubilee was observed. Both the feast of unleavened bread and the feast of tabernacles lasted for seven days. Often special sacrifices were brought which consisted of seven animals or multiples of seven. In addition to the seventh day of every week there were seven special Sabbaths in every year, associated with the seven great feasts. It seems clear that seven is the number of the covenant.

Why God chose the number seven as a symbol of his covenant with Israel is not revealed to us. It has been suggested that three is the number of God and four is the number of this world, and therefore seven is the number that represents the reunion of God with men through his covenant of grace. There is some basis for this view also in Revelation. We already have seen how John's references to God manifest a triadic arrangement. In later chapters the number four becomes prominent in assertions regarding the created world. At any rate, it is not possible to make any dogmatic statements regarding the number seven beyond this that it appears to be the number of God's covenant with men.

Clearly associated with the number seven is the number three and one-half. The number occurs in several variations. Chapter 12 speaks of "a time, and times, and half a time" (12:14). The forty-two months of Revelation 11:2 and the 1260 days of 11:3 and 12 are three and a half years, and the plural "times" of 12:14 is very likely to be understood as a dual, so that "a time, and (two) times, and half a time" equals three and a half years.

The number three and a half is always associated with evil forces that oppress the church. At the same time, these evil forces usually appear to be of a spiritual and religious character. Three and a half may therefore be viewed as the symbol of the broken covenant, half of the number seven, the number of the covenant.

The second most common number in Revelation is twelve, with its multiples 24, 144, 12,000, 144,000. Twelve is without question the number of the church. Ten, with its cube, one thousand, appears to be the number of completeness. The number four is regularly associated with the world.

The First Vision: The Seven Letters (2:1-3:22)

THE INTERPRETATION OF THE SEVEN LETTERS

Many commentators see in the letters to the seven churches a prediction concerning the future of the church on earth, and some even see the seven letters as representative of seven successive ages of church history.

There is clear indication in the text itself that the seven letters are not to be read as symbolic portrayals of the future history of the church. It is strange that the same millennialistic interpreters who accuse amillennialists of not reading the Revelation literally often insist that the seven letters are not real letters to real churches, but predictive portrayals of future ages of history.

First of all, the seven churches are already named in the introduction to Revelation, which speaks of the entire book as being addressed to the seven churches. The writing of the book of Revelation is a real historical fact. We are holding it in our hands. John's experience on Patmos was an actual historical event. The seven churches were located in real cities, listed in a definite geographical order. The significance of that fact becomes rather striking when we compare it to the listing of the twelve tribes of Israel in chapter 7. There we find the names of the tribes given in an unhistorical form and in an order found nowhere else in the Bible. There it is obvious that we are not dealing with the nation of Israel as it ever existed in actual fact. This context, however, gives us no reason to assume that the seven churches and the seven individual letters to the seven churches are anything more than they claim to be. They are real letters, written to real churches, at a specific time in the early history of the Christian church.

This is also clear from the subsequent context. While it is true that in the first verses of the book we learn that this book will deal with future events "that must shortly come to pass," yet

John's actual vision of the future does not begin until chapter 4. Thus in the letters to the seven churches John is writing about "the things which are" (1:19).

THE PATTERN OF THE SEVEN LETTERS

All the letters follow the same general pattern, with a few minor variations. Each letter begins with a command to write which takes exactly the same form in all the letters. The command to write is always followed by a description of the person dictating the letter. This description in almost every case refers to the vision of Jesus in chapter 1.

The description of the speaker is followed, in varying order, by a word of commendation, a word of praise and an admonition usually including a call to repentance. The letters to Smyrna and Philadelphia contain no word of criticism, and the letter to Laodicea lacks the commendation.

The letters all conclude with a call to hear, which again is identical in all the letters, and with a promise to those who take the admonition to heart. The first four letters have these two features in the above order, while the last three letters reverse the order and close with the words, "Whoever has an ear, let him hear what the Spirit says unto the churches." In the following chart, the numbers denote the position of the various parts in the letters.

Congregation	The Command to Write	Description of the Speaker	The Word of Commendation	The Word of Criticism	The Admonition	The Call to Hear	The Promise
Ephesus	1	2	3	4	5	6	7
Smyrna	1	2	3	X	5	6	7
Pergamos	1	2	3	4	5	6	7
Thyatira	1	2	3	4	5	6	7
Sardis	1	2	5	3	4	7	6
Philadelphia	1	2	3	X	5	7	6
Laodicea	1	2	X	4	5	7	6

Note that in a general way the seven letters consist of seven parts, and the arrangment of the letters reflects the general sevenfold pattern of the whole book.

The Letter to Ephesus (2:1-7)

There is in reality no break between chapters 1 and 2. The Savior, who had spoken to John in chapter 1, continues to speak to John in the vision and says, "To the angel of the church in Ephesus write."

The congregation at Ephesus had been founded by the Apostle Paul on his third missionary journey at the beginning of the second half of the first century. When John wrote the Revelation, Christianity had been firmly established in Ephesus for almost a half century.

The command to write illustrates once more the doctrine of verbal inspiration. It is often said that verbal inspiration is not dictation, and while this may be true in most cases, yet here inspiration is definitely portrayed as dictation to a scribe. John serves merely as the penman whose skills the Lord Jesus utilizes in order to convey his message to the church. Jesus dictates the words and John writes them down.

The letter is sent to the "angel" of the church of Ephesus. The angels, the messengers, the pastors of the churches receive their messages from the apostles, and the apostles in turn receive the message from Jesus. This command to write reflects one of the basic themes of the New Testament, namely that Jesus instructed his chosen apostles personally and then sent them out to preach the gospel until the end of time. To this day the application of the words of Jesus, "He that heareth you, heareth me," can be made only to those pastors who proclaim the apostolic message. This is the true and biblical "apostolic succession."

1) Τῷ ἀγγέλῳ τῆς ἐν Ἐφέσῳ ἐκκλησίας γράφον, Τάδε λέγει ὁ κρατῶν τοὺς ἑπτὰ ἀστέρας ἐν τῇ δεξιᾷ αὐτοῦ, ὁ περιπατῶν ἐν μέσῳ τῶν ἑπτὰ λυχνιῶν τῶν χρυσῶν

1) *These things says the one who holds the seven stars in his right hand, the one who walks in the midst of the seven golden candlesticks:*

This description of the speaker echoes words which we already heard in John's report of his vision of the glorified Savior in the first chapter. These words graphically portray the Lord's care and concern for his church. He holds the seven stars, that is, the seven pastors, in his right hand. Holding his people in his hand is a picture that the Savior uses in other contexts to denote the certainty of the salvation that he has prepared for them and the protection with which he defends them. In the Good Shepherd chapter of John's Gospel he says of his sheep, "They shall never perish, neither shall man pluck them out of my hand. My Father which gave them me is greater than all, and no man is able to pluck them out of my Father's hand" (Jo 10:28,29). While this is true of all Christians, in this passage Jesus manifests his special concern for those who are his messengers whom he will protect with his almighty power as they go about his business.

The right hand of God is also often in the Scriptures a symbol of his operative power by which he accomplishes his saving purpose in the world. It would therefore be in harmony with the teaching of Scripture to see these pastors in the right hand of the Savior as his tools or instruments through which he operates in the world today. The Savior has given to his pastors, not only in Asia Minor, but everywhere in the world the task of proclaiming the gospel and of administering the sacraments, through which he brings men out of the kingdom of Satan into the kingdom of God. In this way the pastors are truly the instruments in the right hand of Jesus serving to carry out his will to save men from the consequences of their sin through the message of forgiveness and salvation.

We have already noted that the Savior's walking in the midst of the seven golden candlesticks is a figurative way of expressing his promise, "Where two or three are gathered together in my name, there am I in the midst of them" (Mt 18:20).

2) Οἶδα τὰ ἔργα σου καὶ τὸν κόπον καὶ τὴν ὑπομονήν σου, καὶ ὅτι οὐ δύνῃ βαστάσαι κακούς, καὶ ἐπείρασας τοὺς λέγοντας ἑαυτοὺς ἀποστόλους καὶ οὐκ εἰσίν, καὶ εὗρες αὐτοὺς ψευδεῖς· 3) καὶ ὑπομονὴν ἔχεις, καὶ ἐβάστασας διὰ τὸ ὄνομά μου, καὶ οὐ κεκοπίακες.

2) *I know your works and your labor and your patient endurance, and that you are not able to endure evil men; and you have tested those who say that they are apostles, but are not, and you have found them to be liars.* 3) *But you do have patient endurance, and you have endured (hardships) because of my name and have not become weary.*

These words form the commendation spoken to the congregation in Ephesus. The three words "works," "labor," "patient endurance" are a climactic series dealing in reality with one thought. The Savior is aware of what they have done. He knows also that they had done these things not haphazardly but energetically. The last word indicates that they had carried out this work in spite of opposition and under difficulties.

Two words in this commendation receive special emphasis by repetition. We have tried to reflect that emphasis in our translation. The first word, which we have translated "patient endurance," literally means "a remaining under" and is usually translated as "patience." The second word, which we have translated "endure," literally means to "carry," sometimes with the connotation "to carry a heavy burden."

The Ephesian Christians had demonstrated patient endurance in the hardships under which they had labored, especially in the sufferings they had experienced because of the name of Jesus, that is, because they confessed the Christian message before the world. They had not wearied in this struggle. But while the Savior commends them for this patience he also praises them because they did not allow their patience to lapse into indifference toward the wickedness of many. Suffering, hardships and persecutions they could put up with. But they would not put up with wicked men.

This is a word of commendation that the church in our ecumenical age should take to heart. Modern ecumenism manifests almost complete indifference toward false doctrine in the name of Christian "love" and "patience." Such "love" and "patience" are not pleasing to the Savior.

The context makes clear that the wicked men whom John has in mind here are not irreligious and openly immoral people. They are rather men who claim to be apostles, men who claim to have a special commission from the Lord. An apostle is "a man sent out" — in theological usage, "a man sent out by the Lord Jesus" as his spokesman to the world. These men falsely claimed to have such a position in the church. They repeated the offense of the false prophets of the Old Testament of whom the Lord said, "I have not sent these prophets, yet they ran. I have not spoken unto them, yet they prophesied" (Jer 23:21).

The Ephesians had tested these prophets to see whether their claims were valid. They had taken to heart an earlier admonition which the Apostle John very likely directed especially to them, and in which he said, "Dear friends, do not believe every spirit, but test the spirits to see whether they are from God, because many false prophets have gone out into the world" (1 Jo 4:1). How they tested them John does not say here, but we may assume that they followed the example of the Bereans, who listened to the preaching of Paul and then went home to search the Scriptures to determine whether what Paul had said was true (Ac 17:11). Through this testing they had determined that the claims made by these wicked men were false. The Savior expects his church to carry on such activities still today. He is pleased when his people recognize false teachers for what they are and do not patiently permit them to carry on their activities in their midst.

Yet the Lord also has a word of criticism to direct against the congregation in Ephesus:

4) ἀλλὰ ἔχω κατὰ σοῦ ὅτι τὴν ἀγάπην σου τὴν πρώτην ἀφῆκες.

4) *I have this against you that you have lost the love you had at first.*

Just as man by nature hates the true God because of his demands and threats in the law, so men learn to love God as they come to believe that the God of justice has provided free forgiveness and righteousness for them by the suffering, death and resurrection of Christ. People who have come to see their desperate need and the fulfillment of that need in the promises of the gospel will, without compulsion, be moved to love the Lord. Yet eventually men begin to take the promises of the gospel for granted and treat the threats of the law lightly. As a result, their love also decreases. This was happening in Ephesus.

The Savior's criticism is followed by a call to repentance:

5) μνημόνευε οὖν πόθεν πέπτωκες, καὶ μετανόησον καὶ τὰ πρῶτα ἔργα ποίησον· εἰ δὲ μή, ἔρχομαί σοι καὶ κινήσω τὴν λυχνίαν σου ἐκ τοῦ τόπου αὐτῆς, ἐὰν μὴ μετανοήσῃς. 6) ἀλλὰ τοῦτο ἔχεις, ὅτι μισεῖς τὰ ἔργα τῶν Νικολαϊτῶν, ἃ κἀγὼ μισῶ.

5) *Remember from where you have fallen and repent and do the first works. If you do not, I will come to you and move your candlestick from its place, if you do not repent.* 6) *But this you have that you hate the deeds of the Nicolaitans, which I also hate.*

"To repent" literally means "to change one's mind." In the strictest sense, repentance is the change of mind that takes place when a person no longer desires or expects to be saved through his own works, but wishes instead to be saved through the work of Christ. In other words, repentance is the change that takes place when one becomes a Christian. However, because Christians, too, still have the old Adam, the "change of mind" is wavering and imperfect. Repentance needs to continue and to be renewed in them every day. This need is especially acute where strong influences are striving to draw them away from the faith and love they have toward Christ. A lack of daily repentance may lead finally to a complete loss of faith. When this happens to a whole congregation the Savior "will move the candlestick from its place." He will no longer have a church in that place, a candlestick to light the way to heaven for men through the proclamation of the gospel.

The call to repentance is followed by another short word of commendation. The Lord Jesus praises the Ephesians for their hatred of the deeds of the Nicolaitans. The error of the Nicolaitans is not described in Scripture and the early church fathers say very little about it. Some scholars have suggested that the Nicolaitans were followers of and took their name from Nicolas of Antioch, who was one of the seven deacons appointed by the congregation in Jerusalem shortly after the first Pentecost (Ac 6:5). There is no solid evidence for this view. It seems, however, that the basic tenet of the Nicolaitans was that since we are saved by grace and not by works, it is perfectly permissible for a Christian to lead a dissolute, immoral life. That their hateful deeds were connected with false teaching becomes clear from verse 15, where the Savior says that he also hates the doctrine of the Nicolaitans. It is important to note that the Savior says he hates the deeds of the Nicolaitans and that he praises the Christians of Ephesus for joining him in this hatred. Such remarks help form a correct attitude toward sin and error. We may neither welcome nor ignore sin and error in the name of Christian "love."

7) Ὁ ἔχων οὖς ἀκουσάτω τί τὸ Πνεῦμα λέγει ταῖς ἐκκλησίαις.

7) *He that has ears, let him hear what the Spirit is saying to the churches!*

The admonition to hear is identical in all seven letters, and it once more emphasizes the doctrine of inspiration. Jesus identifies the Spirit of God as the author of the message in the seven letters. Jesus here speaks of the Spirit as a person distinct from himself. At the same time it indicates the unity of the Godhead, since what Jesus says is also what the Spirit says.

The letter closes with a promise:

Τῷ νικῶντι δώσω αὐτῷ φαγεῖν ἐκ τοῦ ξύλου τῆς ζωῆς, ὅ ἐστιν ἐν τῷ Παραδείσῳ τοῦ Θεοῦ.

To the one who is victorious I will give the privilege of eating from the tree of life, which is in the Paradise of God.

"Paradise" is originally a Persian word meaning "park" or "garden," and the reference clearly is to the Garden of Eden. In the Garden of Eden, the tree of life bestowed eternal life on those who ate from it. These words therefore are a figurative way of promising everlasting life to those who resist the efforts of the devil, the world and the flesh to lead them away from Christ. In the last chapter of the book John describes a vision in which he saw this promise fulfilled (22:2).

The promises given in the seven letters are echoed, at least in part, in the vision of the reign of the martyred souls and in the vision of the new Jerusalem, John's last vision on Patmos. The following chart outlines the similarities:

Congregation	Promise	Fulfillment
Ephesus	"the right to eat from the tree of life" (2:7)	"the tree of life . . . for the healing of the nations" (22:2)
Smyrna	"He . . . will not be hurt by the second death" (2:11)	"The second death has no power over them" (20:6)
Pergamos	"a new name" (2:17)	"his name will be on their foreheads" (22:4)
Thyatira	"I will give authority over the nations . . . I will give him the morning star" (2:26-28)	"They will reign forever and ever . . . I am . . . the bright Morning Star" (22:5,16)
Sardis	"I will never erase his name out of the book of life" (3:5)	"only those whose names are written in the book of life" (21:27)
Philadelphia	"the temple of my God . . . the new Jerusalem, which is coming down out of heaven from my God . . . I will also write on him my new name" (3:12)	"the Lord God Almighty and the Lamb are its temple . . . the new Jerusalem, coming down out of heaven from God . . . his name will be on their foreheads" (21:22,2; 22:4)
Laodicea	"I will give the right to sit with me on my throne" (3:21)	"They . . . reigned with Christ a thousand years . . . they will reign forever and ever" (20:4; 22:5)

The Letter to Smyrna (2:8-11)

8) Καὶ τῷ ἀγγέλῳ τῆς ἐν Σμύρνῃ ἐκκλησίας γράψον,

Τάδε λέγει ὁ πρῶτος καὶ ὁ ἔσχατος, ὃς ἐγένετο νεκρὸς καὶ ἔζησεν.

8) *To the angel of the church in Smyrna write: These things says the first and the last, who was dead and came to life again.*

The second letter is addressed to the congregation in Smyrna, about 35 miles northwest of Ephesus. While Ephesus is no longer a city of any importance, Smyrna (Izmir) is still a thriving city with over 350,000 inhabitants.

The description of the Savior in this letter again recalls the vision in chapter 1 (cp 1:17,18). He is described as the first and the last, the one who is before all things (Col 1:17), who was already in the beginning (Jn 1:1), who existed before the creation and will never pass out of existence. He is the eternal one. The words clearly point to the deity of Christ. But he is also true man, for he died and is now alive again. The word translated "is alive" (ἔζησεν) in the KJV is in the original in the past tense and should be translated, as is done in most modern translations, as a reference to the event of the resurrection. "He came to life again." He is the risen Savior, who has conquered death.

This congregation hears no word of criticism, but only a word of praise. The Savior says,

9) Οἶδά σου τὴν θλῖψιν καὶ τὴν πτωχείαν, ἀλλὰ πλούσιος εἶ, καὶ τὴν βλασφημίαν ἐκ τῶν λεγόντων Ἰουδαίους εἶναι ἑαυτούς, καὶ οὐκ εἰσὶν ἀλλὰ συναγωγὴ τοῦ Σατανᾶ. 10) μὴ φοβοῦ ἃ μέλλεις πάσχειν. ἰδοὺ μέλλει βάλλειν ὁ διάβολος ἐξ ὑμῶν εἰς φυλακὴν ἵνα πειρασθῆτε, καὶ ἕξετε θλῖψιν ἡμερῶν δέκα. γίνου πιστὸς ἄχρι θανάτου, καὶ δώσω σοι τὸν στέφανον τῆς ζωῆς.

9) *I know your tribulation and your poverty — but you are rich — and the blasphemy that comes from those who say they are Jews, but are not, but are rather the synagogue of Satan.* 10) *Have no fear of those things which you are about to suffer. Behold, the devil is about to throw some of you into prison that you may be tempted, and you will have tribulation for ten days. Be faithful until death, and I will give you the crown of life.*

The first sentence of this commendation is reminiscent of the beatitude, "Blessed are you who are poor" (Lk 6:20). The Apostle Paul also spoke of being rich in the midst of poverty (2 Cor 6:10). The Christians in Smyrna either belonged to the poorer classes in the city or they had lost their possessions through persecution. While the reference to tribulation in verse 9 does not necessarily indicate persecution, the next verse clearly does. Verse 10 could also be translated, "You will *go on having* tribulation for ten days." The phrase "for ten days" may be a way of expressing the thought that the time of the persecution has been definitely fixed by God and that it will be of relatively short duration. Since the numbers in Revelation are generally symbolic, there is nothing compelling us to understand these ten days as a literal ten days.

Those "who say they are Jews, but are not, but are rather the synagogue of Satan" are racial Jews who have given up the true Jewish faith. John's words here are difficult to understand at first glance, but they become clear when we read them against the background of the rest of the New Testament. The New Testament in many different ways expresses the thought that the true Jews, the "Israel of God," as Paul says (Ga 6:16), are those who accept Jesus as their Savior from sin. Already at the beginning of New Testament times John the Baptist told the Pharisees not to boast of their descent from Abraham, for God could turn stones into children of Abraham (Mt 3:9). When the Jews boasted that they were the children of Abraham, and therefore the children of God, Jesus told them that they were really the children of the devil (Jn 8:33-44). This incident is especially significant for understanding the expression used here since it is reported in the Gospel written by the author of Revelation. It helps to explain why the Jewish synagogue in Smyrna is called the synagogue of Satan. Additional light is cast on this passage by the words of the Apostle Paul, "A man is not a Jew if he is only one outwardly; . . . No, a man is a Jew if he is one inwardly" (Ro 2:28,29), and "Not all who are descended from Israel are Israel" (Ro 9:6). That apostle also says that Abraham is the father of all believers in Christ (Ro 4:11,12) and that "those who believe are children of Abraham" (Ga 3:7).

In the light of all those passages and many more like them we are justified in saying that those "who say they are Jews but are not" were the Jewish inhabitants of Symrna who refused to accept Jesus of Nazareth as the promised Messiah. Instead of being a synagogue devoted to the worship of the true God they were therefore a "synagogue of Satan." The whole context also implies that, as was the case so often, this Jewish community was responsible for much of the persecution and tribulation which the Christians in Smyrna had to endure.

The Savior urges them not to be afraid of what was about to

happen because, in the first place, the time of the persecution would be limited by God and would not last a long time. Secondly, he assured them that if they would remain faithful until death, he would give them a crown of life. This again is a promise of everlasting life — given by the one who described himself as the one who died and came to life again (v. 8). Because he lives they, too, will live forever. The crown (στέφανος) is the kind awarded to the victors in the athletic games (1 Cor 9:25). He compares the life of a Christian to a struggle. Those who keep up the battle faithfully until they die will receive the prize of everlasting life. They, too, will be alive forevermore, like the one who gave them the promise (Re 1:18). The seeming defeat they suffered when they died at the hands of their enemies will become their victory. For Christ, their Savior and Champion, who is "the first and the last" (v. 8), will give them eternal life.

The words at the end of the letter echo this promise, but in negative terms.

11) Ὁ ἔχων οὖς ἀκουσάτω τί τὸ Πνεῦμα λέγει ταῖς ἐκκλησίαις. Ὁ νικῶν οὐ μὴ ἀδικηθῇ ἐκ τοῦ θανάτου τοῦ δευτέρου.

11) *He who has ears, let him hear what the Spirit says to the churches. He who is victorious will not be hurt by the second death.*

This promise is especially emphatic because οὐ μὴ is the strongest possible Greek negative. The "second death" is eternal death in hell (Re 20:14).

The Letter to Pergamos (2:12-17)

12) Καὶ τῷ ἀγγέλῳ τῆς ἐν Περγάμῳ ἐκκλησίας γράψον,

Τάδε λέγει ὁ ἔχων τὴν ῥομφαίαν τὴν δίστομον τὴν ὀξεῖαν,

12) *To the angel of the church in Pergamos write: These things says he who has the two-edged sword, the sharp one.*

Pergamos, which has faded into insignificance in our time, was a city of great importance in the ancient world, situated about 65 miles northwest of Smyrna. It was the capital city of a kingdom by the same name. After the kingdom of Pergamos became part of the Roman empire, the city of Pergamos became a center of Roman provincial administration. The description of the Savior as the one who holds the sharp, two-edged sword is therefore very fitting. The sword is the symbol of authority (Ro

13:4), and in this description the Lord reminds the Christians in Pergamos that his authority supersedes that of the provincial and imperial rulers. This sword, which, in chapter 1, issues from the mouth of the Savior, is the word of God.

To the church in Pergamos the Savior writes,

> **13) Οἶδα ποῦ κατοικεῖς· ὅπου ὁ θρόνος τοῦ Σατανᾶ· καὶ κρατεῖς τὸ ὄνομά μου, καὶ οὐκ ἠρνήσω τὴν πίστιν μου καὶ ἐν ταῖς ἡμέραις Ἀντιπᾶς ὁ μάρτυς μου ὁ πιστός μου, ὃς ἀπεκτάνθη παρ' ὑμῖν, ὅπου ὁ Σατανᾶς κατοικεῖ. 14) ἀλλ' ἔχω κατὰ σοῦ ὀλίγα, ὅτι ἔχεις ἐκεῖ κρατοῦντας τὴν διδαχὴν Βαλαάμ, ὃς ἐδίδασκεν τῷ Βαλάκ βαλεῖν σκάνδαλον ἐνώπιον τῶν υἱῶν Ἰσραήλ, φαγεῖν εἰδωλόθυτα καὶ πορνεῦσαι. 15) οὕτως ἔχεις καὶ σὺ κρατοῦντας τὴν διδαχὴν τῶν Νικολαϊτῶν ὁμοίως. μετανόησον οὖν· 16) εἰ δὲ μή, ἔρχομαί σοι ταχὺ καὶ πολεμήσω μετ' αὐτῶν ἐν τῇ ῥομφαίᾳ τοῦ στόματός μου. 17) Ὁ ἔχων οὖς ἀκουσάτω τί τὸ Πνεῦμα λέγει ταῖς ἐκκλησίαις. Τῷ νικῶντι δώσω αὐτῷ τοῦ μάννα τοῦ κεκρυμμένου, καὶ δώσω αὐτῷ ψῆφον λευκήν, καὶ ἐπι τὴν ψῆφον ὄνομα καινὸν γεγραμμένον, ὃ οὐδεὶς οἶδεν εἰ μὴ ὁ λαμβάνων.**

> 13) *I know where you live — where the throne of Satan is — and you hold fast to my name; and you did not renounce your faith in me in the days when Antipas, my faithful martyr, was put to death in your presence, where Satan lives.* 14) *But I have a few things against you, because you have there some who hold the doctrine of Balaam, who taught Balak how to cast a stumbling-block before the children of Israel, namely, the eating of things offered to idols and fornicating.* 15) *Likewise, you also have some who hold the doctrine of the Nicolaitans (which I hate). Repent, therefore.* 16) *If you do not, I will come to you quickly and I will fight against them with the sword of my mouth.* 17) *He who has ears to hear, let him hear what the Spirit says to the churches. To him who is victorious I will give a portion of the hidden manna and a white stone with a new name written on it, one known only to the one receiving it.*

Some have suggested that the reference to Satan's living and ruling in Pergamos identifies Pergamos as a center of idolatry and emperor worship. In any case, the general meaning is clear. Pergamos was a place where Satan was especially active and exercised a great deal of influence. That influence is directed especially toward winning Christians away from their faith or preventing men from coming to faith. The Savior especially commends the congregation for resisting these efforts of Satan by holding fast to Jesus' name.

The "name" of Jesus has to do with everything we know about Jesus. "Name," both in English and in Greek, is often a synonym for "reputation." A "good name," for example, has to do with all the good things that are known about a man. What we know of Jesus is found in the gospel. To hold fast to the name of Jesus is to hold fast to the gospel, to cling to what we have learned about the Savior.

Jesus further commends them, "You did not renounce your faith in me." "Your faith in me" is literally "my faith" (πίστιν μου). A word in the genitive following the word "faith" in Greek is often an objective genitive, and it should most likely be so understood here. Linguistically it would be possible to translate as the KJV does, "my faith." In that case we could understand it as the doctrine of Jesus, but this would be an unusual use of this phrase.

One of the members of the congregation has been put to death as a faithful martyr. The word "martyr" is derived from μάρτυς, the Greek word for "witness." By being willing to die for the faith, the Christian martyrs testified to their conviction about the truthfulness and the blessings of the Christian religion. It was more valuable to them than life itself. Who Antipas was we do not know. All the outside information we have about him is legendary. We know only that he was willing to die rather than to give up the gospel and to renounce his faith in Jesus.

The congregation is criticized for tolerating in its midst some members who held "the doctrine of Balaam." Balaam was the unfaithful prophet of the Lord who was hired by Balak, the king of the Moabites, to curse the children of Israel. When his triple attempt to pronounce a curse upon Israel failed (Nu 22:1 — 24:25), he suggested to Balak that he might be able to bring about the destruction of Israel by seeking to involve the Israelites in the immoral and idolatrous Moabite worship (Nu 25:1-18; cp. 31:16).

Evidently there were members in the congregation in Pergamos who saw nothing wrong in participating in the heathen sacrificial meals (cp. 1 Cor 8:1-13) and in the fornication which was so common in the heathen world of that time. Immoralities were even part of the worship service rendered to the heathen gods. That these nominal members of the congregation were somehow involved in idolatrous worship is clear from the rest of the New Testament, which distinguishes between participation in idol worship and in eating meat sacrificed to idols if that meat was later sold in the public meat markets (1 Cor 10:25-30).

The congregation also tolerated members who held to the doctrine of the Nicolaitans. Not all the early manuscripts have the words, "which thing I hate." They may have been added by a scribe who from memory introduced them from verse 6 of this same chapter. Nevertheless, it is clearly the Savior's will that congregations should exercise doctrinal discipline and that they should exclude from the congregation those who hold to false teachings. He is evidently displeased when congregations do not do this.

In fact, the Lord threatens to punish the congregation in Pergamos for its failure to expel these members. He calls upon them to repent of this wrong. He had described himself as the one who has the sharp two-edged sword, and now he says that he will use that sword against the false teachers. When we remember that his word is able to cleanse lepers and still storms, the threat to use it against men is a terrifying one.

After the call to hear comes the final promise to those who are victorious. The Lord promises that those who remain firm will be allowed to eat of the hidden manna. Manna was the means with which the Lord preserved the lives of the children of Israel in the wilderness. In John's Gospel this manna is compared to the "bread of life." It is therefore apparent that this is also a promise of everlasting life to those who overcome.

The victors are also promised a white stone. We know that pebbles were used by juries in the ancient Greek law courts as voting ballots. In fact, the word translated "stone" (ψῆφον) also means "vote" in classical Greek. A white pebble was a vote for acquittal. Since the Lord Jesus is the final judge at the last judgment we may see in this white stone the Savior's verdict of not guilty pronounced over all those whose faith remains firm to the end.

On this stone, according to the Savior's promise, "a new name" is written. In biblical terms, to give someone a name means to describe him. When God gives someone a new name, this person is no longer what he was before. There will be a new type of existence for his people. We may think here especially of the exchange of this present troubled world for the bliss of heaven. No one can ever know that bliss fully until he experiences it, and in that sense the new name is unknown to all except those who have received it. It certainly also includes the hidden righteousness of the believing child of God which makes him an heir of the bliss of heaven. Since this is a righteousness we have by faith, and since faith is conviction concerning unseen things (He 11:1), this righteousness is not something anyone knows except the person who has it.

The Letter to Thyatira (2:18-29)

18) Καὶ τῷ ἀγγέλῳ τῆς ἐν Θυατείροις ἐκκλησίας γράψον,

Τάδε λέγει ὁ Υἱὸς τοῦ Θεοῦ, ὁ ἔχων τοὺς ὀφθαλμοὺς αὐτοῦ ὡς φλόγα πυρός, καὶ οἱ πόδες αὐτοῦ ὅμοιοι χαλκολιβάνῳ·

18) *To the angel of the church in Thyatira write: These things says the Son of God, he who has eyes like fiery flames, and his feet are like Lebanese brass.*

The fourth letter is written to the congregation in Thyatira, the home of Lydia, the seller of purple, who helped Paul in Philippi (Ac 16:14). Thyatira is a little over twenty miles southeast of Pergamos.

The description of the Savior is again taken from John's vision except that here, for the first and only time in the book of Revelation, he is called the "Son of God." Note that in the original both nouns have the definite article (ὁ υἱὸς τοῦ θεοῦ; cp. 1:13). We have already seen that the "eyes like fiery flames" seem to emphasize the Savior's omniscience. His feet usually recall his control over his enemies. The thought that the eyes of the Lord pierce to the innermost recesses of men's hearts and minds is repeated in a later verse (23), where the Lord describes himself as the one who searches the kidneys and the hearts. The Bible pictures the heart as the seat of the intellect and the kidneys and other abdominal organs as the seat of the emotions. The NIV translation, which says that the Lord searches the hearts and minds, therefore seems justified, although perhaps the order of the words ought to be reversed.

The commendation of the congregation at Thyatira is very brief.

19) Οἶδά σου τὰ ἔργα καὶ τὴν ἀγάπην καὶ τὴν πίστιν καὶ τὴν διακονίαν καὶ τὴν ὑπομονήν σου, καὶ τὰ ἔργα σου τὰ ἔσχατα πλείονα τῶν πρώτων.

19) *I know your works, and your love and your faith, and your service and your patient endurance, and that you are doing more now than you did at first.*

The criticism is longer. He faults the congregation for tolerating false teachers, and says,

20) ἀλλὰ ἔχω κατὰ σοῦ ὅτι ἀφεῖς τὴν γυναῖκα Ιεζάβελ, ἡ λέγουσα ἑαυτὴν προφῆτιν, καὶ διδάσκει καὶ πλανᾷ τοὺς ἐμοὺς δούλους πορνεῦσαι καὶ φαγεῖν εἰδωλάθυτα·

20) *But I have this against you that you allow that woman Jezebel, the one who calls herself a prophetess, to deceive my servants and to teach them to fornicate and to eat things offered in sacrifice to idols.*

Who this woman Jezebel was we do not know. It is very likely that Jezebel is not her real name, but a name given to her by John in order to characterize her. In the Old Testament, Jezebel was the daughter of the Phoenician King Ethbaal. She was married to King Ahab and introduced Baal worship with its sexual immorality into the northern kingdom. Since this woman evidently advocated similar practices she deserved to be called by that infamous name.

The sharpest words of criticism, however, are directed against this woman herself. The Lord says,

21) καὶ ἔδωκα αὐτῇ χρόνον ἵνα μετανοήσῃ, καὶ οὐ θέλει μετανοῆσαι ἐκ τῆς πορνείας αὐτῆς. 22) ἰδοὺ βάλλω αὐτὴν εἰς κλίνην, καὶ τοὺς μοιχεύοντας μετ᾽ αὐτῆς εἰς θλῖψιν μεγάλην, ἐὰν μὴ μετανοήσουσιν ἐκ τῶν ἔργων αὐτῆς· 23) καὶ τὰ τέκνα αὐτῆς ἀποκτενῶ ἐν θανάτῳ· καὶ γνώσονται πᾶσαι αἱ ἐκκλησίαι ὅτι ἐγώ εἰμι ὁ ἐραυνῶν νεφροὺς καὶ καρδίας, καὶ δώσω ὑμῖν ἑκάστῳ κατὰ τὰ ἔργα ὑμῶν.

21) *I gave her time to repent, but she had no desire to repent of her fornication.* 22) *Behold, I will cast her into a bed and those who commit adultery with her into great tribulation, if they do not repent of her works.* 23) *And her children I will kill with death, and all the churches will know that I am the one who searches the hearts and minds, and I will give to each of you according to your works.*

In spite of her depravity the Lord had given this woman time to repent of her immorality, but she neglected the opportunity. Therefore he says that he will cast her into a bed. What he evidently means is a bed of sickness or suffering. Her sins had in large measure been committed in a bed, and what she had viewed as a place of pleasure was to become for her a place of pain and sorrow. The pleasures of sin last for only a short time (He 11:25) and often bring consequent suffering. The same things which were viewed as a source of pleasure become instead an oppressive burden.

Not only this woman was to suffer, however. Those who had committed adultery with her would be brought into great tribulation, if they did not repent. The woman's children, too, would die because of her sins. Whether her children are her offspring or her followers is not certain, but the basic thought is that all those associated with her would suffer because of her immorality. Her punishment was to show all the churches that the Lord is not as tolerant of sin as churches often are and that finally he is a God who does not allow sin to go unpunished. Each one will be rewarded according to his works, and the wages of sin is death (Ro 6:23).

But the Lord also promises to forgive the sin of tolerating this woman. He says,

> **24) ὑμῖν δὲ λέγω τοῖς λοιποῖς τοῖς ἐν Θυατείροις, ὅσοι οὐκ ἔχουσιν τὴν διδαχὴν ταύτην, οἵτινες οὐκ ἔγνωσαν τὰ βαθέα τοῦ Σατανᾶ, ὡς λέγουσιν, οὐ βάλλω ἐφ' ὑμᾶς ἄλλο βάρος· 25) πλὴν ὃ ἔχετε κρατήσατε ἄχρι οὗ ἂν ἥξω.**
>
> 24) *To the rest of you in Thyatira, who do not hold to this doctrine, who do not know Satan's "deep things," as they call them, I say that I will not lay upon you another burden.* 25) *Only hold fast to what you have until I come.*

The words of the Savior imply that by tolerating this woman they were endangering their own hold on the truth, but as long as they did not "know" her teaching they would not be punished in the same way as she and her supporters would be. To "know" often means "to adopt as one's own." That is evidently its meaning here.

The reference to "deep things" should alert us to a real danger that still threatens Christians today. Men are often inclined to despise the plain and simple teachings of the gospel and to seek for "deeper" insights into the Christian faith. They imagine that such insights are hidden behind the words of the gospel. When they produce out of their imagination all sorts of conclusions not found in the simple words of the text they often speak of these "discoveries" as products of scholarship and wisdom which go far beyond what they consider to be the shallow thinking of ordinary Christians. But John correctly labels these "deep" additions to the gospel as "Satan's deep things." They have their roots, not in the word of God, but in hell itself. For that reason the Savior encourages the members of the congregation to hold fast to the simple promises of the gospel until he comes again at the end of the world.

To those who remain in firm possession of those treasures he gives the promise,

26) Καὶ ὁ νικῶν καὶ ὁ τηρῶν ἄχρι τέλους τὰ ἔργα μου, δώσω αὐτῷ ἐξουσίαν ἐπὶ τῶν ἐθνῶν, 27) καὶ ποιμανεῖ αὐτοὺς ἐν ῥάβδῳ σιδηρᾷ ὡς τὰ σκεύη τὰ κεραμικὰ συντρίβεται, 28) ὡς κἀγὼ εἴληφα παρὰ τοῦ Πατρός μου, καὶ δώσω αὐτῷ τὸν ἀστέρα τὸν πρωϊνόν. 29) Ὁ ἔχων οὖς ἀκουσάτω τί τὸ Πνεῦμα λέγει ταῖς ἐκκλησίαις.

26) *To the one who is victorious and who does to the end what I have commanded I will give authority over the nations,* 27) *just as I myself have received authority from my Father. He will rule them with a rod of iron and shatter them as vessels of pottery.* 28) *I will also give him the morning star.* 29) *He who has an ear to hear, let him hear what the Spirit says to the churches.*

The phrase which we have translated, "who does to the end what I have commanded" literally reads, "who keeps (or observes) my works unto the end." The Greek word does not mean to observe only in the sense of "regard with attention," but also "to adhere to in practice." It is the word that is used when we speak of observing, or obeying, a command. The Savior used the same word when he commanded his apostles to teach men to "observe" all the things he had commanded. "My works" in this context therefore cannot mean "the works I have done," but it must mean "the works that please me" or "the works I have commanded." The NIV translation "who does my will to the end" is therefore not incorrect, even if it is rather free.

The Savior draws the terms of the promise from Psalm 2. In that psalm God promises to give the Messiah authority over all nations and says that he will rule over the nations with a rod of iron and utterly destroy those who oppose him. In the words, "just as I received authority from my Father," the Lord Jesus asserts that the promise of Psalm 2 was fulfilled in him. When the Savior says he will give the same kind of authority to those who remain faithful to him until the end, this is not a new or unusual thought, even though the way of expressing it may be unusual. There are many passages in the Bible that promise that we will reign with Christ, and that we are through faith reigning with him even now. In fact, Christians are called a "royal," or reigning, priesthood by St. Peter (1 Pt 2:5), and John himself in the first chapter of Revelation says that the Savior has made us kings (1:6). The words of this text are therefore a promise of royal rule and authority God offers to those who are oppressed and persecuted in this world. They serve as another illustration of the fact that the book was written to comfort Christians who were suffering for their faith. What John says here in poetic terms is said more directly by Paul when he writes, "If we suffer, we shall also reign with him" (2 Tm 2:12).

The meaning of the promise, "I will give him the morning star," is not clear. In the last chapter of Revelation (22:16) the Savior calls himself "the bright morning star." This is perhaps the only passage that gives us some clue to the meaning of this promise. We can be certain that the Lord in these words promises a precious and glorious gift. What better gift can he give than himself? Perhaps the specific treasure promised here is that we will have the privilege of seeing him in all his glory and of possessing him through all eternity.

The Letter to Sardis (3:1-6)

1) Καὶ τῷ ἀγγέλῳ τῆς ἐν Σάρδεσιν ἐκκλησίας γράψον,

Τάδε λέγει ὁ ἔχων τὰ ἑπτὰ Πνεύματα τοῦ Θεοῦ καὶ τοὺς ἑπτὰ ἀστέρας,

1) *To the angel of the church in Sardis write: These things says he who has the seven spirits of God and the seven stars.*

Sardis, which was about 30 miles southeast of Thyatira, today is an insignificant village. But at one time it was a great and powerful city, the capital of the ancient kingdom of Lydia. When and how the congregation was founded there we do not know, but when John wrote Revelation the congregation was at the point of dying out. It is perhaps for that reason that the Savior, in addressing this congregation, describes himself as the one "who has the seven spirits of God." This description is not from John's vision of Jesus in chapter one, but from the greeting at the beginning of the book, where John had spoken of "the seven spirits that are before his throne" (1:4). At that place we noted that this must be a name for the Holy Ghost. Since it is the Spirit of God that gives life, the hope of this dying congregation lay in the assurance that the Savior was concerned about their welfare. Jesus is the Lord, who has promised to send the Holy Spirit to his church to breathe life into its dry bones (Eze 37:1-14). The reference to the seven stars may serve as a reminder that the Spirit comes to men through the preaching of God's word. The Savior describes the proclamation of the gospel and the work of the Spirit as being closely joined to one another.

Like the commendation in the previous four letters, Jesus introduces his message to Sardis with the words, "I know your works." But in this letter it precedes not a commendation but a sharp criticism. To the congregation in Sardis the Lord says,

> **Οἶδά σου τὰ ἔργα, ὅτι ὄνομα ἔχεις ὅτι ζῇς, καὶ νεκρὸς εἶ. 2) γίνου γρηγορῶν, καὶ στήρισον τὰ λοιπὰ ἃ ἔμελλον ἀποθανεῖν· οὐ γὰρ εὕρηκά σου ἔργα πεπληρωμένα ἐνώπιον τοῦ Θεοῦ μου· 3) μνημόνευε οὖν πῶς εἴληφας καὶ ἤκουσας, καὶ τήρει καὶ μετανόησον. ἐὰν οὖν μὴ γρηγορήσῃς, ἥξω ὡς κλέπτης, καὶ οὐ μὴ γνῷς ποίαν ὥραν ἥξω ἐπὶ σέ.**
>
> *I know your works. You have a reputation of being alive, but you are dead.* 2) *Wake up, and strengthen what is left, which is about to die, for I have not found your works completed in the sight of my God.* 3) *Remember therefore how you received and heard* [*the message of the gospel*]. *Keep it and repent! If, therefore, you do not stay awake, I will come as a thief, and you will not know at what time I will come upon you.*

Evidently the dying condition of this congregation was not apparent to the casual observer. In fact, it had the reputation that it was a congregation with a great deal of life. Its decay must therefore have been an inward, spiritual one. It was very active, but its works were "not completed in the sight of . . . God." In the sight of men those works may have been very impressive. But the Lord says that their good reputation was not deserved, and that the congregation in Sardis was almost completely dead. Its apparently good works were not the kind of works that God expects of his children.

The criticism of Sardis is needed especially in our time, when the visible Christian church has become very activistic and is engaged in many efforts to improve social and economic and political conditions in the world. The church may, because of this activism, appear to be a living force in the world. But often those efforts are linked with an indifference to doctrine and to the Lord's commandments in general. Works not motivated by the gospel are hardly complete before God. They lack the most necessary ingredient, love. And of what value are those works which God has not sanctioned or commanded?

The main task of the church is to preach the gospel in its truth and purity and to administer the sacraments according to the institution of Christ. If this is neglected or if the gospel is obscured by all sorts of false teaching, the church may be busy day after day, from morning to night, but its works will never be "complete" in the sight of God because it is not doing the job that God assigned to it. It is also interesting to observe how much of the church's contemporary concern for the poor and the downtrodden expresses itself not in actual deeds of love and kindness, but rather in political efforts, often through highly paid lobbyists who are devoted to providing for the poor with other people's money. Such works, too, are hardly "complete" in the sight of God, even though they may be politically expedient and a means of maintaining civil order.

Because the congregation at Sardis did not realize its true condition but perhaps even took pride in its reputation as a lively organization, the Savior told it to wake up and to realize its true condition. He admonished the Christians in Sardis to strengthen the little that still remained of true Christianity. Such strengthening was desperately necessary, for even this remainder was at the point of death.

Verse 3 in the original consists almost entirely of verbs. The first half of the verse says only, "Remember therefore how you have received and heard." John does not say what they received, but since he also speaks of their having heard something, it is rather obvious that he had in mind the preaching of the gospel, which had served to establish the church in Sardis. Therefore in our translation we have added the words "the message of the gospel," which are implied in the text of the original. This message they are to keep, that is, observe, take to heart and follow. This would require repentance, a complete change in their attitude.

The admonition and call to repentance is followed by a serious warning. "If you do not stay awake, I will come as a thief." The coming of the last judgment is often compared to the coming of a thief. These words therefore speak of a day of judgment that will involve Sardis. While the Lord Jesus is the gracious Savior, who earnestly desires the salvation of men, yet he is also the just judge who will severely punish those who ignore his call to repentance.

The last words of the admonition express the urgent need for repentance. "You will not know at what time I will come upon you." The Gospels report that Jesus at one time said, "If the owner of the house had known at what hour the thief was coming, he would have kept watch [that is, he would have stayed awake], and would not have let his house be broken into" (Mt 24:43). Since we do not know when the day of judgment will come, we should never put off repentance. The Scriptures often use the metaphors of staying awake and sleeping in connection with that admonition.

Those who attempt to set a date for the second coming of Christ might profitably take note of the Greek construction in this sentence (οὐ μή with an aorist subjunctive). This is the strongest negative expression in New Testament Greek. We would be justified in translating: "You will certainly not know at what time I will come," or, "There is no way for you to find out when I'm coming."

The four previous letters had begun with a commendation, followed, except in the case of Smyrna, by a word of criticism. The letter to Sardis begins with a sharp rebuke, followed by a brief word of praise. Already in verse 2 the Savior had indicated that not all life had completely disappeared in Sardis. Now he expands on that thought:

4) ἀλλὰ ἔχεις ὀλίγα ὀνόματα ἐν Σάρδεσιν ἃ οὐκ ἐμόλυναν τὰ ἱμάτια αὐτῶν, καὶ περιπατήσουσιν μετ' ἐμοῦ ἐν λευκοῖς, ὅτι ἄξιοί εἰσιν.

4) *But you have a few names in Sardis which have not defiled their garments, and they will walk with me in white, for they are worthy.*

The righteousness or unrighteousness of men is often symbolized by clothing. Isaiah, for example, says, "All of us have become as one who is unclean, and all our righteous acts are like filthy rags" (Is 64:6), and in another place, "I delight greatly in the Lord, my soul rejoices in my God. For he has clothed me with garments of salvation and arrayed me in a robe of righteousness" (Is 61:10). St. Paul uses language that reminds us of this symbolism when he says that at our baptism we "put on" Christ (Gal 3:29). In a later chapter of the book of Revelation John speaks of those who have washed their robes and made them white in the blood of the Lamb (Rv 7:14). As scarlet is the color of sin, so white is the color of purity and holiness. Isaiah demonstrates that symbolism when he writes, "Though your sins are like scarlet, they shall be as white as snow" (Is 1:18). Those who have not defiled their garments, therefore, are those who have not through impenitence and unbelief exchanged the pure garment of Christ's righteousness furnished to them in baptism for the filthy rags of their own righteousness.

To such people the Savior promises that they will walk about with him. They will finally be with him in the glories of heaven. They are worthy of this, he says, but we know from the rest of Scripture that their worthiness consists not in what they are or in what they have done but only in what Christ has done for them.

The formal promise that follows in verse 5 makes use of the same symbolism.

> **5) Ὁ νικῶν οὕτως περιβαλεῖται ἐν ἱματίοις λευκοῖς, καὶ οὐ μὴ ἐξαλείψω τὸ ὄνομα αὐτοῦ ἐκ τῆς βίβλου τῆς ζωῆς, καὶ ὁμολογήσω τὸ ὄνομα αὐτοῦ ἐνώπιον τοῦ Πατρός μου καὶ ἐνώπιον τῶν ἀγγέλων αὐτοῦ. 6) Ὁ ἔχων οὖς ἀκουσάτω τί τὸ Πνεῦμα λέγει ταῖς ἐκκλησίαις.**

> 5) *He that is victorious in this way will be clothed in white garments, and I will by no means erase his name out of the book of life, and I will confess his name before my Father and his angels.* 6) *He who has an ear to hear, let him hear what the Spirit says to the churches.*

Jesus here promises a verdict of innocence to his believers in the final judgment. They will be clothed in white, innocent not only in the eyes of men, but even before the judgment throne of God. The wages of sin is death. But the sins of those who believe in Christ are hidden and covered by the white garments of his righteousness. Their names will remain in the book of life. The "book of life" is mentioned seven (!) times in the book of Revelation (here and in 13:8; 17:8; 20:12, 15; 21:27 and 22:19). Paul speaks of it in Philippians (4:3). Even Moses had spoken of such a book in which God has written the names of men (Ex 32:32).

The context makes it clear that the "book of life" is a figurative way of expressing the doctrine of election. This book contains the names of God's elect, those who will finally come to everlasting life through faith in the Lord Jesus because God has chosen and predestined them for this (Eph 1:3-6). When the Savior says that he will not erase their names out of the book of life, he emphasizes the certainty of the salvation that God has prepared for his elect. The thought is the same as when he said that no one should be able to pluck his sheep out of his hand (Jn 10:28), and when he implied that the elect can not be deceived (Mt 24:24).

Finally, he promises those who are victorious and remain faithful unto death that he will confess their names before his Father and the Father's angels. To "confess" is the opposite of to "deny." Peter denied Christ by saying that he did not know him. Christ thus promises that before his Father and the holy angels he will declare that he knows these people. To "know" in biblical terminology often means to acknowledge as one's own. This usage is illustrated in a negative way for example by the Lord's statement that on the day of judgment he will say to those who are lost, "I never knew you" (Mt 7:23). In a human way of speaking, we may say that on the day of judgment Jesus will introduce the faithful believers to his Father and the angels as his friends, his brothers and his sisters. The promise that Jesus gives here to the faithful in Sardis, he had already made during his life here on earth to all those who confess him before men, who acknowledge that he is their Savior and their God (Mt 10:32,33).

The letter closes with the familiar call to hear.

The Letter to Philadelphia (3:7-13)

7) Καὶ τῷ ἀγγέλῳ τῆς ἐν Φιλαδελφίᾳ ἐκκλησίας γράψον,

Τάδε λέγει ὁ ἅγιος, ὁ ἀληθινός, ὁ ἔχων τὴν κλεῖν Δαυίδ, ὁ ἀνοίγων καὶ οὐδεὶς κλείσει, καὶ κλείων καὶ οὐδεὶς ἀνοίγει,

7) *To the angel of the church in Philadelphia write: These things says the holy one, the genuine one, he who has the key of David, the one who opens and no one will close, and closes and no one will open.*

About 30 miles southeast of Sardis lay the city of Philadelphia. The area was subject to earthquakes, and the city had been destroyed by a quake early in the first century. The city is still in existence today. Its modern name is Alasehir.

The description of the Savior in this letter expands upon the vision in the first chapter. The words, "the holy one, the genuine one," mean "the genuinely holy one." This distinguishes his holiness as divine and above every other holiness. A similar phrase occurs in a later chapter (6:10), where the words "holy *and* true" modify the word "Lord." All these words are additional affirmations of the Savior's deity.

The words that follow are from the Old Testament, where the Lord through the Prophet Isaiah says, "I will place on his shoulder the key to the house of David; what he opens no one can shut, and what he shuts no one can open" (Is 22:22). There the words referred to a man named Eliakim. A man by the name of Shebna, who may have been a non-Jew, had been holding the position of the treasurer, or steward, over the royal household in Jerusalem. Evidently he was a proud man, interested in glorifying himself. God said that he would depose

Shebna and give his position to Eliakim, who would be a faithful official and a "father" to the whole kingdom. The keys to the house of David, that is, control over all the royal treasures would be given to him, and in the faithful performance of his duties he would distribute or withhold these treasures.

Since the Savior in our text applies these words to himself, Eliakim is, in this respect, a type of Christ. As the man who had the keys to the royal treasuries, Eliakim had full control of the material blessings of the kingdom and the authority to bestow or to withhold them. The Lord Jesus has the keys to all the treasures of heaven and the power to bestow or to withhold them according to his will.

The Apostle John, in his Gospel, often summarizes the Savior's spiritual treasures in the word "life." The withholding of those treasures are summarized in the word "death." The "key of David" is therefore in some ways parallel to the "keys of hell and of death," mentioned in the earlier vision (1:18). The only two possible alternatives awaiting man in the next world are heaven or hell, life or death. The key that locks hell is the key that opens heaven, and the key that opens hell is the one that closes heaven. The "keys of hell and of death," the "key of David," and the "keys of the kingdom of heaven" (Mt 16:19) are merely different terms for the same concept, slightly different points of view. Here the Savior does not mention the church's function of administering the means of grace, but he dwells on identifying himself as the unfailing and final source of that forgiveness and of the life and salvation to which it leads.

We should keep this in mind when we evaluate what he means by the open door in the body of the letter to Philadelphia, where he says,

8) Οἶδά σου τὰ ἔργα· ἰδοὺ δέδωκα ἐνώπιόν σου θύραν ἠνεῳγμένην, ἣν οὐδεὶς δύναται κλεῖσαι αὐτήν· ὅτι μικρὰν ἔχεις δύναμιν, καὶ ἐτήρησάς μου τὸν λόγον καὶ οὐκ ἠρνήσω τὸ ὄνομά μου.
9) ἰδοὺ διδῶ ἐκ τῆς συναγωγῆς τοῦ Σατανᾶ, τῶν λεγόντων ἑαυτοὺς Ἰουδαίους εἶναι, καὶ οὐκ εἰσὶν ἀλλὰ ψεύδονται· ἰδοὺ ποιήσω αὐτοὺς ἵνα ἥξουσιν καὶ προσκυνήσουσιν ἐνώπιον τῶν ποδῶν σου, καὶ γνῶσιν ὅτι ἐγὼ ἠγάπησά σε. 10) ὅτι ἐτήρησας τὸν λόγον τῆς ὑπομονῆς μου, κἀγώ σε τηρήσω ἐκ τῆς ὥρας τοῦ πειρασμοῦ τῆς μελλούσης ἔρχεσθαι ἐπὶ τῆς οἰκουμένης ὅλης, πειράσαι τοὺς κατοικοῦντας ἐπὶ τῆς γῆς.

> 8) *I know your works (behold, I have set before you an open door, which no one can shut), that you have a little strength, and have kept my word, and you have not denied my name.* 9) *Behold, I will make those who are of the synagogue of Satan, who say they are Jews and are not but are lying, behold, I will cause them to come and bow down before your feet and to know that it is you that I love.* 10) *Because you have kept my word of patience I also will keep you from the hour of testing, which is about to come over the whole inhabited world, to test those who dwell on earth.*

The symbol of an open door is used by the Apostle Paul to denote a great mission opportunity (1 Cor 16:9; 2 Cor 2:12), but in this context the emphasis is not so much on the mission opportunities of the congregation as on the blessings that the Savior will shower upon the Christians of Philadelphia out of the storehouses of his grace. Otherwise the reference to the words concerning Eliakim in verse 7 hardly seem appropriate. No one will be able to shut the door, that is, no one will be able to deny these treasures to them. They are assured of forgiveness, life and salvation.

The words "*that* you have a little strength" can also mean "*because* you have a little strength," as the translators of the KJV rendered it. The Savior, however, is the only one who has the keys to the door, and we are saved by grace alone. The holding open of the door does not depend on the strength of God's people, but on the power and authority of the Lord Jesus. So it is best to let the words we have placed in parentheses stand as an interruption in the flow of thought. The way we have translated it is a normal way of handling this grammatical construction.

The words "you have a little strength" are often understood as a reference to the size of the congregation, as though it was small in numbers. Other translators see this as a subordinate thought and translate the words to mean "although you have only a little strength, yet you have kept my word." However, the words "although . . . only . . . yet," or similar words, have no counterpart in the original text, which simply coordinates the three expressions, "you have a little strength, you have kept my words, and you have not denied my name." The whole context indicates that these words are to be understood as a commendation. In a world where all men are born without strength (Ro 5:6) and are, in fact, by nature spiritually dead (Eph 2:1), even a little strength is a great advantage. It may be true that the congregation was small in numbers (about this we know nothing). The context simply uses the phrase to draw a contrast. While Sardis was dead or about to die, the congregation in Philadelphia still had some strength. The members had kept (observed, taken to heart) the Savior's word and had not denied his name. They still had enough strength to face persecution and to confess Jesus as their Savior and Lord. Unlike Peter, they did not deny that they knew him.

In connection with the letter to Smyrna we have already discussed "the synagogue of Satan which say that they are Jews but are not." Those were racial Jews who had forsaken the religion of the Old Testament and therefore did not accept Jesus as the Messiah. This description of the Jewish synagogue in Philadelphia as well as in Smyrna serves to remind us that Christianity is not a new religion founded by Jesus or the Apostle Paul, as some claim, but it is simply the continuation and fulfillment of the religion of the Old Testament. Jesus himself told the Pharisees that if they really believed the message of Moses they also would have accepted him as their promised Messiah (Jn 5:46).

Millennialists and dispensationalists often interpret the seven letters as being representations of the seven ages of church history. They view the promise, "I will cause them to come and bow down before your feet," as an allusion to a general conversion of the Jews before the end of the world. This view, which is largely based on a mistranslation and misinterpretation of Romans 11:26 ("all Israel shall be saved") finds no justification in this verse. The word for "bow down," προσκυνήσουσιν, is translated "worship" in the KJV. In modern English this word refers almost exclusively to honor paid to God, but in King James English it can also denote honor paid to men. This is true also of the Greek word. Here it does not denote a worshiping of God, as the phrase, "before *your* feet," makes clear. Hence, we have translated "I will make them come and bow down before you." The unbelieving Jews, who claim that they were the chosen people whom God loved, would finally be forced to acknowledge that the Christians are God's beloved people. This does not indicate the conversion of even one Jew, although it does not preclude the possibility. But to cite this passage as a vital proof text for the universal conversion of the Jews during a millennium betrays how desperate they are in their attempt to find this doctrine in Scripture.

The literal translation of the first part of verse 10 is, "Because you have kept my word of patience." Less preferable as a literal translation is "the word of my patience." This, too, is grammatically possible, but the context does not speak about God's patience, nor is this Greek word for "patience" ever applied to God. It is the same word which we have in a previous context translated as "patient endurance" (2:2). Many modern translations have understood the phrase "my word of patience" to mean "my command to be patient." But the phrase really says only that there is a relationship between God's word and patience. It does not define what that relationship is. While it is true that God commands us to be patient, it is also true that the gospel, with its promises of glory at the end of the sufferings of this present time, gives us the strength and the will to endure persecution and pain with patience. To interpret "my word of patience" as a divine command to be patient gives a legalistic coloring to what is an evangelical context. Furthermore, to keep God's word does not only mean to obey a command. Jesus surely meant more than this when he said, "If a man keep my saying (my word), he shall never see death" (Jn 8:51; cp 8:31,32). Note that this passage is from John's Gospel.

Because the Philadelphian Christians had kept Christ's word he promises, "I will also keep you from the hour of testing which is about to come over the whole inhabited world, to test those who dwell on the earth." While these words surely apply to every Christian in every hour of trial, they seem to refer especially to the tribulations that would precede the end of the world.

The words can hardly refer to the severe persecutions that believers everywhere in the Roman empire had to endure in the years that followed the writing of the Revelation. Jesus says that this time of testing is about to come on "those who dwell on the earth" (τοὺς κατοικοῦντας ἐπὶ τῆς γῆς). This phrase occurs a number of times in the book, and each time it describes the unbelieving world. The persecutions tested the believers, not the unbelievers.

Millennialists usually interpret the "hour of temptation" as a reference to what they call "the great tribulation." This, they say, will be a period of seven trouble-filled years following the so-called "rapture." During that time, according to them, there will be no Christians on the earth. They point to the preposition ἐκ, which means "out of" or "from," and maintain that this means God will take the believers out of this world.

But the text does not say that God will take them out of this world. Rather, the Lord says, "I will keep [τηρήσω] you from [ἐκ] the hour of temptation." He promises to keep them safe from all harm. He can do that without taking them out of this world, just as he protected the children of Israel from the last plagues in Egypt even while they remained there. It is safe to say that if men would not come to this passage with preconceived, unbiblical notions of a rapture and of a great tribulation, they would never find in this text an indication that God will take the believers "out of the world" during the "hour of temptation." The text certainly does not say this to anyone who pays attention to the exact words used here. When Jesus spoke of great tribulation (NIV: "great distress") in his eschatological discourses (Mt 24:21), he clearly implied that the believers would be on earth during that time.

The context makes it obvious that here Jesus is speaking about the time before the end. After he promises to keep his people safe from harm, he assures them that he will not delay his return. When he spoke to his disciples about the great distress that would come in the end times, he promised that the time of trouble would be shortened (Mt 24:22). In that same vein he now says to the Christians in Philadelphia,

11) ἔρχομαι ταχύ· κράτει ὃ ἔχεις, ἵνα μηδεὶς λάβῃ τὸν στέφανόν σου.

11) *I am coming quickly. Hold fast to what you have, that no one may take your crown.*

The letter to Philadelphia, like the letter to Smyrna, contains no word of criticism. However, that does not mean these people were sinless. The admonition in this verse makes clear that the Savior's promise to keep them does not imply that it is impossible for a believer ever to fall away from the faith. The promise is a real promise that he will surely keep. At the same time, it is certainly not a license to cultivate carelessness and indifference and lethargy. Christians are to be aware that they can lose their crown. The picture once again is the crown of victory which the winner received in the Greek athletic contests. The whole tenor of the admonition reminds us that the Christian life is a real struggle against real forces that seek to rob us of our faith and thus also of our salvation. The words of Jesus, "I am coming quickly," are another "word of patience," which reminds us that the struggle is of short duration.

To those who "hold fast" the Lord gives the promise,

12) Ὁ νικῶν, ποιήσω αὐτὸν στῦλον ἐν τῷ ναῷ Θεοῦ μου, καὶ ἔξω οὐ μὴ ἐξέλθῃ ἔτι, καὶ γράψω ἐπ' αὐτὸυ τὸ ὄνομα τοῦ Θεοῦ μου καὶ τὸ ὄνομα τῆς πόλεως τοῦ Θεοῦ μου, τῆς καινῆς Ἰερουσαλήμ ἡ καταβαίνουσα ἐκ τοῦ οὐρανοῦ ἀπὸ τοῦ Θεοῦ μου, καὶ τὸ ὄνομά μου τὸ καινόν. 13) Ὁ ἔχων οὖς ἀκουσάτω τί τὸ Πνεῦμα λέγει ταῖς ἐκκλησίαις.

12) *Him that is victorious I will make a pillar in the temple of my God, and he will never again go out, and I will write on him the name of my God and the name of the city of my God, the new Jerusalem which is coming down from heaven from my God, and my new name.* 13) *He who has an ear, let him hear what the Spirit says to the churches.*

The region of Philadelphia was subject to severe earthquakes. This helps us understand John's language here. An earthquake had destroyed the city early in the first century. Undoubtedly some of the local pillars had survived the devastation and were left standing. John now used them as a symbol of the faithful Christians in Philadelphia who would withstand that "hour of temptation." Jesus promises that he himself will make the steadfast Christians in Philadelphia a pillar in the temple of his God. He speaks here again according to his human nature, as he did during his life on earth, e.g., when he called the Father his God (Jn 20:17).

When the struggle is finally over, the Christians will enjoy "eternal security." Never again will they leave the confines of God's temple.

"I will write on him the name of my God, and the name of the city of my God, and my new name." To write one's name on something denotes ownership. Jesus here promises first of all, that steadfast believers will belong to God forever. They will also belong to the city of God. In Old Testament times the city of God was the city of Jerusalem, where the temple of God was built. But this city of God is another Jerusalem, a new Jerusalem, not built with the hands of men, but coming down out of heaven from God. We will hear more of this new city of God in chapter 21.

Jesus also promises to write his own "new name" on the believer. We have already said that a "name" in biblical terminology is that which describes a person or thing. Jesus now has a "new name," he is now described in terms completely different from those which described him in his state of humiliation, when he wore the garb of a servant. Today and forevermore he is the glorious victor over sin and death, over the devil and hell. Once he was despised and rejected by men, but now he is King of kings and Lord of lords, and those on whom he has written his new name belong to him, and will share in the glory of that new name.

Again, the letter closes with the call to hear.

The Letter to Laodicea (3:14-22)

14) Καὶ τῷ ἀγγέλῳ τῆς ἐν Λαοδικίᾳ ἐκκλησίας γράψον, Τάδε λέγει ὁ Ἀμήν, ὁ μάρτυς ὁ πιστὸς καὶ ἀληθινός, ἡ ἀρχὴ τῆς κτίσεως τοῦ Θεοῦ,

14) *To the angel of the church in Laodicea write: These things says the Amen, the faithful and genuine witness, the ruler of God's creation.*

Laodicea lay a little over forty miles to the southeast of Philadelphia. Besides the congregation at Ephesus, the church in Laodicea is the only one of the seven churches to be mentioned elsewhere in the New Testament. It is mentioned in Paul's letter to the Christians in Colossae, a city about a dozen miles to the east. Ancient Laodicea is no longer in existence, although the modern city of Denizli, with a population of almost 50,000, lies near the old site.

John's greeting to the seven churches refers to Jesus as "the faithful witness" (1:5). Here he is called "the faithful and genuine witness" The word for "genuine" can also be translated "true." The same word describes the Savior in the letter to Philadelphia, where the grammatical construction definitely seems to call for the translation "genuine." In this place the translation "true" or "truthful" would fit well into the context, since truthfulness is an obviously desirable characteristic of a witness.

The idea of truthfulness is found already in the word "Amen," which is related to the Hebrew word for truth. It could therefore be translated, "These things says the Truthful One." A faithful witness is one who delivers a message that fully conforms with the facts and withholds nothing of the truth. In this context, therefore, the translation "the faithful and true witness" would seem to add little to the progression of thought. But the translation "genuine" would indicate that we are dealing with a competent witness who is acquainted personally with the facts that underlie his testimony. The thought behind the word "genuine" is that which John expresses in his Gospel, where he writes, "No man has ever seen God, but God the only Son, who is at the Father's side, he has made him known" (Jn 1:18).

Jehovah's Witnesses often translate the words "the ruler of God's creation" to read "the beginning of God's creation." Thus, they say, Jesus is a creature, the first thing to be created by God, and therefore not God himself. As far as the grammar is concerned, this phrase could mean that Jesus is the first thing to be created. However, it can also mean that Jesus is the one who began the process of creation, that he is the cause of all things that exist. The Greek word ἀρχή can mean either "ruler" or "beginning."

When a certain word can have more than one meaning the context must inform us as to which meaning the author intends. The immediate context here is not decisive beyond question, but the wider context of Scripture makes it impossible to translate in such a way as to rob Christ of his divinity. In the first verses of his Gospel, John say of the Eternal Word, "Through him all things were made; without him nothing was made that has been made" (Jn 1:3). If nothing was made without the Second Person of the Trinity and all things were made by him, it is obvious that he himself cannot have been made in the beginning. It is true that millennia after creation he was made of a woman (Gal 4:4), and in that sense, he is a creature. We see how desperately Jehovah's Witnesses must struggle to escape the proper conclusion from the words of Scripture in their translation of the Bible, which reads, "By him were all *other* things created" (Col 1:16), even though the word "other" is not found in the Greek text.

The threats and promises that are made in the seven letters also allude directly to the description of the Savior at the beginning of the letter (cp. 1:8 and 11; 1:12 and 16; 1:18 and 26; 2:7 and 8). The translation, "the ruler of God's creation," would characteristically correspond to the words in v. 21, "I overcame and sat down with my Father on his throne." Therefore, "the ruler of God's creation" provides the most natural translation of ἡ ἀρχὴ τῆς κτίσεως τοῦ Θεοῦ.

To the congregation in Laodicea the Savior writes:

15) Οἶδά σου τὰ ἔργα, ὅτι οὔτε ψυχρὸς εἶ οὔτε ζεστός. ὄφελον ψυχρὸς ἦς ἢ ζεστός. 16) οὕτως ὅτι χλιαρὸς εἶ, καὶ οὔτε ζεστὸς οὔτε ψυχρός, μέλλω σε ἐμέσαι ἐκ τοῦ στόματός μου. 17) ὅτι λέγεις ὅτι Πλούσιός εἰμι καὶ πεπλούτηκα καὶ οὐδὲν χρείαν ἔχω, καὶ οὐκ

οἶδας ὅτι σὺ εἶ ὁ ταλαίπωρος καὶ ἐλεεινὸς καὶ πτωχὸς καὶ τυφλὸς καὶ γυμνός, 18) συμβουλεύω σοι ἀγοράσαι παρ' ἐμοῦ χρυσίον πεπυρωμένον ἐκ πυρὸς ἵνα πλουτήσῃς, καὶ ἱμάτια λευκὰ ἵνα περιβάλῃ καὶ μὴ φανερωθῇ ἡ αἰσχύνη τῆς γυμνότητός σου, καὶ κολλούριον ἐγχρῖσαι τοὺς ὀφθαλμούς σου ἵνα βλέπῃς. 19) ἐγὼ ὅσους ἐὰν φιλῶ ἐλέγχω καὶ παιδεύω· ζήλευε οὖν καὶ μετανόησον. 20) Ἰδοὺ ἕστηκα ἐπὶ τὴν θύραν καὶ κρούω· ἐάν τις ἀκούσῃ τῆς φωνῆς μου καὶ ἀνοίξῃ τὴν θύραν, εἰσελεύσομαι πρὸς αὐτὸν καὶ δειπνήσω μετ' αὐτοῦ καὶ αὐτὸς μετ' ἐμοῦ. 21) Ὁ νικῶν, δώσω αὐτῷ καθίσαι μετ' ἐμοῦ ἐν τῷ θρόνῳ μου, ὡς κἀγὼ ἐνίκησα καὶ ἐκάθισα μετὰ τοῦ Πατρός μου ἐν τῷ θρόνῳ αὐτοῦ. 22) Ὁ ἔχων οὖς ἀκουσάτω τί τὸ Πνεῦμα λέγει ταῖς ἐκκλησίαις.

15) *I know your works, that you are neither cold nor hot. I wish you were cold or hot.* 16) *So, because you are lukewarm and neither hot nor cold, I will spit you out of my mouth.* 17) *For you say, "I am rich. I have become wealthy and am in need of nothing." You do not know that you are miserable and to be pitied, and poor, and blind, and naked.* 18) *I advise you to buy from me gold refined in fire, that you may be rich, and white garments, that you may be clothed and that the shame of your nakedness may not become public, and to anoint your eyes with eyesalve, that you may see.* 19) *As for me, those whom I love I rebuke and discipline. Therefore, take this seriously and repent.* 20) *Behold, I stand at the door and I am knocking. If anyone hears my voice and opens the door, I will come in to him and dine with him and he with me.* 21) *To him who is victorious I will give the right to sit with me on my throne — just as I have conquered and have sat down with my father on his throne.* 22) *Whoever has an ear, let him hear what the Spirit says to the churches.*

Several commentators think the reference to heat, cold and lukewarmness has some connection with the hot springs that were situated near Laodicea. But whether the Savior was alluding to this or not, the meaning of the criticism is clear. Evidently a characteristic sinful weakness of this congregation was spiritual dullness and indifference. Heat is obviously a figure of speech denoting zeal, interest and concern for the things of the Spirit. Coldness, on the other hand, would symbolize opposition to the gospel. Lukewarmness represents indifference and a lack of interest.

It is easy to see why the Savior would want the congregation to be hot. It is not so easy to see at first glance why coldness, or opposition to the gospel is preferable to lukewarmness. But those who actively oppose the gospel at least still demonstrate some interest in spiritual things. They still manifest some concern about the truth. Saul, who persecuted the church, was still intent upon serving God, whereas Pilate, who asks, "What is truth?" is simply not interested. It is said that John Wesley once expressed the opinion that a preacher of the Word ought either to convert people or make them angry. But people who just are not concerned about heaven or hell, life or death make poor mission prospects. In that sense, therefore, even cold opposition to the gospel is preferable to lukewarmness or indifference.

The Christians in Laodicea were guilty of the sin of indifference. Many years had passed since they had first heard the gospel. Like the Ephesians, who had "lost their first love" during the intervening years, so the congregation in Laodicea had grown less and less concerned about spiritual things. The pleasures of this life and the riches of this world had dulled their sense of spiritual need.

The Savior issues one of his sharpest rebukes to the church in Laodicea. "I will spit you out of my mouth," he says. He threatens to reject them completely. The congregation was not aware of its sad condition. Its attitude was summed up in the words, "I am rich, I have become wealthy. There is nothing I need."

Whether these words are especially to be understood in a material sense or in a spiritual sense is not clear. We know that Laodicea was a very wealthy city. When an earthquake destroyed the city in 60 A.D., the citizens rebuilt it without any help from Rome. It was a well-known banking center, and a mint was situated there. It was also the center of a thriving wool industry, and its cloth was famous throughout the Roman world. Finally, it was also renowned for a type of eyesalve that was invented there and was prescribed by physicians who lived far away from Laodicea.

It is not at all impossible that here the Savior is referring to their material wealth, which enabled them to live from day to day without much concern for their daily bread. Just as bodily needs and physical ailments sometimes remind men of their sinfulness and the needs of the soul, so material prosperity in many cases causes men to forget God. Too many days go by when experience does not compel them to be conscious of the awful consequences of the fall into sin (Pr 30:8f). They do not eat their bread in the sweat of their brow. Maybe this is what the Laodiceans meant when they said that they had no need of anything.

It is, however, also possible that here the Savior is describing Laodicea's lack of the awareness of spiritual need. Here, perhaps, were people who were not "poor in spirit," who did not realize that they had nothing to offer God by which they might win his favor. Perhaps they were living under the delusion that they were entitled to God's love and were for that reason assured of everlasting life. They had no more need of God's gracious forgiveness.

In either case, here was a congregation which had in large measure forgotten its great need for God's care and forgiveness. They were neither cold nor hot, but lukewarm.

The Savior describes the self-sufficient attitude of the Laodiceans and then reminds them of their true condition. He says, "You do not know that you are miserable and to be pitied, and poor, and blind, and naked." Does this refer to material wealth? Certainly people who are materially poor and persecuted would know that they are poor and to be pitied. But it is also possible for poverty-stricken people to be proud and spiritually self-satisfied, and not to know that they are miserable.

Christians often speak of unbelievers in general as being miserable. Yet we sometimes forget that this does not mean that they necessarily *feel* miserable and unhappy. A professor at the University of Chicago once said, "Fundamentalistic preachers often speak of how unhappy the people are who don't have faith. Look at me. I don't believe those things and I am a happy man." The misery of unbelief is often not sensed by unbelievers, and we ought to expect this, for the Bible says that they are "dead" (Eph 2:1) and "past feeling" (Eph 4:19). For this, too, they are to be pitied.

If we consider the "wealth" of the Laodiceans as consisting in material prosperity, we have in the words of the Savior a strong sermon against the so-called "social gospel" of the twentieth century. In many areas of Christendom the Christian religion has degenerated into nothing more than concern about the social and economic welfare of men. It is, however, possible to have all one's need adequately supplied, to have all one's civil rights, a beautiful home and a healthy diet, and yet to be miserable and to be pitied, because the needs of the soul are not being met. A religion therefore that prompts men to be overly concerned about food and drink and clothing does little or nothing to bring men the hope and joy that comes from forgiveness through the blood of Christ. Such a religion does not really meet human needs and does not deserve to be called a Christian religion.

Even though the Laodiceans said that they were wealthy and had need of nothing, the Savior says that their needs are great, that they are "poor and blind and naked." He tells them also how those needs can be met. He says, "I advise you to buy from me gold refined in fire that you may be rich, and white garments that you may be clothed and that the shame of your nakedness may not become public, and to anoint your eyes with eyesalve that you may see."

The Laodiceans could not find true wealth at the mint in Laodicea. True wealth is found only in Christ and in the salvation he procured for us in the fire of affliction he endured when he suffered the penalty for our guilt.

The Laodiceans were naked, says the Savior, and they could cover that nakedness only with the "white garments" he had to offer them. It is of some interest to know that the woolen cloth for which Laodicea was famous was either brightly dyed or woven from black wool. We have already read of white raiment in the letter to Sardis (3:4,5), but in a later chapter (7:13) it becomes clear why Christ alone can supply the garments that will cover the shame of their nakedness. Only the blood of the Lamb can wash them and make them white. With these words the Savior speaks of their need of forgiveness.

The next words, concerning eyesalve, address their need of spiritual healing. Scripture often compares the natural spiritual state of man to the darkness and blindness which makes it impossible for natural men to see the real nature of their sinfulness and which keeps them from recognizing Christ as the only Savior. The Laodicean Christians were unconscious of their real condition. They were falling back into the spiritual blindness in which they were born. But the situation was not yet hopeless. In this case, where their own eyesalve would fail, the Savior would provide them with his gospel and its power to heal their deteriorating spiritual eyesight.

There is no word of commendation for Laodicea. This last letter of the seven is the only one which lacks a word of praise. The condemnation of Laodicea is particularly harsh, but these words of criticism are words of love, designed to benefit the Laodiceans. The Lord says, "As many as I love I rebuke and correct." Love will not allow sin to go uncorrected. Therefore the Savior does not want the Laodiceans to pass lightly over his criticism. He says, "Take it seriously and repent."

Verse 20 is well known: "Behold, I stand at the door and knock. If anyone hears my voice and opens the door, I will come in to dine with him and he with me." There are many who force these words to support a synergistic view of conversion. There is no question that we are here dealing with a gospel invitation. The Savior pleads with men to allow him to come into their lives and hearts so that he may share with them all the blessings of his love. His words are simply another way of expressing the same gospel invitation that is expressed in a multitude of ways throughout the Bible. Synergistic interpreters sometimes appeal to the classical artist's conception of this invitation and point out that the door in the picture has no knob on the outside, to indicate that it can be opened only from within.

However, neither this passage nor any other gospel invitation implies that man by nature has the power to respond. The question of man's ability is settled by other statements of Scripture, which clearly teaches that man is by nature spiritually "dead" and therefore unable to accept God's offer of salvation. We are saved by grace alone.

It is, of course, true that some men do respond to the invitation while others do not. Some men open the door and others keep it closed. But the power which makes the response possible lies not in the natural will of man but in the gospel invitation. The Savior whose knock on the door of our hearts summons us to open the door is the same almighty Lord who stood at the grave of Lazarus and called him forth. Likewise, we read that the Lord opened Lydia's heart (Ac 16:14). The gospel invitation is a word of God and therefore has the inherent power to open the heart for the Savior's entrance. That power alone causes man to respond positively.

What we have said here should not be understood to mean that the Savior in this particular case is addressing a church composed of unbelievers. Millennialists teach that the letter to Philadelphia symbolizes the time of the rapture and look upon the church of Laodicea as a church in which there are no believers. They claim that the letter to Laodicea represents the church as it will exist during the seven years of the great tribulation. A church composed of unbelievers is a contradiction in terms, at least in the language of the Bible. The fact that there is no word of commendation in this letter and that the church is called upon to repent does not in any way prove that there are no Christians in Laodicea. The call to repent also is addressed to most of the other six churches in Asia Minor, and the promise of the Savior to enter the heart of anyone who listens to his invitation is very similar to the words Jesus spoke to his disciples in John 14:23, "If anyone loves me, he will obey my teaching. My Father will love him, and we will come to him, and make our home with him."

Those who open the door and are victorious in the battle against sin and unbelief will have the privilege of sitting with the Savior on his throne. This is a lucid figurative way of promising that we will reign with Christ. The dominion over all creatures that God gave Adam and Eve at the time of creation was in large measure lost through the fall into sin. It will once more fully be restored for all eternity, and the words of Psalm 8, which have been fulfilled in Christ, will again be true also of us. In him and through him we will once more regain the full dominion which we had lost in Adam's fall.

The familiar call to hear closes the letter to Laodicea.

The Second Vision: The Seven Seals (4:1 — 7:17)

JOHN'S VISION OF GOD (4:1-11)

John's vision of the Savior in chapter 1 serves as the introduction to the seven letters. In the text there is nothing to indicate a break between the first and second chapter. The writing of the seven letters is a part of the first vision, even though chapters 2 and 3 do not tell us about anything the Apostle John saw. The Savior, who appeared to him, simply dictated the letters. Whether John wrote the letters during the vision or whether he did this later from memory under the inspiration of the Holy Ghost we do not know.

The beginning of chapter 4 is simply the continuation of the story begun in chapter 1. John writes,

> **1) Μετὰ ταῦτα εἶδον, καὶ ἰδοὺ θύρα ἠνεῳγμένη ἐν τῷ οὐρανῷ, καὶ ἡ φωνὴ ἡ πρώτη ἣν ἤκουσα ὡς σάλπιγγος λαλούσης μετ' ἐμοῦ, λέγων, Ἀνάβα ὧδε, καὶ δείξω σοι ἃ δεῖ γενέσθαι μετὰ ταῦτα. 2) εὐθέως ἐγενόμην ἐν πνεύματι·**
>
> 1) *After these things I saw, and behold, a door was opened in heaven, and I heard the first voice like a trumpet speaking to me. It said, "Come up here, and I will show you what must happen after these things."* 2) *And immediately I was in spirit.*

Many millennialists see in this first verse of chapter 4 a reference to the so-called "rapture of the saints." According to a popular form of millennialism the so-called "thousand-year reign of Christ" here on this earth will be preceded by a "rapture." In other words, shortly before the return of Christ to reign visibly on this earth, all believers will suddenly and silently be taken out of this world to join Christ. No believers at all will be left in this world. The rapture will, according to one version of this doctrine, be followed by seven years of troubled times, known as the "great tribulation," after which the "millennium" will begin.

There is, however, nothing in the verse to indicate that John is here speaking of any "rapture of the saints." Rapturists have been heard to insist, as we have already mentioned, that this must be a reference to the rapture since the omission of such a reference would be "unthinkable" in a book which speaks especially of the last things. This argument, however, only helps to prove that the whole concept of a pre-millennial rapture is pure fantasy which some insist on reading into the Bible.

What John describes here is not an event that will take place in the distant future, but something that happened on a particular Sunday in the first century on the island of Patmos. The first words in this chapter, "after these things," clearly refer to events that had already taken place, namely, the appearance of Christ to John and the dictation of the seven letters.

Having heard the words which the Lord had spoken to the seven churches, John looked and saw a door opened in heaven. The primary meaning of the word "heaven" is "sky," and we may also translate, "I saw a door opened in the sky." At the same time John heard a voice, which he calls "the first voice." Obviously this is a reference to the voice which he had heard at the beginning of the vision (1:10). There, too, he had described the voice as being "like a trumpet."

The voice said to him, "Come up here, and I will show you what must happen after these things." And John said, "Immediately I was [or, came to be] in spirit." This, too, reminds us of the beginning of the visions, for there he said, "I was (or came to be) in spirit on the Lord's day" (1:10).

What happened to John here is very similar to an experience which Paul describes in Second Corinthians. There Paul speaks of a revelation in which he was caught up to the "third heaven," where he heard things which are not lawful for a man to utter. We can not be completely certain about what Paul meant by the third heaven, but it is likely that the "first heaven" is the atmosphere in which the birds fly (Gn 1:20), the second heaven is the space beyond the clouds where the sun, moon and stars are situated (Gn 1:14), and the third heaven is the dwelling place of God and the angels. Modern parapsychologists speak of such events as "out-of-the-body" experiences, yet Paul says that he does not know whether he was "out of the body" or "in the body" (2 Cor 12:2,3). Evidently it was something similar to what John here describes as being "in spirit," in a new spiritual state in which he was able to see and hear things which a man in his normal state here in this world cannot see and hear.

It is significant that John was told that he would be shown "what *must* be after these things." In this context "these things" are the world conditions and events of the late first century, specifically the things described in the seven letters. The Lord promises to reveal future events and conditions to the apostle. When the Lord says that these things *must* happen, he indicates clearly that the future is already determined and that what John would see would surely come to pass. The statement is reminiscent of the many passages which say that the Scriptures *must* be fulfilled. These are not guesses concerning the future, but revelations of the God who sees the future as clearly as he sees the present and the past. The foreknowledge of these future events on God's part does not make them happen, but because God sees the future exactly and correctly it is impossible for him and the men through whom he foretells the future to be mistaken. In that sense the event must happen, even though many of them happen through the free choice of men.

John then describes what he saw in the vision. He writes,

> **καὶ ἰδοὺ θρόνος ἔκειτο ἐν τῷ οὐρανῷ, καὶ ἐπὶ τὸν θρόνον καθήμενος, 3) καὶ ὁ καθήμενος ὅμοιος ὁράσει λίθῳ ἰάσπιδι καὶ σαρδίῳ, καὶ ἶρις κυκλόθεν τοῦ θρόνου ὅμοιος ὁράσει σμαραγδίνῳ 4) καὶ κυκλόθεν τοῦ θρόνου θρόνους εἴκοσι τέσσαρας, καὶ ἐπὶ τοὺς θρόνους εἴκοσι τέσσαρας πρεσβυτέρους καθημένους περιβεβλημένους ἐν ἱματίοις λευκοῖς, καὶ ἐπὶ τὰς κεφαλὰς αὐτῶν στεφάνους χρυσοῦς. 5) καὶ ἐκ τοῦ θρόνου ἐκπορεύονται ἀστραπαὶ καὶ φωναὶ καὶ βρονταί· καὶ ἑπτὰ λαμπάδες πυρὸς καιόμεναι ἐνώπιον τοῦ θρόνου, ἅ εἰσιν τὰ ἑπτὰ Πνεύματα τοῦ Θεοῦ· 6) καὶ ἐνώπιον τοῦ θρόνου ὡς θάλασσα ὑαλίνη ὁμοία κρυστάλλῳ·**
>
> *And behold, a throne was set in the sky, and upon the throne a seated one,* 3) *and the seated one was in appearance like a jasper stone and a carnelian, and around the throne there was a rainbow like an emerald in appearance.* 4) *And around the throne were twenty-four thrones, and seated upon those thrones were twenty-four elders in white garments, and upon their heads there were crowns of gold.* 5) *And out from the throne went lightning flashes and sounds and thunders. Burning before the throne were seven lamps of fire, which are the seven Spirits of God.* 6) *And before the throne there seemed to be a glassy sea, like crystal.*

John saw a vision of God. The subsequent context affirms this, but anyone well acquainted with the Old Testament would know from the very beginning that the one sitting on the throne is God himself. Visions of God such as John describes here are reminiscent of the visions of the Old Testament prophets. The description portrays a focal point of multicolored flashing lights under an arch, or within a circle or halo, of bright green light, "like an emerald." In the Old Testament, God often revealed himself in a bright light which was called "the glory of the Lord." Here John sees that glory, and the impression it makes on him is that of the flashing of precious stones.

The significance of the twenty-four thrones is also easy to discover. Several times in the seven letters the Savior promises faithful Christians that they will reign with him in glory. Many years before this, when the Lord Jesus was still on this earth with his disciples, he promised that some day they would be seated on "twelve thrones judging the twelve tribes of Israel" (Mt 19:28). Twelve of the elders sitting around the throne are the twelve apostles, who are often called "elders" in the New Testament and in the literature of the early church.

Some argue that twelve of these elders cannot be the twelve apostles because John was on Patmos at the time and therefore could not be sitting on one of the thrones. But this argument forgets that we are dealing with a vision. Just as a man may see himself in a dream, so it is surely possible for John to see himself in this vision. The words of Jesus to his disciples also give us a clue to the identity of the twelve remaining elders. They are the twelve patriarchs from whom the twelve tribes of Israel, God's Old Testament people, descended. Thus the twenty-four elders represent the Old and New Testament church. The golden crowns on their heads, as well as the thrones upon which they sit, are symbols of their royal authority. Their white garments symbolize the righteousness which is theirs through faith in Christ.

After John finishes viewing the twenty-four elders, the throne once again attracts his attention. He sees flashes of "lightning." He also hears sounds, or voices, and thunderings coming from the throne. In some ways the scene recalls God's revelation of himself at Mt. Sinai, where he also manifested his presence in "thunders and lightnings" (Ex 19:16).

The seven lamps of fire burning before the throne are similar to the seven-branched candlestick that burned in the Old Testament tabernacle (Ex 37:17-24). The text distinctly tells us that the seven flames symbolize the seven Spirits of God, Revelation's way of describing the Third Person of the Trinity (see chapter 1). The Old Testament Prophet Zechariah also drew a symbolic connection between a seven-branched candlestick and the work of the Holy Spirit (cp Zch 4:1-6). Since the Holy Spirit has inspired the Scriptures, which is a lamp unto our feet (Ps 119:105), he himself is compared to a brightly shining lamp. As the seven branches reaching out into the church form one candlestick, so the "seven Spirits of God" are one Holy Spirit.

In the foreground of the whole heavenly scene John saw a sea of glass as clear as crystal. Not a ripple disturbed the complete calm of the sea before the throne. This represents the perfect peace that exists in the presence of God. The description of this glassy sea is especially significant when we remember that almost every reference to the sea in the Old Testament portrays it as a place of danger and trouble. The only time a Jewish king endeavored to develop a navy, for example, it ended in disaster and the ships "were wrecked at Ezion Geber" (1 Kgs 22:48). Isaiah spoke of the "tossing sea which cannot rest" (Is 57:20). But before the throne in heaven John sees a sea that is at perfect rest. There is nothing here to disturb the quiet rest that is enjoyed by those who are gathered around the throne. The crystal clearness of this sea also signifies that there is no pollution or blemish of any kind in the presence of God.

καὶ ἐν μέσῳ τοῦ θρόνου καὶ κύκλῳ τοῦ θρόνου τέσσερα ζῷα γέμοντα ὀφθαλμῶν ἔμπροσθεν καὶ ὄπισθεν. 7) καὶ τὸ ζῷον τὸ πρῶτον ὅμοιον λέοντι, καὶ τὸ δεύτερον ζῷον ὅμοιον μόσχῳ, καὶ τὸ τρίτον ζῷον ἔχων τὸ πρόσωπον ὡς ἀνθρώπου, καὶ τὸ τέταρτον ζῷον ὅμοιον ἀετῷ πετομένῳ. 8) καὶ τὰ τέσσερα ζῷα, ἓν καθ' ἓν αὐτῶν ἔχων ἀνὰ πτέρυγας ἕξ, κυκλόθεν καὶ ἔσωθεν γέμουσιν ὀφθαλμῶν· καὶ ἀνάπαυσιν οὐκ ἔχουσιν ἡμέρας καὶ νυκτὸς λέγοντες,

Ἅγιος ἅγιος ἅγιος Κύριος ὁ Θεὸς ὁ Παντοκράτωρ,
ὁ ἦν καὶ ὁ ὢν καὶ ὁ ἐρχόμενος.

And in the middle, near the throne, and around the throne, there were four living creatures, full of eyes in front and in back. 7) The first living creature was like a lion, the second living creature like an ox, the third living creature had a face similar to that of a man, and the fourth living creature was like a flying eagle. 8) Each one of the four living creatures had six wings, and the wings were full of eyes all around and on the inner surface. And day and night, without pause, they say, "Holy, holy, holy, Lord God Almighty, the one who was and is and is to come."

Literally, the first words of this section read, "And in the middle of the throne (ἐν μέσῳ τοῦ θρόνου) and around the throne there were four living creatures." The genitive case in Greek signifies some kind of connection, but the context must determine the nature of the connection. Since it is clear that the four living creatures were standing around the throne it is also clear that John could not have seen them in the center of the throne, where God was sitting. We must therefore translate either, "in the center, where the throne was," or, "in the center, near the throne." The throne occupied the center of the scene. Around the throne in a larger circle were arranged the twenty-four thrones on which the twenty-four elders sat. In a smaller circle, in the center and closer to the throne, stood the four living creatures.

The significance of the four living creatures is difficult to determine. Some commentators insist that they cannot be angelic beings because in 5:11 they seem to be distinguished from the angels. But this is by no means a decisive argument. It is entirely possible to see in these passages not a distinction between the living creatures and the angels but rather between four angels of high rank near the throne and the multitude of angels who stand farther away from the center.

The elements in the description of the four living creatures bear many similarities to Ezekiel's vision of the glory of the Lord (Eze 1:4-28). In that vision four living creatures also appear, each of which has four faces, the face of a man, a lion, an ox and an eagle. In the book of Revelation each of the four living creatures has but one of the four faces. The living creatures in Ezekiel's vision have four wings. Here they have six. In this respect the four creatures in this vision are similar to the seraphim in the vision of Isaiah (Is 6:2). In Ezekiel's vision each of the four creatures is accompanied by a wheel which rested on the earth and each wheel was full of eyes (Eze 1:18).

A later chapter of Ezekiel identifies the four "living creatures" as cherubim (Eze 10:20). The similarities between the visions of John and Ezekiel would justify classifying the four living creatures in Revelation among the cherubim. The large number of eyes represents the angels' concern for and awareness of what is happening throughout the universe. The angels are agents through whom God governs the world and protects his people. The four faces represent the four great divisions of life on earth — the birds, represented by the eagle; the wild beasts, by the lion; the domestic animals, by the ox; and man, as in a class all by himself. Unlike modern science, the Bible always views man as a creature sharply distinguished from the animal world. While the text does not spell out the significance of this division, it would be in harmony with Scripture to see in the four cherubim a representation of God's government and control over all aspects of his creation.

The text says nothing about the significance of the six wings of each of the four living creatures. We remember, however, that the angels in the vision of Isaiah (Is 6) also had six wings. Isaiah tells us that the seraphim in his vision used two of their wings to cover their feet, two to cover their faces and two to fly. In ancient times the feet of travelers were likely to be soiled. For that reason it was customary to provide guests with water to wash their feet (Lk 7:44). The covering of the feet by the wings of the angel signifies an effort to hide from God's view everything that is impure. While it is true that the good angels are sinless and holy, yet, compared with the pureness and holiness of God, even the holiest of creatures still must stand in reverent shame and humility before the transcendent holiness of God (cp Job 4:18; 15:15; 25:5).

The covering of the eyes by the second pair of wings signifies the inability of the creature to look directly at the glory of the Lord. It is therefore a confession of the awe-inspiring majesty of God, who lives in unapproachable light, whom no one has seen or can see (1 Tm 6:16).

The last pair of wings, with which the seraphim fly, implies the readiness of the angels to carry out their assignments as messengers and agents of God. Those commentators who therefore see in the four living creatures representations of the providence of God are very likely correct.

The unceasing song of the angels echoes the song of the seraphim in Isaiah's vision. "Holy, holy, holy is the Lord God Almighty, who was, and who is, and who is to come." The last words in the song are not found in Isaiah but are a repetition of the words with which the Savior had described himself in the first chapter (1:8). Here, however, the words describe the triune God, whose essence is alluded to in the threefold repetition of the word "holy."

In our comments on 1:4-6, we noted that the description of God in that section falls into groups of three. Here we see that the threefold holy, three names of God — Lord, God, Almighty — and three attributes of God form three lines of poetry with three terms in each line as follows:

Holy	Holy	Holy
Lord	God	Almighty
who was	who is	who is to come

This threefold description is echoed in the threefold doxology in v. 11 as well as in the threefold resumé of this song in v. 9.

In the vision of Isaiah the angels sing, "Holy, holy, holy is the Lord of hosts, the whole earth is full of his glory." The similarity between the two songs is greater than appears at first glance because the words "Lord Almighty" are the words that are used regularly in the Septuagint (the ancient Greek translation of the Hebrew Old Testament) to translate the Hebrew phrase "The Lord of hosts," or *JHVH Sebaoth*. The two terms are closely related. The name "Lord of Hosts" describes God as the mighty and majestic commander of the powerful angel armies, whereas the name "Lord Almighty" is a more prosaic way of emphasizing his power. This verse forms the basis of Reginald Heber's hymn, "Holy, Holy, Holy" (*The Lutheran Hymnal*, 246). This hymn contains a number of allusions to chapters 4 and 5 of Revelation, e.g., "Casting down their golden crowns around the glassy sea" (cp Rev 4:6,10).

The four living cratures who sing this song of praise to God day and night without resting are joined in their praise by the twenty-four elders who surround the throne in a wider circle. John writes,

9) Καὶ ὅταν δώσουσιν τὰ ζῶα δόξαν καὶ τιμὴν καὶ εὐχαριστίαν τῷ καθημένῳ ἐπὶ τῷ θρόνῳ τῷ ζῶντι εἰς τοὺς αἰῶνας τῶν αἰώνων,
10) πεσοῦνται οἱ εἴκοσι τέσσαρες πρεσβύτεροι ἐνώπιον τοῦ καθημένου ἐπι τοῦ θρόνου, καὶ προσκυνήσουσιν τῷ ζῶντι εἰς τοῦς αἰῶνας τῶν αἰώνων, καὶ βαλοῦσιν τοὺ στεφάνους αὐτῶν ἐνώπιον τοῦ θρόνου, λέγοντες,
11) Ἄξιος εἶ, ὁ Κύριος καὶ ὁ Θεὸς ἡμῶν, λαβεῖν τὴν δόξαν καὶ τὴν τιμὴν καὶ τὴν δύναμιν, ὅτι σὺ ἔκτισας τὰ πάντα, καὶ διὰ τὸ θέλημά σου ἦσαν καὶ ἐκτίσθησαν.

9) *And when the living creatures give glory and honor and thanks to him who sits upon the throne, the one who lives to all eternity,* 10) *the twenty-four elders fall down before him who sits upon the throne, and they worship the one who lives forever and ever, and they cast their crowns before him as they say,*
11) *"Worthy are you, our Lord and God, to receive glory and honor and power, for you have created all things, and because of your will they existed and were created."*

The words of the angels' song in verse 8 evidently are not the full text of the hymn they sing before the throne, for these words could hardly be described by saying that they give the Lord "glory and honor and *thanks*." But as the living creatures sing their song and honor and glorify and thank God, the twenty-four elders, as representatives of the church of the Old and New Testaments, also honor the Lord by falling down and worshiping him. The crowns which they wore on their heads at the beginning of the vision (v. 4) they now remove. They cast them before the throne of God. By that act they confess that even though God has bestowed upon them the high honor of having made them kings, ruling the universe with him, they reign not for their own glory but for his. They recognize also that while they have received the high honor of being kings before God, yet in his glorious presence they surrender to him whatever glory they have. The story is told that Queen Victoria of England once expressed a wish to be alive at the time of the Savior's second coming because, as she said, "I would so dearly love to lay my crown at his feet."

The twenty-four elders address the one who sits on the throne as "our Lord and God" (ὁ κύριος καὶ ὁ θεὸς ἡμῶν). The words are almost identical in form to the exclamation of Thomas when he saw the risen Lord, "My Lord and my God" (ὁ κύριος μοῦ καὶ ὁ θεὸς μοῦ).

While the angels give honor and glory and thanks to God, the twenty-four elders declare that God is worthy to receive this glory and honor. When they also say that he is worthy to receive power or might, this, of course, cannot mean that God becomes more powerful. It can only mean that he is worthy of being called the Almighty One. It is right to ascribe omnipotence to him, as the four living creatures did in their song.

The Lord is worthy of such praise because he has created all things. The cause of anything must always be as great as or greater than the effect. The wonders of creation make it clear that God is a glorious and powerful God. The psalmist expresses a thought very similar to John's when he opens Psalm 19 with the words, "The heavens declare the glory of God."

The last clause in the song of the elders, "because of your will they existed and were created," is translated in the King James Version, "for thy pleasure they are and were created." In King James English the preposition "for" often meant "because of." It is still occasionally used in this way today. For example, we say, "He could not speak for anger," meaning, "He could not speak because he was so angry." Here, also, the words of the elders do not mean that the worlds were created to please God, but rather that they were created and therefore existed because it was the will of God that it should be so. In this way also the creation demonstrates the power and glory of God. When he wants something to be, it is.

THE BOOK OF THE SEVEN SEALS (5:1-5)

1) Καὶ εἶδον ἐπὶ τὴν δεξιὰν τοῦ καθημένου ἐπὶ τοῦ θρόνου βιβλίον γεγραμμένον ἔσωθεν καὶ ὄπισθεν, κατεσφραγισμένον σφραγῖσιν ἑπτά. 2) καὶ εἶδον ἄγγελον ἰσχυρὸν κηρύσσοντα ἐν φωνῇ μεγάλῃ, Τίς ἄξιος ἀνοῖξαι τὸ βιβλίον καὶ λῦσαι τὰς σφραγῖδας αὐτοῦ; 3) καὶ οὐδεὶς ἐδύνατο ἐν τῷ οὐρανῷ οὐδὲ ἐπὶ τῆς γῆς οὐδὲ ὑποκάτω τῆς γῆς ἀνοῖξαι τὸ βιβλίον οὔτε βλέπειν αὐτό. 4) καὶ ἔκλαιον πολύ, ὅτι οὐδεὶς ἄξιος εὑρέθη ἀνοῖξαι τὸ βιβλίον οὔτε βλέπειν αὐτό. 5) καὶ εἷς ἐκ τῶν πρεσβυτέρων λέγει μοι, Μὴ κλαῖε· ἰδοὺ ἐνίκησεν ὁ Λέων ὁ ἐκ τῆς φυλῆς Ἰούδα, ἡ Ῥίζα Δαυειδ, ἀνοῖξαι τὸ βιβλίον καὶ τὰς ἑπτὰ σφραγῖδας αὐτοῦ.

1) *And I saw in the right hand of the One who sat upon the throne, a book with writing on the inside and on the back, sealed with seven seals.* 2) *And I saw a mighty angel who was proclaiming with a loud voice, "Who is worthy to open the book and to break its seals?"* 3) *And no one in heaven or upon the earth or under the earth was able to open the book or to look into it.* 4) *And I was weeping much because no one was found who was worthy to open the book or to look into it.* 5) *And one of the elders said to me, "Stop weeping. Look! The Lion who is from the tribe of Judah, the Root of David, has won the victory (and is able) to open the book and its seven seals."*

After John hears the four living creatures and the twenty-four elders sing their songs of praise, he notices a book in the right hand of God the Father, who is sitting on the throne. The "book" is a scroll. Scrolls usually had writing only on one side. This scroll, however, had writing on both sides. Nevertheless it could not be read because it was sealed with seven seals. Seals usually were pressed by a ring into wax that held the scroll in a closed position. They were to keep unauthorized people from reading the scroll.

The context tells us why the book was sealed and its contents kept secret. In the first chapter of Revelation John tells us that he is going to write about the future. In chapters 6 and 7 he carries out this intention and speaks about future events. But John cannot write about these things until the seals are opened and the contents of the book are revealed.

The future is a closed book to men, and any attempt to discover the secrets of the future apart from God's revelation is an illegitimate quest. No man is worthy to open that book or to look into it. Sorcerers, who try to control the future, and fortunetellers of all kinds, who try to predict the future in ways forbidden by God, are guilty of violating God's majesty. At the close of the book of Revelation God excludes all such practitioners of magic arts from the holy city (Rev 22:15).

On the other hand, the children of God have a longing to know what the future has in store. John wept because no man was worthy to open the book. The church was experiencing bitter persecutions at the time of John's vision, and many Christians must have been troubled about the final outcome of this assault. So far as men could know, apart from divine revelation, this might easily end in the total destruction of the infant church. God's people must have yearned for assurance that the gates of hell would indeed never prevail against the church of Christ.

But as John wept over man's incompetence to know the future, one of the twenty-four elders told him to dry his tears. The words, "Stop weeping," are not an absolute prohibition to shed tears. That would be expressed by an aorist imperative. The present imperative with a negative particle, as here (μὴ κλαῖε), usually expresses a command to stop doing something. The command addressed to John here has the same form as the one Jesus spoke to the widow at Nain. There, too, it is not a general prohibition directed against all weeping at the death of a loved one, but rather a gracious announcement that she could dry her tears because the Lord of life was about to bring her son back to life. She had no more reason to cry. So here also the words spoken to John, "Stop weeping," are an indication that there is no need for tears. Someone has been found who is worthy to open the book and to disclose its contents.

The announcement literally reads, "Look! The Lion of the tribe of Judah, the Root of David, has conquered to open the book and its seven seals." The verb "conquered" is not ordinarily followed by an infinitive. The construction is elliptical and relies on the context for the missing words. The infinitive indicates the result of the victory. From the context we must supply either the verb "to be able" (v. 3) or the adjective "worthy" (vv. 2 and 4), so that we translate either "The Lion of the tribe of Judah . . . has conquered (and is able) to open the book" or "The

Lion of the tribe of Judah . . . has conquered (and is worthy) to open the book."

Christians who were well acquainted with the Old Testament would know immediately who is meant by the "Lion of the tribe of Judah." This is a direct reference to the prophecy of Jacob in Genesis 49:9,10. There Jacob says, in blessing his son Judah, "You are a lion's cub, O Judah; you return from the prey, my son. Like a lion he crouches and lies down, like a lioness — who dares to rouse him? The scepter will not depart from Judah, nor the ruler's staff from between his feet, until he comes to whom it belongs and the obedience of the nations shall be his." This is a Messianic prophecy and it illustrates clearly why John calls the Messiah the "Lion of the tribe of Judah."

The designation "the Root of David" is based on Isaiah 11:1-10, especially verses 1 and 10. This is also a Messianic passage. In the first verse of the chapter the Messiah is spoken of as a branch that will grow out of the roots of Jesse, the father of David. In verse 10 he is simply called "a root of Jesse." From that name to the name "the Root of David" is a very short step. The word "root" here evidently means "sprout," a shoot that grows out of the root of David. The name is synonymous with "the Son of David."

The fact that the Messiah is worthy and able to open the book indicates that the future is in his control. This symbolism is another way of saying that he sits at the right hand of God and that all things are under his feet. In more literal terms we would say that all the future developments in history are subject to his knowledge and control. While his believers may sometimes be surprised by developments and be tempted to fear them, yet he will never be in ignorance of the enemies' plan nor will he ever be helpless before them. He holds the book of the future in his hands and only what he in his gracious providence permits will be free to take place. He breaks the seals when it pleases him.

The Messiah is now identified further in terms more familiar to New Testament readers. Having heard the announcement that someone has been found to open the book, John continues his description of the vision.

THE LAMB BEFORE THE THRONE (5:6-8)

6) Καὶ εἶδον ἐν μέσῳ τοῦ θρόνου καὶ τῶν τεσσάρων ζώων καὶ ἐν μέσῳ τῶν πρεσβυτέρων Ἀρνίον ἑστηκὸς ὡς ἐσφαγμένον, ἔχων κέρατα ἑπτὰ καὶ ὀφθαλμοὺς ἑπτά, οἵ εἰσιν τὰ ἑπτὰ Πνεύματα τοῦ

Θεοῦ ἀπεσταλμένοι εἰς πᾶσαν τὴν γῆν. 7) καὶ ἦλθεν καὶ εἴληφεν ἐκ τῆς δεξιᾶς τοῦ καθημένου ἐπὶ τοῦ θρόνου. 8) Καὶ ὅτε ἔλαβεν τὸ βιβλίον, τὰ τέσσερα ζῷα καὶ οἱ εἴκοσι τέσσαρες πρεσβύτεροι ἔπεσαν ἐνώπιον τοῦ Ἀρνίου, ἔχοντες ἕκαστος κιθάραν καὶ φιάλας χρυσᾶς γεμούσας θυμιαμάτων, αἵ εἰσιν αἱ προσευχαὶ τῶν ἁγίων.

6) *And in the center near the throne surrounded by the four living creatures and the twenty-four elders, I saw a Lamb standing. It seemed to have been slain and had seven horns and seven eyes. These are the seven spirits of God that have been sent into all the earth.* 7) *He came and took (the book) out of the right hand of him who sat upon the throne.* 8) *And when he took the book, the four living creatures and the twenty-four elders fell down before the Lamb. Each one had a harp and golden bowls full of incense. These are the prayers of the saints.*

In verse 6 we have the first of twenty-six passages in Revelation in which the Savior is called a Lamb. In all the remaining books of the New Testament this name is given to the Lord Jesus in only four passages, two of which are found in the Gospel according to St. John (Jn 1:29,36). This symbolism, however, has become so common in the church that a modern Christian reader knows immediately the identity of this lamb standing near the throne.

Already in the Old Testament the Prophet Isaiah had spoken of the coming Redeemer as a lamb led to the slaughter, standing silent before its shearers (Is 53:7). This passage is quoted in one of the two non-Johannine passages in which the lamb symbolism is used (Ac 8:32). But the greatest help in understanding this symbolism is found in the Old Testament system of sacrifices. Lambs were sacrificial animals. Through their blood and death, atonement was made for the sins of the people. The Passover lamb, whose blood saved the firstborn in Israel from death in Egypt, was slain every year to commemorate that event. In the only other non-Johannine passage in which Jesus is spoken of as a lamb (1 Pe 1:9) we are told that we have been redeemed with the precious blood of Christ, as of a lamb without blemish and without spot.

John emphasizes this sacrificial and redemptive symbolism when he says that the Lamb standing near the throne gave the appearance of having been slain. John does not give us the details of the scene, but he gives us enough to remind us of the redeeming death of Christ which paid for our sins. John makes no attempt to explain the significance of this symbolism. He assumes that his readers know what it means.

This, however, is not the case when he says that the Lamb has seven horns and seven eyes. Since it would be difficult even for one who is intimately acquainted with biblical symbolism to understand what this signifies, John immediately explains that the seven horns and the seven eyes are "the seven spirits of God that have been sent into all the earth." This is the fourth and last time in which the Holy Ghost is described in these terms (cp 1:4; 3:1; 4:5). In chapter 1 (v. 4), John speaks of seven spirits before the throne. In chapters 3 and 4 they are called the "seven spirits of God." But here the seven spirits are depicted as the seven horns and the seven eyes of the Lamb. In this way John reminds us that the Holy Ghost is not only the Spirit of the Father, but that he proceeds also from the Son. The symbolism echoes the thought Jesus had expressed literally in the Gospel of St. John when he spoke of the Spirit whom he would send from the Father (Jn 15:26), and whom the Father would send in his name (Jn 14:26).

There are, besides Revelation 5:6, only six passages in the New Testament that speak of the Spirit being "sent" — one in Luke's Gospel (24:49), one in Paul's epistles (Ga 4:6), one in First Peter (1:11), and three in John's Gospel (14:26; 15:26; 16:7). Here, then, is another one of the many passages in the book of Revelation which cumulatively establishes a close connection between it and the Gospel of John.

To help us understand the use of symbols and figurative language it is good to point out again that while in these verses Jesus is called a Lamb, just a few verses earlier he had been called a Lion. This emphatically underscores the freedom with which apocalyptic symbols are employed. It cautions the interpreter not to try to explain details for which he can find no interpretation either in the text of Revelation or in other passages of the Bible. Suffice it to say that the word "lion" reminds us of those Old Testament passages which speak of the Messiah as a conquering King and the name "lamb" of those prophecies which depict him as a suffering servant. Those two ways of speaking of the promised Messiah appeared to be so contradictory to some Jews that they taught that there would be two Messiahs.

The freeness of apocalyptic symbolism is also apparent in John's statement that the Lamb now took the book out of the right hand of him who sat upon the throne. The one who holds the future in his hand conveys his power of control to the Lamb. It is not difficult to see in this symbolic act a representation of the truth that Christ sat down at the right hand of God. By that action God bestowed on the man Jesus of Nazareth, the child born of Mary, all the majesty and power that God has possessed from all eternity.

The four living creatures and the twenty-four elders acknowledge this truth when they fall down in worship before the Lamb and offer him the same type of devotion they had offered to God (cp 4:10). The Lamb that has been slain receives the same honor as God the Father. In a symbolic way the apostle here expresses the truth Jesus proclaimed in the fourth Gospel, "All men should honor the Son even as they honor the Father" (Jn 5:23).

Not only do the elders and the four living creatures bestow divine honor on the Lamb by falling down before him as they had fallen down before the throne (4:10), but they also offer their prayers to him. Incense is offered to him, and this incense is identified as the prayers of the saints. Thus the vision symbolizes the elevation of the man Jesus to a position of divine majesty and glory at the right hand of God.

THE NEW SONG IN PRAISE OF THE LAMB (5:9-14)

9) ᾄδουσιν ᾠδὴν καινὴν λέγοντες,
Ἄξιος εἶ λαβεῖν τὸ βιβλίον καὶ ἀνοῖξαι τὰς σφραγῖδας αὐτοῦ, ὅτι
ἐσφάγης καὶ ἠγόρασας τῷ Θεῷ ἐν τῷ αἵματί σου ἐκ πάσης φυλῆς
καὶ γλώσσης καὶ λαοῦ καὶ ἔθνους, 10) καὶ ἐποίησας αὐτοὺς τῷ
Θεῷ ἡμῶν βασιλείαν καὶ ἱερεῖς, καὶ βασιλεύσουσιν ἐπὶ τῆς γῆς.
11) καὶ εἶδον, καὶ ἤκουσα φωνὴν ἀγγέλων πολλῶν κύκλῳ τοῦ
θρόνου καὶ τῶν ζώων καὶ τῶν πρεσβυτέρων, καὶ ἦν ὁ ἀριθμὸς
αὐτῶν μυριάδες μυριάδων καὶ χιλιάδες χιλιάδων, 12) λέγοντες
φωνῇ μεγάλῃ,
Ἄξιός ἐστιν τὸ Ἀρνίον τὸ ἐσφαγμένον λαβεῖν τὴν δύναμιν
καὶ πλοῦτον καὶ σοφίαν καὶ ἰσχὺν καὶ τιμὴν καὶ δόξαν καὶ
εὐλογίαν.
13) καὶ πᾶν κτίσμα ὃ ἐν τῷ οὐρανῷ καὶ ἐπὶ τῆς γῆς καὶ ὑποκάτω
τῆς γῆς καὶ ἐπὶ τῆς θαλάσσης [ἐστίν], καὶ τὰ ἐν αὐτοῖς πάντα,
ἤκουσα λέγοντας,
Τῷ καθημένῳ ἐπὶ τῷ θρόνῳ καὶ τῷ Ἀρνίῳ ἡ εὐλογία καὶ
ἡ τιμὴ καὶ ἡ δόξα καὶ τὸ κράτος εἰς τοὺς αἰῶνας τῶν
αἰώνων.
14) καὶ τὰ τέσσερα ζῷα ἔλεγον, Ἀμήν, καὶ οἱ πρεσβύτεροι ἔπεσαν
καὶ προσεκύνησαν.

9) *And they sang a new song, saying,*
"You are worthy to take the book

and to open its seals,
because you were slaughtered
and bought us (NIV: men) *for God*
with your blood
out of every tribe and language
and people and nation,
10) *and you made them* (us) *a kingdom and priests*
for our God,
and they (we) *will keep on reigning*
on the earth."

11) *And I saw and heard the voice of many angels surrounding the throne and the living creatures and the elders. Their number was ten thousand times ten thousand and thousands of thousands.* 12) *With a loud voice they were saying, "Worthy is the Lamb that was slaughtered to receive power and riches and wisdom and strength and honor and glory and blessing."*
13) *And every created thing which is in heaven and upon the earth and under the earth and upon the sea and everything in them I heard saying, "To him who sits upon the throne and to the Lamb be blessing and honor and glory and might forever and ever."*
14) *And the four living creatures were saying, "Amen," and the elders fell and worshiped.*

In the song of the elders there are noteworthy variations in the Greek manuscripts. The variations in the Greek can be seen in a comparison between the NIV and the KJV in verses 9b and 10, and they are indicated by the words in parentheses. Most Greek manuscripts in verse 9 have the word "us" as the object of the verb bought, but one ancient manuscript has no object for this verb. The NIV adds the word "men" in this verse because what the Lamb bought came out of the tribes and nations of the earth, and because it conforms with the following third person pronouns. What the Lamb bought would naturally be men or human beings. In verse 10 most Greek manuscripts do not have "us" as the object of the verb "made" but "them," and the great majority of manuscripts have at the end of verse 10 "they will reign" and not "we will reign." Our translation follows the majority of the manuscripts.

There are only two passages in the New Testament, both of them in Revelation, that speak of a new song sung to the Lord. The Old Testament has at least seven passages that use this expression (Ps 33:3; 40:3; 96:1; 98:1; 144:9; 149:1; Is 42:8). The context of each of those passages alludes to the salvation God will prepare for his people. The psalmist, for example, calls upon God's people to sing a new song to the Lord because he has declared his salvation and has revealed his righteousness to the nations (Ps 98:1-3).

The "new song" in Revelation is likewise a song of praise for God's salvation. The gospel as good *news* calls for a *new* song on the part of those who have received the blessings of the new covenant.

Our first question, however, has to do with the subject of the verb "sing." The previous verses mention the four beasts and the twenty-four elders. At first glance it would therefore appear that these two groups are the singers of the new song. If this is the case, and if we adopt the reading, "you have redeemed *us*," then it will be necessary to revise our interpretation of the four living creatures. The singers of this new song say that they have been redeemed by the blood of Christ. In view of Hebrews 2 it is evident that angelic beings cannot make such a statement. The writer of Hebrews says (2:16) that "it is not angels he helps."

We might, on the other hand, ask whether the singing might not have been antiphonal, partly sung by the four living creatures and partly by the twenty-four elders. If the singing is antiphonal that would explain why so many manuscripts have "us" in the first part of the song and "they" in the second half. It would also explain why copyists had difficulty with the pronouns here. It could well be that because they did not consider that the two halves may have been sung by two different groups, they tried to bring consistency into the use of the pronouns. It is significant that almost all the manuscripts have "us" in verse 9 and almost all the manuscripts have "them" and "they" in verse 10. The manuscripts that omit "us" in verse 9 do not have an object for the verb "bought." No manuscript listed in the UBS text of the New Testament has the word "men," which the NIV adds here.

On the other hand, if the four living creatures join in singing the words, "You bought us," then those interpreters who think that the living creatures are representative of all believers may be correct in their opinion. They explain that the fact that there are four of them signifies that the believers had come out of every tribe, language, people and nation. While such an interpretation would not be contrary to any doctrine of Scripture, it is difficult to see a parallel between a lion, an ox, a man and an eagle, and tribes, languages, people and nations. The similarity of the four creatures to those in Ezekiel's vision are enough to convince this interpreter that they are cherubim.

Those who see in the four living creatures representatives of all animate creation — man, domestic animals, wild animals and birds — would also have difficulty making the four living creatures subjects of the verb "sing," unless the singing is antiphonal. For although all of animate creation is a beneficiary of the work of Christ (Ro 8:21), yet it could hardly be said of animals and birds that they have been made priests unto God. It would, therefore, be preferable to say that the subjects of the verb "sing" are simply the twenty-four elders. However, before making a final decision on this point, a person should consider the variations in the original text. The NIV translation holds the view that the four living creatures are cherubim.

The song first of all praises the Lamb as one worthy to open the book. No one else in heaven or on earth, no man or created angel, was fit for that honor (5:3). He won this honor of governing the course of history by giving his life and shedding his blood. Thus he purchased men for God out of every tribe and language and people and nation. The dative "for God" may be viewed as a dative of advantage or interest. Through the purchase price of Jesus' blood we now belong to God.

By paying this price for us he has made us a "kingdom." In the final analysis it makes no difference here if we read "us" or "them," for the context indicates that the kingdom is composed of those who have been bought for God by the blood of the Lamb. Some manuscripts say, "You have made us kings."

There is really no significant difference of meaning between these two variant readings. In either case, the redeemed have received a position of authority because of Christ's work. When Adam and Eve were created God gave them a position of rulership over all his creation (Gn 1:28). All things were put under their feet (Ps 8). Through the fall into sin man's dominion over nature was lost, or at least corrupted. The earth now rebels against man's effort to wring his livelihood from it (Gn 3:17-19). Animate creation no longer renders him willing service but is kept in check by force and fear (Gn 9:2). This lost dominion has been restored to the human race only in Christ, whose victory we share as his brothers and childen of God by faith (Ps 8; He 2:6-11). Thus he has made those who are joined with him by faith partners in his rule of the world. This statement, that he has made us a kingdom, repeats in almost identical words what we already have read in the first chapter (v. 6).

In that passage, as here, John also tells us that the Savior has made us priests. In the Old Testament the children of Israel were not allowed to offer sacrifices or to approach God directly in his Temple. They offered their sacrifices, including the sacrifice of incense, and they approached God in the holy places of the Temple through intermediaries, namely, the Levitical priests. Now, however, since Christ, our great high priest and the Lamb of God, has made the one perfect sacrifice and has taken away the sins of the world (Jn 1:29), the way into God's presence is open to all believers (He 10:14-22). Peter expresses both this truth and the thought of the preceding paragraph when he calls Christians a "royal priesthood" (1 Pe 2:9).

The fact that Christ has made his people into a "kingdom" is the basis for the concluding statement in this song of praise to the Lamb: "And they (or, we) will reign on the earth." Millennialists see in these words a reference to the millennial reign of Christ. However, the "millennial" reign spoken of in Revelation 20, as we shall see, is not a temporal reign of God's saints on the earth. It is the reign of the souls of "beheaded" believers in heaven. Nothing is said here about a reign of a thousand years.

The future tense in Greek either denotes an act which will take place at some time in the future or something that will continue into the future. The context here indicates that this reign has alrady begun. The first part of the sentence tells us that the believers are already kings. This can only mean that they are already ruling. It would therefore be more in keeping with the context to translate, "And they (or, we) will continue to rule on the earth."

This is a statement that called for great faith on the part of the Christians who read the book of Revelation in John's day. They were being persecuted. The Roman government was confiscating their property, exiling them from their homes and putting many of them to death. They were undergoing tremendous hardships, and their enemies appeared to have the upper hand. Yet John reminds them that they are kings, that they will continue to reign on the earth as they learn more and more to walk by faith and not by sight.

Even if the future tense of the verb is a reference to a future reign this still would not be a proof passage for any kind of millennial reign. The reign of Christ and of his people in the "new heaven and new earth" will not be a millennial reign. Just as Christ shall reign forever and ever, so any future reign of God's people on the new earth will not last for so short a time as a thousand years. Of that kingdom "there will be no end."

The universality of Christ's redemption is alluded to in the phrase: "out of every tribe and language and people and nation." While those words do not necessarily teach that Christ died for all men, yet they do emphasize that his redemptive work is not limited to the Jewish people but that it is for men from every nation.

This is the first of seven phrases that describe the population of the earth. While the variations in wording are slight, in every one of the seven passages four words are used to comprehend all the inhabitants of the earth. This is one of the features of Revelation that leads us to the conclusion that four is the symbolic number of the earth and its people. The seven phrases are:

1) 5:9 — every tribe and language and people and nation
2) 7:9 — every nation and tribe and people and language
3) 10:11 — peoples and nations and languages and kings
4) 11:9 — peoples and tribes and languages and kings
5) 13:7 — every tribe and people and language and nation
6) 14:6 — every nation and tribe and language and people
7) 17:15 — peoples and multitudes and nations and languages

When the twenty-four elders ended their song John heard another group in heaven begin to sing praises to the Lamb. He says, "I saw and heard the sound of many angels." The figure of speech is a zeugma. John means to say that he saw many angels and heard their voices. This multitude of angels encircled the throne and the four living creatures and the twenty-four elders (see the illustration). John gives the number of angels as "ten thousand times ten thousand and thousands of thousands." The Prophet Daniel, who reports a similar vision, speaks of thousands of thousands who stood before God and ten thousand times ten thousand who served him (Dn 7:10).

These millions of angels join in the praise of the Lamb as they sing, "Worthy is the Lamb that was slain to receive power and riches and wisdom and strength and honor and glory and blessing." This song of the angels contains seven words of praise. It thus follows the sevenfold pattern common to this book. Interestingly, the song of praise to God in 4:11 contains three words of praise and the song of all created things, addressed to the Father and the Lamb in 5:13, contains four words of praise. Whether there is any special significance in this arrangement is difficult to say. Since the hymn in 4:11 is addressed to the triune God (cp v. 8), the three words of praise seem appropriate. The song of creation in verse 13 of this chapter is

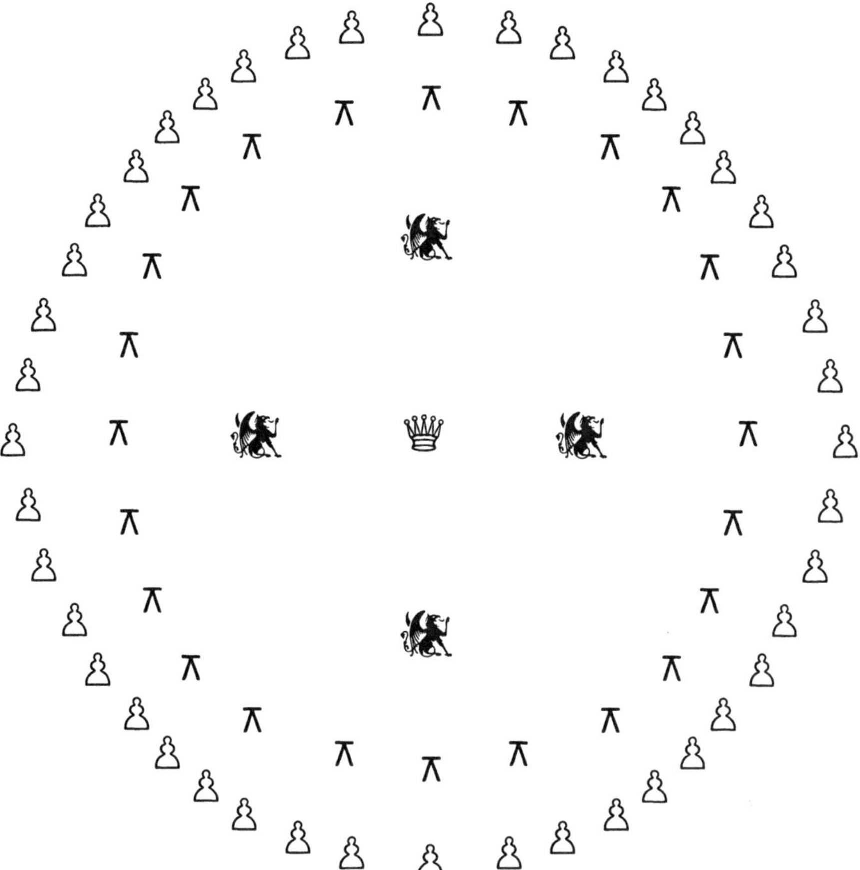

introduced by a reference to four classes of creatures, namely, those in heaven, on earth, under the earth, and in the sea. Since the number four in Revelation is regularly associated with the earth, the four words of praise from the created world seem to be part of a deliberate pattern.

When we note that the song of the angels in honor of the Lamb contains seven words of praise, we may recall that through his redeeming work Christ restored between God and the world (three plus four) that fellowship which the fall into sin had destroyed.

The angels' seven words of praise reflect the exaltation of Jesus. Two of the words speak of the power which he is worthy to receive. After his resurrection Jesus told his disciples, "All power is given to me in heaven and in earth" (Mt 28:20). He is worthy to receive riches. He had become poor for our sakes (2 Cor 8:9), so poor that he had no place to lay his head (Lk 9:58), but in his exaltation all things in heaven and earth are put under his control. He is worthy to receive wisdom. The full and constant use of God's own omniscience becomes his prerogative in his state of exaltation. The last three words speak of the divine honor and glory which are now his in exchange for the shame and disgrace that came upon him when he was slain. The last word "blessing" is especially significant. Countless Hebrew prayers, the kind of prayers John had known from his childhood, begin with the words "Blessed art thou, O Lord, King of the universe." Such prayers are properly addressed to the exalted Son of Mary.

Finally all creation joins in the heavenly hymnody. This third, and last, hymn in this chapter is addressed to the one who sits on the throne, and to the Lamb. We may read the sentence as a wish, "May blessing and honor and glory and might be given to the one who sits on the throne and to the Lamb," or as a confession of faith, "Blessing and honor and glory and might should belong to the one who sits on the throne and to the Lamb."

The four living creatures express their agreement with these sentiments by saying "Amen." John here uses an imperfect tense, which indicates that they said it not only once but a number of times. We may conclude that they spoke their "Amen" at the close of each one of the three hymns.

The twenty-four elders who had begun this symphony of praise and had given us a glimpse of the joys of heaven, now fall to the ground and worship. The stage is set for the actual opening of the book with seven seals.

THE VISION OF THE SEVEN SEALS (6:1 — 8:5)

When we bear in mind that at the time of St. John's exile on Patmos the Christian church was a persecuted minority, largely made up of people from the lower classes, many of whom were slaves, we must recognize that John's statement that they were a kingdom and that they would continue to reign on the earth must have sounded like irrational nonsense. If it was really true that all power and might and wisdom and wealth belong to the Lamb who had bought them for God at the price of his own blood, then they might reasonably expect that the whole world would not only be ruled for their benefit, but that this benefit would be apparent to all. The whole concept of a millennial kingdom is the result of this kind of false concept of what it means to be a child of God in this sin-cursed world. In spite of its apparently fundamentalistic cast and of its prevalence in circles that express a desire to be loyal to Scripture, millennialism is at heart closely related to the Social Gospel, which holds out the hope for a better world where there is no war, no sickness, no hunger, no inequity of any kind, without the renewal which will take place on the final day of judgment. Men have always yearned for a golden age where peace and harmony and justice prevail everywhere.

The vision of the seven seals which begins in chapter 6 is a rejection of all such hopes for a golden age in this present world. Instead of outward peace and materialistic prosperity the church must expect to share in the sufferings that are common to men and even experience added hardship and grief at the hands of a sinful world. This vision is an affirmation of the truth of the apostolic words which tell us that we must through much tribulation enter into the kingdom of God.

Before considering the details of this vision it is helpful to view it in broad outline. There is a great similarity between this vision and the Savior's words about the signs of the end in Matthew 24. Not only does this vision speak of the same signs of the second coming but even in close to the same order. While there is some disagreement also among orthodox commentators about the meaning of the rider on the white horse, there can be no dispute whatever about the second through the sixth seal. The red horse obviously is war; the black horse, famine; the pale horse, various kinds of pestilence and calamity; the souls under the altar speak of persecution; and in the sixth seal we find a description of the end of the world.

This list of calamities ending with the last judgment clearly indicates that we have here a symbolic representation of one aspect of the entire New Testament era. These are "the things that are to come hereafter" (4:1). The events described here in symbols are signs and foreshadowings of the end of the world ending with the last judgment itself. For the sake of comparison, a listing of the main features in the pertinent section of Matthew 24 and the sixth chapter of Revelation follows. The signs and the order in which they are mentioned generally agree also in Mark and Luke (cp Mk 13:6-13 and Lk 21:8-17).

Matthew 24	Revelation 6
false Christs v. 5	the white horse (?) v. 1-2
wars and rumor of wars v. 6	the red horse (war) v. 3-4
famines v. 7	the black horse (famine) v. 5-6
pestilences (v. 7) (cp Lk 21:11)	the pale horse (death) v. 7-8
earthquakes v. 7	earthquake v. 12
persecution v. 9	the souls under the altar v. 9-11
apostasy v. 10	
false prophets v. 11	
love growing cold v. 12	
the worldwide spread of the gospel v. 14	the white horse (?) v. 1-2
"Then shall the end come" v. 14	the end v. 12-17

This comparison should demonstrate beyond question that what we have in this chapter of Revelation is a symbolic representation of the truths the Savior taught in regard to the signs of the last times. When we compare the list of signs in Mark and Luke, we see that the early church preached about them in the general order in which they occur here.

This is also a helpful directive as to how we should read and understand the book of Revelation. Just as the Savior, for example, does not have in mind any particular war but every war and every rumor of war, each one is to remind us that he was telling the truth when he said that the world would some day come to an end. So the red horse in this chapter is not to be understood as some particular war which will take place sometime in the distant future to usher in a millennium. The rider on the red horse is riding throughout history wherever war and bloodshed break out. The same can be said about the black and pale horses. Likewise the souls under the altar are told, in answer to their plea, about numerous other persecutions that will take place before the end — not just one isolated, specific persecution.

The text also indicates that all of this ends not in a millennium but in the last judgment. In this chapter we have nothing new and nothing different from the Savior's teaching about the last things in Matthew's Gospel. John depicts for us common signs that will occur repeatedly during the New Testament era foreshadowing the final destruction of the wicked at the last day, which, already in the Old Testament, is spoken of as the day of the Lord's wrath (*e.g.*, Zph. 1:18).

THE FOUR HORSEMEN OF THE APOCALYPSE (6:1-9)

The First Seal: The Rider on the White Horse (6:1,2)

1) Καὶ εἶδον ὅτε ἤνοιξεν τὸ Ἀρνίον μίαν ἐκ τῶν ἑπτὰ σφραγίδων, καὶ ἤκουσα ἑνὸς ἐκ τῶν τεσσάρων ζώων λέγοντος ὡς φωνῇ βροντῆς, Ἔρχου. 2) καὶ εἶδον, καὶ ἰδοὺ ἵππος λευκός, καὶ ὁ καθήμενος ἐπ' αὐτὸν ἔχων τόξον, καὶ ἐδόθη αὐτῷ στέφανος, καὶ ἐξῆλθεν νικῶν καὶ ἵνα νικήσῃ.

1) *And I saw when the Lamb opened the first of the seven seals. And I heard one of the four living creatures saying with a voice like thunder, "Come."* 2) *And I looked, and there was a white horse, and he who sat on it had a bow and was given a crown, and he went out conquering and to conquer.*

It is strange that commentators have difficulty agreeing on the identity of the rider on the white horse. Many commentators hold that since all the other seals in this chapter represent calamities that overtake the world and aggravate the church, the rider on the white horse must also be one of the church's enemies or a danger that threatens the church. A rather common view is that this rider represents civil government in its antichristian aspect.

However, all through the book of Revelation, white is the color of purity and goodness. Moreover, in chapter 19 we again meet a rider on a white horse who is definitely identified as the Savior. It is sometimes argued that the two riders cannot represent the same person because the rider in chapter 6 wears only one crown (στέφανος) whereas the rider in chapter 19 wears many crowns (διαδήματα) (19:12). Entirely aside from the fact that John uses symbolism with the utmost freedom, the rider in this chapter is going out to conquer. By chapter 19 he has won many victories and therefore is entitled to wear many crowns.

Another argument that this rider cannot be Christ is that here he carries a bow while in chapter 19 he is armed with a sword. But apocalyptic symbolism is not that restrictive in other places, so why press the detail here? The Messiah has all weapons at his disposal. In the Old Testament the Messiah is pictured as a conquering king whose "arrows are sharp" in the heart of his enemies (Ps 45:5).

An alternate interpretation which is somewhat more tenable is that this rider is either the Antichrist or a false Messiah, as representative of all the false Messiahs whose coming was foretold by Jesus. This might explain why he wears a crown and is dressed in white — as an attempt on his part to give the impression that he is the Messiah. But the only indication that he might be a pretender is the parallel position of the prophecy of false Christs at the beginning of the list of signs in Matthew, Mark and Luke (Mt 24:5; Mk 13:5; Lk 21:8). Because of the rather remarkable parallelism between Revelation 6 and Matthew 24, the position of the white horse at the head of the procession here seems significant.

Another argument used in favor of the interpretation that the rider cannot be Christ is that the Savior is the one who opens the seals and therefore cannot be a part of the scene depicted in the seven seals. Such a conclusion, however, is unwarranted. It would be like saying that no one can show others a picture of himself. Jesus is showing John a vision. If the above argument were true, it would end up proving that Jesus is absent from all of the visions.

While it is impossible to speak on this point with dogmatic certainty, yet the whole symbolism of the book of Revelation points to the conclusion that the rider on the white horse is Jesus; or, if not Jesus himself, the gospel, the Word of God. In the list of signs of the last times which we cited from the Gospels there are five which have no positively identified counterpart in Revelation 6. Of these five, four are very closely related, false Christs and false prophets, apostasy and love growing cold. The last two are so much alike that it is questionable that they should be listed as separate items. One of these remaining five signs, however, is completely different from the rest. The worldwide proclamation of the gospel stands out as a bright ray of hope in a list otherwise composed wholly of calamities and catastrophes. This should dispose of the argument which says that since all the other symbols of this chapter represent dangers that confront the church in this world, the rider on the white horse must also represent some evil thing.

By way of anticipation we may also note at this time that the vision of the seven trumpets, which is at the same time the vision of the seventh seal, undoubtedly deals with the curse of false doctrine and apostasy. The antichristian forces in the world also receive a great deal of attention in later chapters. Thus the seventh seal treats of the sign of false teaching and apostasy.

All this makes a strong case for saying that the white horse represents the worldwide preaching of the gospel. It is through the preaching of the gospel that Christ rides out to conquer. With this identification of the white horse every one of the signs Jesus mentioned in Matthew 24:4-14 and the parallel passages in Mark and Luke is covered in the vision of the seven seals and in the vision of the seven trumpets, which is, in turn, the vision of the seventh seal.

Perhaps we should add a word about a variant reading found in the manuscripts. According to the KJV, in each of the first four visions John hears one of the four living creatures say, "Come and see." Many of the Greek manuscripts omit the last two words.

This variant reading raises a question: "To whom is the command 'Come' addressed?" The KJV and the manuscripts on which it is based view the command as spoken to John. The added words "and see" are clearly echoed by John's statement, "And I saw." However, the opening words of chapter 4 have already told us that John was caught up to heaven "in spirit" so that he could see the things that would come in the future. If addressed to John, the command would seem redundant.

Those manuscripts and translations which omit the words, "and see" indicate that the command "Come" is addressed to each of the four horsemen in turn. This would fit the context better. Since both readings make perfectly good sense, and the manuscript evidence is about evenly divided, it is impossible to decide with certainty which of the two readings is correct. And the adoption of one or the other does not significantly affect the message of the vision.

The Second Seal: the Rider on the Red Horse (6:3,4)

3) Καὶ ὅτε ἤνοιξεν τὴν σφραγῖδα τὴν δευτέραν, ἤκουσα τοῦ δευτέρου ζώου λέγοντος, Ἔρχου. 4) καὶ ἐξῆλθεν ἄλλος ἵππος πυρρός, καὶ τῷ καθημένῳ ἐπ' αὐτὸν ἐδόθη αὐτῷ λαβεῖν τὴν εἰρήνην ἐκ τῆς γῆς καὶ ἵνα ἀλλήλους σφάξουσιν, καὶ ἐδόθη αὐτῷ μάχαιρα μεγάλη.

3) *And when he opened the second seal I heard the second living creature say, "Come."* 4) *And another horse went out, a red one, and to the one who sat on it power was given to take peace from the earth and to cause men to kill one another. And a great sword was given to him.*

There is no difficulty whatever in the interpretation of this vision. All competent commentators will agree that this horse represents war. Millennialistic interpreters see it as a prediction of a specific war, but there is no justification for seeing it as anything other than what our Savior expressed literally when he spoke of wars and rumors of wars as signs of the end of the world. This vision is one of the two passages in Revelation in which the color red (πυρρός) plays a role. The other passage calls the devil a "great red dragon" (12:3). Several synonyms of πυρρὸς are used also. The color of the breastplates of the horsemen in the vision of the sixth trumpet is πυρίνους, fire-red (9:17) and the color of the beast on which the harlot Babylon sits and the color of clothing of the harlot is κόκκινον (17:3,4; 18:16; cp 18:12). From this we may conclude that red is the color of wickedness and evil. Isaiah had spoken of it as the color of great sin (Is 1:18).

The Third Seal: The Rider on the Black Horse (6:5,6)

5) Καὶ ὅτε ἤνοιξεν τὴν σφραγῖδα τὴν τρίτην, ἤκουσα τοῦ τρίτου ζώου λέγοντος, Ἔρχου. καὶ εἶδον, καὶ ἰδοὺ ἵππος μέλας, καὶ ὁ καθήμενος ἐπ' αὐτὸν ἔχων ζυγὸν ἐν τῇ χειρὶ αὐτοῦ. 6) καὶ ἤκουσα ὡς φωνὴν ἐν μέσῳ τῶν τεσσάρων ζώων λέγουσαν, Χοῖνιξ σίτου δηναρίου, καὶ τρεῖς χοίνικες κριθῶν δηναρίου· καὶ τὸ ἔλαιον καὶ τὸν οἶνον μὴ ἀδικήσῃς.

5) *And when he opened the third seal I heard the third living creature say, "Come." And I looked, and there was a black horse. And the one who sat on it had a balance scale in his hand.* 6) *And I heard what sounded like a voice from among the four living creatures. It said, "A choinix of wheat for a denarius, and three choinixes of barley for a denarius, and do not adulterate the oil and the wine."*

There can be no doubt about this vision either. "A choinix of wheat for a denarius and three choinixes of barley for a denarius!" A denarius was the standard day's pay. A choinix held about a quart. The voice is apparently offering for sale the equivalent of a loaf of bread for a day's wages. Barley was cheaper than wheat but three quarts of barley for a day's pay indicates that the price of food is impossibly high. Only those who are rich can in such times afford to buy food. For others there is only the prospect of starvation. Obviously we are here dealing with famine, which Jesus also listed as a sign of the approaching end.

The word which we have translated "adulterate" literally means to do wrong to, to spoil, or to damage. The voice cautions against doing damage to the oil and the wine. In times of great scarcity there would be a temptation to stretch the supply of olive oil and wine by adding water or some other liquid. It is therefore likely that the word means "adulterate" here.

The color black is used only twice in Revelation, here and in the vision of the sixth seal (6:12). It appears to be the color of calamity.

The Fourth Seal: The Rider on the Pale Horse (6:7,8)

7) Καὶ ὅτε ἤνοιξεν τὴν σφραγῖδα τὴν τετάρτην, ἤκουσα φωνὴν τοῦ τετάρτου ζώου λέγοντος, Ἔρχου. 8) καὶ εἶδον, καὶ ἰδοὺ ἵππος χλωρός, καὶ ὁ καθήμενος ἐπάνω αὐτοῦ, ὄνομα αὐτῷ Ὁ Θάνατος, καὶ ὁ Ἅιδης ἠκολούθει μετ' αὐτοῦ, καὶ ἐδόθη αὐτοῖς ἐξουσία ἐπὶ τὸ τέταρτον τῆς γῆς, ἀποκτεῖναι ἐν ῥομφαίᾳ καὶ ἐν λιμῷ καὶ ἐν θανάτῳ καὶ ὑπὸ τῶν θηρίων τῆς γῆς.

7) *And when he opened the fourth seal I heard the voice of the fourth living creature saying, "Come."* 8) *And I looked and there was a pale horse. And the one who sat on it was named Death, and Hades followed along with him. Authority over a quarter of the earth was given to them, to kill with the sword and with famine, and with death, and by the wild animals of the earth.*

The rider on the pale horse is identified as Death. The Greek word for "pale" is χλωρός, which really means "green" — related to our word chlorophyll. It was the word that Greek doctors used to describe the color of a sick person, just as we sometimes describe a person who looks ill as being "green around the gills." The rider on the pale horse is a symbolic representation of widespread illness or pestilence. The symbol includes those deaths which are the result of the calamities symbolized by the red and black horses, namely, war and famine and attacks by wild beasts.

The rider on the pale horse, identified as Death, is followed by Hades. In the New Testament Hades is a name for hell. (Compare what was said of Hades in connection with 1:18.) Hades is not further described. Some commentators speculate that Hades rides the pale horse seated behind Death. Others imagine that he rides a second horse. Artists have pictured Hades as a fearsome figure of a man walking behind the pale horse. The last picture would seem to fit best with the language of the text, although there is nothing to prevent us from visualizing Hades as a voracious beast ready to devour the men who have been killed by war, famine, pestilence and wild animals.

The Apostle John in this way reminds us of the fact that physical death is not the only wages of sin. There is always "the dread of something after death" (Hamlet, III, i). Far more fearful than temporal death is the eternal death that threatens those who die without faith in the Lamb, who have rejected the gospel promises which the rider on the white horse proclaimed.

The Fifth Seal: The Souls under the Altar (6:9-11)

The next vision also speaks of death. But in this case death is not accompanied by Hades. John continues,

> **9) Καὶ ὅτε ἤνοιξεν τὴν πέμπτην σφραγῖδα, εἶδον ὑποκάτω τοῦ θυσιαστηρίου τὰς ψυχὰς τῶν ἐσφαγμένων διὰ τὸν λόγον τοῦ Θεοῦ καὶ διὰ τὴν μαρτυρίαν ἣν εἶχον. 10) καὶ ἔκραξαν φωνῇ μεγάλῃ λέγοντες, Ἕως πότε, ὁ Δεσπότης ὁ ἅγιος καὶ ἀληθινός, οὐ κρίνεις καὶ ἐκδικεῖς τὸ αἷμα ἡμῶν ἐκ τῶν κατοικούντων ἐπὶ τῆς γῆς; 11) καὶ ἐδόθη αὐτοῖς ἑκάστῳ στολὴ λευκή, καὶ ἐρρέθη αὐτοῖς ἵνα ἀναπαύσωνται ἔτι χρόνον μικρόν, ἕως πληρωθῶσιν καὶ οἱ σύνδουλοι αὐτῶν καὶ οἱ ἀδελφοὶ αὐτῶν οἱ μέλλοντες ἀποκτέννεσθαι ὡς καὶ αὐτοί.**

> 9) *And when he opened the fifth seal I saw under the incense altar the souls of those who had been butchered because of the Word of God and because of the testimony they kept on giving.* 10) *And they called out with a loud voice, "Until when, O Lord, holy and true, are you putting off your judging and your avenging of our blood from those who are dwelling on the earth?"* 11) *And a white robe was given to each one of them and they were told to rest a little longer until also their fellow servants and their brothers, who would be put to death as they were, would all be there.*

The Savior had spoken of the persecution of his people as one of the signs of the end times. John here also speaks of persecution. The souls which he sees have been put to death because of the Word of God and the testimony to which they held fast in spite of all the efforts of the persecutors to persuade them to deny the faith. Their constancy in holding fast to their confession is indicated by the imperfect tense of the Greek word εἶχον, which we have translated, "they kept on giving," literally, "they kept on holding."

The souls he sees are under the altar. No such altar had been mentioned in any of the preceding context and yet the word has the definite article, the significance of which we might reproduce in English by translating: "under the well-known altar." To John's readers the well-known altar cannot be the one in the tabernacle in the wilderness or in the Temple at Jerusalem. Both of them had been destroyed by the time John wrote these words. But the book of Hebrews, which was certainly known to the Christians of John's time, did speak of the tabernacle in the wilderness as a symbolic representation of God's house in heaven. These souls of Christian martyrs who had died for their faith thus are living in the heavenly tabernacle with God, which Revelation regularly describes in terms of the wilderness tabernacle.

The word that John uses to describe the killing of the martyrs is the word that is usually used for the slaughter of animals. We therefore translate it with the word "butcher." It reflects the inhumanity of the persecutors in their treatment of God's people. The word is also used for the killing of sacrificial animals. Some commentators view the altar mentioned here as the altar of burnt offering and comment that the killing of the martyrs is in this way portrayed as a sacrifice to God. While such a thought is surely not out of harmony with biblical truth, it is not certain that it is in harmony with the intentions of the author. One thing is completely sure. If the death of the martyrs is to be considered a sacrifice, it cannot be a propitiatory sacrifice that atones for sin. That honor belongs to Christ alone.

John hears the souls of these martyrs asking God how long it will be before he sits in judgment on their persecutors and avenges their death. These slain martyrs not only expect God to punish their persecutors but they desire that God should do so.

At first glance the prayer of these martyrs may seem to be in conflict with the spirit of Jesus who calls upon us to forgive those who sin against us and to pray for those who persecute us. In this respect this prayer of the martyrs is reminiscent of the imprecatory psalms, in which the psalmist prays for vengeance on his enemies.

Neither the prayer of these martyrs nor the imprecatory psalms, however, are unworthy prayers. The difficulty which many people and even many theologians see in them stems from a failure to understand the biblical distinction between law and gospel. The law, which is the expression of God's holy, immutable will, calls for the punishment of evildoers. This prayer of the sainted martyrs as well as the imprecatory psalms are to remind God's enemies that their sins will surely be punished if they continue in their impenitence. It is the will of the just God that those who sin against him and his people should be punished, and the prayer of these martyrs is in accord with this holy will of God. The prayer can therefore be made with a loud voice. It is a prayer of which they need not be ashamed and which they can pray with confidence.

The prayer is addressed to "the Lord, holy and true." The word "Lord" here in the original is not the Greek word κύριος but δεσπότης, a word that stresses absolute lordship, and which the NIV translates with the phrase "Sovereign Lord." This is the only time this word is used in Revelation. The reference to God's holiness in this context points especially to his opposition to all sin and to his holy will, which calls for the punishment of the persecutors of his people. The martyrs for that reason express surprise over his seeming delay in avenging the wrongs done to them. He is also called the "true" Lord, not in the sense that he is truthful but rather that he is a real and genuine Lord over all, who therefore has the might and the authority to punish the earthly authorities who are responsible for the persecution of his people.

God does not directly answer the question of the martyrs when they ask how long a time will pass before he will avenge their blood. They are simply told that they should rest a little bit longer, for God intends to allow the murderers of his people to continue in their evil ways. Literally, the martyrs are told that the judgment of God will be delayed until "also their fellow servants and their brothers, who are about to be put to death as they were, would all be there." The statement, while rather unusual, is nevertheless clear. It means that there is a fixed number of martyrs known to God and God will allow the enemies of the church to continue their opposition until the full number of those destined for martyrdom has been reached.

John in this way reminds the persecuted Christians in his own time and for all times that the sufferings of the church are by no means an indication that the faith of the church, which confesses that Jesus Christ is Lord, is a vain or mistaken faith. The persecution of the church is a part of God's gracious plan according to which he exercises his lordship. When the persecutors have fulfilled God's purpose for the ultimate benefit of his people, then he will demonstrate his sovereign lordship also over his enemies by avenging the blood of the martyrs.

In the meantime, a white robe is given to each of the martyrs. White robes are a very common symbol in Revelation. The symbolism is fully explained in 7:14. The robes represent the forgiveness of sins which is ours through the blood of Christ. The sainted martyrs are thus reminded that their righteousness before God is a gracious gift of God's love to them. It is not a reward for martyrdom. If God would deal with them according to their merits they would deserve punishment as much as their persecutors do. God thus reminds them that the God of justice who punishes sin is also the God of grace who forgives sin. Therefore God's delay in punishing their persecutors is a sign of his grace and mercy according to which he gives even the enemies of the church time for repentance. While God's people rightly pray that sin might be punished and that the blood of the martyrs might be avenged, yet they also ought to pray that the enemies of the church will turn from their evil way and find salvation and forgiveness in the blood of the Lamb who was slain also for them.

The "short time" during which the martyrs are to wait patiently for God's avenging justice is evidently the whole New Testament period. Many of the persecutors of the church will not receive public punishment until the day of judgment. While we are not told this in so many words, yet it is evidently God who speaks of their period of waiting for vengeance as a "short time," or "a little longer." To God, the nearly twenty centuries of the New Testament era are indeed a little while. A thousand years in his sight are but as yesterday when it is past (Ps 90:4; 2 Pe 3:8).

On the other hand, the time evidently appears to be long to the souls of the martyrs. Many orthodox Lutheran commentators have been of the opinion that after death souls are not conscious of the passage of time. They define eternity as the absence of time, or timelessness. While the Bible makes it clear that eternity as an attribute of God is timelessness, it never indicates that the word eternity has the same meaning when it is applied to creatures. Time is a creation of God, and God therefore exists outside of and beyond time. It is also clear from Scripture that there is a tremendous difference between God's eternity and ours. His eternity has no beginning, but our eternal life has a beginning. It is thus certainly possible that while God's eternity is timelessness, our eternity is endless time, and because of that, even the souls in heaven are conscious of the passage of time, as seems to be the case here. However, we must be careful not to become too dogmatic on this point. This question will arise once more in connection with the words of chapter 10 where the KJV translates, "There shall be time no longer."

The Sixth Seal: The Last Judgment (6:12-17)

12) Καὶ εἶδον ὅτε ἤνοιξεν τὴν σφραγῖδα τὴν ἕκτην, καὶ σεισμὸς μέγας ἐγένετο, καὶ ὁ ἥλιος ἐγένετο μέλας ὡς σάκκος τρίχινος, καὶ ἡ σελήνη ὅλη ἐγένετο ὡς αἷμα, 13) καὶ οἱ ἀστέρες τοῦ οὐρανοῦ ἔπεσαν εἰς τὴν γῆν, ὡς συκῆ βάλλει τοὺς ὀλύνθους αὐτῆς ὑπὸ ἀνέμου μεγάλου σειομένη, 14) καὶ ὁ οὐρανὸς ἀπεχωρίσθη ὡς βιβλίον ἑλισσόμενον, καὶ πᾶν ὄρος καὶ νῆσος ἐκ τῶν τόπων αὐτῶν ἐκινήθησαν. 15) καὶ οἱ βασιλεῖς τῆς γῆς καὶ οἱ μεγιστᾶνες καὶ οἱχιλίαρχοι καὶ οἱ πλούσιοι καὶ οἱ ἰσχυροὶ καὶ πᾶς δοῦλος καὶ ἐλεύθερος ἔκρυψαν ἑαυτοὺς εἰς τὰ σπήλαια καὶ εἰς τὰς πέτρας τῶν ὀρέων, 16) καὶ λέγουσιν τοῖς ὄρεσιν καὶ ταῖς πέτραις, Πέσετε ἐφ' ἡμᾶς καὶ κρύψατε ἡμᾶς ἀπὸ προσώπου τοῦ καθημένου ἐπὶ τοῦ θρόνου καὶ ἀπὸ τῆς ὀργῆς τοῦ Ἀρνίου, 17) ὅτι ἦλθεν ἡ ἡμέρα ἡ μεγάλη τῆς ὀργῆς αὐτῶν, καὶ τίς δύναται σταθῆναι;

12) *And I saw when he opened the sixth seal, and there was a great earthquake and the sun became black as sackcloth made of hair, and the moon, all of it, became as blood,* 13) *and the stars of heaven fell to the earth as a fig tree drops its summer figs when it is shaken by a strong wind.* 14) *And the sky was removed like a scroll being rolled up, and every mountain and island was moved from its place.* 15) *And the kings of the earth and the mighty men and the captains of thousands and the rich and the strong and every slave and every free man hid themselves in the caves and rocks of the mountains,* 16) *and they say to the mountains and the rocks, "Fall on us and hide us from the face of the one who sits on the throne and from the wrath of the lamb,* 17) *for the great day of their wrath has come, and who is able to stand?"*

The unprejudiced reader, whose mind has not been captured by millennial heresy, can only conclude that this passage describes the end of the present world and the last judgment. What Paul describes in the prosaic statement, "The fashion of this world passes away" (1 Cor 7:31), here unfolds in graphic detail. Every earthquake throughout history is but a foreshadow of this great earthquake which moves every mountain and island from its place. Not only the earth but the whole universe undergoes a radical change. The imagery here does not speak of an annihilation of the created universe. The sun loses its light and becomes completely darkened. The moon takes on the appearance of blood. The stars fall from heaven to the earth, and the sky itself appears to roll up like a scroll.

It is foolish to speculate on how all this can happen. This is a vision and depicts truths in fantastic images. To John, the stars of heaven falling to the earth evidently appear to be as small as when they shine in the sky. That becomes evident when he compares them to figs falling from a tree. We need not ask how the moon can take on the color of blood if the sun has been completely darkened. In visions anything can happen.

But what is happening here is easy to understand. This present world as we know it will some day come to an end.

The day of the end of the world will also be the great day of God's wrath. This is the final day of judgment to which every other day of judgment has been pointing. Paul describes the last judgment as the "day of wrath when the righteous judgment of God will be revealed" (Ro 2:5). Every time the Lord of history acts in judgment on men and nations is a day of the Lord's wrath. The Old Testament prophets spoke in this way of the Lord's punishing activity. Ezekiel spoke of the destruction of Jerusalem by the Babylonians as "the day of the wrath of the Lord" (Eze 7:19). A generation before Ezekiel, Zephaniah had also foreseen the same event, and he evidently saw it as a type of the last great judgment when he wrote (1:14-18),

> The great day of the Lord is near —
>   near and coming quickly.
> Listen: The cry on the day of the Lord will be bitter,
>   the shouting of the warrior there.
> That day will be a day of wrath,
>   a day of distress and anguish,
>   a day of trouble and ruin,
>   a day of darkness and gloom,
>   a day of clouds and blackness,
>   a day of trumpet and battle cry
>   against the fortified cities
>   and against the corner towers.
> I will bring distress on the people
>   and they will walk like blind men,
>   because they have sinned against the Lord.
> Their blood will be poured out like dust
>   and their entrails like filth.
> Neither their silver nor gold
>   will be able to save them
>   on the day of the Lord's wrath.
> In the fire of his jealousy

the whole world will be consumed,
for he will make a sudden end
of all who live in the earth.

On the "great" day of his wrath God will finally avenge the blood of the martyrs. The great and mighty men who persecuted them will then receive the due reward of their deeds. John mentions seven classes of men who will be the objects of God's wrath. Some commentators who hold that the number six represents the forces of evil in the symbolism of Revelation, count six classes of men here by combining "every slave and free man" into one group. However, the number six is never used in the book except in the statement that each of the four living creatures had six wings (4:8) and in "the number of the beast," namely, 666 (13:18). No one can say with certainty whether there is any significance in the division into six or seven groups.

But just as we can say with certainty that, as the first three verses depict the passing away of this present world on the day of judgment, so the last three verses clearly describe the punishment of those men who are the enemies of God and of his church. They recognize that the wrath of God is about to fall on them and that death and annihilation would be preferable to the fate in store for them. They therefore seek to hide from his wrath in the caves and rocks of the mountains. They recognize, however, that no effort of theirs will rescue them from the punishment they have deserved. In desperation they pray to the mountains and hills and plead for a burial that will hide them from the sight of God and of the Lamb. They quote from the Old Testament (Ho 10:8) the words which Hosea had put into the mouth of sinners on the day of God's judgment, "Fall on us and hide us." Jesus had quoted those same words to the weeping women of Jerusalem when he had spoken to them of God's wrath which was to come upon the Jews (Lk 23:30).

It should be noted that the wrath of God is here described as the wrath of the Lamb. In most other passages of Revelation it is simply called the wrath of God (cp 14:10,19; 15:1,7; 16:1; 19:15). We are in this way reminded that there is no dispute between the persons of the Trinity regarding the punishment of the wicked. Some Christians have a tendency to visualize God the Father as a stern and angry judge and God the Son as the gracious person of the Trinity who seeks to persuade his Father not to punish men. But the day of God's wrath is the great day of the Lamb's wrath also. Jesus, the Lamb of God, is both the gracious Savior who redeemed us to God with his blood and the angry judge who will some day say to his unbelieving enemies, "Depart from me, ye cursed, into everlasting fire prepared for the devil and his angels" (Mt 25:41).

The question with which the chapter closes, "Who is able to stand?" is a rhetorical question that implies that no man will be able to stand before the wrath of God. The unbelieving world on the day of judgment will recognize the truth that the church continually warned them about when it spoke of the wrath to come. None of them will be able to stand with the hope of acquittal before this court because they rejected the message of forgiveness proclaimed in the gospel. Their question echoes the question of the psalmist, "If you, O Lord, kept a record of sins, O Lord, who could stand?" (Ps 130:3). Because of their unbelief God will judge them according to the record of their sins. They will be without the hope the psalmist expresses when he continues, "But with you there is forgiveness; therefore you are feared" (v. 4).

Earlier in this chapter (v. 11) John had spoken of this forgiveness under the symbol of the white robe which the martyrs received. The martyrs therefore will be able to stand before this judgment of God in the great day of his wrath. As John meditated on this vision after that day on Patmos when God had showed him these things, he often must have recalled the parable of the wedding garment (Mt 22:1-14) where Jesus said that only those who were wearing the white robe of his righteousness would be able to stand before God's throne.

But God himself answers the question, "Who shall be able to stand?" in the next two scenes in this vision, which picture for us all those who will be safe when God destroys the world.

THE 144,000: THE CHURCH ON EARTH (7:1-8)

1) Μετὰ τοῦτο εἶδον τέσσαρας ἀγγέλους ἑστῶτας ἐπὶ τὰς τέσσαρ-
ας γωνίας τῆς γῆς, κρατοῦντας τοὺς τέσσαρας ἀνέμους τῆς γῆς,
ἵνα μὴ πνέῃ ἄνεμος ἐπὶ τῆς γῆς μήτε ἐπὶ τῆς θαλάσσης μήτε ἐπὶ
πᾶν δένδρον. 2) καὶ εἶδον ἄλλον ἄγγελον ἀναβαίνοντα ἀπὸ ἀνα-
τολῆς ἡλίου, ἔχοντα σφραγῖδα Θεοῦ ζῶντος, καὶ ἔκραξεν φωνῇ
μεγάλῃ τοῖς τέσσαρσιν ἀγγέλοις οἷς ἐδόθη αὐτοῖς ἀδικῆσαι τὴν
γῆν καὶ τὴν θάλασσαν, 3) λέγων, Μὴ ἀδικήσητε τὴν γῆν μήτε τὴν
θάλασσαν μήτε τὰ δένδρα, ἄχρι σφραγίσωμεν τοὺς δούλους τοῦ
Θεοῦ ἡμῶν ἐπὶ τῶν μετώπων αὐτῶν. 4) Καὶ ἤκουσα τὸν ἀριθμὸν
τῶν ἐσφραγισμένων, ἑκατὸν τεσσεράκοντα τέσσαρες χιλιάδες
ἐσφραγισμένοι ἐκ πάσης φυλῆς υἱῶν Ισραηλ·

5) ἐκ φυλῆς Ἰούδα δώδεκα χιλιάδες ἐσφραγισμένοι,
ἐκ φυλῆς Ῥουβὴν δώδεκα χιλιάδες,
ἐκ φυλῆς Γὰδ δώδεκα χιλιάδες,
6) ἐκ φυλῆς Ἀσὴρ δώδεκα χιλιάδες,
ἐκ φυλῆς Νεφθαλεὶμ δώδεκα χιλιάδες,
ἐκ φυλῆς Μανασσὴ δώδεκα χιλιάδες,
7) ἐκ φυλῆς Συμεὼν δώδεκα χιλιάδες,
ἐκ φυλῆς Λευεὶ δώδεκα χιλιάδες,
ἐκ φυλῆς Ἰσσαχὰρ δώδεκα χιλιάδες,
8) ἐκ φυλῆς Ζαβουλὼν δώδεκα χιλιάδες,
ἐκ φυλῆς Ἰωσὴφ δώδεκα χιλιάδες,
ἐκ φυλῆς Βενιαμεὶν δώδεκα χιλιάδες ἐσφραγισμένοι.

1) *After this I saw four angels standing on the four corners of the earth, holding the four winds of the earth to keep them from blowing on the earth or on the sea, or on every tree.* 2) *And I saw another angel coming up from the east, having the seal of the living God, and he cried with a loud voice to the four angels to whom was given (the power) to hurt the earth and the sea,* 3) *"Do not hurt the earth nor the sea nor the trees until we have set a seal on the foreheads of the servants of God."* 4) *And I heard the number of those sealed, 144,000, sealed out of every tribe of the children of Israel:*

5)	*out of the tribe of Judah,*	*12,000 sealed*
	out of the tribe of Reuben,	*12,000*
	out of the tribe of Gad,	*12,000*
6)	*out of the tribe of Asher,*	*12,000*
	out of the tribe of Naphtali,	*12,000*
	out of the tribe of Manasseh,	*12,000*
7)	*out of the tribe of Simeon,*	*12,000*
	out of the tribe of Levi,	*12,000*
	out of the tribe of Issachar,	*12,000*
8)	*out of the tribe of Zebulun,*	*12,000*
	out of the tribe of Joseph,	*12,000*
	out of the tribe of Benjamin,	*12,000 sealed*

This is one of the passages in Revelation that leads us to conclude that the number four is the number of the earth. It speaks of the four corners of the earth and the four winds of the earth. The four winds of the earth are portrayed as wild and destructive beasts which are held on a leash by four angels. The four winds have the power to "hurt" the earth, which implies that once unleashed they have the power of complete destruction — down to the last tree. The first three verses indicate that the complete destruction of the earth is to be delayed until the angel and his unnamed assistants ("we") are able to finish the task of "sealing" the servants of God.

To set one's seal on something means basically to assert and to claim ownership. A modern parallel practice is the custom of putting a brand on cattle. The people who are sealed are the servants of God, the people who belong to God. God's seal is set on men when God claims them as his own, when God says to them, "You are mine." In keeping with that thought, the Apostle Peter called the Christians to whom he wrote a λαὸς εἰς περιποίησιν, "a people belonging to God."

Sinful human beings are delivered and set free from the bondage of the devil and become servants of God in the moment of their conversion. The angel says, in effect, "Do not destroy the earth totally until all the elect have been brought into God's kingdom." This vision is a symbolic way of expressing the thought that the present world continues to exist for the sake of the elect and that the world will not be destroyed until the last elect person has been brought to faith.

There is another way to interpret these verses. In the book of Ezekiel there is a vision in which the prophet saw six men with swords who were commissioned to destroy the inhabitants of Jerusalem without mercy. Before these six destroyers were allowed to begin their work, however, another man clothed with linen and carrying an inkhorn at his side was sent into the streets of the city to place a mark on the forehead of all those who were penitent, all the believers in the city. Thereafter the destroyers were commanded to slay all the inhabitants of Jerusalem, but not to lay a hand on any of those who had the mark on the forehead (Eze 9:1-10,22).

In the final analysis, it makes little difference if the seal is interpreted as a mark of ownership or as a sign indicating that the bearer of the seal is not to be harmed. In either case, the message remains the same, namely, the destruction of the earth is not to take place until all those predestined for salvation have been made servants of God. The rider on the white horse is to be given time to complete his mission first. The gospel of the kingdom is to be preached in all the world for a witness to all nations. After that the end will come.

Some object to this interpretation and say that the events described in 7:1-8 must follow the judgment day described at the end of chapter 6 because the first words of chapter 7 say "after this." This phrase, however, belongs with the words "I saw." John is not proposing a chronological framework for the contents of the visions. He is simply recalling the order in which he saw them. The visions, like novels, histories and many literary works, use "flashbacks" to help us understand what is happening in the present. Even in the biblical historical books, events are not always recorded in the order in which they happened. (cp. *e.g.*, the order in Gn 1 and 2).

The scenes described in Revelation 7 are the first of a number of visions in which the Holy Ghost portrays the glorious hope that ought to live in the heart of a believing child of God. In the midst of war and famine, pestilence and persecution we need to hear again and again that finally we will be delivered from these great tribulations and find an incomparably happy existence in the glories of heaven.

The present scene of the 144,000 who were sealed prevents John and his readers from drawing a wrong conclusion from the scene of the final judgment which he had just witnessed. The awful calamities of war, famine, pestilence and persecution finally reached a climax in the utter destruction of heaven and earth, a destruction which those earlier calamities had foreshadowed.

If this were the whole story, however, the history of the world would be a hopeless story of despair, in which every one might be advised to grasp whatever the present moment might offer and say, "Let us eat and drink and be merry for tomorrow we die." To correct that false impression God lets John see that in the midst of all this great tribulation that leads eventually to total destruction of the present order of things, there is a small group that the Lord has determined to keep in safety and who will not be harmed in the great day of the Lord's wrath because they are his people. For their sake the destruction of the world will be delayed. The four angels will keep the four winds on a leash until the last one of the elect has been effectively made God's own through baptism and the gospel.

The vision of the 144,000 and the subsequent vision of the great white host before the throne are typical of a number of such scenes in the book. Often after John has seen a cluster of catastrophic events, he is granted a vision of the saints in glory or at least one which reminds him of the security and hope of God's people (cp. 11:15-19; 14:1-5; 19:1-8; 21:1 — 22:5). In one case the scene of glory precedes the announcement of destruction (15:1-4). This is John's way of reminding us of the truth which Paul taught, "Our present sufferings are not worth comparing with the glory that will be revealed in us" (Ro 8:18).

Many commentators insist that the 144,000 are converted Jews because they are said to come from "every tribe of the children of Israel." This interpretation is impossible. While there are twelve tribes listed with exactly 12,000 from each tribe being sealed, the list does not agree with any listing that was used in the Old Testament for the literal, historical twelve tribes of the children of Israel. In the Old Testament the tribe of Levi was not counted with the tribes among whom the promised land was divided. Yet Levi is included here. On the other hand, the tribe of Dan is omitted. Commentators who insist that the literal tribes of Israel are meant struggle to explain why Dan is not mentioned. Yet these explanations satisfy only those who have prejudged the case. It may be a little easier to explain why Ephraim is not mentioned. Ephraim and Manasseh were sons of Joseph, and mention of the tribe of Joseph in the eleventh place may be a substitute for Ephraim. Yet, in the Old Testament Ephraim is one of the most important tribes. The whole northern kingdom was sometimes called Ephraim. So even this variation from the standard Old Testament terminology supports the fact that here we are not dealing with the literal twelve tribes of the nation of Israel.

Earlier in the book of Revelation Jesus had spoken to the church of Smyrna about the blasphemy of "those who say they are Jews but are not," but instead are "the synagogue of Satan." The same kind of language is used in the letter to Philadelphia. Words like this reflect the common teaching of the New Testament that the true Jews, the true children of Abraham. are those who share Abraham's faith. This is why at the dawn of the New Testament era John the Baptist tells the Jews not to take pride in their physical descent from Abraham. God, he says, could make children of Abraham out of the stones on the desert floor. Jesus echoed this teaching of John when he told the Pharisees, outwardly the most pious among the Jews, that they were the children of the devil.

The Apostle Paul spelled out this doctrine concerning the true children of Abraham in great detail. His letter to the Galatians opposed the Judaizers, who insisted that anyone who became a Christian should also become a Jew. To combat this error, Paul called the church, which included uncircumcised believers, "the Israel of God." Those who have become new creatures through regeneration and conversion are the true Israelites in God's sight.

In his letter to the Romans Paul emphasizes this truth again and again. In Romans 2 he says that those who are Jews only outwardly are not really Jews. In chapter 4 we are told that only believers are children of Abraham. In chapter 9 he makes the assertion that Israel is not completely made up of Israelites and that not all of Abraham's descendants are his children. In chapter 11 he clearly teaches that those Jews who do not have faith are expelled and excluded from the chosen people, but Gentiles who believe are a part of the spiritual Israel.

The question of what constitutes true Jewishness or what really makes a person one of the children of Israel is illustrated in a negative way by a development in the modern state of Israel. Early in 1979 the highest court of Israel handed down a ruling which stated that no one who accepted Jesus as the Messiah could be considered a Jew, even if that person had not joined a Christian congregation and wanted to be considered a Jew. According to Israeli law one can still be considered a Jew even if he rejects the religion of Moses, or if he accepts any religion other than Christianity. But under no circumstances can he be considered a Jew if he accepts Jesus of Nazareth as the Messiah. A sharper contrast to the Bible's teaching concerning Jewishness can scarcely be imagined (cp *Biblicum* 3-4, 1979, 138ff). John's characterization of apostate Judaism as the "synagogue of Satan" and the whole teaching of the New Testament on this matter finds a concrete illustration in this decision of the modern Israeli courts.

Against the background of the clear teaching of the New Testament the significance of the 144,000 Israelites who are sealed also becomes crystal clear. It is so clear that it leaves us in no doubt as to the significance of the number 144,000. It represents the whole church on earth. Everywhere in Revelation, twelve is the number associated with the church. Twelve squared is 144. Squaring or cubing the symbolic numbers occurs several times in the book, but without affecting the basic symbolism. The 144,000 are the full number of the elect, or the whole church as it is known to the omniscience of God. The number 1,000 is ten cubed, and therefore the number for completeness.

THE GREAT WHITE HOST: THE CHURCH IN HEAVEN (7:9-17)

In the first eight verses of this chapter John learned that the church on earth was safe and secure for all time, even though the earth itself was destined for destruction. Now he sees another vision in which the church is no longer on earth but in heaven before the throne of God. He writes,

9) Μετὰ ταῦτα εἶδον, καὶ ἰδοὺ ὄχλος πολύς, ὃν ἀριθμῆσαι αὐτὸν οὐδεὶς ἐδύνατο, ἐκ παντὸς ἔθνους καὶ φυλῶν καὶ λαῶν καὶ γλωσσῶν, ἑστῶτες ἐνώπιον τοῦ θρόνου καὶ ἐνώπιον τοῦ Ἀρνίου, περιβεβλημένους στολὰς λευκάς, καὶ φοίνικες ἐν ταῖς χερσὶν αὐτῶν· 10) καὶ κράζουσιν φωνῇ μεγάλῃ λέγοντες,

Ἡ σωτηρία τῷ Θεῷ ἡμῶν τῷ καθημένῳ ἐπὶ τῷ θρόνῳ καὶ τῷ Ἀρνίῳ.

11) καὶ πάντες οἱ ἄγγελοι εἱστήκεισαν κύκλῳ τοῦ θρόνου καὶ τῶν πρεσβυτέρων καὶ τῶν τεσσάρων ζῴων, καὶ ἔπεσαν ἐνώπιον τοῦ θρόνου ἐπὶ τὰ πρόσωπα αὐτῶν καὶ προσεκύνησαν τῷ Θεῷ, 12) λέγοντες,

Ἀμήν, ἡ εὐλογία καὶ ἡ δόξα καὶ ἡ σοφία καὶ ἡ εὐχαριστία καὶ ἡ τιμὴ καὶ ἡ δύναμις καὶ ἡ ἰσχὺς τῷ Θεῷ ἡμῶν εἰς τοὺς αἰῶνας τῶν αἰώνων· ἀμήν.

13) Καὶ ἀπεκρίθη εἷς ἐκ τῶν πρεσβυτέρων λέγων μοι, Οὗτοι οἱ περιβεβλημένοι τὰς στολὰς τὰς λευκὰς τίνες εἰσὶν καὶ πόθεν ἦλθον; 14) καὶ εἴρηκα αὐτῷ, Κύριέ μου, σὺ οἶδας. καὶ εἶπέν μοι, Οὗτοί εἰσιν οἱ ἐρχόμενοι ἐκ τῆς θλίψεως τῆς μεγάλης καὶ ἔπλυναν τὰς στολὰς αὐτῶν καὶ ἐλεύκαναν αὐτὰς ἐν τῷ αἵματι τοῦ Ἀρνίου. 15) διὰ τοῦτό εἰσιν ἐνώπιον τοῦ θρόνου τοῦ Θεοῦ, καὶ λατρεύουσιν αὐτῷ ἡμέρας καὶ νυκτὸς ἐν τῷ ναῷ αὐτοῦ, καὶ ὁ καθήμενος ἐπὶ τοῦ θρόνου σκηνώσει ἐπ᾽ αὐτούς. 16) οὐ πεινάσουσιν ἔτι οὐδὲ διψήσουσιν ἔτι, οὐδὲ μὴ πέσῃ ἐπ᾽ αὐτοὺς ὁ ἥλιος οὐδὲ πᾶν καῦμα, 17) ὅτι τὸ Ἀρνίον τὸ ἀνὰ μέσον τοῦ θρόνου ποιμανεῖ αὐτοὺς καὶ ὁδηγήσει αὐτοὺς ἐπὶ ζωῆς πηγὰς ὑδάτων· καὶ ἐξαλείψει ὁ Θεὸς πᾶν δάκρυον ἐκ τῶν ὀφθαλμῶν αὐτῶν.

9) *After these things I saw, and behold! a great multitude, whom no man could number, out of every nation and tribe and people and language standing before the throne and before the lamb, clothed with white robes, and in their hands (they carried) palms.* 10) *And they cried with a loud voice,*

"Salvation comes from our God who sits on the throne and from the Lamb."

11) *And all the angels had placed themselves in a circle around the throne and the elders and the four living creatures. They fell on their faces before the throne and worshiped God,* 12) *saying,*

"Amen. Blessing and glory and wisdom and thanks and honor and power and might
belong to our God forever and ever. Amen."

13) *And one of the elders spoke to me and said, "These men clothed in white robes — who are they and where did they come from?" And I answered him, "My lord, you know."* 14) *And he said, "These are the ones who are coming out of the great tribulation, and they washed their robes and made them white in the*

blood of the Lamb.
15) *Because of this they are before the throne of God,*
and serve him day and night in his temple,
and he that sits on the throne shall dwell among them.
16) *They shall hunger no more,*
nor thirst any more,
nor shall the sun fall upon them,
nor any heat,
17) *because the Lamb in the center near the throne shall be their shepherd,*
and he will lead them to the watersprings of life;
and God will completely wipe away every tear from their eyes.

Verses 1-3 of chapter 7 show that the 144,000 of the previous vision were on earth prior to the destruction of the earth. They therefore symbolize the whole church on earth or the church militant. The people described in the second part of the chapter, however, have come out of the great tribulation described in chapter 6. They were no longer victims of the horrors of war and famine, pestilence and persecution. Nor were they among the number of those who called upon the mountains and hills to fall on them in order to hide them from the wrath of the Lamb.

Millennialists speak of the "great tribulation" as a period of seven years and associate it with what they call the "rapture of the saints." Yet they do not all agree on whether to place the so-called rapture before, during or after the tribulation. Hence they are divided into three camps, namely, pre-, post- and mid-tribulation rapturists.

But Revelation 7 makes no reference to any such rapture. We have translated the Greek present participle in the text as "the ones who are coming out." The doctrine of the rapture would be easier to reconcile with an aorist participle, which we could translate, "the ones who have come out," or "the ones who came out." John sees their "coming out" of the great tribulation as a continuous and ongoing process. Every time one of the 144,000 who are marked with the seal of God dies, he "comes out of" the great tribulation, i.e., the "many tribulations" (Ac 14:22) through which we must enter the kingdom of God.

While the Scriptures clearly teach that as the world nears its end, there will be especially great calamities and that evil men will grow worse and worse (2 Tm 3:13), there is not one passage of the Scripture that says that the church will escape this tribulation by being "raptured" out of this world for seven years. The preposition "out of" implies that the Christians are in the great tribulation. They must suffer along with the unbelieving world. The repeated assurance of Revelation that they will not be "hurt" merely echoes the promise that all the sufferings of this present time will work together for good to them that love God (Rm 8:18,28).

Jesus also had spoken of a great tribulation in Matthew 24 in his prophecy concerning the end times. There Jesus prophesied the destruction of Jerusalem in 70 A.D. and also the final destruction of the world at his second coming. It is not always easy in that chapter to distinguish the prophecies that refer to the first event from those that refer to the second. Some of the Savior's words apply only to the destruction of Jerusalem, some only to the second coming and some to both. The reference to a great tribulation (Mt 24:15-28) seems to apply first of all to the days before the fall of Jerusalem, although that tribulation may be understood as foreshadowing another great tribulation that will afflict men prior to the second coming. It is true that the Christians in 70 A.D. recognized the signs and escaped from Jerusalem in time. Still, they were not spared from tribulation. The Savior's words leave no doubt that many hardships would accompany their flight. Here we especially note that the Savior's description of the great tribulation contains no hint that there will be a rapture of the saints either preceding, interrupting or following the time of tribulation.

Even the words of Christ, "The one shall be taken and the other left," which occur in a later eschatological discourse (Mt 24:40,41), do not speak of a pretribulation rapture. If a house is burning and one occupant is taken out while the other is left, it can only mean that the second is left to perish in the flames. All that can be concluded with certainty from these words of Christ is that some will be spared the destruction that is to come upon the earth. Only in that sense will there be a "rapture."

In an effort to confine the "great tribulation" in 7:14 to a seven-year period of extraordinary suffering, millennialists often point to the definite article before the words "great tribulation." This article, they say, distinguishes this tribulation from the common troubles that affect men. Such a conclusion is not valid. The scene which John recorded in chapter 6 is full of references to calamities and troubles. Therefore it is only natural to interpret the definite article here as an article of previous reference. And even apart from that, the text says nothing to the effect that it will last seven years or that it will be preceded by a rapture of the church. Nowhere in Scripture are the words "great tribulation" used in conjunction with a reference to "seven years."

The great multitude which John saw in this vision was so great that John says no one could number them. In this context with its reference to the twelve tribes of Israel, it reminds us that God had promised Abraham and Jacob that their descendants would be as innumerable as the stars of heaven and the sand on the seashore (Gn 15:5-6; 22:17; 32:12; He 11:12).

The reference to an unnumbered multitude is another piece of evidence to support the interpretation that "Israel" in the first part of this chapter is the spiritual Israel of God. The statement that the individuals in this group have come from every nation and tribe and people and language is natural to this interpretation. It is a part of the general New Testament picture of the new Israel. When Paul in Romans 4 speaks of Abraham as the father of all believers, whether Jews or Gentiles, circumcised or uncircumcised, he finds justification in the Old Testament promise that Abraham would be the "father of many nations."

The fact that the glorified believers around the throne of God are from every nation and tribe and people and language is also evidence that the mission of the rider on the white horse, who had ridden out "conquering and to conquer" (6:2), had been successful. The gospel of the kingdom was preached for a witness to all nations, as Jesus had said (Mt 24:14), and it bore fruit everywhere (Is 55:10,11).

This is the second time in Revelation that the people of the world have been described as "nations and tribes and people and languages." The same words, but in a different order, describe those who were redeemed by the blood of the Lamb in chapter 5. In the following chapters of Revelation the population of the earth is described in this same or a very similar way: 10:11; 11:9; 13:7; 14:6; 17:15. Once the word "kings" is used (10:11) and once the word "multitudes" instead of "tribes" (17:15). It is likely that since four is the number which is associated with the earth John uses four words to describe the totality of the earth's people. He does this seven times in the book. This is interesting in view of the importance of the number seven in the structure and symbolism of Revelation.

These multitudes that have come out of every nation and tribe and people and language are standing before the throne and before the Lamb. They have joined the ten thousand times ten thousand holy angels whom John had seen encircling the throne and the living creatures and the elders in an earlier vision (5:11). These multitudes, unlike the 144,000, thus are not on earth. This contradicts the doctrine of the Jehovah's Witnesses that the 144,000 will be kings with Christ in heaven while the great multitude of those who have led good lives and worshiped Jehovah as a Unitarian type of God will live in a renewed earth after the final judgment. This chapter gives no support whatever to an idea like that.

Like the martyrs under the altar (6:11) these multitudes are also clothed in white robes. White is the color of purity. Even the Prophet Daniel had spoken of the multitudes who would be purified and made white (Dn 12:10 KJV). In their hands they carried palm branches. Already in classical Greek literature palm fronds were symbols of victory. Seven times in the seven letters (2:7,11,17,26; 3:5,12,21) the Savior made a promise to those who are victorious. The palm branches identify these multitudes as the victorious ones, as those who have overcome. One of the promises the Savior made to the victorious ones was that they would be clothed in white (3:5).

Having described the multitudes in glory John records the song which they sing around the throne. Literally translated the song reads,

> Salvation to our God who sits upon the throne and to the Lamb!

Some modern translations view the dative as a dative of possession and translate, "Salvation belongs to our God" (RSV, NIV). This is an unusual way of speaking, but the meaning is clear. The saints here confess that all the credit for their salvation belongs to God. It is also possible to interpret the dative here as being the translation of an equivalent Hebrew expression (cp 3:9) which indicates authorship. In such a case we could translate: "Salvation comes from our God," or, "Our God is the author of salvation." This is the grammatical basis of Beck's translation of this song, "We are saved by our God who sits on the throne and by the Lamb."

The holy angels standing in a circle around the throne echo the song of the redeemed with a second sevenfold doxology (cp 5:12). They express their agreement with the confession of the saints with an "Amen," which might be translated in English as "That is absolutely true." To this they then add their own song of praise in which they say that blessing and glory and wisdom and thanksgiving and honor and power and might belong to our God forever. They add a second "Amen" at the end as an indication of the conviction that their confession is firmly founded in fact. This high praise is not exaggerated as might be the case if they were singing the praises of some earthly ruler.

One of the twenty-four elders who were seated around the throne then asked John whether he knew the identity and the origin of these white-robed multitudes. And John said, "My lord, you know." John's reply is identical to that of Ezekiel in the vision of the dry bones (Eze 37:3), and it evidently means, "You will have to answer that question for me."

The elder then answers his own question by telling John first of all that this multitude is composed of people who "are coming out" of the great tribulation. They have now been delivered from all the suffering that a hostile world had been able to inflict on them. We have already taken note of the present participle, which indicates that day by day this multitude is growing as additional believing children of God reach the heavenly mansions through the portals of death.

The white robes that they wear are now fully explained. They were not white in themselves. They needed to be washed and made clean. It recalls the words of Isaiah's confession, "All our righteous acts are like filthy rags" (Is 64:6). But Isaiah also spoke of a robe of righteousness with which the Lord clothes his people (Is 61:10). The same prophet also spoke of scarlet sins which by God's gracious verdict would become as white as snow (Is 1:18).

The cleansing agent that made their robes as white as snow was the blood of Christ. The "blood of Christ" is a figure of speech representing the "death of Christ" as the payment for our sins. Because Christ died for us after our sins were laid on him we are now free from all sin. What John says here about washing our robes in the blood of the Lamb he had expressed in less symbolic but still figurative terms in his first epistle, where he wrote, "The blood of Jesus, his Son, purifies us from every sin" (1 Jn 1:7).

The perfect bliss of this heavenly host of redeemed people is then described in a series of ten statements:

1) They are before the throne of God
2) and serve him day and night in his temple
3) and he that sits on the throne shall dwell among them.
4) They shall hunger no more

5) nor thirst any more,
6) nor shall the sun fall upon them,
7) nor any heat,
8) because the Lamb in the center near the
 throne shall be their shepherd
9) and he will lead them to the watersprings
 of life
10) and God will completely wipe away every tear
 from their eyes.

Remembering that ten is the number of completeness, we may contemplate in these ten statements the complete release from all evil and the complete "fullness of joy" (Ps 16:11) which will be ours at God's right hand.

John introduces this description of the glory of God's people with "therefore," or "because of this." It is a reference to the washing of their robes in the blood of the Lamb. The redeemed are in glory because of what Christ has done for them by his redeeming work. Only the blood of the Lamb, which has freed them from every trace and stain of sin, has made it possible for them to stand before the throne of the holy God with whom no sin can dwell (Ps 5:4,5). In this way John once more reminds his readers that the song of the redeemed in verse 10 is true and that salvation comes only from our God, who sits on the throne, and from the Lamb.

The first three lines of this poem on the blessedness of the redeemed give us a beatific vision of God. The redeemed are in God's presence, before his throne of glory. There they spend their days and nights serving God. Later in the book John tells us that there will be no night there (21:25). Before we see a contradiction in this we must remember that these are visions, and we are not allowed to press the details. The picture expressed the truth that their bliss will not be interrupted, as is so often the case in this world. Here we are indeed already kings and priests, but the sufferings and tribulations of this life make it plain that we are not yet what we shall be (1 Jn 3:2). On this earth and in this life we must walk by faith and not by sight (2 Cor 5:7).

The service that the saints perform before the throne is worship service (λατρεύουσιν). They spend their days and nights in praise and adoration. It would be a mistake to limit the activity of the saints in heaven to such praise and adoration. The word which denotes the worship of the saints before the throne is the one Paul uses to describe the service we are to perform by using our body and all of its members to do the Lord's work in this world (Ro 12:1-21). While the word lays stress on honoring God by what we do, it does not define any particular type of service. At the same time, however, it reminds us that a very important part of our worship service here on earth is the praise and adoration that we render to God.

The next four lines of the poem depict the freedom of God's people from the effects of sin. When God cursed the ground after the Fall, it became difficult for man to wrest his daily bread from the soil. Hunger and thirst, which were easy to satisfy in the Garden before the Fall, became a common source of suffering in a fallen world. The sun, which was created to serve man, became for many a burning instrument of discomfort and even torture. Here the relentless heat of the oriental sun serves as a symbol of all the natural evils that have come into this world because of sin. But all this is now past. Hunger and thirst and the burning heat of the sun bring no more discomfort and pain.

After John describes the bliss of heaven in negative terms, he once more sounds a positive note in the concluding lines of the poem. Freedom from the sufferings of this present time (Ro 8:18) and bliss in the presence of God (Ps 16:11) come to God's people "because the Lamb who is in the center near the throne will be their shepherd and will lead them to the water-fountains of life." While water is a common Old Testament symbol of salvation, John's Gospel and the book of Revelation are the only books of the New Testament that use this symbolism. This is one of the many places in Revelation where John's Gospel helps to shed light on the meaning of a symbol. In John's Gospel we hear Jesus telling the Samaritan woman at Jacob's well, "Whoever drinks of the water I give him will never thirst. Indeed, the water I give him will become in him a spring of water welling up to eternal life" (Jn 4:14).

John uses not only the Old Testament symbol of water to represent salvation, but also the Old Testament symbol of the shepherd, a symbol which is common in the New Testament, but again, most often in John's Gospel and Revelation. When John wrote that the Lamb would be their shepherd and would lead them to the watersprings of life, he must have remembered the 23rd Psalm, "The Lord is my shepherd . . . He leadeth me beside the still waters." The shepherd is the Lamb. The Lamb is the Lord, and "the Lord" in the 23rd Psalm is Jahweh, the Hebrew proper name of God.

The last of the ten blessings that come to those who have washed their robes in the blood of the Lamb is that "God will completely wipe away every tear from their eyes." Everything that caused them to weep during the great tribulation — persecution and death, famine, war and pestilence — will then forever be a thing of the past.

This scene of God's elect and redeemed people enjoying the bliss of heaven must have been a source of encouragement to persevere in those days of bitter persecution. It is still a source of encouragement, comfort and hope today as we in the sufferings of this present time wait for the glory that shall be revealed in us.

You will notice that the second and third visions overlap. The seventh seal introduces the vision of the trumpets.

The Third Vision: The Seven Trumpets (8:1 — 11:19)

The first six seals in the vision of the seven seals used symbols that are relatively easy to interpret. This is not the case with the vision of the seven trumpets. This vision evidently covers the same period of time as the seven seals since both visions end with judgment day. Both visions view that day as a day of wrath for God's enemies (cp 6:17 and 11:18), but also as a day of vindication and glory for the saints (cp 7:9-17 and 11:18).

While the details of this vision are difficult to interpret, its general thrust is very clear. First of all, there is a very close connection between the seals and the trumpets. The opening of the seventh seal serves as the introduction to the seven trumpets.

The first six seals had depicted the signs of the end followed by the last judgment. When we compared the signs in Revelation 6 with the list of signs Jesus gave in his eschatological discourse in Matthew 24, we noted that Revelation 6 omits four of the signs. These four are false Christs, apostasy, false prophets and love growing cold. False Christs and false prophets are, however, so closely related that we may view the two as one sign. The same can be said of apostasy and of the deterioration of love in the church. We may summarize these four signs as representing false doctrine and ungodly living. This is a basic clue to help us understand the trumpets.

It is a long-standing tradition in the history of biblical interpretation that the seven trumpets symbolize various false religions or heresies that have plagued the church throughout its history. Some commentators, among them Dr. Martin Luther, have attempted to identify the specific heresies symbolized by the individual trumpets. Usually that has been done by listing the outstanding heretics of the church in chronological order and then correlating them in some way with the trumpets. But it is difficult in most cases to make an absolutely convincing identification.

Yet insofar as the visions depict the damage done by false doctrine, there is good reason to go along with the traditional interpretation.

Commentators who view the trumpets as symbolic foreshadowings of physical calamities will, of course, consider them a review of the vision of the seals.

Many, Christians included, have difficulty with the traditional interpretation because they generally fail to understand the danger that heresies pose and the destruction and misery that they bring. We know from many passages of Scripture that false doctrine leads men astray from the faith and that unbelief ends in eternal death and everlasting destruction. If we remember this, it will not be hard to see in the calamities of Revelation 8 and 9 a graphic portrayal of the effects of heresy.

THE SEVENTH SEAL: THE SEVEN ANGELS WITH THE SEVEN TRUMPETS (8:1-5)

**1) Καὶ ὅταν ἤνοιξεν τὴν σφραγῖδα τὴν ἑβδόμην, ἐγένετο σιγὴ ἐν
τῷ οὐρανῷ ὡς ἡμιώριον. 2) Καὶ εἶδον τοὺς ἑπτὰ ἀγγέλους οἳ
ἐνώπιον τοῦ Θεοῦ ἑστήκασιν, καὶ ἐδόθησαν αὐτοῖς ἑπτὰ σάλπιγ-
γες.**

**3) Καὶ ἄλλος ἄγγελος ἦλθεν καὶ ἐστάθη ἐπὶ τοῦ θυσιαστηρίου
ἔχων λιβανωτὸν χρυσοῦν, καὶ ἐδόθη αὐτῷ θυμιάματα πολλά, ἵνα
δώσει ταῖς προσευχαῖς τῶν ἁγίων πάντων ἐπὶ τὸ θυσιαστήριον τὸ
χρυσοῦν τὸ ἐνώπιον τοῦ θρόνου. 4) καὶ ἀνέβη ὁ καπνὸς τῶν
θυμιαμάτων ταῖς προσευχαῖς τῶν ἁγίων ἐκ χειρὸς τοῦ ἀγγέλου
ἐνώπιον τοῦ Θεοῦ. 5) καὶ εἴληφεν ὁ ἄγγελος τὸν λιβανωτόν, καὶ
ἐγέμισεν αὐτὸν ἐκ τοῦ πυρὸς τοῦ θυσιαστηρίου καὶ ἔβαλεν εἰς τὴν
γῆν· καὶ ἐγένοντο βρονταὶ καὶ φωναὶ καὶ ἀστραπαὶ καὶ σεισμός.**

1) *And when he opened the seventh seal there was silence in
heaven for about half an hour.* 2) *And I saw the seven angels that
stand before God, and they were given seven trumpets.*

3) *And another angel came and stood near the altar with a
golden censer and he was given much incense to offer together
with the prayers of all the saints on the golden altar which was
before the throne.* 4) *And the smoke of the incense went up before
God together with the prayers of the saints from the hand of the
angel.* 5) *Then the angel took the censer, filled it with fire from
the altar, and flung it on the earth. And there came claps of
thunder, and crashes, and flashes of lightning, and an earthquake.*

The opening of the seventh seal was followed by half an hour of silence in heaven. Public speakers know that a deliberately long pause, the "pregnant pause," is a sure way to get the attention of every person in the audience. At the same time it indicates that he believes that what he is about to say is very important. Jesus wants his church to know that what he is about to reveal in the seventh seal is of great significance for the church. In other words, the false doctrines that will arise to endanger the faith of the church and the apostasy that will lead the church away from her love of the Savior are dangers far greater than war and famine, pestilence and persecution. The half hour of silence teaches us that the church should not treat these dangers lightly. War, famine, pestilence and persecution can at their worst only rob us of physical life. False doctrine and apostasy can deprive us of eternal salvation.

During that half hour of silence John saw "the seven angels that stand before God." The definite article would normally be understood as denoting these as seven particular angels who are well known for their service to God. Many commentators so interpret it and see here a reference to the seven archangels, or the seven angels "of the presence." However, there is nowhere in Scripture any reference to seven archangels, unless this isolated passage is to be understood in that way. It is true that the angel Gabriel describes himself as "the one who stands before God" (Lk 1:19), but nowhere in Scripture do we read of seven special angels of high rank who are described in such terms. It might also be noted that the Bible never uses the word "archangel" in the plural. So far as the revelation of Scripture goes, we know of only one archangel, whose name is Michael. There may be seven archangels, as some have asserted, but this is the only passage in all of Scripture that could be cited for that opinion.

A study of John's use of the definite article in Revelation will convince the student that in this book John is quite free in using the article in what grammarians call the "deictic" sense. One use of the deictic article is to denote objects which are so vividly present to the mind of the speaker that he assumes that they are well-known to his hearers also. The definite article here therefore may mean nothing more than "the seven angels who appeared to me in the vision standing before God." Another example of such an article is found in 10:3, where John speaks of "*the* seven thunders," even though seven thunders are mentioned nowhere else in the whole Bible.

The significance of the half-hour of silence becomes even more pronounced when John tells us that the seven angels were given seven trumpets. The sound of trumpets is especially penetrating, and it was often used to warn of danger. This was such a common use of the trumpet that the Prophet Amos can ask, "When a trumpet sounds in a city, do not the people tremble?" (Am 3:6). The anticipation of the blast of the seven trumpets coupled with the half hour of silence heightens the sense of foreboding and the realization that what is about to be revealed is of the utmost importance and poses a terrible danger to the world and the church.

But before the seven angels sounded the seven trumpets, John saw another angel who came and stood near the altar. He was carrying a censer and was given a large quantity of incense. The altar is obviously the incense altar, as is further demonstrated by the fact that it is called the golden altar. The golden incense altar in the tabernacle stood just before the entrance to the holy of holies, where God was enthroned above the mercy seat between the cherubim. And here in the temple of heaven John sees a similar altar standing before the throne of God. This is the second passage in Revelation which compares heaven to the tabernacle in the wilderness.

The dative case, ταῖς προσευχαῖς, must be a dative of accompaniment. The incense was given to the angel in order that he might offer it as an accompaniment to the prayers of all the saints. We read that the smoke of the incense went up before God together with their prayers. It is clear that in this context the incense is not a symbol for the prayers of God's people, as was the case in chapter 5 (cp 5:8). Later (v.4), the implication is that our prayers and the prayers of all the saints need something to make them acceptable to God. The Bible tells us that the prayers of those who do not obey God's law are an abomination to God (Pr 28:9). Insofar as we are all sinners we, in and by ourselves, have no right to approach God in prayer. In a certain sense the blind man whom Jesus healed was right when he said, "We know that God doesn't hear sinners" (Jn 9:31, Beck).

While John does not tell us what this incense symbolizes, yet the Biblical teaching about prayer is so definite on this point that there can be no doubt that this incense is the merit of Christ. God does not hear sinners, and as sinners, so Luther says, we deserve nothing but punishment. But Jesus has washed us clean from all sins in his blood. In that way he has given us the right to approach God in prayer. His atoning merit makes our prayers, tainted with sin as they are, acceptable to God. We are all the children of God by faith in Christ Jesus (Ga 3:28), and only those who have faith in Christ Jesus have a right to say, "Our Father who art in heaven." When John here speaks of incense that is offered up *with* our prayers, he is teaching us in symbolic language the same truth which Jesus expressed, when he said, "My Father will give you whatever you ask *in my name*" (Jn 16:23).

The same angel, however, who serves God's people by offering the incense with their prayers, uses the same incense burner to afflict the wicked world. He took the censer, filled it with fire from the altar, and flung it to the earth. There can be no doubt that this action represents some kind of punishment for the earth. God's people can be confident and patient because through Christ their prayers are acceptable to God. But the earth, that is, the world of unbelievers, can only expect evidences of God's anger. When the angel flung the censer filled with fire to the earth, there were thunderings and crashes, flashes of lightning and an earthquake — all of which are symbols of God's wrath against sin.

The mention of "another angel" raises the question whether in Revelation an angel ever represents the Lord Jesus. The angel of 7:2, for example, is evidently an authority figure who gives orders to other angels. That evidence alone, however, hardly suffices to identify this angel as Christ.

The angel of 8:3 manifestly demonstrates the same kind of authority. Moreover, the fact that he offers the incense that makes the prayers of the saints acceptable to God may be a reference to the intercession of Christ. The fact that the incense was "given" to him might be an argument against identifying this angel with Christ. On the other hand, it may be viewed as a parallel to other statements of Scripture in which divine prerogatives (authority, Mt 28:19; judgment, Jn 5:27) are "given" to him according to his human nature.

THE FIRST FOUR TRUMPETS (8:6-13)

The remaining verses of chapter 8 describe great calamities which inflict horrible damage on the earth. John writes,

> **6) Καὶ οἱ ἑπτὰ ἄγγελοι οἱ ἔχοντες τὰς ἑπτὰ σάλπιγγας ἡτοίμασαν αὑτοὺς ἵνα σαλπίσωσιν.**
> **7) Καὶ ὁ πρῶτος ἐσάλπισεν· καὶ ἐγένετο χάλαζα καὶ πῦρ μεμιγμένα ἐν αἵματι καὶ ἐβλήθη εἰς τὴν γῆν· καὶ τὸ τρίτον τῆς γῆς**

κατεκάη, καὶ τὸ τρίτον τῶν δένδρων κατεκάη, καὶ πᾶς χόρτος χλωρὸς κατεκάη. 8) Καὶ ὁ δεύτερος ἄγγελος ἐσάλπισεν· καὶ ὡς ὄρος μέγα πυρὶ καιόμενον ἐβλήθη εἰς τὴν θάλασσαν· καὶ ἐγένετο τὸ τρίτον τῆς θαλάσσης αἷμα, 9) καὶ ἀπέθανεν τὸ τρίτον τῶν κτισμάτων τῶν ἐν τῇ θαλάσσῃ, τὸ ἔχοντα ψυχάς, καὶ τὸ τρίτον τῶν πλοίων διεφθάρησαν. 10) Καὶ ὁ τρίτος ἄγγελος ἐσάλπισεν· καὶ ἔπεσεν ἐκ τοῦ οὐρανοῦ ἀστὴρ μέγας καιόμενος ὡς λαμπάς, καὶ ἔπεσεν ἐπὶ τὸ τρίτον τῶν ποταμῶν καὶ ἐπὶ τὰς πηγὰς τῶν ὑδάτων. 11) καὶ τὸ ὄνομα τοῦ ἀστέρος λέγεται, Ὁ Ἄψινθος. καὶ ἐγένετο τὸ τρίτον τῶν ὑδάτων εἰς ἄψινθον, καὶ πολλοὶ τῶν ἀνθρώπων ἀπέθανον ἐκ τῶν ὑδάτων ὅτι ἐπικράνθησαν. 12) Καὶ ὁ τέταρτος ἄγγελος ἐσάλπισεν· καὶ ἐπλήγη τὸ τρίτον τοῦ ἡλίου καὶ τὸ τρίτον τῆς σελήνης καὶ τὸ τρίτον τῶν ἀστέρων, ἵνα σκοτισθῇ τὸ τρίτον αὐτῶν καὶ ἡ ἡμέρα μὴ φάνῃ τὸ τρίτον αὐτῆς, καὶ ἡ νὺξ ὁμοίως. 13) Καὶ εἶδον, καὶ ἤκουσα ἑνὸς ἀετοῦ πετομένου ἐν μεσουρανήματι λέγοντος φωνῇ μεγάλῃ, Οὐαὶ οὐαὶ οὐαὶ τοὺς κατοικοῦντας ἐπὶ τῆς γῆς ἐκ τῶν λοιπῶν φωνῶν τῆς σάλπιγγος τῶν τριῶν ἀγγέλων τῶν μελλόντων σαλπίζειν.

6) *And the seven angels which had the seven trumpets prepared to blow them.*
7) *And the first blew his trumpet. And there was hail and fire mixed with blood which fell on the earth. Then one third of the earth was burned up and one third of the trees was burned up, and all the green grass was burned up.*
8) *And the second angel blew his trumpet. And what looked like a great mountain burning with fire fell into the sea. And one third of the sea became blood.* 9) *And one third of the creatures in the sea that have life died, and one third of the ships was destroyed.*
10) *And the third angel blew his trumpet. And a great star, like a burning lamp, fell from the sky, and it fell on one third of the rivers and on the water springs.* 11) *And the name of the star was Wormwood. And one third of the waters became wormwood, and multitudes of men died from the waters because they had been made bitter.*
12) *And the fourth angel blew his trumpet. And one third of the sun was struck, and one third of the moon, and one third of the stars, so that a third part of them became dark. As for the day, there was no light for a third part of it, and the night likewise.*
13) *And I saw and heard a single eagle flying in midair saying with a loud voice, Woe, woe, woe to those whose home is on the earth because of the remaining trumpet blasts of the three angels who are about to blow their trumpets.*

The calamities pictured here are in many ways similar to the plagues of Egypt. In the seventh Egyptian plague hail and fire which ran along the ground destroyed the crops and killed many animals and men who did not take shelter after Moses had issued his warning (Ex 9:18-25). The first trumpet signals a devastation by fire and hail. As a result, one third of the earth, one third of the trees and all the green grass were burned up.

In the vision of the second trumpet John saw what appeared to be a great mountain of fire which fell into the sea and turned it into blood, killing one third of all the living creatures in the sea and destroying one third of the ships. This reminds us of the first plague in Egypt, in which God turned the water in Egypt into blood. The other similarity between the second trumpet vision and the Egyptian plague has to do with the death of the fish in the Nile (Ex 7:21).

While formally there seems to be little similarity between the vision of the third trumpet and the plagues of Egypt, yet it may be noted that the waters of Egypt became undrinkable in the first plague (Ex 7:21) just as in this vision the fresh water of the earth became poisonous when it was mixed with wormwood, or vermouth, which is a very bitter herb.

The darkness in the vision of the fourth trumpet is reminiscent of the ninth plague of Egypt, in which all of Egypt except the land of Goshen was covered by thick darkness for three days. In the vision of the fifth trumpet swarms of locusts afflict the earth, just as locusts devoured Egypt in the eighth plague.

Finally, just as the plagues of Egypt resulted in deliverance for God's people even though they brought much suffering to the Egyptians, so we may conclude that these plagues, though they bring much suffering to the people of the world, will not harm the children of God. In fact, they are a sign of deliverance.

John knew from his association with the Lord Jesus (see Mt 24) that false doctrines would be a sign that the end of the world is near.

False doctrine is a significant sign of the end, especially in view of the conclusions which the people of this world, and also some Christians in their weakness, draw from its presence. There are many who say that if the Bible were a clear book, false doctrine would not exist. Others simply try to write false doctrines off as a legitimate "variety of interpretations." They assert that men have a right to such interpretations because no one can be sure of what the words really mean.

However, the presence of false doctrines in the world is by no means an indication of lack of clarity in Scripture. Rather, it is evidence of the Bible's clearness as well as its truth. For the Bible clearly foretold that there would be false doctrines and apostasy from the faith.

Moreover, the fact that false doctrine follows the angel's flinging of the incense burner teaches in a symbolic way that false doctrine is a punishment from God. When men turn a deaf ear to the truth and refuse to take the words of Scripture at face value, error and deception are natural punishments that come as a direct consequence of the rejection of God's Word. Because men turn away their ears from the truth, all that is left for them is to believe in fables (2 Tm 4:4). And because men have refused to love the truth, God will send them strong delusions so that they firmly believe lies instead (2 Th 2:10f).

In each of these four trumpet visions John tells us that a third of the affected areas are destroyed. The hail and fire and blood of the first trumpet burn up one third of the earth and one third of the trees, as well as all the green grass. The great burning mountain that fell into the sea turned one third of the sea into blood, killed one third of the living creatures found in the sea, and destroyed one third of the ships. The great star named Wormwood turned one third of the waters in the rivers and water springs into wormwood, rendering them lethal for multitudes of men. And finally, at the blast of the fourth trumpet, one third of the sun, the moon, and the stars was turned into darkness.

The significance of these thirds is difficult to discover. All that we can say for certain is that these heresies will not cause total destruction. Even though they bring great danger and damage to the world by obscuring the light of God's Word (one third of the sun), by poisoning the waters of life (by turning them into blood and wormwood), and by robbing men of spiritual sustenance (the destruction of the earth, the trees and the green grass), yet they are never able to blot out the truth of God's Word completely. Also in this sense, the gates of hell are not able to destroy the church.

While the angels blowing the first four trumpets announce dire calamities for the world, greater evils than these are in store. After the fourth trumpet there is a brief interruption in the sequence of events. Then John tells us that he saw a single eagle flying in midair. The KJV translates "angel" instead of "eagle." That translation is based on late manuscripts. The earliest copies of Revelation and the greatest number of extant copies all have the word "eagle" here. Later copyists may have concluded that since the eagle is represented as speaking the context called for the word "angel" instead. However, in a book so highly figurative a speaking eagle does not come as a surprise.

The eagle announces a threefold woe and implies that the three remaining trumpets will usher in calamities even greater and false doctrines even more dangerous than those described up to this point. Immediately John continues,

THE FIFTH TRUMPET: THE LOCUSTS OUT OF HELL (9:1-11)

1) Καὶ ὁ πέμπτος ἄγγελος ἐσάλπισεν· καὶ εἶδον ἀστέρα ἐκ τοῦ οὐρανοῦ πεπτωκότα εἰς τὴν γῆν, καὶ ἐδόθη αὐτῷ ἡ κλεὶς τοῦ φρέατος τῆς ἀβύσσου. 2) καὶ ἤνοιξεν τὸ φρέαρ τῆς ἀβύσσου· καὶ ἀνέβη καπνὸς ἐκ τοῦ φρέατος ὡς καπνὸς καμίνου μεγάλης, καὶ ἐσκοτώθη ὁ ἥλιος καὶ ὁ ἀὴρ ἐκ τοῦ καπνοῦ τοῦ φρέατος. 3) καὶ ἐκ τοῦ καπνοῦ ἐξῆλθον ἀκρίδες εἰς τὴν γῆν, καὶ ἐδόθη αὐτοῖς ἐξουσία ὡς ἔχουσιν ἐξουσίαν οἱ σκορπίοι τῆς γῆς. 4) καὶ ἐρρέθη αὐτοῖς ἵνα μὴ ἀδικήσουσιν τὸν χόρτον τῆς γῆς οὐδὲ πᾶν χλωρὸν οὐδὲ πᾶν δένδρον, εἰ μὴ τοὺς ἀνθρώπους οἵτινες οὐκ ἔχουσιν τὴν σφραγῖδα τοῦ Θεοῦ ἐπὶ τῶν μετώπων. 5) καὶ ἐδόθη αὐτοῖς ἵνα μὴ ἀποκτείνωσιν αὐτούς, ἀλλ' ἵνα βασανισθήσονται μῆνας πέντε· καὶ ὁ βασανισμὸς αὐτῶν ὡς βασανισμὸς σκορπίου, ὅταν παίσῃ ἄνθρωπον. 6) καὶ ἐν ταῖς ἡμέραις ἐκείναις ζητήσουσιν οἱ ἄνθρωποι τὸν θάνατον καὶ οὐ μὴ εὑρήσουσιν αὐτόν, καὶ ἐπιθυμήσουσιν ἀποθανεῖν καὶ φεύγει ὁ θάνατος ἀπ' αὐτῶν. 7) καὶ τὰ ὁμοιώματα τῶν ἀκρίδων ὅμοιοι ἵπποις ἡτοιμασμένοις εἰς πόλεμον, καὶ ἐπὶ τὰς κεφαλὰς αὐτῶν ὡς στέφανοι ὅμοιοι χρυσῷ, καὶ τὰ πρόσωπα αὐτῶν ὡς πρόσωπα ἀνθρώπων, 8) καὶ εἶχον τρίχας ὡς τρίχας γυναικῶν, καὶ οἱ ὀδόντες αὐτῶν ὡς λεόντων ἦσαν, 9) καὶ εἶχον θώρακας ὡς θώρακας σιδηροῦς, καὶ ἡ φωνὴ τῶν πτερύγων αὐτῶν ὡς φωνὴ ἁρμάτων ἵππων πολλῶν τρεχόντων εἰς πόλεμον. 10) καὶ ἔχουσιν οὐρὰς ὁμοίας σκορπίοις καὶ κέντρα, καὶ ἐν ταῖς οὐραῖς αὐτῶν ἡ ἐξουσία αὐτῶν ἀδικῆσαι τοὺς ἀνθρώπους μῆνας πέντε. 11) ἔχουσιν ἐπ' αὐτῶν βασιλέα τὸν ἄγγελον τῆς ἀβύσσου, ὄνομα αὐτῷ Ἑβραϊστὶ Ἀβαδδών, καὶ ἐν τῇ Ἑλληνικῇ ὄνομα ἔχει Ἀπολλύων.

1) *And the fifth angel blew his trumpet. And I saw a star falling out of heaven to the earth, and the key of the pit of the abyss was given to him.* 2) *And he opened the pit of the abyss, and smoke came up out of the pit as smoke from a great furnace, and the sun and the air were darkened by the smoke of the pit.* 3) *And out of the smoke came locusts upon the earth and the kind of power that the scorpions of the earth have was given to them.* 4) *And they were told not to harm the grass of the earth, nor any green thing,*

nor any tree, but only those human beings who do not have the seal of God on their foreheads. 5) *And [power] was given to them not that they might kill them but that they might be tortured for five months. And the pain they cause is like the pain caused by a scorpion when it strikes a person.* 6) *And in those days men will seek death but will surely not find it, and they will long to die, but death will flee from them.*
7) *And the appearance of the locusts was like that of horses ready for battle, and upon their heads they seemed to wear crowns that appeared to be of gold, and their faces looked like human faces.*
8) *And they had hair that looked like female tresses, and their teeth were like lions' teeth.* 9) *And they had breastplates that appeared to be made of iron, and the sound of their wings was like the sound of many chariot horses charging into battle.*
10) *And they had tails, that is, stingers like those of scorpions, and in these tails of theirs they had the power to hurt men for five months.* 11) *They have the angel of the abyss as their king. His name in Hebrew is Abaddon and in Greek he has the name Apollyon.*

Interpreting the book of Revelation could in some respects be compared to solving a difficult crossword puzzle. We may read through the whole list of clues and at first be able to identify only a few of the words, but each word helps in some way to identify others.

At first glance these first eleven verses of chapter 9 contain very few symbols that we can quickly identify. Perhaps the easiest to identify is the "abyss." The word ἀβύσσος, besides the four times it appears in Revelation, is used in only two other passages in the New Testament. In the account of the Gadarene demoniac, the legion of demons who possessed him asked Jesus not to send them into the abyss. The word evidently denotes the deepest depths of hell. Literally it means a bottomless pit.

While some commentators are hesitant to identify "the angel of the abyss" as Satan, yet it is diffcult to conceive of any other firm interpretation of that term. It is true that Satan is nowhere else in the Bible called Abaddon or Apollyon. These two words both mean "Destroyer." The first is Hebrew and the second Greek. This is, however, surely a very fitting name for the devil, who brought all of God's creation to the brink of destruction through his temptation of Eve.

Moreover, many of the opposing arguments are not in harmony with Scripture. Poellot, for example, repeats Little's argument that this star cannot represent the devil "for he fell not 'unto the earth' but into the abyss itself." As proof he cites Jude

6. But the fact that the devil is cast into hell and bound in everlasting chains does not mean that he cannot roam over the face of the earth. Because the angels are always in heaven (Mt 18:11) does not prevent them from being present on earth. The limitations and the laws that govern spirits are not known to us. Besides this, we are not to press symbolic or figurative language in this way.

A second argument that Poellot uses to prove that this star cannot be Satan is that "he has no key or power to open its (the abyss') shaft and release himself or any of his followers." The symbolism of this chapter does not in any way suggest that the key given to the "star" enables him to release himself. He has the power to release a swarm of "locusts." There are many passages that speak of the devil's power to unleash manifest and diverse evils on our world as well as on the church, even though he will never be able to destroy it.

All these counterarguments, however, are unnecessary when we note that the claim that the devil "fell not unto the earth" contradicts the statement of chapter 12, where we read that Satan was indeed "cast out into the earth" (v. 9).

The "star" that fell from heaven is undoubtedly the same person who is later called the angel of the bottomless pit (v. 11). The word "star" denotes an outstanding personality (cp the "star" that comes out of Jacob [Nu 24:17], *i.e.*, the Messiah). The devil seems to have been an angel of high rank (see Jude 6 regarding "the angels who did not keep their position of authority"). The word "heaven" here does not necessarily take us back to the time of the beginning when the angels who sinned were cast out of heaven and God's presence. "Heaven," in biblical usage, most often means simply "the sky." It is the place where the birds fly (Gn 1:20) and where God placed the sun, moon and stars (Gn 1:14). In those passages from the first chapter of the Bible many modern versions translate the Hebrew word for "heaven" with the word "sky." Since the star that fell out of heaven has the key to the bottomless pit and controls the movements of the locusts, it is natural to speak of him as the "king" of these locusts (v. 11). All this reinforces the identification of the fallen star as Satan.

Having made these identifications it now becomes possible for us to say that the locusts that come out of the bottomless pit are a plague of some kind that the devil is able to call out of hell and unleash on the world. It is not a literal plague of locusts. We know this from the command that they are not to harm any of the vegetation on earth. The damage they do is done directly to men, but only to those men who do not have the seal of God on their foreheads, that is, the elect of God (cp 7:3).

This statement should help to convince the reader that the locusts, like the hail, the mountain, the star and the darkness of chapter 7 are also false doctrines. Many years before John wrote Revelation he had heard Jesus preach about the signs of the last times. As John wrote these early chapters of Revelation he must have reflected on some of the things that Jesus had said in that sermon.

At that time the Savior had assured his disciples that the elect could not be led astray. He said, "False Christs and false prophets will appear and perform great signs and miracles to deceive even the elect — if that were possible" (Mt 24:24). Wars, famines, pestilence and persecution may touch the lives of God's elect and bring earthly harm to them, but false doctrine will never lead them astray or permanently deceive them. The Savior has promised, "My sheep listen to my voice . . . and they shall never perish; no one can snatch them out of my hand" (Jn 10:27,28).

The swarming locusts are unable to harm those men who have the seal of God on their foreheads. This suggests that the plague portrays a host of false teachers disseminating their misleading doctrines in this world. This conclusion is supported by the description of the locusts as a cloud of smoke issuing out of the abyss and obscuring the light of the sun. The Bible in many ways makes it clear that false doctrine has its origin in hell. Since the beginning, the devil has raised doubts about God's word ("Did God really say . . . ?") and even has denied it outright ("You will not surely die!"). He is called the father of lies (Jn 8:44), and the most destructive lies of all are those that lead men away from God's Word. Paul speaks of men abandoning the faith by following deceiving spirits and things taught by demons (1 Tm 4:1). The same apostle spoke of the coming of the Antichrist, the greatest false teacher of them all, as being the work of Satan (2 Th 2:9). The author of Revelation himself had alluded to the ungodly spirits who work through false prophets (1 Jn 4:1). It is therefore certainly in harmony with the clear teaching of Scripture to say that the locusts that come pouring out of hell in this vision of the fifth trumpet are the innumerable lies that false prophets have proclaimed in this world. These heresies have kept men from coming to faith in the Savior. They have helped to lead astray those who only believed for a while but in time of temptation fell away (Lk 8:13) and who thus demonstrate that they do not belong to the elect.

This interpretation is strengthened by the symbolic obscuring of the sun. The sun is the great light God made on the fourth day, so that men might see clearly and not walk in darkness. In a physical sense the sun is the light of the world. In a spiritual sense Christ is the light of the world (Jn 8:12). Jesus also told his disciples, "You are the light of the world" (Mt 5:14). And there are many other passages which echo the words of the psalmist, "Your word is a lamp to my feet, and a light for my path" (Ps 119:105). Those three statements complement one another. Jesus is the "true light that gives light to every man" (Jn 1:9). But Jesus also commissioned his disciples, the church, to carry his testimony to the ends of the earth so that all might learn to know his name, the truth he revealed about himself. Therefore the church also can properly be called the light of the world. But since the church can make known the truth about Jesus only if it proclaims the word of God in its truth and purity, the word itself is likewise called a "light that shines in a dark place" (2 Pe 1:19). Anything that obscures God's word — and that is done chiefly, if not exclusively, by false doctrine — anything that makes the message of the church less than or different from what it ought to be is like a smoke screen coming out of the opening of hell to obscure the light and the healing rays of the "sun of righteousness" (Mal 4:2). The hymn writer had good biblical reasons for calling Jesus the "sun of my soul." In his first chapter the writer of Revelation compared the face of Jesus to the sun at its brightest. In the second last chapter he will write that the new Jerusalem has no need of a sun, for "the Lamb is its light" (21:23). That light is obscured only by false teachings.

The remaining symbolism of this section is not easy to interpret. If, however, we have correctly identified the locusts as the false doctrines the devil lets loose on the world, we can see in the remaining symbols the power and effect of these heresies. John says that the locusts were not given power to kill men but only to torment them. Here we are led to consider that the damage done by false doctrine is not as easy to detect as that done by persecution. The persecutors, whose destructive effect we alluded to in chapter six, brought death to the Christians. The destructive effect of false doctrine is not so easily perceived. But every false doctrine in the final analysis brings torment to the hearts and souls of men by cutting off or hindering the hope and comfort brought by the Word and by weakening or destroying the assurance of forgiveness and salvation.

One of the ancient pagan writers said that there is no torment known to man that exceeds the pain caused by a bad conscience. The only real and lasting cure for such a conscience is the gospel message of full and free forgiveness proclaimed without conditions of any kind. Anything that obscures that message, that blots out the light of that sun, brings terrible torment to the souls of men. It is a torment which finally culminates in the suffering of hell. John compares the anguish of a guilty conscience to the intense pain caused by the sting of a scorpion.

The despair that overwhelmed the heart of Judas drove him to suicide. Likewise, many human beings who have been tormented by an evil conscience have been tempted to see in death a way of release from their pain. Yet these very torments of conscience remind them that death may only increase their suffering. Shakespeare has given us an eloquent description of that dilemma in the soliloquy of Hamlet, where he spoke of that "dread of something after death" that "makes us rather bear those ills we have than fly to others that we know not of."

The spiritual significance of the statement that the locusts are given power to cause affliction for five months is difficult to say. The only comment we can make with confidence is that real locust plagues often last for five months before they abate. Many of the numbers used in Revelation have general symbolic significance, but "five," which is used very seldom (only here and in 17:20), does not seem to be such a number. We may see in it, however, an indication of how false doctrines, like locust swarms, have a tendency to fade away and lose their power, only to appear again for a new season of seeming success. Thus, for example, Arianism, the denial of the deity of Christ, which threatened to destroy the church in the fourth century, faded away, only to rear its head again and again during the history of the visible church.

The militancy of many heretical sects and their zeal in search of proselytes may be compared to the appearance of the locusts as horses ready for battle. The crowns on their heads point to the success of their efforts. The Greek language has two common words for "crown." The one used most often (στέφανος), while it sometimes is a badge of office or symbol of authority, most often was a prize given in recognition of a victory of some kind. The other (διάδημα) is always a sign of authority and rule.

The first of these is the word used here. In their militant missionary efforts — as we see, for example, in the Mormons and the Jehovah's Witnesses — they often appear to achieve astonishing successes and victories. But the crowns which they wear are not real. They look "like gold" but really are made of something like colored paper.

The locusts are described as having the faces of human beings and the hair of women but the teeth of lions. This parallels the concept that the Savior expressed when he spoke of false teachers as ravening wolves in sheep's clothing. In their human appearance they appear harmless, even peaceful and effeminate, but when they open their mouths their lions' teeth betray them as servants of the angel of the bottomless pit, of that roaring lion in search of prey (1 Pe 5).

The iron breastplates and the chariot horses charging into battle elaborate on the militant spirit of heretics. And the description closes with the repeated warning: the pain they cause is like that inflicted by the sting of scorpions.

Ours is an ecumenical age, which writes off almost all Christian doctrine as being little more than human opinion and tolerates every form of doctrinal apostasy and heresy in the church. The people of our day need to hear this description of the damage that heresy does to the souls of men, that it deprives them of true hope and finally robs them of the will to live. Because people have grown insensitive to doctrinal differences, false teachers have become a fearful and ubiquitous plague. Their teachings are still as dangerous as the sting of scorpions, as threatening as the snarling of ravenous wolves, and as destructive as lions' teeth.

But the demonic plague of locusts is not the last effort to alert the church to the danger of false doctrine. The flying eagle of 8:13 had spoken of three woes that were still to come. The first of these was the pain inflicted by the hellish locusts. The second woe is now described.

THE SIXTH TRUMPET: THE ARMY FROM THE EUPHRATES (9:12-19)

12) Ἡ Οὐαὶ ἡ μία ἀπῆλθεν· ἰδοὺ ἔρχεται ἔτι δύο Οὐαὶ μετὰ ταῦτα.
13) Καὶ ὁ ἕκτος ἄγγελος ἐσάλπισεν· καὶ ἤκουσα φωνὴν μίαν ἐκ τῶν τεσσάρων κεράτων τοῦ θυσιαστηρίου τοῦ χρυσοῦ τοῦ ἐνώπιον τοῦ Θεοῦ,
14) λέγοντα τῷ ἕκτῳ ἀγγέλῳ, ὁ ἔχων τὴν σάλπιγγα, Λῦσον τοὺς τέσσαρας ἀγγέλους τοὺς δεδεμένους ἐπὶ τῷ ποταμῷ τῷ μεγάλῳ Εὐφράτῃ.
15) καὶ ἐλύθησαν οἱ τέσσαρες ἄγγελοι

οἱ ἡτοιμασμένοι εἰς τὴν ὥραν καὶ ἡμέραν καὶ μῆνα καὶ ἐνιαυτόν, ἵνα ἀποκτείνωσιν τὸ τρίτον τῶν ἀνθρώπων. 16) καὶ ὁ ἀριθμὸς τῶν στρατευμάτων τοῦ ἱππικοῦ δισμυριάδες μυριάδων· ἤκουσα τὸν ἀριθμὸν αὐτῶν. 17) καὶ οὕτως εἶδον τοὺς ἵππους ἐν τῇ ὁράσει καὶ τοὺς καθημένους ἐπ' αὐτῶν, ἔχοντας θώρακας πυρίνους καὶ ὑακινθίνους καὶ θειώδεις· καὶ αἱ κεφαλαὶ τῶν ἵππων ὡς κεφαλαὶ λεόντων, καὶ ἐκ τῶν στομάτων αὐτῶν ἐκπορεύεται πῦρ καὶ καπνὸς καὶ θεῖον. 18) ἀπὸ τῶν τριῶν πληγῶν τούτων ἀπεκτάνθησαν τὸ τρίτον τῶν ἀνθρώπων, ἐκ τοῦ πυρὸς καὶ τοῦ καπνοῦ καὶ τοῦ θείου τοῦ ἐκπορευομένου ἐκ τῶν στομάτων αὐτῶν. 19) ἡ γὰρ ἐξουσία τῶν ἵππων ἐν τῷ στόματι αὐτῶν ἐστιν καὶ ἐν ταῖς οὐραῖς αὐτῶν· αἱ γὰρ οὐραὶ αὐτῶν ὅμοιαι ὄφεσιν, ἔχουσαι κεφαλάς, καὶ ἐν αὐταῖς ἀδικοῦσιν.

12) *One woe is past. Look! After these things two more woes are coming.*
13) *And the sixth angel blew his trumpet. And I heard a voice from the four horns of the golden incense altar which is before God.* 14) *It said to the sixth angel, the one with the trumpet, "Untie the four angels that are bound at the great river Euphrates."* 15) *And the four angels, who had been prepared for this hour, day, month and year, were untied so that they might kill a third of mankind.* 16) *And the number of cavalry regiments was 20,000 of 10,000 each. I heard the number.* 17) *And this is the way I saw the horses in the vision and those who rode on them: They had breastplates of fire-red, pale blue, and sulfur-yellow. And the heads of the horses were lionlike, and out of their mouths went fire and smoke and sulfur.* 18) *By these three plagues, by the fire and the smoke and the sulfur that came out of their mouths, the third part of mankind was killed.* 19) *For the power of the horses is in their mouths and in their tails, for their tails are like serpents. They have heads and with these they cause damage.*

The voice that comes from the incense altar is not further identified, but its command to untie the four chained angels reminds us that God is holding the forces of evil in check and that he will not unloose them until the world is ready for the judgment. We have not met these four angels before. They apparently are not the same four angels mentioned in 7:1, although the definite article here might be viewed as an article of previous reference. The descriptive participle which follows, however, is reason enough to use the deictic article here. If anything, we ought to compare these four angels to the four winds that are held in check by the four angels of chapter 7. These four angels represent forces of evil, and they are free to do their destructive work only at that exact time which God has appointed. The view that they are good angels in control of evil forces is hard to justify. It would be difficult to conceive of good angels as being "bound." They gladly do God's will. In any case, the symbolism reminds us that God controls the destiny of the world and the church. He determines "the times before appointed" (Ac 17:26). This thought is reinforced when the angels are described as "having been prepared." In this context the past passive participle indicates that God uses them as his agents to inflict damage on the world. We are, however, not told how or by whom they were prepared. God makes use of evil to carry out his purposes (cp, *e.g.*, Gn 50:20).

There is very likely no special significance in most of the other details mentioned in verses 13-15. The four horns of the incense altar were four projections at the four corners of the top of the altar. Also in the Old Testament these horns do not seem to have any special significance, although we are told that both Adonijah and Joab fled to take hold of the horns of the altar in the tabernacle (1 Kgs 1:50; 2:28) in the apparent belief that this was a position of safety. It may have been no more than a superstitious opinion on their part. The NIV translates "from the horns of the altar" because the earliest manuscripts only speak of the horns of the altar and do not mention how many there were.

The altar is "before God." This is undoubtedly not a reference to the position of the incense altar in the Old Testament tabernacle but only an echo of the first verses of chapter 8, where we read that this altar was "before the throne."

The reference to the Euphrates, however, may be of some special significance, especially when we compare this vision with the previous one. There we learned that the damage was the work of swarms of locusts that issued out of the mouth of hell. The enemies described here have a more earthly origin. They come from the region of the Euphrates.

In later Old Testament times all the great enemies of God's chosen people came from this area of the world. Assyria, Babylonia and Persia were all based in the valley of the Tigris and Euphrates rivers. Later in Revelation the great enemy of the church will receive the name Babylon. Just as Jerusalem is a New Testament name for the church, so the name of Babylon, historically one of the great enemies of the earthly Jerusalem, symbolizes the great spiritual enemy of the spiritual Jerusalem. Here the great forces of evil assemble in the region of the Euphrates.

There is a difference between the two visions in chapter 9. The vision of the locusts reminds us that the devil is intent upon sowing the seeds of false doctrine in the world and that he is able to summon out of hell many delusions to lead men astray. But wicked men do not need the direct inspiration of the devil to conceive of falsehoods. They are able to invent them on their own. The Bible often speaks of the "world" as an enemy of God's people. We often speak of the devil, the world and the flesh as the three great foes that God's people must struggle against and overcome. There can be no doubt that of all the evils that have their origin in the world, the false philosophies and heretical theologies are far more injurious to the souls of men than the moral evils which lead men astray. Where the gospel of grace and free forgiveness is proclaimed, even publicans and harlots can find salvation. But where that gospel is obscured or completely hidden by humanism, materialism, evolutionism, communism and countless other false world views, men are finally robbed of all hope of salvation. These horsemen that come from the region of the Euphrates are symbols of these false doctrines that the world invents and proclaims.

We are invited to ponder the great number and diversity of false teachings in the world as they march into view in the form of 200-million horses (twenty-thousand regiments of ten thousand each). Truth has only one form. It is a unified whole. But falsehood can take on innumerable forms. Two contrary statements cannot both be true, but a hundred conflicting statements can all be false.

Having stated the number of the horses, John then describes the riders and the horses in some detail. There is an obvious parallelism in the description of the breastplates of the riders as fire-red, pale blue and sulfur yellow (πυρίνους καὶ ὑακινθίνους καὶ θειώδεις) and the fire, smoke and sulfur (πῦρ καὶ καπνὸς καὶ θεῖον) that come out of the mouths of the horses. The word which we have translated "pale blue" is the color of hyacinth. The word is used only once in the New Testament. The noun from which it is derived is also used only once as the name of the eleventh of the twelve precious stones that form the foundation of the heavenly Jerusalem (21:20). According to lexicographers it is either a sapphire or an aquamarine. While it is generally agreed that the color referred to in the description of the breastplates is a shade of blue, the lexicographers and commentators are not agreed on whether it is a light or dark blue. The reason for translating "pale blue" is based on the fact that when sulfur burns it burns with a very pale blue flame. Burning sulfur does not produce smoke, yet the pale blue color would be reflected in the smoke breathed out by the horses.

Fire and sulfur in the book of Revelation are definitely symbols of hell. In addition to these verses, there are four other passages in the book (14:10; 19:20; 20:10; 21:8) that use the phrase. In each of these four verses the connection with hell is indisputable. Thus while these riders and their horses do not, like the locusts, come out of hell, but from the region of the Euphrates, they still stand in the service of Satan and wear his colors.

Another indication of their hellish intent may be seen in the lions' heads possessed by these horses. The locusts of the previous vision had the teeth of lions. The lion-like character of these horses is easier to recognize than that of the locusts, which does not become apparent until they open their mouths and bare their teeth. The heresies depicted in the vision of the fifth trumpet are those that rise within the church itself while those symbolized in this vision come from the open enemies of the church, the avowed Babylonians. In this context the reader will again recall the roaring lion who walks about seeking men to devour (1 Pe 5:8,9). The fearsome appearance of these horses and riders ought to alert all of God's saints to the terrifying and destructive nature of false doctrines, which many in our day simply view as relatively harmless differences of opinion among religious people. At the same time, confessing Christians who deny fellowship to the purveyors of false doctrine are despised and dismissed as loveless and un-Christian. While these words were being written a member of the Gay Peoples Union accused the writer of a lack of Christian love because of his insistence that homosexuality is a damnable sin.

Verse 18 contains an exegetical difficulty. It says that by means of the three plagues that came out of the mouths of the horses, that is, by the fire, smoke and sulfur, the third part of mankind was killed. Does this mean that they were put to death physically or robbed of spiritual life? In view of the command given to the locusts, forbidding them to kill men (v. 5), it would seem that in this verse physical death is meant. Some commentators have seen in these verses a prophecy concerning the holy wars which the Mohammedans carried on against Christian nations for centuries, in which the Mohammedan warriors were promised salvation for slaying the infidels. While there can be no doubt whatever that Mohammedanism has been one of the most destructive of heresies and that it has risen from outside the Christian church, yet it would be a mistake to apply these words to Islam exclusively.

In light of the total context, however, it would seem that the killing performed by these horses definitely includes the concept of causing, or at least insuring, spiritual death. The next verse says that the power of the horses is in their mouths, as well as in their tails. The apocalyptic symbolism of Revelation justifies our conclusion that the smoke and fire and sulfur that come out of their mouths, like the smoke from the abyss, represent the false doctrines which these horses and riders spread through the world. This whole section deals with doctrinal delusions that obscure the light of God's Word.

The tails of the horses are like serpents and have heads with which they cause damage. This description emphasizes once more the terrifying nature of these enemies. The damage they cause is not specified. But the picture leads the reader to remember the story of the Fall, in which the mouth of a serpent deceived and brought disaster on the whole human race.

Because of God's mercy, the whole human race can no longer be deceived in this way. That was indicated in the previous vision where the locusts were commanded not to harm the elect. It is indicated here when we are told that the fire, smoke and sulfur killed the third part of mankind. The phrase echoes the words of the previous chapter, which had mentioned a third of the earth (8:7), a third of the sea (8:8), a third of the fresh waters (8:10), and a third of the sun, moon and stars (8:12). We cannot say that these words teach that two-thirds of mankind is saved, but only that these armies from the Euphrates cause the death of a third part of the human race. The earlier sections of this vision have shown that there are also other destructive enemies at large in this world. The point is that none of them can ever bring total destruction to the whole human race. Yet the last verses of this chapter demonstrate that the remaining two-thirds of men will not be saved.

THE IMPENITENCE OF THOSE WHO REMAIN (9:20-21)

20) καὶ οἱ λοιποὶ τῶν ἀνθρώπων, οἳ οὐκ ἀπεκτάνθησαν ἐν ταῖς πληγαῖς ταύταις, οὐδὲ μετενόησαν ἐκ τῶν ἔργων τῶν χειρῶν αὐτῶν, ἵνα μὴ προσκυνήσουσιν τὰ δαιμόνια καὶ τὰ εἴδωλα τὰ χρυσᾶ καὶ τὰ ἀργυρᾶ καὶ τὰ χαλκᾶ καὶ τὰ λίθινα καὶ τὰ ξύλινα, ἃ οὔτε βλέπειν δύνανται οὔτε ἀκούειν οὔτε περιπατεῖν, 21) καὶ οὐ μετενόησαν ἐκ τῶν φόνων αὐτῶν οὔτε ἐκ τῶν φαρμακιῶν αὐτῶν

οὔτε ἐκ τῆς πορνείας αὐτῶν οὔτε ἐκ τῶν κλεμμάτων αὐτῶν.

20) *But the rest of men, who were not killed by these plagues, did not even repent of the works of their hands, so that they might stop worshiping demons and idols of gold, silver, brass, stone or wood, which cannot see or hear or walk;* 21) *neither did they repent of their murders, and their sorceries, and their fornications, and their thefts.*

These words indicate that when God sends mental and spiritual pain and sorrow as a direct punishment flowing naturally from falsehood and heresy his purpose is to call men to repentance. But these words also make clear to God's people that they are not to expect a mass conversion of mankind. The great majority of men will always turn a deaf ear to God's call to repentance, even though the unsatisfying character of the teachings they espouse ought to make them realize that those teachings are wrong. The people of God therefore are not to become discouraged when they see widespread impenitence and unbelief. Rather, they ought to see even in this another evidence of the truth of God's Word.

Even the severest chastisements of God do not cause the mass of mankind to repent, to change their way of thinking. Literally the text says that "they do not change their mind out of the works of their hands." If men begin to think differently, if they adopt a different philosophy of life, that inner change will become evident in their outward behavior. When in their hearts they no longer find their evil works attractive or desirable then they will forsake them. In that way men repent "out of" their wicked deeds.

In Romans 1, the Apostle Paul points out that the immoral and unrighteous behavior of men is a direct consequence of their failure to recognize and to worship the true God. The Apostle John in these verses indicates the same sort of relationship when he describes the impenitence of men. First, he speaks of their impenitence in regard to their worship of false gods. This reference to idolatrous worship is especially significant in this context, which deals with false doctrine. False teaching always leads to idolatry. When men worship a god other than the one who has revealed himself in the Bible, they give honor to a man-made god, a god who might just as well be made of gold or silver or brass or wood. John speaks of this also as a worship of demons. Paul speaks of idolatry in the same terms when he says that the sacrifices offered in an idol temple are sacrifices offered to demons (1 Cor 10:20). This, too, is significant in this context. Early in this chapter the false teachings that obscure the truth of God's Word had been symbolized by a swarm of locusts released on the world by the devil. When men accept those false teachings and assist in spreading them, they are giving honor to the devil. The Lutheran Confessions say that the highest honor we can pay to God is that we believe what he says. When men believe the devil's lies in preference to God's truth, they are, in reality, offering their worship to the devil.

The description of these idols as gods which cannot see or hear or talk echoes many Old Testament passages. The psalmist, for example, wrote of idols of silver and gold that have mouths but cannot speak, eyes but cannot see, and ears but cannot hear (Ps 115:4-6). The false religions invented by devils and unbelieving men cannot bring men true hope or relief from the nagging pain of unsatisfied hearts.

After he describes the impenitence of men in respect to the sin of idolatry, John proceeds to point out that they continue also in their sins against the rest of the law — murder, magic, fornication and theft. Where man's relation to God is not right, his relationships with his neighbor are also vitiated. In the world in which we live we see not only the false doctrines of materialism, evolutionism, humanism, secularism and countless other delusions, but also multitudes who murder unborn babies without shame and with the permission of the courts, who openly engage in sorcery and witchcraft and call it religion, who look upon sexual immorality as love and liberation, and who believe that they have a moral right to the property of others. And this is the kind of world that John describes for us in chapters 8 and 9 of this book.

Over against the gloomy perspective of these two chapters the tenth chapter holds out the hope that the forces of falsehood will never be able totally to obscure the truth.

THE ANGEL WITH THE LITTLE BOOK (10:1-7)

1) Καὶ εἶδον ἄλλον ἄγγελον ἰσχυρὸν καταβαίνοντα ἐκ τοῦ οὐρανοῦ, περιβεβλημένον νεφέλην, καὶ ἡ ἶρις ἐπὶ τὴν κεφαλὴν αὐτοῦ, καὶ τὸ πρόσωπον αὐτοῦ ὡς ὁ ἥλιος, καὶ οἱ πόδες αὐτοῦ ὡς στῦλοι πυρός, 2) καὶ ἔχων ἐν τῇ χειρὶ αὐτοῦ βιβλαρίδιον ἠνεῳγμένον. καὶ ἔθηκεν τὸν πόδα αὐτοῦ τὸν δεξιὸν ἐπὶ τῆς θαλάσσης, τὸν δὲ εὐώνυμον ἐπὶ τῆς γῆς, 3) καὶ ἔκραξεν φωνῇ μεγάλῃ ὥσπερ λέων μυκᾶται. καὶ ὅτε ἔκραξεν, ἐλάλησαν αἱ ἑπτὰ βρονταὶ τὰς ἑαυτῶν φωνάς. 4) Καὶ ὅτε ἐλάλησαν αἱ ἑπτὰ βρονταί, ἤμελλον γράφειν·

καὶ ἤκουσα φωνὴν ἐκ τοῦ οὐρανοῦ λέγουσαν, Σφράγισον ἃ ἐλάλησαν αἱ ἑπτὰ βρονταί, καὶ μὴ αὐτὰ γράψῃς. 5) Καὶ ὁ ἄγγελος, ὃν εἶδον ἑστῶτα ἐπὶ τῆς θαλάσσης καὶ ἐπὶ τῆς γῆς, ἦρεν τὴν χεῖρα αὐτοῦ τὴν δεξιὰν εἰς τὸν οὐρανόν, 6) καὶ ὤμοσεν ἐν τῷ ζῶντι εἰς τοὺς αἰῶνας τῶν αἰώνων, ὃς ἔκτισεν τὸν οὐρανὸν καὶ τὰ ἐν αὐτῷ καὶ τὴν γῆν καὶ τὰ ἐν αὐτῇ καὶ τὴν θάλασσαν καὶ τὰ ἐν αὐτῇ, ὅτι χρόνος οὐκέτι ἔσται, 7) ἀλλ' ἐν ταῖς ἡμέραις τῆς φωνῆς τοῦ ἑβδόμου ἀγγέλου, ὅταν μέλλῃ σαλπίζειν, καὶ ἐτελέσθη τὸ μυστήριον τοῦ Θεοῦ, ὡς εὐηγγέλισεν τοὺς ἑαυτοῦ δούλους τοὺς προφήτας.

1) *And I saw another angel, a strong one, coming down out of heaven, clothed with a cloud, and the rainbow was over his head, and his face was like the sun, and his feet like pillars of fire,* 2) *and he had in his hand a little book, held open.*
And he placed his right foot on the sea, and the left on the earth, 3) *and he cried with a loud voice, just as a lion roars. And when he cried, the seven thunders uttered their sounds.* 4) *And when the seven thunders spoke, I was about to write. But I heard a voice out of the sky which said, "Put a seal on the things the seven thunders said, and do not write them."*
5) *And the angel whom I saw standing on the sea and on the earth raised his right hand into the sky* 6) *and he swore by the one who lives forever and ever, who created the sky and the things that are in it, and the earth and the things that are in it, and the sea and the things that are in it, that there will be no more time,* 7) *but in the days of the sound of the seventh angel, when he is about to blow his trumpet, indeed the mystery of God will be completed, as he made this good news known to his servants the prophets.*

The angel of this chapter is not identified, but the description seems to indicate that this is more than a created angel. Some of the things said about this angel parallel the description of Christ in chapter 1. There we are told that his face shone as the sun and that his feet were like red-hot brass (1:15,16). Here we read that his face was like the sun and his feet like pillars of fire. In all of Scripture there is no other passage that speaks of any created angel as having a face that shines as the sun. The only identifiable person in the Bible of whom this is ever said is the Lord Jesus (Mt 17:2; Re 1:16). We are told also that a rainbow was over his head. In all of Scripture there is no passage that speaks of a created angel as being adorned with the rainbow. In the vision of the Lord's glory in Revelation 4 the throne of God is surrounded by a rainbow (4:3). The only other passage in Scripture in which the rainbow is spoken of as a personal adornment is found in the vision of the glory of the Lord granted to the Prophet Ezekiel. In that vision the radiance that surrounds the Lord is said to be "like the appearance of a rainbow in the clouds on a rainy day" (Eze 1:28).

That this is not one of God's created angels also seems to be indicated by the fact that he is "clothed with a cloud." Both in the Old and in the New Testament the Lord made his presence known by the appearance of a cloud. God accompanied Israel in the desert in the pillar of cloud and fire, and his presence at Sinai was manifested in the thick cloud that covered the mountain. At the transfiguration the voice of the Lord came out of the cloud that overshadowed the disciples. At the ascension John and the other disciples saw a cloud that received Jesus out of their sight. And we are often told that he will come again in the clouds of heaven. With the possible exception of this passage in Revelation, no other passage in the Bible ever speaks of any created angel as being clothed, or covered, or surrounded by a cloud. But of the Lord we are told, "Clouds and thick darkness surround him, righteousness and justice are the foundation of his throne" (Ps 97:2). That passage is only one of many that speak in similar terms.

The opinion that this strong angel is the Lord Jesus cannot be refuted by a dogmatic statement that the Lord Jesus is never called an angel in the book of Revelation. That sort of remark only begs the question.

The symbolism and language of Revelation is often that of the Old Testament prophets. In the Old Testament the second person of the Trinity is in many passages called the "angel of the Lord." The word angel is an Anglicized Greek word which means "messenger." Malachi calls the promised Messiah the angel, or messenger, of the covenant (Mal 3:1). There are also many New Testament passages that speak of Jesus as the messenger of his Father. He was sent into the world to make God and his will known to men. So why should it surprise us if Revelation speaks of him as an angel? Revelation regularly describes the Savior as a lamb, which is Old Testament symbolism. Revelation is the only New Testament book that speaks of the Savior as a lion (5:5), which is also Old Testament symbolism. While the symbol of the lion is not restricted to the Lord, the words of verse 3, "as a lion roars," clearly echo several Old Testament passages. The Prophet Amos writes, for example, "The lion has roared — who will not fear? The Sovereign Lord has spoken — who can but prophecy?" (Am 3:8) Hosea uses the same imagery when he says, "They will follow the Lord; he will roar like a lion" (Ho 11:10). While we therefore cannot insist that this strong angel is the Lord Jesus, there is good biblical evidence for making this identification, and in our comments we will assume this is correct.

There are many passages in the New Testament that portray the Savior's power and control over all creation by saying that all things have been put under his feet. This strong angel stands with his right foot on the sea and his left on the earth and raises his right hand into the sky, a symbol of his absolute control over the world. As such, the vision of this chapter injects a note of hope into the gloomy picture painted by the first six trumpets. In spite of all the delusions and deceptions of heretical teachers, the angel of the bottomless pit and the 200-million horsemen from the Euphrates, God's people can still find comfort and assurance in the conviction that their Lord and Savior is still ruler of sky and land and sea.

The mighty angel, the Lord Jesus, has in his left hand "a little book, held open." The word ἠνεῳγμένον, which we have translated "held open," is a perfect participle. The participial form indicates that this is a continuing condition of this little book. The perfect tense often describes something that came to pass in the past but continues into the present.

The end of the chapter will reveal what is in the book. At this point we simply learn that the message is not a secret, unlike the book in chapter 5, which was sealed with seven seals. The secrets of that book became public knowledge only after the Lion of the tribe of Judah opened the seals. Yet the opening of the seven seals did not lead to a detailed revelation of the coming history of the world. Instead, it reminded John and his fellow sufferers that even though the Lord God Almighty was sitting on his throne and the rider on the white horse was riding to many victories, yet in this fallen world God's people would see as preludes and signs of his final victory wars and rumors of wars, famines, pestilences, persecutions and multitudes of heretics and heresies. This was the "great tribulation" out of which they would come to glory.

It had been difficult for the disciples to learn that the Messiah's pathway to victory would wind its way through the valley of suffering and death. Peter's first reaction to that suggestion was, "This shall never happen" (Mt 16:22). It must have been just as difficult for God's persecuted people in those days of the church's infancy to cling to the assurance that they were kings and priests, a royal priesthood, when so many of them were suffering exile, confiscation of property and even death. On the night before his death, the Savior had spoken to his disciples about the hatred and persecution that they would endure in this world. It was something they needed to know. Jesus said, "I have told you this, so that when the time comes, you will remember that I warned you" (Jn 16:4). The fulfillment of the prophecies concerning tribulation was to be for them a strong argument for the truth of the promises concerning the victory that would be theirs even if they should die. The vision of the seven seals is another way of stating the truth which Paul had expressed regarding our suffering, "In all these things we are more than conquerors through him that loved us" (Ro 8:37).

Like an amplified echo, the seven thunders add a divine reminder that we should take the message of the seven trumpets and seven seals to heart. Since seven thunders are spoken of nowhere else in the book or anywhere in Scripture, the article must again be deictic, pointing to a phenomenon that was still so vivid in the mind of the writer that he speaks of them as though they were well-known. But when John was just about to record the message of the seven thunders, he was told to leave the words unwritten. We assume that they had spoken of calamities of some kind, since thunder is a common symbol of God's wrath (cp *e.g.* Ex 9:23; 1 Sa 7:10; Is 29:6). The command to John not to write reminds us that there are many things about the future that God does not want us to know.

But God did not hide the contents of the little book that is permanently open in the hand of the Savior. While the seven thunders symbolize what we are not allowed to know about the future, the open book in the hand of the Savior tells us all we need to know. The poet spoke of those twofold areas of knowledge when he wrote,

> I know not what the future hath
> Of marvel or surprise;
> I only know that life and death
> His mercy underlies.
>
> I know not where his islands lift
> Their fronded palms in air;
> I only know I cannot drift
> Beyond his love and care.

After he heard the command not to write the message of the seven thunders, John fixed his attention once again on the angel, who now raised his right hand into the sky and swore by the one who had created all things. This is a feature of this vision that seems at first glance to speak against the identification of the angel as the Son of God. But God swears by himself, according to the Bible (Gn 22:16; He 6:13), and it would not be out of harmony with the Scriptures to say that the Son of God swears by his Father. Nor is it unbiblical to see in the words "who lives forever and ever, who created the sky . . . the earth . . . and the sea" a description of God the Father, for it is a common practice in Scripture to say that God (the Father) created the world *through* his Son.

When the angel swears that there will be no more time, there arises a question of interpretation that we cannot answer with certainty. It is possible to translate, as the NIV does, that "there will be no more delay." This would fit very well into the context which tells us that the mystery of God will be completed. The "mystery of God" is his plan for men and the universe as he has revealed it in the gospel promises. In the light of 1 Corinthians 2 we might say that the mystery of God includes all the things which God has prepared for those who love him. The mystery of God will be completed when these things will become visible, tangible realities for those who now walk by faith and not by sight. History will then have reached the goal God set for it in his eternal predestination, and God's people will need to wait no longer for the fulfillment of all the promises in which they found hope and comfort in times of suffering and persecution. When that moment comes there will also be no more time for repentance on the part of those who, in spite of all God's warnings, continued to worship false gods and to carry on immoral practices (Re 9:20f).

Many Lutheran interpreters, however, understand these words, "there will be no time," in an absolute sense. They are of the opinion that the last day will literally see the cessation of time itself, so that the completion of the mystery will mean that everything passes out of time into the timelessness of eternity.

The question is really a philosophical one. Under the influence of neo-Platonism many Christians and also many Lutherans have developed a tendency to disparage all material things. In keeping with this, they favor the view that the destruction of the world in the fire of the last judgment means the annihilation of matter. In such a world view it would be consistent to assume the destruction or annihilation of time. But there is no Bible passage that teaches that our eternity is timeless. All that we can be sure of is that it is endless. In fact, the question of the disembodied souls in 6:10, "How long, O Lord," would seem to indicate that souls are conscious of the passage of time after death. If it is argued that those words are found in a vision and therefore cannot be pressed in this way, we can only reply that the words, "there will be no more time," are also found in a vision. We are here speaking of things beyond our experience and therefore beyond our capacity fully to understand. It behooves us therefore to speak of these things with great reserve and humility. We do not know for sure whether time will come to an end or not. What we can be sure of is that when the mystery of God is complete, there will be no more time during which God's people will need to ask, "How long, O Lord, how long?" and likewise there will be no more time during which the ungodly will have an opportunity to repent. When the mystery of God is finished the time of suffering for believers and the time of grace for unbelievers will come to an end.

This completion of the mystery of God will come in fulfillment of prophecy. We are told that God announced this good news to his servants the prophets. The word which we have translated "has announced the good news" is εὐηγγέλισεν, which usually means "to preach the gospel." It would also be valid to translate, "as he preached the gospel to his servants the prophets." In any case, this remark serves as a transition to the last part of this chapter, where John is commissioned to carry on the same task. Just as God had communicated the good news to his prophets, so he also communicated it to John.

JOHN'S COMMISSION TO PREACH (10:8-11)

8) Καὶ ἡ φωνὴ ἣν ἤκουσα ἐκ τοῦ οὐρανοῦ, πάλιν λαλοῦσαν μετ' ἐμοῦ καὶ λέγουσαν, Ὕπαγε λάβε τὸ βιβλίον τὸ ἠνεῳγμένον ἐν τῇ χειρὶ τοῦ ἀγγέλου τοῦ ἑστῶτος ἐπὶ τῆς θαλάσσης καὶ ἐπὶ τῆς γῆς. 9) καὶ ἀπῆλθα πρὸς τὸν ἄγγελον, λέγων αὐτῷ δοῦναί μοι τὸ βιβλαρίδιον. καὶ λέγει μοι, Λάβε καὶ κατάφαγε αὐτό, καὶ πικρανεῖ σου τὴν κοιλίαν, ἀλλ' ἐν τῷ στόματι σου ἔσται γλυκὺ ὡς μέλι. 10) καὶ ἔλαβον τὸ βιβλαρίδιον ἐκ τῆς χειρὸς τοῦ ἀγγέλου καὶ κατέφαγον αὐτό, καὶ ἦν ἐν τῷ στόματί μου ὡς μέλι γλυκύ· καὶ ὅτε ἔφαγον αὐτό, ἐπικράνθη ἡ κοιλία μου. 11) καὶ λέγουσίν μοι, Δεῖ σε πάλιν προφητεῦσαι ἐπὶ λαοῖς καὶ ἔθνεσιν καὶ γλώσσαις καὶ βασιλεῦσιν πολλοῖς.

8) *And the voice which I heard out of the sky (I heard) speaking with me again, saying, "Come, take the book that is held open in the hand of the angel who is standing on the sea and on the earth."* 9) *And I came to the angel telling him to give me the little book. And he said to me, "Take it and eat it up, and it will make your stomach bitter, but in your mouth it will be sweet like honey."* 10) *And I took the little book out of the hand of the angel and ate it up, and it was sweet like honey in my mouth, but when I ate it my stomach became bitter.* 11) *And they say to me, "It is necessary for you to prophesy again before many peoples, and nations and languages and kings."*

The scene is reminiscent of Ezekiel's call to the prophetic office (Eze 2:1 — 3:11). In a vision Ezekiel saw a hand holding a scroll. Like John, he was commanded to eat this scroll and then to prophecy to the children of Israel. The Old Testament prophet also says that the scroll was as sweet as honey in his mouth. Later he speaks of the bitterness and anger he experienced as a result of this vision (3:14).

The basic teaching set forth in both visions is the doctrine of inspiration. After Ezekiel had eaten the scroll God said to him, "Speak my words to them." The words of God were evidently written on the scroll which Ezekiel had eaten. After he made those words his own, by eating the scroll, the prophet was to share those words with the people to whom he was sent. This is symbolized also by the unrolled scroll and the open book. The message was not to remain secret. But while Ezekiel was to go to the children of Israel, John was to share the message of the open book with many peoples and nations and languages and kings.

The NIV translation of verse 11 says that John was to preach "about" many peoples, nations, languages and kings. This is most likely incorrect. It is much more in keeping with the wide context of the New Testament to understand the words of the angel as another form of Christ's great commission (Mt 28:1). The preposition ἐπί very rarely means "about." Moreover, the message of John is really not about nations. It is a message about Jesus which John was to proclaim to and "before" the nations. While ἐπί is usually followed by the genitive case, the NIV does translate ἐπί with the dative in a similar way in 22:16, when it renders the phrase ἐπὶ ταῖς ἐκκλησίαις "for the churches." That sort of treatment of the prepositional phrase in this passage would have resulted in an appropriate translation, "You must prophesy again *for* many peoples, nations, languages, and kings."

Both Ezekiel and John found the taste of the book to be sweet like honey. The psalmist spoke of the Word of God in the same terms when he said that the words of God are sweeter than honey in the comb (Ps 19:10). Jeremiah expresses it more literally, but just as eloquently. "When your words came, I ate them; they were my joy and my heart's delight" (Jr 15:16). John graphically portrays the hope and joy and comfort that the gospel of God's grace and forgiveness brings to the hearts of men. His words echo the promise of the angel, "It was sweet like honey in my mouth."

Yet he also experienced the truth of the angel's words, "It will make your stomach bitter." The message of the gospel is not compatible with the false philosophies and theologies of this world. The smoke from the bottomless pit constantly obscures the light of this sun. As a result of man's impenitence, which John had depicted in the last verses of the previous chapter, it is not an easy lot to preach this alien message to many people and nations and languages and kings. As the world hated Christ, so it will also hate those who preach his gospel and who have been called to bear the cross after their Lord. So the message which brings much joy also invites bitterness and persecution. The earthly lot of the Christian will not always be a happy one. Even God's kings and priests must through much tribulation enter into the kingdom of God. The rider on the white horse is followed by three other horses. Those who accept his message can expect persecution at the hands of an evil world.

Yet in spite of bitterness and persecution, "it is necessary . . . to prophesy." Those words stand in sharp contrast to the gloomy picture we saw in the previous two chapters. Those chapters displayed the great multitude of delusions and heresies that evil men and demons would devise to keep men from finding repentance and forgiveness through the pure word of God. This chapter assures us that the Lord will not allow the preaching of the gospel to perish. John and the whole church hear the message, "It is necessary for you to prophesy again before many peoples, nations, languages and kings." It is "necessary" for at least two reasons. First, the risen Savior had commanded his apostles to preach the gospel to every creature and to make disciples of all nations. And he promised that the gates of hell will never prevail against it. Secondly, it is "necessary" for the Scriptures to be fulfilled. In the week before he died the Lord told his apostles that "this gospel of the kingdom will be preached in the whole world as a testimony to all nations," and when that has been done "the end will come" (Mt 24:14).

This preaching of the gospel side by side with the proclamation of countless heresies in a largely impenitent world will bear consequences for the visible church. These consequences follow in the next chapter.

THE CHURCH IN THE "CHURCH" (11:1-14)

1) Καὶ ἐδόθη μοι κάλαμος ὅμοιος ῥάβδῳ, λέγων, Ἔγειρε καὶ μέτρησον τὸν ναὸν τοῦ Θεοῦ καὶ τὸ θυσιαστήριον καὶ τοὺς προσκυνοῦντας ἐν αὐτῷ. 2) καὶ τὴν αὐλὴν τὴν ἔξωθεν τοῦ ναοῦ ἔκβαλε ἔξωθεν καὶ μὴ αὐτὴν μετρήσῃς, ὅτι ἐδόθη τοῖς ἔθνεσιν, καὶ τὴν πόλιν τὴν ἁγίαν πατήσουσιν μῆνας τεσσεράκοντα καὶ δύο. 3) καὶ δώσω τοῖς δυσὶν μάρτυσίν μου, καὶ προφητεύσουσιν ἡμέρας χιλίας διακοσίας ἑξήκοντα περιβεβλημένοι σάκκους. 4) Οὗτοί εἰσιν αἱ δύο ἐλαῖαι καὶ αἱ δύο λυχνίαι αἱ ἐνώπιον τοῦ Κυρίου τῆς γῆς ἑστῶτες. 5) καὶ εἴ τις αὐτοὺς θέλει ἀδικῆσαι, πῦρ ἐκπορεύεται ἐκ τοῦ στόματος αὐτῶν καὶ κατεσθίει τοὺς ἐχθροὺς αὐτῶν· καὶ εἴ τις θελήσῃ αὐτοὺς ἀδικῆσαι οὕτως δεῖ αὐτὸν ἀποκτανθῆναι. 6) οὗτοι ἔχουσιν τὴν ἐξουσίαν κλεῖσαι τὸν οὐρανόν, ἵνα μὴ ὑετὸς βρέχῃ τὰς ἡμέρας τῆς προφητείας αὐτῶν, καὶ ἐξουσίαν ἔχουσιν ἐπὶ τῶν ὑδάτων στρέφειν αὐτὰ εἰς αἷμα καὶ πατάξαι τὴν γῆν ἐν πάσῃ πληγῇ ὁσάκις ἐὰν θελήσωσιν. 7) καὶ ὅταν τελέσωσιν τὴν μαρτυρίαν αὐτῶν, τὸ θηρίον τὸ ἀναβαῖνον ἐκ τῆς ἀβύσσου ποιήσει μετ' αὐτῶν πόλεμον καὶ νικήσει αὐτοὺς καὶ ἀποκτενεῖ αὐτούς. 8) καὶ τὸ πτῶμα αὐτῶν ἐπὶ τῆς πλατείας τῆς πόλεως τῆς μεγάλης, ἥτις καλεῖται πνευματικῶς Σόδομα καὶ Αἴγυπτος, ὅπου καὶ ὁ Κύριος αὐτῶν ἐσταυρώθη. 9) καὶ βλέπουσιν ἐκ τῶν λαῶν καὶ φυλῶν καὶ γλωσσῶν καὶ ἐθνῶν τὸ πτῶμα αὐτῶν ἡμέρας τρεῖς καὶ ἥμισυ, καὶ τὰ πτώματα αὐτῶν οὐκ ἀφίουσιν τεθῆναι εἰς μνῆμα. 10) καὶ οἱ κατοικοῦντες ἐπὶ τῆς γῆς χαίρουσιν ἐπ' αὐτοῖς καὶ εὐφραίνονται, καὶ δῶρα πέμψουσιν ἀλλήλοις, ὅτι οὗτοι οἱ δύο προφῆται ἐβασάνισαν τοὺς κατοικοῦντας ἐπὶ τῆς γῆς. 11) καὶ μετὰ τὰς τρεῖς ἡμέρας καὶ ἥμισυ πνεῦμα ζωῆς ἐκ τοῦ Θεοῦ εἰσῆλθεν ἐν αὐτοῖς, καὶ ἔστησαν ἐπὶ τοὺς πόδας αὐτῶν, καὶ φόβος μέγας ἐπέπεσεν ἐπὶ τοὺς θεωροῦντας αὐτούς. 12) καὶ ἤκουσαν φωνῆς μεγάλης ἐκ τοῦ οὐρανοῦ λεγούσης αὐτοῖς, Ἀνάβατε ὧδε· καὶ ἀνέβησαν εἰς τὸν οὐρανὸν ἐν τῇ νεφέλῃ, καὶ ἐθεώρησαν αὐτοὺς οἱ ἐχθροὶ αὐτῶν.
13) Καὶ ἐν ἐκείνῃ τῇ ὥρᾳ ἐγένετο σεισμὸς μέγας, καὶ τὸ δέκατον τῆς πόλεως ἔπεσεν, καὶ ἀπεκτάνθησαν ἐν τῷ σεισμῷ ὀνόματα ἀνθρώπων χιλιάδες ἑπτά, καὶ οἱ λοιποὶ ἔμφοβοι ἐγένοντο καὶ ἔδωκαν δόξαν τῷ Θεῷ τοῦ οὐρανοῦ.
14) Ἡ Οὐαὶ ἡ δευτέρα ἀπῆλθεν· ἰδοὺ ἡ Οὐαὶ ἡ τρίτη ἔρχεται ταχύ.

1) *And a reed like a rod was given to me, and he said "Rise and measure the incense altar and the temple of God and those who worship in it.* 2) *But the outer court of the temple exclude and do not measure it, because it is given to the heathen and they will trample the holy city for forty-two months.* 3) *And I will commission my two witnesses and they will prophesy for one thousand two hundred and sixty days, clothed in sackcloth.* 4) *These are the two olive trees and the two lampstands that stand before the Lord of the earth.* 5) *And if anyone wishes to harm them, fire comes out of their mouths and consumes their enemies. And if any should wish to harm them, it is necessary that he be killed in this way.* 6) *These men have the authority to shut up the sky so that no rain may fall during the days of their prophesying and they have authority over the waters, to turn them into blood, and to strike the earth with every plague as often as they want.*
7) *And when they finish their testimony the beast that comes up from the abyss will make war with them and conquer them and kill them.* 8) *And their bodies will lie on the street of the great city, which spiritually is called Sodom and Egypt, where also their Lord was crucified.* 9) *And men from peoples and tribes and languages and nations will see their bodies for three and a half days, and they will not permit their bodies to be placed in a tomb.*
10) *And those who dwell on the earth will rejoice over them and be glad, and they will send gifts to one another, because these two prophets tormented those who dwell on the earth.* 11) *And after three and a half days a breath of life from God came into them and they stood on their feet, and great fear fell on those who saw them.* 12) *And they heard a great voice from the sky saying to them, "Come up here." And they went up into the sky in the cloud, and their enemies watched them.* 13) *And at that moment there was a great earthquake and the tenth part of the city collapsed and seven thousand people were killed by the earthquake, and the survivors became terrified and gave praise to the God of heaven.*
14) *The second woe is past. Behold, the third woe is coming, soon.*

The second woe, or the vision of the sixth trumpet, begins at 9:13. Even though there are three rather distinct parts to the vision — the 200-million horsemen from the Euphrates (9:13-21), the little book (10:1-11), and the two witnesses (11:1-14) — yet there is a concrete relationship between these sections. The 200-million horses out of whose mouths came flame, smoke and sulphur are symbolic of the countless delusions that keep men from finding life. The vision of the little book assures us that false teachings will not have the field all to themselves. God will see to it that his word is also preached side by side with these many heresies. But this will result also in a corruption of the visible church. This corruption of the visible church is the subject of this last part of the vision of the sixth trumpet.

In the first verses of chapter 11 John is commanded to measure the temple. This, too, is reminiscent of a vision in the book of Ezekiel, where the temple was measured with a reed (Eze 40-48). While there are many difficulties of interpretation in Ezekiel's long vision, orthodox commentators are agreed that this is a vision of the New Testament church.

This must also be the interpretation of the temple in John's vision. In the figurative language of the New Testament the temple of God is either the body of the Christian (1 Cor 3:16,17; 6:19) or the holy Christian church (2 Cor 6:16; Eph 2:21; 2 Th 2:4). In this chapter the temple that John is told to measure must be the church. The holy city is clearly the city of Jerusalem, where the Old Testament temple was situated. In the symbolism of the New Testament Jerusalem is a figurative name for the church. Paul speaks of two Jerusalems in his letter to the Galatians (4:25-27), and it is obvious that the "Jerusalem that is above" is the city in which all believers have their citizenship. In the letter to the Hebrews the believers are said to have come "to the city of the living God, the heavenly Jerusalem" (12:22), and this city is then specifically identified as "the church of the first-born, which are written in heaven" (12:23), which is a clear designation of all of God's elect.

John hears that he is to measure only the temple and the altar and those who worship there, but to exclude the court of the temple. This underscores the doctrine that the church as it is seen by men is different from the church as defined by God. One of the parables of Jesus speaks of the church as a net full of good and bad fish which will not be separated until the last day. This same truth is contained in the statement that the court of the temple is not to be included as part of the temple proper, because it is given to the Gentiles who will trample upon the holy city for 42 months. Gentiles in this context are obviously unbelievers, the opposite of spiritual Israel. In spite of their unbelief they are temporary residents of the holy city. Thus John sets the stage for what is to follow. He reminds us that not all those who appear to be members of the Christian church and hold outward citizenship in the holy city really belong there. They say they are Jews, but God says they are not (2:9; 3:9). They are intruders whose presence in the church tramples on areas where they do not belong and in many ways keeps the church from being what it ought to be.

The period of 42 months plays a significant role in the following chapters. We should note that 42 months is equivalent to 1260 days. It is also three and a half years. While the phrase "three and a half years" is not used in the book, the 1260 days are in chapter 12 equated to "a time, and times, and half a time" (12:6,14), which is undoubtedly to be understood as one time (or year) and two times (years) and half a time (year), or three and a half years, since that would be the equivalent of 1260 days.

What is meant by these 42 months? On the basis of the context it is the period of time during which the court of the temple is given over to unbelievers and during which these unbelievers will be permitted to occupy the holy city as an alien force. Unbelievers will not be separated out of the visible church until the day of judgment. Only then will the sheep be separated from the goats, the grain from the chaff, the good fish from the bad fish. That event is mentioned a number of times in the last chapters of Revelation. Then the holy city, which is trampled by the Gentiles, will be replaced by the heavenly Jerusalem that comes down from God out of heaven (21:2). That city will never be entered by anything that defiles or promotes abominations and lies (21:27). Those who love or invent lies will be "outside" (22:15), just as they are even now outside the boundaries of the church as John defines it with his measuring reed.

The 42 months therefore must be a designation of the whole New Testament period. Here they represent the time during which Gentiles, or unbelievers, occupy large areas of the visible church. Much of that unbelief is caused and sustained by the false doctrines whose destructive force has been described in chapters 8 and 9. In Revelation 13:15 the 42 months are the time during which the beast from the sea is able to speak his great blasphemies against God.

The same 42 months, designated as 1260 days, are spoken of in the following verse of this chapter as the time during which God's two witnesses will proclaim God's message. That period begins with the sending out of the apostles to proclaim the fulfillment of the promises given by the prophets and it also will continue until the end time. "Then the end will come" (Mt 24:14).

In chapter 12 we meet the 1260 days once more. There they represent the period during which the church is kept safe even though she is persecuted by the devil (12:6). When the persecution of the devil is prominent in the discussion the period is spoken of as "a time and times and half a time," or three and a half years (12:14). If we ask how long the church must spend in the desert pursued by the devil, we can only answer on the basis of Scripture that this again must be the New Testament period up to the end of the world, or, in the symbolism of Revelation, until Satan and the two beasts are thrown into the lake of fire (20:10).

For the sake of continuity we may here mention that the number three and a half occurs twice more in Revelation, both times in this context (11:9,11). The two witnesses who testify for 1260 days are finally killed, and their dead bodies lie in the street unburied for three and a half days before they are resurrected and taken to heaven. The number three and a half and its variants, 42 and 1260, are obviously associated with the persecution of the church, just as seven is the number of God's covenant with his people. Some assert that since three and a half is half of seven, or seven broken in half, it indicates that the enemies are intent upon making God's covenant inoperative. This is a possible interpretation and would not violate any Scriptural truth.

After he speaks of the Gentiles who trample the holy city and the court of the temple for 42 months, John then proceeds to describe two witnesses who testify for the Lord and prophesy during this whole period, which now is referred to as 1260 days. The word "prophesy" here stands in close proximity to the same word in the last verse of the previous chapter; it refers to the proclamation of the contents of the "little book," *i.e.*, the gospel.

John had heard that eating the little book would make his stomach bitter. In a parallel figure, the two witnesses prophesy "clothed in sackcloth." The wearing of sackcloth is a common indication of repentance and sorrow. Penitence must be a mark of every true preacher of the gospel, for unless he knows how much he himself as a sinner needs the comfort of the gospel, he will never preach it in the proper spirit to others. But even though this is true, the context here seems to lay stress on the sorrow and the suffering that the witnesses will experience at the hands of the unbelievers who occupy so much of the holy city. Just as in John's case, the gospel brings bitterness with it for the two witnesses.

The fact that there are only two witnesses in this "great city" (v. 8) is a graphic portrayal of the Savior's words, "The laborers are few" (Mt 9:37). Yet two is enough. According to the Old

Testament ordinance no one was ever put to death on the basis of the testimony of one man. The well-known rule was that in the mouth of two or three witnesses every word shall be established. Remembering that the 1260 must be the whole New Testament period, we can conclude that the Lord is here reminding John and the infant church that in spite of the seemingly overwhelming numbers of false teachers and false doctrines, God will always preserve enough witnesses to keep the message of the gospel alive, even in an apostate church and an unbelieving world.

The two witnesses are called "the two olive trees and the two lampstands which stand before the Lord of the earth" (v. 4). The "two olive trees" must be a reference to a vision of Zechariah. That prophet had a vision in which he also saw two olive trees which supplied an unceasing stream of oil to light one golden candlestick or lampstand. The symbolism of the olive trees is explained to Zechariah. He lived at the time when the Jews were returning from the Babylonian Captivity to rebuild the temple. The two olive trees represented the two anointed men who were responsible for directing the rebuilding of the temple — Zerubbabel, the civil ruler, and Joshua, the high priest (Zch 4:1-14). In connection with that vision Zechariah was told that the Lord's work would not be accomplished and perfected by human might or power, but solely by the Spirit of God (Zch 4:6).

The interpretation of Zechariah's vision provides the clue for the interpretation of this verse. The two witnesses are the two olive trees that supply the oil for the lampstands. Oil in the symbolism of the Bible is used to denote the Holy Spirit. When Samuel anointed Saul with oil, we are told that the Holy Spirit came upon him (1 Sm 10:1-10). Psalm 45 prophesies that the Messiah will be anointed with the oil of gladness (v. 7), and the New Testament records the fulfillment of that prophecy when it says, "God anointed Jesus of Nazareth with the Holy Ghost" (Ac 10:38). In 2 Corinthians (1:21,22) Paul equates our anointing by God with his gift of the Holy Spirit. The two witnesses thus are the channels through whom the Holy Spirit, who alone can build the church, comes to men.

The Holy Spirit comes to men through word and sacrament, that is, through the gospel, which enables the church to show men the way to forgiveness and eternal life. Thus these two witnesses are at the same time the lampstands which bring light to the world. Earlier in Revelation the seven lampstands had been symbols of the seven churches (1:20). What those seven churches were for Asia Minor in the early days of the church, these two witnesses are for the unbelieving world during the whole New Testament age. This is the truth Jesus proclaimed when he told his apostles that they were the light of the world.

Because the two witnesses have the Holy Spirit and the word of "the Lord of the earth," they exercise an influence which is out of all proportion to their numbers. "If anyone wishes to harm them, fire comes out of their mouths and consumes their enemies" (v. 5). Fire is a symbol either of the consuming wrath of God (cp *e.g.*, 2 Kgs 1:10; Lk 3:9; 2 Th 1:8; He 12:29) or of the converting and sanctifying power of the Holy Spirit (cp Mt 3:11; Ac 2:3). It would be consistent with the rest of Scripture to say that the fire which comes out of their mouths is the word of God which they proclaim. Jeremiah, for example, was told by God, "I will make my words in your mouth fire" (5:14; cp Jr 23:29). The word of God as law and gospel demonstrates both the consuming wrath and the redeeming and sanctifying grace of God. In this context it would seem that the wrath of God especially is in the forefront, since the fire out of the mouth of the witnesses consumes, literally "eats down," the enemies. While the preaching of God's word is a savor of life unto life for some, it is a savor of death unto death for others (2 Cor 2:16). Those who refuse to listen to the two witnesses will die as a result of that opposition.

That truth is emphasized and repeated in the words, "If anyone should wish to harm them, it is necessary that he be killed in this way" (v. 5). The first sentence in this verse is a simple condition. This second sentence seems to be an irregular form of a present general condition, indicating that this is a fixed rule. This is what always happens. That thought is further strengthened by the word δεῖ, it is necessary. That particular word in Scripture often denotes a necessity which is ordained by God. The word of God in the mouth of his witnesses says, among other things, "He that believeth not shall be damned," and, "The soul that sinneth it shall die." Those are never empty words. When God said, "Let there be light," there was light. When God's word condemns a sinner to death, that word is just as effective as the creative word he spoke at the beginning. For this reason the word that comes out of the mouth of God's spokesmen must bring death to those who oppose it in unbelief and continue in their sin by impenitence.

These two witnesses also "have the authority to shut up the sky so that no rain may fall during the time of their prophesying." This is manifestly an assertion based on the Old Testament account of the ministry of Elijah, who during the days of Ahab predicted that it would not rain, and it did not rain for three and a half years (1 Kgs 17; Lk 4:25; Jas 5:17). Like the two witnesses, Elijah too belonged to what seemed a very small minority of Israelites who were faithful to God's word, yet the word which he spoke controlled the destiny of Israel. His history was to be an abiding comfort to the "little flock" to whom it is God's pleasure to give the kingdom.

There is another illustration of the same truth in the assertion that the two witnesses have authority and power to turn water into blood and to strike the earth with every plague as often as they want. Every student of the Bible will immediately remember Moses and Aaron and the ten plagues that forced Pharaoh finally to let the children of Israel go out of their slavery. Here two witnesses, seemingly powerless by nature, were endued with supernatural power when they were given the authority to speak for God. This account, too, is a constant source of hope for the church as it looks forward to the day when the holy city will no longer be trampled by the Gentiles.

After the two witnesses "have finished their testimony, the beast that comes up from the abyss will make war with them and conquer them and kill them" (v. 7). The Savior's prediction that the end will come when the gospel has been preached as a testimony to all nations (Mt 24:14) makes it clear that the time spoken of here is shortly before the end of the world. This is very likely the time of the "little season" spoken of in 20:3. When the two witnesses finish their testifying, all nations will have heard the gospel.

At that time the church will suffer one final, and apparently successful, persecution. The beast that comes out of the abyss is able to silence the voice of the witnesses. The preaching of the gospel will seem to be ended forever. Orthodox commentators are not agreed on the specific identification of the beast, other than that it is a powerful opponent. Those Lutheran commentators who have identified the beast as the Roman Antichrist have some justification for that view. How can there be a greater danger to the preaching of the gospel than that which is posed by a church that retains so many of the outward trappings of Christianity but officially damns the doctrine of justification by faith, the very heart and life-blood of the Christian religion! Yet not only the heresies of Rome, but every "Christian" heresy and every pagan religion and every secular world view and man-made philosophy is a threat to the continued preaching of the gospel. Those commentators who see this beast as a symbol of every anti-Christian movement, civil or ecclesiastical, may also have a valid claim.

On the other hand, there are good reasons for being more specific and for viewing this beast as Satan. The term "abyss" is most certainly a designation of hell itself. If this verse refers to what is called the "little season" in chapter 20, then this description of a beast coming up out of hell is parallel to the release of Satan mentioned in 20:3. Of added significance for seeing these verses as a parallel is the fact that chapters 11 and 20 are two of the four places in the book that use the word "abyss" as a name for hell. Those who see this beast as identical with the two beasts of chapter 13, and following chapters, should note that this beast comes out of the abyss. The two beasts of chapter 13 come out of the sea and the earth. The word translated "beast" is the Greek word for any wild and dangerous animal. It is therefore a very fitting term for the "roaring lion who walks about seeking whom he may devour" (1 Pt 5:8).

There is no significant difference between these various views insofar as their final lesson is concerned. Yet it may help us understand chapter 20 if we view these passages as different ways of describing the same event. All commentators will have to agree that the beast from the abyss is a great enemy of those who preach the gospel, and finally every heresy finds its source in the devil, who is the father of lies.

When the devil succeeds in his attempt to kill the two witnesses "their bodies lie on the street of the great city, which spiritually is called Sodom and Egypt, where also our Lord was crucified." The last phrase clearly identifies the "great city" as Jerusalem. It is the same city which had been called the "holy city" earlier in this chapter. Because the "holy" city is occupied by unbelievers it deserves rather to be called Sodom and Egypt. Sodom is a symbol of immorality and Egypt a symbol of rebellion against God's words and of the oppression of God's people. When the Old Testament Jerusalem, where the temple of Solomon was the central sanctuary, became immoral and unbelieving, the Prophet Isaiah gave it the name of Sodom and Gomorrah (Is 1:10). When the New Testament Jerusalem, the visible church, becomes a center of immorality in which prominent churchmen defend homosexuality and where practicing homosexuals demand and are given the right to be communed and even ordained, and in which there is open rebellion against God's word, it no longer deserves the honored name of Jerusalem but instead, from a spiritual point of view, it ought to be called Sodom, a seat of immorality, and Egypt, a center of disobedience.

The remark, "where also their Lord was crucified," reminds us that the visible church is often the center of the oppression and persecution of God's people. In his Gospel, John had written, "He came to that which was his own, and his own did not receive him" (Jn 1:11). If there was any place on earth which should have received the Messiah with open arms it was Jerusalem, the center of worship for the chosen people. But instead, this is the place where he was crucified. The lesson that we ought to learn for the New Testament Jerusalem is that the greatest enemies of the holy Christian church are to be found in the "holy city," in the visible church. The reason why John was told not to measure the court and the city but only the central sanctuary becomes more clear. This would be the place to speak of the anti-Christian character of official Roman Catholic theology, historical criticism, synergism, and many of the popular trends in Protestant and even Lutheran circles. The enmity and the ridicule that is directed against those who are faithful to the teachings of Scripture parallel the hatred directed against the Messiah by the religious leaders of his time.

The NIV has rendered the word πνευματικῶς as "figuratively." It is questionable whether in New Testament times the word ever was understood in that way, even though in later ages the allegorical interpretation of Scripture was called "spiritual." It is best translated "spiritually," or "from a spiritual point of view." Outwardly defenders of the worst heresies and immoralities still pass as part of the Christian church, but in reality, from the point of view of the Holy Spirit, they are among the worst enemies of God's people and trample the holy city underfoot. The picture of faithful witnesses lying dead in the streets of the "holy" city is of special significance in our time when recognized leaders of "Christendom" pour contempt on those whom they call, among other things, "the superorthodox brethren."

The Gentiles in the holy city are joined by men from the rest of the world, "from the peoples and tribes and languages and nations." For three and a half days they look at the dead bodies of the two witnesses, whom they refuse to bury. They find satisfaction in seeing them dead and do not want to lessen that pleasure. Their intense hatred against God's witnesses becomes manifest, not only in their desire to gloat over the dead bodies but also in the gifts that they send to one another as evidence of their celebration.

This hardened hatred, depraved beyond normal understanding, is explained by the words, "These two prophets tormented those who dwell on the earth." With one possible exception (14:6) John always uses this rather common phrase, "those who dwell on the earth," to describe the impenitent mass of mankind. The message which is preached to them rebukes them either for their ungodly life or their wrong religious opinions. To the impenitent this message is unwelcome, and it rouses them to anger and hatred. John Wesley is quoted as saying that a true preacher of God's word should either convert men or make them angry.

The number three and a half occurs only here in the book of Revelation. As we have seen, this number is related to a series of other numbers (*e.g.*, 42 months, 1260 days, and "a time and times and half a time") which are always associated with the enemies of the church and their hatred or persecution of the church. That association is also evident here. The bodies lie in the street for three and a half days, but then they become alive again and are taken to heaven. This is a symbolic way of expressing the truth set forth by the hymn writer,

> His seeming triumph o'er God's saints
> Lasts but a little hour.

The number three and a half indicates that this is still the time of the Gentiles. But since the period of Satan's triumph is only three and a half days at the end of forty-two months this number emphasizes that the time of Satan's apparent triumph over the gospel witnesses is indeed only a "little season," as John describes it in 20:3.

Satan's triumph was short-lived because at the end of the three and a half days "a breath of life from God" came into the two witnesses, "and they stood on their feet, and a great fear fell upon those who saw them" (v. 11). At the time of creation God had breathed life into the nostrils of Adam. He now repeated this great miracle for the two witnesses. Life-giving breath enters their bodies and they stand up on their feet. The Greek words πνεῦμα ζωῆς should very likely be translated "a breath of life" rather than "the Spirit of life" because of the absence of the article and the whole tenor of the context.

The joy that the enemies had felt as they gazed on the dead bodies of the witnesses for three and a half days was changed into "a great fear" when they saw them alive once more. Not only was their celebration cut short, but the resurrection of the men who had tormented them with their preaching was clear evidence that their message had been divine and therefore true.

The victory of the witnesses in their testimony to the truth became complete when "they heard a great voice from the sky saying to them, 'Come up here.' And they went up into the sky in the cloud, and their enemies watched them" (v. 12). It is usually difficult to decide whether ὀυρανός should be translated as "sky" or "heaven," especially since in modern English there is a tendency to look upon those two words as being somewhat divorced from one another. In the Bible "heaven" means either the atmosphere, where the birds fly (Gn 1:20), or the entire space above the earth (Gn 1:16), or the abode of God. Any one of these three meanings would fit very well here. The mention of a cloud would seem to favor the translation "sky." The article with cloud must again be deictic.

This part of the vision reminds us again that Christianity is an "other-world religion." The real victory of the witnesses does not come in this world. The believers' greatest joys are those that will come when the voice from the sky summons them into God's presence. The ascension of the two witnesses is reminiscent of the ascension of Christ, who also disappeared in a cloud. Like the Savior's ascension, the ascension of the two witnesses ought to encourage the suffering and persecuted church to set its affection on things above and not on the things of this earth (Col 3:1).

When they ascended, "at that moment there was a great earthquake, and the tenth part of the city collapsed, and 7,000 people were killed in the earthquake, and the survivors became terrified and gave praise to the God of heaven."

Earthquakes are often spoken of in Scriptures as a sign of the end. In Hebrews 11:26f the shaking of the earth is evidence of its impermanence. This particular earthquake is especially significant when we remember that only a few verses back the unbelievers who were rejoicing over Satan's apparent victory had been described as those "who dwell on the earth." Their dwelling-place is not a permanent home. Every earthquake ought to remind them of this.

In the earthquake a tenth part of the city collapsed. This holy city is the visible Christian church, a reminder that the visible church is of itself not a place of safety. Most of the visible church finally must perish with the rest of the unbelieving world. In the collapse of the tenth part of the city 7,000 people died. Literally the text says, "seven thousand names of men were killed in the earthquake." "Names" is sometimes used in the New Testament as a figurative expression for "person" or "people" (cp Ac 1:15). It is tempting, but not possible, to find a relationship between these 7,000 and the 7,000 in the days of Elijah who had not bowed their knees before Baal (1 Kgs 19:18).

It is tempting also to see in the last detail of this vision some evidence of a mass conversion of the impenitent in the visible church. We read that when a tenth part of the city fell into ruins and 7,000 people died, "the survivors became terrified and gave praise to the God of heaven." While becoming terrified is one step in repentance, "terrors of conscience" alone do not make a person a Christian. As the Lutheran confessions say, these terrors must be "relieved by faith" if they are to be part of a real conversion. While the words, "they gave praise to the God of heaven," might possibly be understood as a fruit of faith, yet St. Paul says that finally every tongue will confess that Jesus Christ is Lord to the glory of God the Father (Php 2:11). They will in the end be compelled to speak of God's glory, for they will no longer be able to deny it when they see it. So the magicians of Pharaoh were finally forced to acknowledge the superior power of Moses and Aaron when they said, "This is the finger of God" (Ex 8:19). It seems fitting to understand the reaction of these survivors of the earthquake in the same way.

The name "the God of heaven" is a rather rare term. In the New Testament it is used only in Revelation, and in the Old Testament chiefly in Daniel, Ezra and Nehemiah. It is another example of strong Old Testament influence on the imagery and vocabulary of Revelation.

The second of the three woes in 8:13 is now concluded. This final onslaught on the church is quickly to be followed by the third and last woe (v. 14).

THE SEVENTH TRUMPET: THE END OF THE WORLD (11:15-19)

15) Καὶ ὁ ἕβδομος ἄγγελος ἐσάλπισεν· καὶ ἐγένοντο φωναὶ μεγάλαι ἐν τῷ οὐρανῷ, λέγοντες,

Ἐγένετο ἡ βασιλεία τοῦ κόσμου τοῦ Κυρίου ἡμῶν καὶ τοῦ

Χριστοῦ αὐτοῦ, καὶ βασιλεύσει εἰς τοὺς αἰῶνας τῶν αἰώνων.
16) καὶ οἱ εἴκοσι τέσσαρες πρεσβύτεροι, οἱ ἐνώπιον τοῦ Θεοῦ καθήμενοι ἐπὶ τοὺς θρόνους αὐτῶν, ἔπεσαν ἐπὶ τὰ πρόσωπα αὐτῶν καὶ προσεκύνησαν τῷ Θεῷ, 17) λέγοντες,

Εὐχαριστοῦμέν σοι, Κύριε ὁ Θεὸς ὁ Παντοκράτωρ, ὁ ὢν καὶ ὁ ἦν, ὅτι εἴληφας τὴν δύναμίν σου τὴν μεγάλην καὶ ἐβασίλευσας· 18) καὶ τὰ ἔθνη ὠργίσθησαν, καὶ ἦλθεν ἡ ὀργή σου καὶ ὁ καιρὸς τῶν νεκρῶν κριθῆναι καὶ δοῦναι τὸν μισθὸν τοῖς δούλοις σου τοῖς προφήταις καὶ τοῖς ἁγίοις καὶ τοῖς φοβουμένοις τὸ ὄνομά σου, τοῖς μικροῖς καὶ τοῖς μεγάλοις, καὶ διαφθεῖραι τοὺς διαφθείροντας τὴν γῆν.

19) καὶ ἠνοίγη ὁ ναὸς τοῦ Θεοῦ ὁ ἐν τῷ οὐρανῷ καὶ ὤφθη ἡ κιβωτὸς τῆς διαθήκης αὐτοῦ ἐν τῷ ναῷ αὐτοῦ, καὶ ἐγένοντο ἀστραπαὶ καὶ φωναὶ καὶ βρονταὶ καὶ σεισμὸς καὶ χάλαζα μεγάλη.

15) *And the seventh angel blew his trumpet. And there were loud voices in the sky which said,*

The kingdom of the world has become
the kingdom of our Lord and of his
Anointed One.
And he will reign forever and ever.

16) *And the twenty-four elders, seated before God on their thrones fell on their faces and worshiped God,* 17) *saying,*

We thank you, O Lord, the almighty God, who is and was; because you have taken your great power and reigned; 18) *and the nations were angered, and your anger has come, even the time when the dead are to be judged and when you will give the reward to your servants the prophets and to your saints and those who fear your name, the small and the great, and when you will destroy those who destroy the earth.*

19) *And the temple of God which is in heaven was opened and the ark of his covenant was seen in his temple, and there were lightnings and voices and thunders and an earthquake and great hail.*

Like the sixth seal, the seventh trumpet brings us to the day of judgment. Loud voices announce from the sky that the kingdom of the world has come to be the kingdom of the Lord and of his Anointed One, his Christ. Those words can only refer to the outward manifestation of the Lord's rule of the world. He is the everlasting king (Jr 10:10) who has always ruled over all things in heaven and on earth. Yet the Bible often speaks of the present world as being under the rule of the devil, who is even called in one place, "the god of this world" (2 Cor 4:4). But when the seventh trumpet sounds it will become evident that this world is the Lord's kingdom. At that time God's people will see what they have always believed, namely, that Christ, the son of Mary, is seated at the right hand of the Father with all things under his feet. This state of things will then continue into all eternity.

The loud voices heard in the sky, whose origin is not specified, are then joined by the voices of the twenty-four elders, whom we have met many times before. They express their thanks to God for this manifestation of his ruling power. The word with which they address God is κύριε, Lord, which is here obviously the translation of the Hebrew name Jahweh, by which God made himself known in the Old Testament. Jahweh, the Lord, is then, in the fashion of the Old Testament, described as the almighty and eternal God. The name Jahweh in itself points to his eternality. Jahweh means "HE IS." This thought is picked up in the second phrase, "the one who is and the one who was." The phrase, "the one who is to be," which is added in chapter 1, is not found here in the earliest manuscripts.

After the twenty-four elders rephrase the thought which the voices had expressed at the beginning of this vision, they speak of the significance of this event for believers and unbelievers alike. First, they say that the heathen, the Gentiles, became angry. These are the Gentiles who had trampled on the holy city for 42 months and who only a short time before were rejoicing over Satan's apparent victory. The beginning of the visible reign of God over the earth means that they will no longer be able to carry out their plans and see the world governed according to their desires. Since they will no longer be able even in appearance to influence the course of history, their only recourse is anger.

In the vision of the sixth seal the day of judgment had been called the day of God's wrath. That thought is repeated here in the words, "Your wrath has come." Already the Old Testament prophets had spoken of "the day of the Lord" as a "day of wrath." Before that final day it often appeared that God was closing his eyes to the immorality and wickedness that characterizes this present world. But now the time has come to punish all wickedness.

This is the last day, when the dead will be judged. Some have concluded from the last verse in this chapter that this is a day of judgment but not *the* day of judgment. But such an interpretation would require several general resurrections, a concept which the Bible nowhere teaches.

The subsequent words clearly teach that this will be a resurrection of both believers and unbelievers. For believers it will not be a day of wrath. Rather, it will be, first of all, a day when God will give *the* reward to his servants, the prophets. These words, "his servants the prophets," are a common Old Testament phrase. One of the greatest rewards will be that the prophets will see with their own eyes the establishment of that kingdom which they had often described, a kingdom where swords will be beaten into plowshares and spears into pruning hooks.

On that day God will give the same reward to the saints and those who fear his name. The Greek word, τοῖς ἁγίοις, which we have translated "saints," means "holy ones." In Scripture it is a designation either for the holy angels or for believers, who are called holy because of the forgiveness of sins which they have through faith in Christ. The two terms, "saints" and "those who fear your name," are really synonymous. So we could also translate, "your saints, namely, those who fear your name."

The name of God includes everything that God has made known to us about himself. One of the greatest Lutheran dogmaticians in America said that the whole Bible is an expanded name of God. Those who "fear God's name" are those who "tremble at his word" (Is 66:2), who take seriously what God says about his wrath against all sinners and who believe everything God says about his forgiving grace in Christ. Those who fear his name, who stand in reverent awe before everything God says, are the believers, the saints. The use of two articles (τοῖς ἁγίοις καὶ τοῖς φοβουμένοις) might indicate that we are here dealing with two groups of people, but if we translate the Greek word καὶ between the two nouns as if it were an epexegetical καὶ no problem remains.

This reward of the believers is given to both "small and great." Some manuscripts have these words in the accusative rather than the dative. The accusative is very difficult to explain and many commentators therefore conclude that the dative found in most of the later manuscripts is actually the original reading. While the grammar is difficult, the sense is obvious, and we must translate as though it were a dative, unless, perhaps, we would want to view it as an accusative of respect and translate, "in respect to both small and great." All Christians, without regard for their importance in the eyes of the world, will share in the reward. The article with "reward" is a deictic article, which refers to a reward that was well-known to John's readers.

After they speak about the reward the believers would receive, the twenty-four elders speak once more about the unbelievers, the objects of God's wrath. This time of reward for the saints will be a time of punishment for the Gentiles, the non-believers, who are now described as those who "are destroying the earth." As a result of the sin of our first parents, the ground was cursed and all of creation was made subject to decay (Ro 8:2). The blood of Abel caused the fertility of the ground to decrease (Gn 4:12). Here the "destruction of the earth" is something far beyond that which attracts the concern of modern ecologists. It is destruction that comes as a divinely ordained consequence of immorality and unrighteousness. By their wickedness men bring destruction on the earth, just as the sins of Sodom brought fire and brimstone upon that city. And as a just recompense the destroyers are themselves to be destroyed. The specifics follow in later chapters.

After John heard the song of the elders, he saw "the temple of God which is in heaven" (v. 19). The chapter had opened with the command that John should measure the temple of God in the holy city on earth, that is, the church surrounded on all sides by its enemies. The temple on earth has its counterpart in heaven, the church set free from all the threatening dangers that bring oppression and persecution. In a later chapter John will speak in similar terms of the holy city. Here he sees the holy city trampled underfoot by its enemies. In chapter 21 he will see the holy city coming down out of heaven from God. There is no question that in this verse οὐρανός should be translated "heaven" and not "sky," for the context clearly speaks of the place of God's presence.

John saw the temple opened and the ark of the covenant inside. In a very special sense the ark of the covenant in the Old Testament was a symbol of God's presence with his people. And yet the ark of the covenant was seen by very few people. In the tabernacle it was hidden behind the two veils. When it was transported from place to place by the Levites it was covered so that it could not be seen. For the most part, only the high priest was permitted to see it, and even he saw it very seldom. But now the temple is opened so that the ark is visible to all. Those who reach the heavenly temple will have free access into the presence of God. They will be with him, and he will be with them. This is the way John will express the significance of this vision in a later chapter.

But again, before the chapter ends, attention once more shifts to a manifestation of God's wrath. "There came lightnings and voices and thunders and an earthquake and great hail." Evidently the lightnings and the voices and the thunders are expressions of God's wrath. The earthquake and the hail are symbols of the destruction that God's anger finally will bring on an impenitent world population. There had been a great hailstorm in Egypt at the time of the Exodus. It killed all those who did not seek shelter (Ex 9:19). In another vision of the judgment (16:19) we will read about hailstones weighing a hundred pounds. John's readers who knew their Old Testament would realize that the only shelter that could protect men against such destruction is the merit of Christ, who has turned away God's wrath by redeeming us with his blood (5:9).

The Fourth Vision:
The Seven Visions (12 — 15)

Up to this point the text has announced its own major divisions — the seven letters, seven seals and seven trumpets. Another main division, the seven bowls, will follow in chapter 16. The chapters between the seven trumpets and the seven bowls are not explicitly called the seven visions. Yet even superficial attention to the text will make it clear that in this section we again have seven distinct subdivisions. After the first vision (12:1-18) each individual vision is introduced by the Greek words καὶ εἶδον (13:1; 14:1,6,14; 15:1), "and I saw," which unfortunately neither the KJV nor the NIV translates in a uniform way. Just as the opening of the seventh seal introduced the vision of the seven trumpets, so the seventh vision in this series introduces the vision of the seven bowls.

THE FIRST VISION:
THE GREAT RED DRAGON (12:1-17)

The first of these seven visions portrays the efforts of the devil to destroy Christ and his church. The vision consists of three distinct scenes. In the first, we see the devil attacking Christ himself.

The Dragon and the Child (12:1-6)

1) Καὶ σημεῖον μέγα ὤφθη ἐν τῷ οὐρανῷ, γυνὴ περιβεβλημένη τὸν ἥλιον, καὶ ἡ σελήνη ὑποκάτω τῶν ποδῶν αὐτῆς, καὶ ἐπὶ τῆς κεφαλῆς αὐτῆς στέφανος ἀστέρων δώδεκα, 2) καὶ ἐν γαστρὶ ἔχουσα, καὶ κράζει ὠδίνουσα καὶ βασανιζομένη τεκεῖν. 3) καὶ ὤφθη ἄλλο σημεῖον ἐν τῷ οὐρανῷ, καὶ ἰδοὺ δράκων πυρρὸς μέγας, ἔχων κεφαλὰς ἑπτὰ καὶ κέρατα δέκα καὶ ἐπὶ τὰς κεφαλὰς αὐτοῦ ἑπτὰ διαδήματα, 4) καὶ ἡ οὐρὰ αὐτοῦ σύρει τὸ τρίτον τῶν ἀστέρων τοῦ οὐρανοῦ, καὶ ἔβαλεν αὐτοὺς εἰς τὴν γῆν. Καὶ ὁ δράκων ἕστηκεν ἐνώπιον τῆς γυναικὸς τῆς μελλούσης τεκεῖν, ἵνα ὅταν τέκῃ τὸ τέκνον αὐτῆς καταφάγῃ. 5) καὶ ἔτεκεν υἱὸν ἄρσεν, ὃς μέλλει

ποιμαίνειν πάντα τὰ ἔθνη ἐν ῥάβδῳ σιδηρᾷ. καὶ ἡρπάσθη τὸ τέκνον αὐτῆς πρὸς τὸν Θεὸν καὶ πρὸς τὸν θρόνον αὐτοῦ. 6) καὶ ἡ γυνὴ ἔφυγεν εἰς τὴν ἔρημον, ὅπου ἔχει ἐκεῖ τόπον ἡτοιμασμένον ἀπὸ τοῦ Θεοῦ, ἵνα ἐκεῖ τρέφωσιν αὐτὴν ἡμέρας χιλίας διακοσίας ἑξήκοντα.

1) *And a great sign was seen in the sky — a woman clothed with the sun, with the moon under her feet, and on her head a crown of twelve stars.* 2) *She was pregnant, and she cried out in labor, suffering to give birth.* 3) *And another sign was seen in the sky, and, see, a great red dragon, with seven heads and ten horns and on his heads seven crowns.* 4) *And his tail swept away a third of the stars in the sky and threw them to the earth.*
And the dragon stood before the woman who was about to give birth, that he might devour the child as soon as it would be born.
5) *And she gave birth to a son, a male child, who will rule all the nations with an iron rod. And her child was snatched up to God and to his throne.*
6) *And the woman fled into the wilderness, where she has a place prepared by God in order that they might feed her there for 1260 days.*

There is little in this part of the vision that creates difficulty for the interpreter. We are told that the great dragon is Satan, and the child caught up to God is obviously Christ. These verses focus our attention on the efforts of the devil to destroy Christ during his earthly life.

Popular Roman Catholic thought has seen in the first verses of this text a description of the Virgin Mary as the queen of heaven. Artists have painted portraits of the virgin which are based on this description. However, Roman commentators often recognize that this woman cannot be the blessed virgin. To those who have recognized that the number twelve is the number of the church, the twelve stars that she wears in her crown already indicate that this woman is a symbol of the church. Moreover, after the ascension of Christ, the woman flees into the wilderness where she remains for 1260 days (v. 6).

The 1260 days equal the 42 months of chapter 11. This is the New Testament era, the time during which there is a temple of God on earth situated in a holy city that is trampled by the Gentiles. This is the time when the church is in the desert, the time when the church is far removed from her real home. Because she has not yet ascended into heaven to be with her Lord, she is in exile in a world where she does not belong. The woman represents the church during the period of the New Testament as she waits in the wilderness of this world for her final redemption from the sufferings of this present time. In the last verse of the chapter this woman is declared to be the mother of all believers. Such language is never used of the Virgin Mary in the New Testament. But of the church, the heavenly Jerusalem, St. Paul says that she is the mother of us all (Ga 4:26). The glory of the church is represented by the fact that she is clothed with the sun, and her influence in the government of the universe is symbolized by the fact that the moon is under her feet.

In the first six verses of this chapter we do not see future events. In a symbolic way John takes us back to the time of the birth of Christ. The woman in his vision was pregnant and ready to give birth. But John saw more than the impending birth of the Savior. He saw a great red dragon, who, as we have already seen, is a representation of Satan (v. 9). The dragon has seven heads and ten horns, with seven crowns on his heads. This is one of several similar passages (*e.g.*, 13:1; 17:3) in which the number seven is associated with the devil and those who serve him. This seems rather strange since in the book of Revelation seven generally is a symbol of God's dealing with men. We have called it the number of the covenant. The symbolism of the seven heads is not explained here as it is in a later context (17:9). But that explanation does not fit here. We can only suggest that the seven heads and the seven crowns represent the devil's desire to substitute himself for God as ruler of the universe. The ten horns, since they obviously bear neither logical nor natural symmetry with seven heads, may serve to alert us to the falseness of his claims by which he seeks to present himself as a substitute for the God of the covenant.

This interpretation is supported by the fact that the dragon wears seven crown on his seven heads. The word for crown here is διάδημα, rather than στέφανος, the crown of victory. The διάδημα, the "diadem," was the crown of the rulers of ancient Persia. Caligula was the first Roman emperor to use this particular emblem of royalty. The citizens of Rome saw this as evidence of Caligula's insanity because the person who wore such a crown considered himself to be a god. After Caligula, no Roman emperor wore it until Diocletian, who also adopted the Persian custom which required anyone who approached the one wearing the diadem to fall prostrate on the ground before him.

While John's Revelation was written about two hundred years before the time of Diocletian, the self-deifying pride which moved that emperor to put on the diadem already was making itself evident in the claims of Domitian, who most likely ruled as emperor when John was exiled to Patmos. While Domitian did not wear the diadem, he did demand that he be called "*dominus et deus*," "Lord and God." John's readers surely knew the significance of the diadem and were familiar with Domitian's attempts to have himself worshiped as "Lord and God." So they very likely recognized the diadems on the heads of the dragon as just another of Satan's attempts to claim divine honor for himself. Mazieh Gail, in her book, *The Three Popes*, says that the diadem later was "adopted by the popes."

The great power and influence of the devil is portrayed for us where we see his tail tearing a third of the stars out of the sky and throwing them to the earth. In an earlier chapter (9:11) Satan himself was symbolized by a star falling from heaven. This picture of the dragon sweeping one-third of the stars out of the sky may symbolize the original fall of the angels. While the Bible tells us very little about that fall, it does indicate that one angel of high rank rebelled first and persuaded a large number of other good angels to join him in rebellion. These angels may be represented by the stars swept out of heaven by the dragon's tail. On the other hand it is possible that John is here only calling attention to the great power of the dragon. Whether we understand the word οὐρανός here as "sky" or as "heaven," the original abode of the evil angels, will depend on our understanding of this part of the vision.

This powerful dragon was intent upon destroying the woman's child as soon as it would be born (v. 4). But in this he was completely frustrated. There can be no question about the identity of this child. It was a male child who "will rule all nations with a rod of iron (*i.e.*, an iron scepter)." The Lord Jesus had spoken of himself in exactly those same terms in the letter to Thyatira (2:27,28). In that connection we already noted that both of these passages, as well as a later passage (19:15), contain an allusion to Psalm 2, which describes the promised Messiah. The words, "Her child was snatched up to God and to his throne," are a clear portrayal of the ascension of Christ, which in a certain sense forever put him beyond the devil's reach. In all of this the human nature of Christ is in the forefront.

From the Gospels we know of the devil's intent to destroy Christ or to undermine his work. These verses portray in a general way the slaughter of the babies of Bethlehem, the temptation in the wilderness, the many cases of devil possesion which Christ encountered, the suggestion of Peter that Jesus ought not to suffer (Mt 16:22), and the betrayal by Judas (Jn 13:2). The woman who had given birth to the child, evidently sensing what the devil would try to do when he failed in his attempt to devour the child, "fled into the wilderness, where she has a place prepared by God." The phrase ἡτοιμασμένον ἀπὸ τοῦ θεοῦ, "prepared by God," is an example of the use of the preposition ἀπὸ to denote the direct agent, a use that becomes more common in later Greek.

In a hostile world God has prepared for his church a place of safety. Jesus during his days on earth had promised that the gates of hell would not be able to destroy his church (Mt 16:18). When John saw this vision, it must have reminded him of the words of Jesus, "My prayer is not that you take them out of the world but that you protect them from the evil one. They are not of the world, even as I am not of it" (Jn 17:15,16). In those days of persecution Christians might have wondered why God did not deliver them from their suffering by snatching them also to heaven. While this vision does not answer that question, it did make clear to them that their ascension to the presence of God would be delayed. They would be in a "desert," a place of discomfort and suffering, but nevertheless a place prepared by God. It was God's intention and purpose (the ἵνα clause) that "there they should feed her for 1260 days." Who "they" are is not specified. In the Hebrew language the third person of the active voice with an indefinite subject is often used in a sentence in which Greek would usually use a passive verb. We could translate, "where she will be fed." God will provide for his church in some way, just as he provided for Elijah when the ravens fed him at the brook Cherith and the widow fed him at Zarephath.

John resumes the description of the woman's flight into the wilderness in verse 13. In the meantime, the scene once more shifts to the sky.

The War in the Sky (12:7-12)

7) Καὶ ἐγένετο πόλεμος ἐν τῷ οὐρανῷ, ὁ Μιχαὴλ καὶ οἱ ἄγγελοι αὐτοῦ τοῦ πολεμῆσαι μετὰ τοῦ δράκοντος. καὶ ὁ δράκων ἐπολέμησεν καὶ οἱ ἄγγελοι αὐτοῦ, 8) καὶ οὐκ ἴσχυσεν, οὐδὲ τόπος εὑρέθη αὐτῶν ἔτι ἐν τῷ οὐρανῷ. 9) καὶ ἐβλήθη ὁ δράκων ὁ μέγας, ὁ ὄφις ὁ ἀρχαῖος, ὁ καλούμενος Διάβολος καί Ὁ Σατανᾶς, ὁπλανῶν τὴν οἰκουμένην ὅλην, ἐβλήθη εἰς τὴν γῆν, καὶ οἱ ἄγγελοι

αὐτοῦ μετ' αὐτοῦ ἐβλήθησαν. 10) καὶ ἤκουσα φωνὴν μεγάλην ἐν τῷ οὐρανῷ λέγουσαν,
Ἄρτι ἐγένετο ἡ σωτηρία καὶ ἡ δύναμις καὶ ἡ βασιλεία τοῦ Θεοῦ ἡμῶν καὶ ἡ ἐξουσία τοῦ Χριστοῦ αὐτοῦ, ὅτι ἐβλήθη ὁ κατήγωρ τῶν ἀδελφῶν ἡμῶν, ὁ κατηγορῶν αὐτοὺς ἐνώπιον τοῦ Θεοῦ ἡμῶν ἡμέρας καὶ νυκτός.
11) καὶ αὐτοὶ ἐνίκησαν αὐτὸν διὰ τὸ αἷμα τοῦ Ἀρνίου καὶ διὰ τὸν λόγον τῆς μαρτυρίας αὐτῶν, καὶ οὐκ ἠγάπησαν τὴν ψυχὴν αὐτῶν ἄχρι θανάτου.
12) διὰ τοῦτο εὐφραίνεσθε, οὐρανοὶ καὶ οἱ ἐν αὐτοῖς σκηνοῦντες· οὐαὶ τὴν γῆν καὶ τὴν θάλασσαν, ὅτι κατέβη ὁ διάβολος πρὸς ὑμᾶς ἔχων θυμὸν μέγαν, εἰδὼς ὅτι ὀλίγον καιρὸν ἔχει.

7) *And there was a war in the sky. Michael and his angels were to fight with the dragon. And the dragon and his angels fought.*
8) *But he was not strong enough, nor was there a place for them in the sky any longer.*
9) *And the great dragon was cast out, the ancient serpent, the one who is called Devil and Satan, the one who leads astray the whole inhabited earth — he was thrown to the earth, and his angels were thrown (down) with him.*
10) *And I heard a loud voice in the sky, saying:*

Now has come the salvation and the power and the kingdom of our God and the authority of his Anointed One, because the accuser of our brothers is thrown (down), the one who accuses them before our God by day and by night.
11) *And they conquered him because of the blood of the Lamb and because of the word of their testimony, and they did not love their lives unto death.*
12) *Exult on this account, O you heavens, and those who dwell in them.*

Woe be the earth and the sea,
for the devil has come down to you.
He is very angry,
knowing that he has little time.

Many commentators have understood this battle to be one that took place soon after the beginning of creation and before the fall of man. They have seen these verses as a description of the original fall of the evil angels at the time of creation. But the evidence indicates that these verses do not refer to the original fall of the angels. Therefore we have translated, "There was a war in the sky," rather than, "There was a war in heaven." An earlier verse in this chapter had spoken of "the stars of heaven," and in that context "heaven" may mean "sky" (see the comments on v. 4).

That this is not a war that took place millennia before the

time of John seems evident from the song of victory that is sung after the battle is over. While it would not be impossible to view the description of this battle as a "flashback" to a past event similar to that found in the description of the birth of the child in the previous scene, yet the words of that song indicate that this war which John saw fought in the sky over Patmos was a representation of the battle in which the devil lost the ability to accuse John's brethren before the throne of God. There is only one battle of which this was the outcome, namely, the battle that Jesus fought when he came in the flesh to destroy the works of the devil (1 Jn 3:8). Moreover, when Jesus spoke of his impending death, he called it the time when the prince of this world would be "thrown out" (Jn 12:31).

The word for "thrown out" which he uses in John 12, ἐκβληθήσεται, is closely related to the word he uses here, ἐβλήθη. We should remember that both of these passages are found in the writings of John. There is also a related passage in the Gospel of Luke. When the seventy disciples returned from their mission and rejoiced over the success that they had, the Savior said to them, "I saw Satan fall like lightning from heaven." Many interpreters hold that these words do not refer to the original fall of the evil angels but rather to the defeat of Satan which takes place when the Gospel message is proclaimed. That is the interpretation which fits best into the context.

That the good angels were actively engaged in that struggle with the devil and his evil angels is hinted at even if not discussed in any detail in the Gospels (see, *e.g.*, Lk 22:43; Mt 28:5; Jn 13:2). Side by side with the great physical struggle that men saw in Gethsemane and on Calvary, there was a great battle being fought in the spiritual realm.

The leader of the army of the good angels is Michael. The name Michael is really a Hebrew question which means, "Who is like God?" The identity of Michael has been disputed, also in Lutheranism. Some have argued that Michael is a name for the Savior, who in his human nature is "like God," having received all the divine attributes in the incarnation. It can be argued also that the word "archangel" might mean not "ruling angel" but "the ruler of the angels." Add to this the fact that the word archangel is never used in the plural, which might lead us to infer that there is only one. This could then lead to the conclusion that this ruler of the angels is the Son of God. He is spoken of as such in the book of Joshua. The "man" who appeared in a vision to Joshua at Jericho and who is later called "the LORD," or "Jahweh," calls himself "the captain of the host of the Lord" (Jos 5:13—6:2). In that place the second person of the Holy Trinity really calls himself the ruler of the angel armies. Also supportive of this view is what is said about Michael in Daniel 12:1. There Michael is called "the great prince who protects your people," and it is said that when he arises, Daniel's people will be delivered. Those words could easily be applied to the Savior.

There are also passages that weigh rather heavily against the view that Michael is the Lord Jesus. In Jude it is said that Michael did not dare to bring a railing accusation against the devil but said instead, "The Lord rebuke you!" (Jude 9). One could perhaps argue that those words could be understood of Christ against the background of the Trinity, which enables the "Lord" to speak of the "Lord" as a distinct person. But this would hardly do justice to the context. A fairly decisive argument lies in the words of Daniel, who identifies Michael as "one of the chief princes" (10:13). This seems to identify Michael as one of a number of angels of superior rank, and this, by the way, is the only substantial biblical evidence for the claim that there are more archangels than one. (See the comments on 8:1.)

Actually it makes little difference whether one considers Michael to be a created angel or the "Angel of the Lord," who is the "captain of the hosts of the Lord." The significance of these verses is that there was a great battle fought between the good and evil angels in connection with the redemptive work of Christ. In this battle the devil and his angels were decisively defeated. They were thrown out of the sky to the earth. The NIV translation, "They lost their place in heaven," while possible, leaves the conflicting impression that this refers to the fall of the angels in the beginning.

At this point the dragon is identified. He is first called the ancient serpent. The reference is, of course, to the serpent who deceived Eve (Gn 3:1; 2 Cor 11:3) in the garden of Eden. He is "the one who is called Devil and Satan." The word devil, διάβολος, means "slanderer." He is the one who spreads lies, especially about God. The word "devil" is really, in the New Testament, a proper name which is reserved for the leader of the evil angels. The evil angels themselves are always called demons, δαιμόνια, a word which the KJV translates "devils," but which the NIV regularly translates "demons." "Satan" is a Hebrew word which means "the Accuser." In the song of victory which John here heard from the sky, Satan is said to be the one who accuses God's people continually (v. 10). Finally, he is characterized as the one who leads the whole inhabited world astray. His influence is seen everywhere in the depravity of men.

After the devil was cast down, John heard a loud voice in the sky which, in poetic rhapsody, celebrated the victory over the devil. The first sentence of this song proclaims a truth which was of the utmost importance for the persecuted church and which ought to be studied very carefully by every millennialist. It reminded the suffering saints of that time that salvation did not consist in their being protected against the sword of the persecutors and the mouth of the lions in the arena. It ought to remind millennialists of our time that the kingdom does not consist primarily in the suppression of the ungodly. Rather, the salvation of God comes, his power is manifested, his kingdom is established, and the authority of Christ is demonstrated in this that the accuser of God's people is no longer able to accuse them. Satan, the accuser, is pictured as a prosecuting attorney who appears before God regularly to bring charges against the Christians. First he tempts them to sin and then, having accomplished his purpose, he hurries to the throne of God to demand that they be punished.

There are many things of which they could be accused, yet Satan has lost his power to accuse them. They have won the victory over him "because of" (not "by" as the KJV and the NIV translate) the blood of the Lamb and because of the word of their testimony. The blood of the Lamb cleanses us from all sin (1 Jn 1:7). In that blood the saints have washed their robes and made them white (Rv 7:14). Because of that blood, because the Son of God died to pay the wages of sin in place of all men, the devil no longer can accuse us before the judgment throne of God.

This victory is also won "because of the word of their testimony." In his Gospel, John had told of how Jesus appointed his apostles to be his witnesses. The Savior, on the night before he died, gave them the promise that the Holy Ghost would come to them to testify concerning Jesus and then added, "But you must also testify, for you have been with me from the beginning" (Jn 15:27). The form of the great commission as we have it in the book of Acts is couched in those same terms. The Savior said to his followers, "You will be my witnesses" (Ac 1:8). In his first epistle, John describes the gospel as "the testimony that God testified concerning his Son" (1 Jn 5:10). In John's form of the great commission, the heart of the message is clearly the good news of forgiveness (Jn 20:23; cp Lk 24:47). The "word of their testimony" is the gospel. The gospel message of forgiveness freely offered to all men to be accepted by faith makes it evident that when the devil accuses us before God he is a liar and cannot succeed, because the judge before whom he accuses us has already acquitted us (Ro 8:33). For this reason it can be said that Christians conquer the devil "because of" the gospel. There is no need to translate διὰ as "by" or "by means of," which would be an irregular rendering of the preposition with the accusative.

The "brothers" whom Satan cannot accuse are then described as people who "did not love their lives unto death." The thought is compressed into very few words, but the NIV has undoubtedly caught the meaning when it expands the wording of the original and paraphrases the Greek preposition ἀχρὶ with "so much as to shrink from." These words again remind us that John wrote Revelation in a time of persecution, when many Christians had to make a choice between remaining faithful to the Savior or denying him. That choice often meant a choice between life and death. Like all normal people, Christians also love life. The life that is spoken of here is physical, bodily life. This is indicated by the use of ψυχή rather than ζωή. They did not love their lives so much that they refused to suffer death for their faith. Love, in the common sense of the term, is basically the desire to possess. They were not so desirous of keeping their physical life that when it came to the point of dying for their faith, they were ready to deny the testimony they had given. God's message of forgiveness was dearer to them than physical life (ψυχή) because that message was the source of true life (ζωή), the life that could never be extinguished.

Because the devil has lost the power to accuse God's people, the heavens and those who dwell in them are then called upon to exult. Here the word "heavens" denotes the abode of the angels and the blessed dead. Our joy in heaven, too, is based on the forgiveness of sins which we have through the blood of the Lamb. The redeeming love of God will be our theme not only till we die, but to all eternity. While peace and freedom from want and from fear will be part of our life in heaven, yet true exulting joy is never possible except διὰ τοῦτο, "because of this," that the accuser has been cast down because of the blood of the Lamb. The Social Gospel, Judaism, Mohammedanism, as well as many other "Christian" and non-Christian heresies forget this.

It is a pity that many fundamentalistic millennialists do not recognize that their error draws men away from the true joy we have in Christ. In spite of millennialistic and Social Gospel denials, the kingdom of our God came when Satan was defeated in the great war in the sky.

Nevertheless, the devil has not yet been cast into the lake of fire, where all his power to harm God's people will be destroyed forever (20:10). Because of the blood of the Lamb and the testimony of the church he has lost his power to accuse. But, as the previous chapters pointed out, he still seeks to obscure and to silence that testimony by darkening the sun with his locusts from hell and by slaying God's witnesses. We are still in the 1260 days during which Jerusalem is trampled by the Gentiles, and therefore the voice from heaven continues,

> Woe to the earth and the sea,
> for the devil has come down to you.
> He is very angry
> knowing that he has little time.

Because of the resurrection and ascension of Christ the devil knows that he has lost the war. But like a defeated tyrant who knows that the day of total defeat can only be delayed he is intent upon taking as many people as possible with him to destruction.

Both Peter and Paul pointed out that this raging enemy can be withstood only by faith (Eph 6:16; 1 Pe 5:8,9). While John does not explicitly introduce this thought into his solemn warning, yet it is implicit in the earlier statement that the brethren overcome the devil because of the word of their testimony. Testimony is always given in order to persuade, to arouse certainty. And the certainty that is created by the testimony of the church is the Christian faith.

The scene of the vision at this point once more shifts back to the earth. In the verse immediately before the vision of the war in heaven we had read about the flight of the woman to the wilderness. John now returns to that point in the vision and sets forth the reason for the warning that the voice from the sky had directed to the earth and the sea.

The Dragon Persecutes the Woman (12:13-18)

13) Καὶ ὅτε εἶδεν ὁ δράκων ὅτι ἐβλήθη εἰς τὴν γῆν, ἐδίωξεν τὴν γυναῖκα ἥτις ἔτεκεν τὸν ἄρσενα. 14) καὶ ἐδόθησαν τῇ γυναικὶ αἱ δύο πτέρυγες τοῦ ἀετοῦ τοῦ μεγάλου, ἵνα πέτηται εἰς τὴν ἔρημον

εἰς τὸν τόπον αὐτῆς, ὅπου τρέφεται ἐκεῖ καιρὸν καὶ καιροὺς καὶ ἥμισυ καιροῦ ἀπὸ προσώπου τοῦ ὄφεως. 15) καὶ ἔβαλεν ὁ ὄφις ἐκ τοῦ στόματος αὐτοῦ ὀπίσω τῆς γυναικὸς ὕδωρ ὡς ποταμόν, ἵνα αὐτὴν ποταμοφόρητον ποιήσῃ. 16) καὶ ἐβοήθησεν ἡ γῆ τῇ γυναικί, καὶ ἤνοιξεν ἡ γῆ τὸ στόμα αὐτῆς καὶ κατέπιεν τὸν ποταμὸν ὃν ἔβαλεν ὁ δράκων ἐκ τοῦ στόματος αὐτοῦ. 17) καὶ ὠργίσθη ὁ δράκων ἐπὶ τῇ γυναικί, καὶ ἀπῆλθεν ποιῆσαι πόλεμον μετὰ τῶν λοιπῶν τοῦ σπέρματος αὐτῆς, τῶν τηρούντων τὰς ἐντολὰς τοῦ Θεοῦ καὶ ἐχόντων τὴν μαρτυρίαν Ἰησοῦ· 18) καὶ ἐστάθη ἐπὶ τὴν ἄμμον τῆς θαλάσσης.

13) *And when the dragon saw that he was thrown to the earth, he pursued the woman who had given birth to the child, a boy,* 14) *and the two wings of the great eagle were given to the woman, in order that she might fly to her place in the wilderness, where she is fed for a time and times and half a time away from the presence of the serpent.* 15) *And the serpent gushed out of his mouth water like a river after the woman in order to cause her to be carried away by the river.* 16) *And the earth helped the woman, and the earth opened her mouth and swallowed the river which the dragon had poured out of his mouth.* 17) *And the dragon was angry over the woman and he went away to make war with the rest of her children, who keep the commandments of God and who have the testimony of Jesus.* 18) *And he stood on the shore of the sea.*

Having failed in his assault on the angelic armies, the devil once more turns his attention to the woman who had begun her flight into the desert (v. 6). Because of the imminent danger from the devil, the woman is given the two wings of the great eagle. The articles again are deictic.

The basic significance is clear. The devil persists in his persecution of the church, and the church is given supernatural help to escape from the pursuing enemy. The context does not assign any specific significance to the two wings. Usually the wings of eagles and of other birds in the figurative language of the Bible signify God's care and concern for his people. He bears them "on eagles' wings" (Ex 19:4), and under the shadow of his wings they find refuge and shelter (Ps 91:4; Mt 23:37). The Prophet Ezekiel speaks of two great eagles (17:2ff), but these are manifestly the enemies who carry God's people into captivity. All that we can say for certain is that the church receives divine help in her efforts to escape the machinations of the devil. While the two wings remind some of the two sacraments that God has given the church as weapons for her warfare against the devil, we cannot say with certainty that the Spirit intended this interpretation.

For an explanation of "a time and times and half a time," see the comments on verse 6.

The dragon in John's vision then released a huge river of water out of his mouth in an effort to carry the woman away. But the earth came to the woman's rescue by opening up and swallowing the stream. Here we may be more specific and say that this stream represents the demonic doctrines (1 Tm 4:1ff) by which the devil seeks to rob the church of her faith in God's word and leads many astray (2 Tm 4:3f). The swallowing of the river by the earth may point to the fact that false doctrines have a way of going out of style and of being discredited. In any case, both the eagle wings and the swallowing of the waters remind us again that "the gates of hell shall not prevail" against the church, but that God will always find a way to preserve his church against all the wiles of the devil.

The devil's inability to get at the woman filled him with rage. Most of the translations imply that his rage was directed against the woman. While it is true that in later Greek ἐπὶ with the dative occasionally means "against," the normal translation fits well into this context. He was angry "over" the woman. His experiences with the woman were the occasion of his rage, which is directed primarily against God.

Since he could not get at the church he "went away to make war with the rest of her children." The "children" of the church are the members of the church, those who believe in Jesus as their Savior, who by his blood protected them from the accusations of the devil. Since Satan failed in his efforts to destroy the church as an organism, he now directs his attacks against individual members. We know that his only hope of success is to separate them from the church, and the only way he can do that is by destroying their faith.

The children of the church are described as those "who keep the commandments of God and have the testimony of Jesus." The testimony of Jesus is the gospel message, "the testimony that God testified concerning his Son" (1 Jn 5:10, author's translation). To "have" that testimony must mean more than to possess it in a printed form or to have heard it. A person does not really "have" that message until he has made it his own by appropriating it to himself by faith — or, as Luther said, "He who believes it, has it."

Since they have learned to love God as their forgiving Father, the believers are people "who keep the commandments." Their obedience is far from perfect, but at least through faith they are no longer "in the flesh," unable to please God (Ro 8:7,8). Love for God, from which all obedience to the law must flow, is possible only for believers, because the inborn attitude of all men toward God is one of hatred (Rom 8:7). Through faith alone they possess the obedience that Christ rendered to God by keeping all the commandments.

This description of the believers is by no means inconsistent with the doctrine of salvation by faith without works. Whenever men by faith make the "testimony of Jesus Christ" their own, so that they truly believe that because of the shedding of the blood of Christ their sins are fully forgiven, they will always begin to love the Lord and thus take the first step toward obeying and fulfilling the law. Only those who have learned where their salvation lies can truly be said to keep the commandments.

The first words of the next chapter really belong here also. The KJV translation, which has John standing on the shore of the sea, not only does not fit the context well but it is also based on late manuscripts. The earliest manuscripts read, "And he [that is, the dragon] stood on the shore of the sea." The next vision concerns a beast that comes out of the sea, and these words hint very strongly at a connection between the dragon and this beast, a connection which is established in the course of the vision. The rise of the beast from the sea and the second beast from the earth is the devil's opportunity to find willing tools to serve his purposes.

THE SECOND VISION: THE BEAST FROM THE SEA (13:1-10)

The Beast Described (13:1-8)

1) Καὶ εἶδον ἐκ τῆς θαλάσσης θηρίον ἀναβαῖνον, ἔχον κέρατα δέκα καὶ κεφαλὰς ἑπτά, καὶ ἐπὶ τῶν κεράτων αὐτοῦ δέκα διαδήματα, καὶ ἐπὶ τὰς κεφαλὰς αὐτοῦ ὀνόματα βλασφημίας. 2) καὶ τὸ θηρίον ὃ εἶδον ἦν ὅμοιον παρδάλει, καὶ οἱ πόδες αὐτοῦ ὡς ἄρκου, καὶ τὸ στόμα αὐτοῦ ὡς στόμα λέοντος. καὶ ἔδωκεν αὐτῷ ὁ δράκων τὴν δύναμιν αὐτοῦ καὶ τὸν θρόνον αὐτοῦ καὶ ἐξουσίαν μεγάλην. 3) καὶ μίαν ἐκ τῶν κεφαλῶν αὐτοῦ ὡς ἐσφαγμένην εἰς θάνατον, καὶ ἡ πληγὴ τοῦ θανάτου αὐτοῦ ἐθεραπεύθη. καὶ ἐθαυμάσθη ὅλη ἡ γῆ ὀπίσω τοῦ θηρίου, 4) καὶ προσεκύνησαν τῷ δράκοντι, ὅτι ἔδωκεν τὴν ἐξουσίαν τῷ θηρίῳ, καὶ προσεκύνησαν τῷ θηρίῳ λέγοντες, Τίς ὅμοιος τῷ θηρίῳ, καὶ τίς δύναται πολεμῆσαι μετ'

αὐτοῦ; 5) καὶ ἐδόθη αὐτῷ στόμα λαλοῦν μεγάλα καὶ βλασφημίας, καὶ ἐδόθη αὐτῷ ἐξουσία ποιῆσαι μῆνας τεσσεράκοντα καὶ δύο. 6) καὶ ἤνοιξεν τὸ στόμα αὐτοῦ εἰς βλασφημίας πρὸς τὸν Θεόν, βλασφημῆσαι τὸ ὄνομα αὐτοῦ καὶ τὴν σκηνὴν αὐτοῦ, τοὺς ἐν τῷ οὐρανῷ σκηνοῦντας. 7) καὶ ἐδόθη αὐτῷ ποιῆσαι πόλεμον μετὰ τῶν ἁγίων καὶ νικῆσαι αὐτούς, καὶ ἐδόθη αὐτῷ ἐξουσία ἐπὶ πᾶσαν φυλὴν καὶ λαὸν καὶ γλῶσσαν καὶ ἔθνος. 8) καὶ προσκυνήσουσιν αὐτὸν πάντες οἱ κατοικοῦντες ἐπὶ τῆς γῆς, οὗ οὐ γέγραπται τὸ ὄνομα αὐτοῦ ἐν τῷ βιβλίῳ τῆς ζωῆς τοῦ Ἀρνίου τοῦ ἐσφαγμένου ἀπὸ καταβολῆς κόσμου.

1) *And I saw a beast rising out of the sea, having ten horns and seven heads, and upon his horns ten crowns, and there were blasphemous names on his heads.* 2) *And the beast which I saw was like a leopard, but his feet were like those of a bear, and his mouth like the mouth of a lion. And the dragon gave him his power and his throne and great authority.* 3) *One of his heads seemed to have been butchered to death, but its mortal wound was healed. And the whole world, following the beast, was filled with admiration,* 4) *and they worshiped the dragon because he gave authority to the beast, and they worshiped the beast, saying, "Who is like the beast, and who can go to war against him?"*

5) *And he was given a mouth speaking great things, yes, blasphemous things, and he was given authority to work (or, to continue) for 42 months.* 6) *And he opened his mouth to speak blasphemies against God, to blaspheme his name and his tabernacle, those who dwell in heaven.*

7) *And he was given power to wage war with the saints and to be victorious over them, and he was given authority over every tribe and people and language and nation.* 8) *And all those who dwell on the earth will worship him, whose names have not been written from the beginning of the world in the book of life, which belongs to the lamb that was slain.*

There are two truths with which all commentators must agree regarding this beast. First, the beast receives his power from the devil and serves the devil's purposes. Secondly, the beast is a powerful enemy of the church, but he will not be able to do any permanent damage to the elect. This vision, therefore, once more sets before us the basic message of Revelation, namely, that the church will have enemies who will try to destroy it but God will keep his elect safe in the midst of all danger.

The identity of the beast is not as obvious as this general message of comfort for a persecuted and suffering church. The Christians of that time might well have seen this beast as representing any enemy that made their lives miserable. The most manifest enemy who was persecuting them when John wrote the book was the imperial government of Rome.

Many Lutheran commentators have also seen this beast as a symbol of the Roman empire, which in the early centuries of the church's history sought repeatedly to wipe out the Christian religion. While this interpretation seems valid, we would be shortsighted to limit the interpretation to the persecutions carried on by imperial Rome.

The imagery of Revelation is often the imagery of the Old Testament. To anyone who is well-acquainted with the Old Testament, this vision of John will immediately call to mind a similar vision described by the Prophet Daniel. In the seventh chapter of his book, that prophet spoke of four beasts that came out of the sea. The beast from the sea which John describes here is in some ways like the four beasts of Daniel. The first of those four is described as being "like a lion"; John's beast has the mouth of a lion. Daniel's second beast looked "like a bear"; John's beast has feet like those of a bear. Daniel's third beast was "one that looked like a leopard"; the beast which John saw was like a leopard. The fourth beast is not compared to any wild animal but it has ten horns; John's beast also has ten horns. The third beast described by Daniel has four heads, which means that the four beasts together have seven heads, just as the single beast seen by John. One of the ten horns of Daniel's beast is described as "waging war against the saints and defeating them." Allowing for difference in language, those very words are reproduced by John in his description of the beast (Re 13:7).

In the book of Daniel the significance of the four beasts is directly stated. We are told that "the four great beasts are four kingdoms." When we compare this vision of the four beasts with Daniel's interpretation of Nebuchadnezzar's dream (Dn 2), these four kingdoms are easy to identify. They are 1) the kingdom of Nebuchadnezzar, 2) the Medo-Persian empire, 3) the empire of Alexander and his successors, and 4) the Roman empire. The four heads of the third beast evidently symbolize the four kingdoms into which Alexander's realm was divided after his death, and the ten horns of the fourth beast represent the many nations or kingdoms that developed out of the ruins of the Roman empire.

The four beasts of Daniel's vision are such clear representations of secular rulers that there scarcely can be any doubt that the beast which John saw coming out of the sea is also a symbol of secular government. The clear parallelism between the two visions requires such an interpretation. Having established that, the rest of the details of the vision fall into place.

In the previous chapter we saw the devil frustrated in his attempts to destroy the church by a flood of false doctrine that poured out of his mouth like a roaring river. But as he stood on the shores of the sea he saw in the rise of the beast out of the sea another opportunity to attack the church.

As we have seen, this terrifying beast is a symbol of secular government. While it is true that secular governments are all institutions of God, nevertheless they can because of their power become especially efficient tools of Satan, just as other good creatures of God can become instruments of evil. The beast is not a creation of the devil. Just as the earth and the sea brought forth living creatures at the time of creation (Gn 1:20,24), so this beast rises out of the sea. It is orginally part of the natural order of the world.

However, from the very beginning its demonic character is apparent. The beast has ten horns and seven heads. Exactly the same terms had been applied the great red dragon. The vision establishes the close alliance that exists between this beast and the devil.

On its ten horns the beast wears ten crowns. The crowns are διαδήματα, diadems, such as we saw in the vision of the dragon. The wearing of such a crown was viewed as a claim to divine honor. The wearer was viewed as an incarnate god. Civil governments often have a tendency to claim for themselves the kind of authority that belongs only to God, and at times such governments directly attempt to dethrone God. The godless communistic governments of our time are a case in point. But here we may also think of governments that set aside the divine command, "Thou shalt not kill," in the case of unborn babies. Such governments, too, usurp divine prerogatives. While governments have the power of the sword, or the right to kill, they have this right only in the case of "evildoers" (Ro 13:3ff).

"On his heads were blasphemous names." Literally, the text says, "On his heads were names of blasphemy," but the genitive is certainly a genitive of description. Some manuscripts read, "On his heads there was a blasphemous name." The variant does not alter the sense. The word "name," especially in biblical usage, often means much more than the arbitrary designation we apply to a person or thing. The word "name" is often used to denote that which describes a person and tells us what he is. We use the word in that sense when we speak of a man's "good name." His "good name" includes all the good things that are said about him.

"Blasphemy" literally is "evil-speaking" or "slander." The very name of this beast speaks evil of someone. Who is blasphemed or slandered by the name or names of the beast is not made clear at this point, but verse 6 indicates that this blasphemy is directed against God. We might say that a person's name consists of all the things that are said about him, and many of the things that are said about civil governments are in reality blasphemies against God. While this is to a certain degree true of all governments, it is especially true of those governments that are openly anti-Christian or even professedly atheistic, such as the governments of communist countries. When a government claims, for example, that it is the source of all the blessings that come to the nation or when it arrogates to itself the right to punish men for their thoughts and attitudes, these very claims are a denial and usurpation of the prerogatives and sovereignty of God. What is said of them is a "name of blasphemy," a reputation that involves blasphemy and insults God.

The dangerous, the destructive power of the beast is portrayed in its appearance as a leopard with the feet of a bear and the mouth of a lion. These three animals often fill men with fear, and thus, from a human point of view, God's people will often be tempted to be afraid when they contemplate the power of civil governments and know how easily their power can be enlisted in the service of Satan. Before that power, Christians often feel helpless and frustrated. This can be true even of those governments that are most benign. When Christians are forced by the government's divinely given authority to pay taxes to support an educational system that seeks to inculcate anti-Christian evolutionary theories and a religion of secular humanism, the government takes on the appearance of a leopard, bear, and lion in the eyes of a Christian.

Thus the civil government becomes an instrument of Satan. "The dragon gave him his power and his throne and great authority." At first glance, this sentiment seems to contradict the biblical doctrine which teaches that the power and authority of *all* civil governments comes from God (Ro 13:1). Paul says that no civil authority exists except by God's ordinance. It could therefore be argued that the interpretation that identifies the beast as symbol of civil government must be wrong, since the beast receives his authority and ruling power from Satan. But the biblical doctrine of divine concurrence, which teaches that God uses evil men and even Satan to carry out his divine purposes, makes such a conclusion unnecessary and even untenable. We are told, for example, that it was the devil who bereaved Job of his children and robbed him of his possessions, but Job could still say, "The Lord . . . has taken away" (Job 1:21). And when the devil afflicted Job with boils, Job described his misery and pain in the words: "The arrows of the Almighty are in me" (Job 6:4). So also the Bible teaches that both Satan and God moved David to take a census in Israel (2 Sm 24:1; 1 Chr 21:1). Against the background of divine concurrence it should not be difficult to see how it is possible for John to say that the beast receives his power and authority from Satan without contradicting the truth that ultimately all authority derives from God.

John continues, "One of his heads seemed to have been butchered to death, but its mortal wound was healed." A more literal translation might read, "One of his heads appeared to be slain to death, but the wound that caused its death was healed." The Greek word ἐσφαγμένην means more than "mortally wounded" (NIV), especially since this form is a perfect participle.

This verse has created difficulties for commentators. Some of them have seen it as a reference to Christ's redemptive work and the victory which he won over Satan at the empty tomb. All that can be said without fear of contradiction, however, is that this severe wounding and death of one of the seven heads evidently represents some sort of reversal suffered by the beast as it attempts to carry out its service to the devil and to exercise the demonic power bestowed on it by Satan. Nevertheless this reversal is only temporary. The mortal wound was healed and the church can expect renewed persecution from civil governments. The wounding of one of the heads of the beast may be a symbol to indicate to the church that there will be periods of respite when the open hostility of civil governments will be muted for a time.

It is possible, however, to see in this deadly wound, a specific event in history which illustrates how the civil government temporarily seems to lose its power to serve Satan. The periodic bloody persecutions of the church at the hands of the Roman government seemed to have come to an end when the Emperor Constantine was converted and Christianity became the established religion of the empire. Instead of being a persecutor of the church, the civil government became a promoter of the Christian religion. Civil government as a tool of Satan seemed to have suffered an incurable wound. But the resultant state-church system became one of history's greatest enemies of true piety and orthodox Christianity. The mortal wound was healed, at least from the devil's point of view.

When John then tells us that the whole earth, that is, the inhabitants of the world, followed the beast and was filled with admiration, he does not tell us what gave rise to the awe with which men regarded the beast. The admiration might have resulted from the seemingly miraculous recovery from the deadly wound or it might have been wonder at the great power and authority of the beast. The context seems to favor the second alternative. The world admires power and prestige and does not ask whether that power is used in the service of God or of the devil. When governments use their great power to attack the church, the people of God cannot expect to find sympathy from the general populace.

The popular admiration of the beast is connected with honor paid to the devil. John saw the people of the earth bowing down before the dragon because he was the one who had given the beast his authority. The non-Christian world may on the surface recoil from overt devil worship, and yet Paul tells us that all worship that is not directed toward the true God is in reality offered to devils (1 Cor 10:20). Thus John can also say that the whole earth worships the dragon when it bestows idolatrous honor on earthly governments.

The unbelieving world also worships the beast and says, "Who is like the beast, and who can go to war against him?" Those words ascribe omnipotence to the beast. Both questions are rhetorical and imply that the beast is superior to all other beings and that no one is able to fight a victorious battle against the government that has entered the service of Satan. The beast is accorded honor that belongs only to God. The Old Testament several times emphasizes the incomparable majesty of God by asserting that there is no one like him. After the crossing of the Red Sea the Israelites asked, "Who is like you — majestic in holiness, awesome in glory, working wonders?" (Ex 15:11; cp Is 46:5; 1 Kgs 8:23; 2 Chr 6:14; Ps 35:10; 71:19). Here that same kind of majesty is ascribed to the beast. The second question concedes that the beast will be victorious over all his enemies. The world expects that the church will finally suffer total defeat at the hands of a persecuting government. Through the prophecies in this book John assures God's people that this will not happen, yet he forewarns the members of the church that there will be times when the outlook for the church will be so bleak that its enemies will be confident of victory. But just as the imperial government of Rome and its heathen subjects learned that there was a power that could go to war successfully against them, so the atheistic rulers of modern communist countries will also learn that their confident predictions concerning the annihilation of Christianity will come to nothing.

Not only do the followers of the beast ascribe omnipotence and majesty to him. But the beast himself was given "a mouth to speak great things, yes, blasphemous things." Literally the text says, "great things and blasphemies." The "and" is explanatory, telling us the nature of the "great things." Just as the praise heaped on the beast by his followers is blasphemous, so the claims that the beast makes for himself are likewise an insult to God.

Yet God does not destroy this great enemy immediately as God's people might hope and expect. The beast is given authority "to work [or, to continue] for 42 months." We have already seen that the 42 months is the time during which the unbelievers trample the holy city underfoot — namely, the whole New Testament period. While the Greek word ποιῆσαι means "to do" or "to work," yet when it has a word or phrase denoting time as its object it means "to spend" or "to pass" the designated period of time (cp Jas 4:13). In this context it is not clear whether the phrase "42 months" is the object of the verb or a simple accusative denoting duration. In any case, the vision makes clear that God's people are not to expect complete deliverance from the threatening dangers posed by godless governments until the end of the world. The enemies of the church will continue during the whole New Testament era ("42 months"). The kingdom of God on earth will be a kingdom of the cross until its consummation in eternal glory.

The beast does not hesitate to use "the mouth" given to him. "He opened his mouth to speak blasphemies against God, to blaspheme his name and his tabernacle, those who dwell in heaven" (v. 6).

First of all he blasphemes God's name. The name of God includes all the things we know about God. It is God's revelation about himself in the Holy Scriptures. It would be a mistake for us to imagine that this kind of blasphemy is found only in communist governments. When our own government supports the denial of God's creation in our public school system and the ridicule of Christianity in our universities, it joins in this blasphemy and demonstrates how easy it is for a secular government to become the devil's instrument. When Sweden, a nominally Lutheran country, requires religious education in its public school system but makes it difficult for teachers to defend an orthodox Lutheran interpretation of the Bible, it also promotes blasphemy against God's word.

The blasphemy of the beast is also directed against God's "tabernacle, those who dwell in heaven," or, more literally "those who tabernacle in heaven." Many modern translations, as well as some of the Greek manuscripts, read instead, "his tabernacle *and* those who dwell in heaven." It would seem that the best reading is the one we have adopted as the basis for our translation. The absence of "and" between the two phrases indicates that the second phrase "those who dwell in heaven" stands in apposition to "his tabernacle." The men who copied the text seem to have had difficulty with this identification, and they very likely simplified the text by adding the "and."

However, the description of "his tabernacle" as "those who dwell in heaven" is not foreign to New Testament thought. It is well known that the New Testament speaks of the church as the temple of God and of the individual members of the church as the stones used to build that temple (Eph 2:19-21). "Those who dwell in heaven" are the believers, who already here on earth have everlasting life (Jn 5:24; 1 Jn 3:14) and whose citizenship is in heaven (Php 3:20). To call these believers "his tabernacle" is no more surprising than to call them "his temple."

The word σκηνοῦντας, which we have translated "dwell" or "tabernacle," often denotes a temporary stay in a certain place. That meaning, however, does not fit into this context. The noun related to this verb, tabernacle, σκηνή, is also used here, clearly in its specific Old Testament sense. While the Old Testament tabernacle was also a temporary place of worship used by the children of Israel during their wanderings in the wilderness and for several centuries after the conquest of Canaan, yet the emphasis here seems to be on the fact that the tabernacle was the place where God dwelled in the midst of his people. Those who "dwell in heaven" are therefore those who live with God, God's chosen people, the invisible church.

Thus the blasphemies of the beast are also directed against the church. John's readers would recognize what these slanders against the church of their time were. Christians were called haters of men and atheists because they refused to join in the idolatrous worship and orgiastic festivals of the heathen. They were called cannibals because of their celebration of the Lord's Supper and incestuous people because husbands and wives referred to each other as brother and sister. They were called enemies of the state because they refused to worship the emperor or to burn incense to his image. And they were charged with infanticide because of the practice of infant baptism. Similar charges are still made against the church today. Christians today are called anti-social because they refuse to join in worship with false teachers. They are called obscurantist because they refuse to accept some of the theories of modern science, so-called. They are called loveless because they refuse to admit unbelievers to the sacrament. In communist countries their loyalty to the state is suspect because they refuse to give up their worship of God, and Christian young people are considered unfit for higher education because they are given to "religious superstition."

The animosity of the beast against the church is not limited to verbal abuse. "He was given power to wage war with the saints and to be victorious over them, and he was given authority over every tribe and people and language and nation." We have translated in this way with some hesitation. Literally the Greek text reads, "It was given to him to wage war." The Greek word δίδωμι (give) with the infinitive sometimes means "to permit someone to do something." If we were to translate, "He was permitted to wage war," this would imply that it was allowed by what we call the permissive will of God. While this would not be in conflict with the analogy of faith, it is perhaps better to translate the clause, "He was given power to wage war with the saints," as an action of the devil. The context seems to require this. In verse 4 we were told, "The dragon gave to the beast his *authority*." This thought is echoed in the second part of verse 5, which says that *authority* was given to him to work for 42 months, and in the second half of verse 7, which says that *authority* was given to him over all the nations of the earth. In other words, John's vision not only tells the church that the beast will continue to exercise authority to the end of time, but also that there is no place on this earth where the church can escape from the attacks of this beast.

This war which the devil encourages the beast to wage against the saints results in the defeat of God's people. The devil gives the beast power and authority to win a victory over the Christians. But the victory cannot be total or final. That would be diametrically opposed to the whole message of the book which assures us at many times and in many ways that in the end the victory will always belong to the church. Our text describes the apparent victory which the civil government wins over God's children when it is able to persecute them, kill them and drive them into the catacombs.

Once more we hear that the beast is worshiped. This time the worshipers are described as "all those who dwell on the earth." This phrase is used eight times in Revelation, and each time it clearly designates unbelievers and enemies of the church. Here the phrase stands in contrast to "his tabernacle, those who dwell in heaven" (v. 6).

Those who dwell on the earth are further described as "those whose names have not been written from the beginning of the world in the book of life which belongs to the Lamb that was slain." Many translators treat the phrase "from the beginning of the world" as an adverbial modifier of "slain" and translate, "the book of life of the Lamb slain from the foundation of the world." It seems to be correct to view it instead as a modifier of the word "written." There are several reasons for this. Almost the same description of the unbelievers is found in a later chapter (17:8); in that place there can be no question that the phrase modifies "written," because the phrase "of the Lamb slain" does not occur there. Moreover, nowhere else in Scripture do we have any statement that says that Christ was slain from the creation of the world. But many passages speak of our eternal election, which took place before the world's beginning, and the writing of our names in the book of life is evidently a symbolic way of speaking of our election.

The mention of the book of life leads John to quote a passage in which the Prophet Jeremiah (Jr 15:2; 43:11) asserts divine providence in concrete terms.

Overruling Providence (13:9-10)

9) εἴ τις ἔχει οὖς ἀκουσάτω. 10) εἴ τις εἰς αἰχμαλωσίαν, εἰς αἰχμαλωσίαν ὑπάγει· εἴ τις ἐν μαχαίρῃ ἀποκτενεῖ, δεῖ αὐτὸν ἐν μαχαίρῃ ἀποκτανθῆναι. Ὧδέ ἐστιν ἡ ὑπομονὴ καὶ ἡ πίστις τῶν ἁγίων.

9) *If anyone has ears let him listen:*
10) *If anyone is destined for imprisonment,*

into prison he will go.
If anyone is destined to be killed with a sword,
by a sword he must be killed.
Here is the patience and the confidence of the saints.

John here reminds a suffering church that the calamities that were overtaking them and that would overtake them in all of history were not chance happenings. God would not forget them or lose control of the situation. God had foreseen all these things and had taken them into account when he planned the pathway by which those whose names were written in the book of life would finally reach their eternal goal.

These words also help to define the type of victory that the beast would win over the saints (v. 7). They would be imprisoned and put to death, but only as part of God's plan of salvation for them.

The last words of this section, "Here is the patience and the faith of the saints" is translated thus by the NIV: "This calls for patient endurance and faithfulness on the part of the saints." The context, however, hardly justifies that translation. The words in the original "call for" nothing to be performed by God's people. Rather, they are assured that they have been elected and predestined for everlasting life. If on the way to heaven they are also destined for imprisonment and martyrdom, they can endure all this with patience and with confident hope. They know that this, too, has been ordained for them by their gracious Lord and Savior. The book of life belongs to him who had been slain to redeem them to God by his blood.

THE THIRD VISION: THE BEAST FROM THE EARTH (13:11-18)

11) Καὶ εἶδον ἄλλο θηρίον ἀναβαῖνον ἐκ τῆς γῆς, καὶ εἶχεν κέρατα δύο ὅμοια ἀρνίῳ, καὶ ἐλάλει ὡς δράκων. 12) καὶ τὴν ἐξουσίαν τοῦ πρώτου θηρίου πᾶσαν ποιεῖ ἐνώπιον αὐτοῦ. καὶ ποιεῖ τὴν γῆν καὶ τοὺς ἐν αὐτῇ κατοικοῦντας ἵνα προσκυνήσουσιν τὸ θηρίον τὸ πρῶτον, οὗ ἐθεραπεύθη ἡ πληγὴ τοῦ θανάτου αὐτοῦ. 13) καὶ ποιεῖ σημεῖα μεγάλα, ἵνα καὶ πῦρ ποιῇ ἐκ τοῦ οὐρανοῦ καταβαίνειν εἰς τὴν γῆν ἐνώπιον τῶν ἀνθρώπων. 14) καὶ πλανᾷ τοὺς κατοικοῦντας ἐπὶ τῆς γῆς διὰ τὰ σημεῖα ἃ ἐδόθη αὐτῷ ποιῆσαι ἐνώπιον τοῦ θηρίου, λέγων τοῖς κατοικοῦσιν ἐπὶ τῆς γῆς ποιῆσαι εἰκόνα τῷ θηρίῳ, ὃς ἔχει τὴν πληγὴν τῆς μαχαίρης καὶ ἔζησεν. 15) καὶ ἐδόθη αὐτῷ δοῦναι πνεῦμα τῇ εἰκόνι τοῦ θηρίου, ἵνα καὶ λαλήσῃ ἡ εἰκὼν τοῦ θηρίου, καὶ ποιήσῃ ἵνα ὅσοι ἐὰν μὴ προσκυνήσωσιν τῇ εἰκόνι

τοῦ θηρίου ἀποκτανθῶσιν. 16) καὶ ποιεῖ πάντας, τοὺς μικροὺς καὶ τοὺς μεγάλους, καὶ τοὺς πλουσίους καὶ τοὺς πτωχούς, καὶ τοὺς ἐλευθέρους καὶ τοὺς δούλους, ἵνα δῶσιν αὐτοῖς χάραγμα ἐπὶ τῆς χειρὸς αὐτῶν τῆς δεξιᾶς ἢ ἐπὶ τὸ μέτωπον αὐτῶν, 17) καὶ ἵνα μή τις δύνηται ἀγοράσαι ἢ πωλῆσαι εἰ μὴ ὁ ἔχων τὸ χάραγμα τὸ ὄνομα τοῦ θηρίου ἢ τὸν ἀριθμὸν τοῦ ὀνόματος αὐτοῦ. 18) Ὧδε ἡ σοφία ἐστίν. ὁ ἔχων νοῦν ψηφισάτω τὸν ἀριθμὸν τοῦ θηρίου· ἀριθμὸς γὰρ ἀνθρώπου ἐστίν. καὶ ὁ ἀριθμὸς αὐτοῦ ἑξακόσιοι ἑξήκοωτα ἕξ.

11) *And I saw another beast coming up out of the earth, and he had two horns like the Lamb, but he spoke like the dragon.* 12) *And he exercises all the authority of the first beast before him. And he makes the earth and those who dwell in it worship the first beast, whose mortal wound was healed.* 13) *And he does great miracles so that he even makes fire come down out of heaven on the earth in the sight of men.* 14) *And he deceives those who dwell on the earth because of the miracles which are given to him to perform before the beast, telling those who dwell on the earth to make an image for the beast who had the sword wound but lived.*

15) *And it was given to him to give breath to the image of the beast so that the image of the beast spoke and caused all those who did not worship the image of the beast to be killed.* 16) *And he makes all men, small and great, rich and poor, free and slave, receive a mark on their right hand or on their foreheads,* 17) *in order that no one might buy or sell unless he has the mark, the name of the beast, or the number of his name.* 18) *Here is wisdom: Let him who has understanding calculate the number of the beast, for it is the number of a man. And his number is 666.*

The first verse in this section presents a problem in translation which also has an effect on the interpretation of the verse. Both the word "lamb" and "dragon" are anarthrous, that is, they have no article. This would be normal the first time the words are used, as in the case in 5:6, where the word "lamb" is used for the first time, and in 12:3, where the word "dragon" is used for the first time. The word "lamb" is used twenty-six times in later chapters, and in every case except here it has the definite article, which would be the article of previous reference. The word "dragon" is used eleven more times; again, in every passage except here it has the definite article.

The common translation of this verse reads, "He had two horns like a lamb, but he spoke as a dragon." The absence of the article in Greek does not always call for an indefinite article in English (Greek has no indefinite article). The absence of the article sometimes indicates that a word is being treated as a proper name. It would be possible to view the absence of the article here in this way, especially because in Revelation the word "lamb" is always a name for Jesus and the word "dragon" is always a name for the devil. We could then very properly capitalize the two words in English and translate, "He had two horns like Lamb but he spoke as Dragon."

At other times the absence of the article indicates quality. The anarthrous noun in Greek is almost equivalent to an English adjective. The English language has the same idiom. An English-speaking person senses that it makes a difference whether we translate "God is a spirit" or "God is spirit" (Jn 4:24). The second sentence really says that God is spiritual. It would be perfectly permissible to translate this verse therefore, "Lamblike, he had two horns, but his speech was dragonlike."

Because both translations, however, are clumsy in English, we have chosen instead to translate with a definite article, "He had two horns like the Lamb, but he spoke like the dragon." We have done that because, even though Christians are also called lambs or sheep, the word here refers to the Lord Jesus. The thought is not that the beast from the earth looks like a Christian (cp Jn 10:28,29; 21:13), but that he actually looks like Christ.

The only argument from Revelation against this interpretation is the ascription of seven horns to the lamb in 5:6. But we have no way of knowing whether the lamb which John saw in these visions always had seven horns. The reader may recall the comments regarding the single crown the rider on the white horse wears in chapter 6 and the many diadems he wears in chapter 19. Many times in Revelation when the Savior is called the lamb there is no reference to his appearance at all. Those passages are similar to the words of John the Baptist when he pointed to the Savior in his human form and called him the Lamb of God that takes away the sins of the world (Jn 1:29).

There can be no doubt in the mind of the interpreter that the lamblike beast in the vision is a great enemy of the church. While the beast from the sea was obviously a fearsome and dangerous foe of God's people, the beast from the earth at first glance appears to be completely harmless. It actually takes on the appearance of Christ, or at the very least, (if one insists on translating, "a lamb") of one of Christ's followers.

Orthodox Lutheran commentators have generally seen in this beast from the earth a representation of the great Antichrist and, in harmony with the Lutheran confessions, have identified him with the pope of Rome. While the identification of the Antichrist rests primarily on what the Apostle Paul teaches concerning "the man of sin" in 2 Thessalonians 2, there are still some things said here that help to undergird the confessional Lutheran doctrine which says that "*papam esse ipsum verum antichristum*" (the pope is himself the true Antichrist) (S.A.II, iv,10).

It is significant that the Greek preposition ἀντί (*anti*) in Koine usage almost always has the meaning "instead of" and not "against." When the New Testament, therefore, uses the name "Antichrist," the common understanding would be that he is a "substitute" Christ, and not just someone who is against Christ. With this in mind, it is doubly significant that the appearance of this beast is lamblike, that is, having the appearance of Christ. In this connection we may be reminded that when the pope visited America a few years ago a number of people were reported in the newspapers to have said that when they met the pope they felt that they were in the very presence of Christ. One of the canonized saints of the Roman Church, Catherine of Siena, called the pope "Jesus Christ on earth." There are those who argue that the pope cannot be the Antichrist today because modern popes are such Christlike men. This verse affords us a powerful antidote to the temptation in that argument. The popes who have been outwardly wicked and depraved are in the minority. Most of them have appeared to be "Lamblike."

But the destructive nature of this beast becomes evident in what he says. His speech is dragonlike, that is, the message he proclaims is the devil's message. What that message is in its essence becomes clear from the first words spoken by the devil in Eden. On the surface that message does not appear to be depraved. Satan at times appears as an angel of light (2 Cor 11:14). After all, he did not urge Adam and Eve to commit adultery or murder. But he did deny the clear word of God and urged Eve to seek her happiness, her "salvation," as it were, in what she could do for herself rather than in all the good things which God had done and supplied for her and her husband. The basic doctrine of the devil is the message of salvation by works. In the canons and decrees of the Council of Trent the Roman church officially condemns and consigns to hell anyone who teaches that men are justified by faith alone and that good works are not necessary for salvation. It has, by that very act, adopted the message of the dragon from hell as its official position and, in effect, has officially declared the clear teaching of Scripture to be untrue. Through the official theology of the Roman Church the devil still tells men that they will not perish if they do the deeds suggested by the church. Many of these deeds sound deceptively biblical. The Roman Church recommends contrition, faith, prayers and fastings as meritorious deeds by which we earn forgiveness and salvation.

But while Rome and the papacy deserve to be identified with this lamblike beast from the earth we should not forget that modern Protestantism has in large measure adopted the dragon's message. Salvation through human effort, to a greater or lesser degree, is a common theme in current Protestant thought. As a result, men seek their salvation not in the grace of God and the merits of Christ apprehended by faith alone but in their own efforts, conversion experiences, and the like. Thus much of Protestantism, though it appears to be "lamblike," has also begun to deliver a dragonlike message. This beast is referred to in all later chapters as "the false prophet."

The beast thus sets himself up as a substitute Christ. The Old Testament prophets had spoken of the coming Savior as a great prophet, and this theme recurs again and again in the New Testament. His message proclaims salvation by grace without works. All those who turn the gospel into a new law and turn even faith and contrition into good works that men must perform as conditions of forgiveness are offering a substitute prophetic message, and not the gospel of Christ. The message still, to many, seems Christlike because it uses all the right words. But it really robs Christ of his glory by ascribing a certain amount of the credit for our salvation to our own works. And no one in the church does that with greater skill than the pope of Rome. While Lenski, Poellot, Little, and other commentators therefore may be justified in saying that the beast from the earth represents "antichristian propaganda," yet they may also be faulted for not seeing the close connection between this verse and the verdict of the Smalcald Articles that "the pope is himself the true Antichrist." Still, in a broader sense, we may say that this beast also represents all doctrine which undermines the gospel and serves the devil's purposes.

Each generation of Christians will have to grapple with heresy where it arises. So in our time we recognize the dragon's voice in humanism, evolutionism, pentecostalism, Mormonism, Russelism, Armstrongism, and other modern heresies —

all of which are the more dangerous because the men who promote them appear to be lamblike. The false teachers still maintain a wardrobe of sheep's clothing.

This beast is a far greater threat to the church than the open enemy represented by the first beast, for false doctrine robs men of life in a far higher sense than the murderous persecutions carried on by the beast from the sea. Persecution may deprive God's children of physical life but false doctrine robs men of spiritual and eternal life.

Yet the two beasts clearly cooperate in their campaign against God and his church. The beast from the earth "exercises all the authority of the first beast before him." Instead of the phrase, "before him" the NIV has the translation, "on his behalf." While "before him" or "in his presence" is the literal translation of the original, yet the equivalent Hebrew phrase, when used in relation to a person with authority, indicates an official position, authorizing the person who stands "before" the ruler to act on his behalf. Thus the phrase may indicate that the second beast serves the purposes of the first beast, just as that beast serves the purposes of the devil, from whom he derives his power and authority (13:2).

The context clarifies the meaning of "all the authority of the first beast." It does not refer primarily to the authority and power that all civil government receives directly from God, but rather to the power and authority it receives from the devil with God's permission. The first beast has authority and power 1) to demand and receive worship and honor from the unbelieving world (13:4), 2) to speak great blasphemies, 3) to endure to the end of time (13:5), 4) to blaspheme the revelation of God and the church (13:6), 5) to persecute the believers, and 6) to enjoy worldwide rule (13:7). The second beast, therefore, in spite of its harmless appearance, is indeed a great enemy of the church. It adds to its own scope of activity that of the first beast.

Paul had said of the false teachers who would come that they would proclaim "doctrines of devils" (1 Tm 4:1). In John's language, they would speak "as the dragon" (13:11). While we may therefore include all false teachers who teach devilish doctrines when we speak of the significance of this beast, yet in the Roman papacy the total activity described here is manifested more clearly than anywhere else. Earlier popes have claimed worldwide secular authority, and later popes have never repudiated that claim. The papacy was the prime mover of many of the bloody persecutions of Christians in the late Middle Ages and in early modern times. With its curse on the biblical doctrine of salvation by grace without works the papacy blasphemes the revelation of God and with its worldwide sacrifice of the mass it denies the all-sufficiency of the one sacrifice by which all those who are sanctified have been forever perfected (He 10:14). By anathematizing as heretics those who teach the biblical doctrine it also slanders the church. The papacy will also endure to the end of time, for the Lord will not destroy that great "man of sin" until the brightness of his coming (2 Th 2:8). By substituting for the invisible kingdom of God its own visible kingdom, the papacy becomes something very much like an earthly government and thus reinforces the tendency of men to look upon worldly rulers as a final source of blessings rather than as instruments of God through whom the Lord wishes to bestow his blessings on men. In this way "he makes the earth and those who dwell in it worship the first beast whose mortal wound was healed" (v. 12).

When Paul describes the activity of the Antichrist he speaks of the "lying wonders" with which he would deceive men (2 Th 2:9,10). John echoes the thought of Paul when he says that this beast "does great miracles so that he even makes fire come down out of heaven on the earth in the sight of men. And he deceives those who dwell on the earth because of the miracles which are given him to perform before the beast, telling those who dwell on the earth to make an image for the beast who had the sword wound but lived."

In the Old Testament the Prophet Elijah had demonstrated that Jahweh is the true God by calling down fire from heaven (1 Kgs 18:24ff). The beast mimics this miracle, and with this sign and others like it he is able to deceive the unbelieving world, "those who dwell on the earth," so that they believe his devilish lies. When Roman Catholic writers, therefore, cite the miracles done by the Roman Church (at Lourdes, for example) as proof for the claim that the Roman Church is the true catholic church, we remember that such miracles are here described as lying wonders (2 Th 2:10) by which the beast deceives the world. While miracles can support true doctrine, it is also true that doctrine is a criterion by which true miracles are to be tested (Dt 13:1ff; Is 8:19,20).

Not only does the beast deceive the world with these false miracles but he persuades those who dwell on the earth to make an idolatrous image of the first beast. The two beasts now join their forces to carry out the devil's intention to destroy the true church. Civil government in its antichristian aspect and the apostate church, which speaks the devil's message rather than the truth of God, combine their power and authority in an effort to destroy the people of God. Church historians will be able to cite countless examples of how the church has called upon the civil authorities to imprison and burn those whom the church had condemned as heretics. Lutheran Christians will in this connection think of the Diet of Worms, where leaders of the Roman Church persuaded the emperor to issue the decree that condemned Martin Luther to death.

This same truth is set before us again in symbolic language when we are told that the false prophet was able to give breath to the image that had been set up so that the image was able to speak and to order the death of all those who refused to worship the image. We know that in later Roman persecutions Christians were often given a choice between death or burning incense before an image of the emperor. This particular loyalty test, it seems, was already applied in John's time. There was, for example, in Pergamos a temple dedicated to emperor worship. Commentators suggest that Antipas (2:13) may have been put to death for refusing to participate in that kind of worship. In any case, John in his vision foresaw the time when the false church would approve of and even encourage the execution of those who would not give idolatrous worship to the anti-christian civil government. Such worship takes place whenever men are ready to obey men rather than God (Ac 4:19).

Death by execution is, however, not the only means employed by the antichristian powers to enforce their demands. The beast also uses economic pressures to achieve its ends and causes all classes of men, the small and the great, the rich and the poor, freemen and slaves, to receive a mark on their right hands or on their foreheads. The word translated as "mark" denotes a brand, or the impression left by a seal. Such a "mark" indicates ownership. Just as God's people in chapter 7 were marked with a seal to show that they had become God's possession, so these people are marked with a seal to indicate that they belong to the beast. This mark gives them the right to engage in commerce and to participate in the economic activity of the community. The sort of thing spoken of here is illustrated in many communist countries, where one must openly demonstrate allegiance to the atheistic form of government in order to participate fully in the business world as well as in the world of politics. In many of those countries, for example, young people are denied a higher education and entrance into the professions unless they join organizations for communist youth. Thus, in a sense, they cannot "buy or sell" unless they have "the mark, the name of the beast or the number of his name." The phrases, "the name of the beast" or "the number of his name," apparently stand in apposition to "the mark," so that the seal impresses either the beast's name or the beast's number on the person who receives the mark.

It is necessary at this point to ask which of the two beasts is meant here. After the first verse and up to the last two verses in the chapter, the name "beast" always refers to the beast from the sea. It is twice identified as "the first beast" and twice as the beast that had recovered from a deadly wound (v. 3,11,14). Three times the name occurs within the phrase, "the image of the beast" (v. 15). The context shows that this is an image of the beast from the sea. Following this chapter, "the beast" designates the first beast and "the false prophet" the second beast.

From all this it would seem that the beast spoken of in the last two verses of this chapter must also be the first beast, the beast from the sea. But, while it is true that the first beast is mentioned by name more frequently, this particular section focuses on the activity of the second beast. The beast from the earth exercises the power of the first beast. He causes the earth and the unbelieving world to worship the beast whose wound had been healed. He does great miracles. He deceives the nations. He causes the people to erect an image to the first beast, and he gives it breath. Finally, he causes men to receive a mark, which includes the name, or number, of the beast. Since this whole section began with the description of this beast from the earth, who now causes men to be branded with a mark of ownership, it is likely that the number is the number of this second beast. But the question cannot be answered with finality. Perhaps the name and number can be assigned to both beasts. We will discuss this question again in our comments on 15:2.

The last verse of this chapter has been the occasion for endless speculation. John writes, "Here is wisdom: Let him who has understanding calculate the number of the beast, for it is the number of a man. And his number is 666."

From the earliest centuries of the church's history many attempts have been made to calculate this number. The church father Irenaeus, who was only one generation removed from St. John, referred to the "many names" that could be found to fit this calculation. In the Greek language every letter of the alphabet has a numerical value, and, because the numerical value of many names is 666, Irenaeus said that it was safer to wait for the fulfillment of the prophecy than to guess and to look for names that would fit. Nevertheless he says a very likely solution could be found in the name Λατεῖνος, the Greek word for "Latin." The numerical value of this combination of Greek letters is 666 (Λ = 30, A = 1, T = 300, E = 5, I = 10, N = 50, O = 70, and Σ = 200).

Some commentators have objected to solutions of this kind because they insist that this type of calculation (called gematria) is found nowhere else in Scripture. This is a weighty argument, but it is by no means conclusive. The word which we have translated "calculate" is used in only one other passage in the New Testament. Jesus speaks of a man who "calculates" the cost of the tower he is planning to build (Lk 14:28). That certainly involves adding the cost of the various items needed for the tower, just as here it would describe the process of adding the numerical value of all the letters in a name.

If this suggestion of Irenaeus is correct it would become apparent why it makes little difference whether it is the first or second beast to whom the number belongs. At John's time the great secular antichrist was the Roman government, and, in connection with the solution proposed above, Irenaeus notes that "those who now govern are Latins." So also the great ecclesiastical Antichrist is the papacy, whose official language to this day is Latin, even if the mass in our time is celebrated in the vernacular. Since the time of the Reformation and the Council of Trent, when the pope was clearly revealed as the Antichrist, we have even more reason to approve of this as a probable solution than Irenaeus did, who said that it was safer to wait for the fulfillment of the prophecy.

But because there is no clear passage of Scripture that demands the type of calculation suggested above, it is probably better to seek a solution more in keeping with the way in which numbers are otherwise used in Revelation. We have seen that the number twelve is a symbol of the church, ten the symbol of completeness, four the number of the world, and seven the number of the covenant or the symbol of God's dealing with men. It has been suggested that six, being very close to, yet always short, of seven, should be viewed as a symbol of the devil's attempt to usurp God's place in the hearts of men and the foreordained failure of that attempt. In the context it would be more fitting to see in this number a symbol of the attempt of

Antichrist to seat himself in the temple of God and to claim divine prerogatives for himself, as Paul describes him (2 Th 2:3-9). Since ten is the number of completenes and 666 is six plus ten times six plus ten times ten times six, this number symbolizes the fact that the Antichrist will never be able to enter into the same kind of covenant relationship with his followers that God has entered with his people. Since three and a half, or half of the covenant number seven, is the number of evil, it is not unthinkable that the number six, or half of twelve, represents the church's enemies. Such an interpretation would fit very well into the context. Irenaeus, in addition to the speculations noted earlier, spoke rather positively about 666 as a summary of all the apostasy which occurred in the beginning, in the intermediate periods, and which will take place at the end.

Some modern Lutheran commentators who reject the interpretation that the beast from the earth is above all else the pope of Rome have argued that the translation, "It is the number of a man" is incorrect, and that we should translate instead, "It is a human number." It is true that neither the word "number" nor the word "man" has an article in the original Greek. For that reason it might be better to translate as the NIV does, "It is a man's number." But the argument that it cannot be the number of a man because it is specifically called the number "of the beast" is untenable. If the Savior can be pictured as a lamb and the devil as a dragon, there is no reason why a man cannot be pictured as a beast.

There are in this chapter a number of details about which we must speak with reserve, but the main thoughts are very clear. The visions tell us plainly that the devil will have two great allies in his attempt to destroy the church. One is the civil government, which uses its brute power to war against the people of God. The other is the apostate church, which still has the outward trappings of Christianity but which undermines faith and even makes it impossible by proclaiming a message that is not the gospel but rather the teaching of the devil. Martin Luther applied this revelation to his own time when, in one of his hymns, he spoke of "the murderous pope and Turk." The Turkish government was an antichristian government which often sought by force of arms to impose Mohammedanism on its subjects and to destroy the Christian church in the countries under its control. The pope also was antichristian and was trying to prevent the reemergence of the gospel by condemning Luther and the message of salvation by grace alone in favor of the devilish doctrine of salvation by works. It behooves Christians of all time, however, to know that great forces are arrayed against them so that they may be moved to watch and pray lest they be pressured into apostasy by wicked governmental agencies or misled into unbelief and false worship by false teachers.

John not only warns against the danger. Having portrayed the terrible enemies intent on destroying the church he now sees another vision in which he reassures his readers that the devil and the two beasts, these three great foes who have been called the "unholy trinity," will not succeed in their efforts.

THE FOURTH VISION: THE 144,000 WITH THE LAMB (14:1-5)

1) Καὶ εἶδον, καὶ ἰδοὺ τὸ Ἀρνίον ἑστὸς ἐπὶ τὸ ὄρος Σιών, καὶ μετ᾽ αὐτοῦ ἑκατὸν τεσσεράκοντα τέσσαρες χιλιάδες ἔχουσαι τὸ ὄνομα αὐτοῦ καὶ τὸ ὄνομα τοῦ Πατρὸς αὐτοῦ γεγραμμένον ἐπὶ τῶν μετώπων αὐτῶν. 2) καὶ ἤκουσα φωνὴν ἐκ τοῦ οὐρανοῦ ὡς φωνὴν ὑδάτων πολλῶν καὶ ὡς φωνὴν βροντῆς μεγάλης, καὶ ἡ φωνὴ ἣν ἤκουσα ὡς κιθαρῳδῶν κιθαριζόντων ἐν ταῖς κιθάραις αὐτῶν. 3) καὶ ᾄδουσιν ᾠδὴν καινὴν ἐνώπιον τοῦ θρόνου καὶ ἐνώπιον τῶν τεσσάρων ζώων καὶ τῶν πρεσβυτέρων· καὶ οὐδεὶς ἐδύνατο μαθεῖν τὴν ᾠδὴν εἰ μὴ αἱ ἑκατὸν τεσσεράκοντα τέσσαρες χιλιάδες, οἱ ἠγορασμένοι ἀπὸ τῆς γῆς. 4) οὗτοί εἰσιν οἳ μετὰ γυναικῶν οὐκ ἐμολύνθησαν· παρθένοι γάρ εἰσιν, οὗτοι οἱ ἀκολουθοῦντες τῷ Ἀρνίῳ ὅπου ἂν ὑπάγῃ. οὗτοι ἠγοράσθησαν ἀπὸ τῶν ἀνθρώπων ἀπαρχὴ τῷ Θεῷ καὶ τῷ Ἀρνίῳ, 5) καὶ ἐν τῷ στόματι αὐτῶν οὐχ εὑρέθη ψεῦδος· ἄμωμοί εἰσιν.

1) *And I saw, and behold, the Lamb standing on Mt. Zion, and with him a hundred-forty-four thousand who had his name and the name of his Father written on their foreheads.* 2) *And I heard a sound from heaven like the sound of much water and like the sound of heavy thunder, and the sound which I heard was like the sound of harpists playing on their harps.* 3) *And they sang a new song before the throne and before the four living creatures and the elders. And no one was able to learn that song except the hundred-forty-four thousand, the ones purchased from the earth.* 4) *These are the ones who were not defiled with women, for they are virgins. These are the ones who keep on following the Lamb wherever he goes. These were purchased from among mankind, firstfruits to God and the Lamb.* 5) *And in their mouths there was not found a lie. They are blameless.*

Just as the description of the great tribulation that is to come on the earth (6:2-17) is followed by the vision of the 144,000 who were sealed on earth and the innumerable host around the throne in heaven (7:1-17), so the fearful picture of the damage done by what has been called "the unholy trinity" (the dragon and the two beasts who serve him) is followed by a vision of the 144,000 in heaven.

We have already noted in our comments on chapter 7 that the 144,000 are the whole invisible church. In chapter 7 the 144,000 are described as people for whose sake the destruction of the world was delayed so that there might be time for them to receive the seal of God on their foreheads. The seal there, of course, is a figure of speech denoting the mark left by the seal. Here they are described as having the name of the Lamb and of his Father written on their foreheads. There is really no difference between the two statements, and the second statement only makes clear what type of seal the angel used in chapter 7. Many of the seals that have been uncovered by archaeologists include the name of the owner in the design. Very often the name is preceded by a preposition indicating that the object stamped with the seal belongs to the man whose name is engraved on the seal.

All of the 144,000 have both the name of the Lamb and the name of his Father written on their foreheads. This is a clear indication that no one belongs to the true God who does not also belong to Christ. He is the only way to the Father, and no one comes to the Father except through him (Jn 14:6). Similarly, no one comes to Jesus unless the Father draws him (Jn 6:44). We have here, therefore, a symbolic representation of the truth which Peter and John proclaimed when they said to the members of the Sanhedrin, "Salvation is found in no one else, for there is no other name under heaven given to men by which we must be saved" (Ac 4:12).

In this vision the 144,000 who belong to God are no longer on earth. They were in the company of the Lamb who was standing on Mt. Zion. Like Jerusalem, Mt. Zion, on which the temple in Jerusalem was built, is in the Bible a symbol of the New Testament church (He 12:22; cp Is 2:1ff; Ro 11:26; Ps 46; Ga 4:26). It would be possible to see in this verse only a symbolic representation of the Savior's presence with his people, but verse 3 places the 144,000 around the throne and in the presence of the four living creatures and the twenty-four elders whom we already met at the beginning of John's vision of the future.

Here we are dealing with the church triumphant. Mt. Zion is in this passage a name for the heavenly Jerusalem, where God's people are forever free from the dangers that threaten them at the hands of the unholy trinity.

And so we have in these verses another representation of the final triumph of the church over all her enemies. John speaks of the joy of that victory when he writes, "I heard a sound from heaven . . . like the sound of harpists playing (literally, "harping") on their harps." Harps (κιθάρα) are mentioned three times in the book of Revelation. In each case they are used to accompany singing around the throne of God. In John' first vision of heaven he saw that the four living creatures and the twenty-four elders had harps with which they accompanied their song of praise to the Lamb (5:8,9). In the introduction to the vision of the seven bowls those who had been victorious over the beast likewise accompanied their singing with harps (16:2,3). The fact that harps accompany the singing of the 144,000 is another indication that Mt. Zion in this vision is a symbolic name for the church triumphant in heaven.

The sound of the harps is described as being "like the sound of much water (literally, "the voice of many waters") and like the sound of heavy thunder." In the opening vision of Revelation the voice of the Savior had been compared to the sound of much water (1:15), or "a thundering waterfall." The same phrase is used for a third time to describe the singing of the victorious saints in a later vision (19:6).

In that later vision, as in the present one, the music is described as a sound of "strong thunders." The phrase "the sound of thunder" is also used three times in Revelation. It is used once to describe the voice of one of the four living creatures in the vision of the four horsemen (6:1), and twice to describe the music of the saints (14:2; 19:6). In the first of those two passages it is spoken of as "great (or heavy) thunder" (βροντῆς μεγάλης), describing the sound of the harps; and in the second as "strong thunders" (βροντῶν ἰσχυρῶν), describing the singing of the redeemed in heaven. This description of the heavenly harping gives emphasis to the large number of the saints, and it must have been a source of comfort to the early church which so often saw itself as a besieged little flock that was in danger of being silenced by imperial persecution. It still offers the same kind of comfort to us today as we see the widespread apostasy of the visible contemporary church, in which the sound of the pure word of God seems to be drowned out by the many voices which spread the message of the unholy trinity.

To the accompaniment of the thundering harps the 144,000 "sing a new song before the throne and before the four living creatures and the elders." Earlier the phrase "a new song" had been used to describe the singing of the elders and the four living creatures (5:9). In that connection we cited a number of passages from the Psalms and Isaiah where this phrase was used. In all these cases there is a clear reference to the salvation that God is preparing for his people. The "new song" is a song of praise in which the believers express gratitude and joy over their salvation.

It is a song that only the redeemed can sing. "And no one was able to learn that song except the hundred-forty-four thousand, the ones purchased from the earth." The article before "song" is an article of previous reference and is therefore very properly translated as a demonstrative pronoun. The perfect tense of the participle "redeemed" reminds us that this is a finished work, the results of which continue into the present. We contributed nothing to bring about our redemption from the earth.

The words of the "new song" are not given, since it can be learned only by those who were purchased, or redeemed, from the earth. The other passage which speaks of a "new song" (5:8,9) speaks of the redemption which the Lamb has accomplished with his blood.

The redeemed are then described in all their innocence and perfection. "These are the ones who were not defiled with women, for they are virgins. These are the ones who follow the Lamb wherever he goes. These were purchased from mankind, firstfruits to God and the Lamb. And in their mouths there was not found a lie. They are blameless."

We noted earlier that the number 144,000 is a symbolic number indicating that we are here dealing with the entire invisible church, the full number of all the elect. They are called "Firstfruits." At first, this sounds as if they are only a portion of the harvest, as if the 144,000 were a special group among the redeemed. The Apostle Paul regularly used the term "firstfruits" to denote the first portion of a larger gift or harvest (Ro 8:23; 11:16; 16:5; 1 Cor 15:2; 16:15). In the Old Testament, however, the firstfruits were the part of the harvest that was brought to the temple as an offering to the Lord. The rest of the harvest was to be used for food and in this sense was reserved for destruction. When this group is therefore called "firstfruits to God and the Lamb," we understand it as the part of the harvest of mankind that is brought to the temple in heaven. As we heard in the first verse of this chapter, they carry the seal and name of God on their foreheads. This clearly distinguishes them from the rest of men who have the mark and name of the beast on the right hand or on the forehead (13:16). This contrast between those who have the mark of the beast and those who bear the seal of God (14:1) also shows that we are here dealing with the whole invisible church. Moreover, the fact that no one can learn the words of the "new song" except the 144,000 also indicates that John is using the word "firstfruits" in the sense of all those who share in the bliss of heaven and escape destruction.

The terms in which the 144,000 are described also lead us to the same conclusion. Because they are described as "virgins who were not defiled with women," popular Roman Catholic thought has sometimes seen in them the celibate priesthood, but even Roman Catholicism's Jerusalem Bible indicates that virginity in this context is a figurative term for faithfulness to God. St. Paul compared the congregation in Corinth to a virgin when he wrote, "I have promised you to one husband, to Christ, so that I might present you as a pure virgin to him" (2 Cor 11:2). In the Old Testament the chosen people were called "virgin" by several prophets (Is 37:22; Jr 14:17; 18:13; 31:4,21; Lm 1:15; 2:13; Am 5:2). This figure of speech is related to the very common designation of the Old Testament church as the wife of Jahweh and the New Testament church as the bride of Christ or the wife of the Lamb. Also closely related is the common designation of idolatry as adultery. In his commentary on Hosea, Luther says that in the imagery of the Old Testament "committing harlotry means practicing idolatry" (LW, vol. 18, p. 4). These 144,000 refused to receive the mark of the beast. They rejected all idolatry and refused to be unfaithful to God and to the Lamb. They remained faithful to the bridegroom who would come at the end of time to claim them as his bride (cp 19:6-8).

It is said of them also that they "keep on following the Lamb wherever he goes." The present participle, "following," indicates that this is a continuous action on their part. The Lord Jesus himself had described his elect in those terms in John's Gospel. He said, "My sheep listen to my voice; I know them, and they follow me. I give them eternal life, and they shall never perish; no one can snatch them out of my hand" (Jn 10:27f). John had heard the Savior speak those words, and those of John's hearers who knew his Gospel well must have remembered that when they heard pastors read these verses.

The words, "These were purchased from among mankind," at first seem to present a difficulty. It would be easy to read into them the idea of a limited atonement, as though the rest had not been purchased. But the Bible teaches very clearly that the Lord Jesus is the Savior of all men, that he shed his blood for all and thus redeemed all men from sin, death and the power of the devil. Peter uses the same word that John uses here (ἀγοράζειν) when he says that the false teachers who deny the Lord and bring upon themselves swift destruction were nevertheless bought by him (2 Pe 2:1). Yet here we are told that these 144,000 are the ones who were purchased, or redeemed, from among mankind, just as several verses earlier they were described as having been purchased from the earth. But the word "redemption" (ἀπολύτρωσις) is used at times to denote our final release from the pains and sorrows of this world (Ro 8:23; Lk 21:28; Eph 1:14; 4:30). Evidently the word "purchase" is also used in a wider sense, denoting not only the payment of the purchase price but also the act of taking to oneself the purchased possession. Since these 144,000 are in heaven it is clear that in their case the Savior not only has paid the price of their redemption (1 Cor 6:20) but also has come to take these purchased people to himself.

Finally, it is said of them that there is no lie in their mouths and that they are blameless. John in this place does not tell us in what their blamelessness consists, but in view of the description of the saints around the throne of God in chapter 7 we can say that they are blameless because they were cleansed from every spot and blemish by the blood of the Lamb. The word John uses here, ἄμωμος, is also used by Paul to describe the church when he says that Christ gave himself for the church to make it holy and blameless (Eph 5:27). Peter used the same word to describe Christ when he spoke of him as a lamb "without blemish" (1 Pe 1:19). Our blamelessness is the imputed righteousness of Christ.

It may seem that John points only to the sanctified lives of the 144,000 when he writes, "In their mouth there was not found a lie." Actually, however, the statement that there is no lie in their mouths is a concrete expression of the blamelessness that is ascribed to them. James says that if any one is never at fault in what he says, he is a perfect man who is able to keep all the members of his body under control (Jas 3:2). To be free of lying is therefore equivalent to being free of every sin. This close relation between being free of lying and being blameless is illustrated when the Lord Jesus is described as one who committed no sin and in whose mouth no deceit was found (1 Pe 2:22; Is 53:9).

Lying is a sin which is often singled out in Scripture as being especially hateful to God (see, *e.g.*, Pr 6:17; Ps 5:6). It is also a sin with which all men are charged (Ro 3:4), and for which men will finally be cast into the lake of fire (21:8). Since lying is such a common sin, we see in this verse not merely a reference to the sanctified lives of God's people, but particularly to that forgiveness which cleanses their lips from all iniquity (Is 6:7). The words are a concrete example of the blamelessness that is a characteristic of these followers of the Lamb, a blamelessness that finally always is a gift which God bestows on them through his Son and his atoning blood. This Lamb, before whom they stand, is after all the Lamb of God which takes away the sin of the world (Jn 1:29), the Lamb that was slain and has redeemed us to God by his blood (5:9), the Lamb in whose blood the saints have washed their robes and made them white (7:14). Because of what he has done for them they are blameless. The lies of which they, like Peter, may have been guilty have been forgotten by the God who promises not to remember our sins (Jr 31:34).

The scene now shifts back to the earth and John describes the fifth vision in this series.

THE FIFTH VISION: THE THREE ANGELS (14:6-13)

6) Καὶ εἶδον ἄλλον ἄγγελον πετόμενον ἐν μεσουρανήματι, ἔχοντα εὐαγγέλιον αἰώνιον εὐαγγελίσαι ἐπὶ τοὺς καθημένους ἐπὶ τῆς γῆς καὶ ἐπὶ πᾶν ἔθνος καὶ φυλὴν καὶ γλῶσσαν καὶ λαόν, 7) λέγων ἐν φωνῇ μεγάλῃ, Φοβήθητε τὸν Θεὸν καὶ δότε αὐτῷ δόξαν, ὅτι ἦλθεν ἡ ὥρα τῆς κρίσεως αὐτοῦ, καὶ προσκυνήσατε τῷ ποιήσαντι τὸν οὐρανὸν καὶ τὴν γῆν καὶ θάλασσαν καὶ πηγὰς ὑδάτων. 8) Καὶ ἄλλος ἄγγελος δεύτερος ἠκολούθησεν λέγων, Ἔπεσεν ἔπεσεν Βαβυλὼν ἡ μεγάλη, ἣ ἐκ τοῦ οἴνου τοῦ θυμοῦ τῆς πορνείας αὐτῆς πεπότικεν πάντα τὰ ἔθνη. 9) Καὶ ἄλλος ἄγγελος τρίτος ἠκολούθησεν αὐτοῖς λέγων ἐν φωνῇ μεγάλῃ, Εἴ τις προσκυνεῖ τὸ θηρίον καὶ τὴν εἰκόνα αὐτοῦ, καὶ λαμβάνει χάραγμα ἐπὶ τοῦ μετώπου αὐτοῦ ἢ ἐπὶ τὴν χεῖρα αὐτοῦ, 10) καὶ αὐτὸς πίεται ἐκ τοῦ οἴνου τοῦ θυμοῦ τοῦ Θεοῦ τοῦ κεκερασμένου ἀκράτου ἐν τῷ ποτηρίῳ τῆς ὀργῆς αὐτοῦ, καὶ βασανισθήσεται ἐν πυρὶ καὶ θείῳ ἐνώπιον ἀγγέλων ἁγίων καὶ ἐνώπιον τοῦ Ἀρνίου. 11) καὶ ὁ καπνὸς τοῦ βασανισμοῦ αὐτῶν εἰς αἰῶνας αἰώνων ἀναβαίνει, καὶ οὐκ ἔχουσιν ἀνάπαυσιν ἡμέρας καὶ νυκτὸς οἱ προσκυνοῦντες τὸ θηρίον καὶ τὴν εἰκόνα

αὐτοῦ, καὶ εἴ τις λαμβάνει τὸ χάραγμα τοῦ ὀνόματος αὐτοῦ.
12) Ὧδε ἡ ὑπομονὴ τῶν ἁγίων ἐστίν, οἱ τηροῦντες τὰς ἐντολὰς
τοῦ Θεοῦ καὶ τὴν πίστιν Ἰησοῦ. 13) Καὶ ἤκουσα φωνῆς ἐκ τοῦ
οὐρανοῦ λεγούσης, Γράψον, Μακάριοι οἱ νεκροὶ οἱ ἐν Κυρίῳ ἀποθνήσκοντες ἀπ᾽ ἄρτι. ναί, λέγει τὸ Πνεῦμα, ἵνα ἀναπαήσονται ἐκ τῶν κόπων αὐτῶν· τὰ γὰρ ἔργα αὐτῶν ἀκολουθεῖ μετ᾽ αὐτῶν.

6) *And I saw another angel flying in midheaven, having the everlasting gospel to preach to those who live on the earth, namely, to every nation and tribe and language and people,*
7) *saying with a loud voice, "Fear God and give him praise, because the hour of his judgment has come, and worship him who made the sky and the earth and the sea and fountains of water."*

8) *And another angel, a second one, followed, saying, "Fallen, fallen is Babylon the Great which made all nations drink of the wine of her adulterous desire."*

9) *And another angel, a third one, followed them, saying with a loud voice, "If anyone worships the beast and his image and*
receives a mark on his forehead or on his hand, 10) *he will also*
drink of the wine of God's wrath which is poured unmixed into the cup of his anger, and he will be tormented in burning sulphur
before the holy angels and before the Lamb. 11) *And the smoke of*
their torment rises forever and ever, and those who worship the beast and his image, and anyone who receives the mark of his
name, have no rest by day and by night." 12) *Here is the patient*
endurance of the saints who keep the commands of God and their faith in Jesus.

13) *And I heard a voice from the sky saying, "Write! Blessed are the dead who die in the Lord from now on. Yes, says the Spirit, that they may rest from their labors, for their works accompany them."*

The vision of the angel flying in midheaven with the everlasting gospel to preach has in Lutheranism traditionally been interpreted as a prophecy concerning the Reformation. The verses portraying this vision constitute one of the historic epistle lessons for the Reformation Festival. We have no quarrel with this interpretation if these verses are not treated as a direct prophecy pointing specifically and only to the work of Dr. Martin Luther. It is in keeping with the idealistic method of interpreting the book, however, to read these verses as a message of God's comfort addressed to the church after the previous chapter's alert against false doctrine.

The first three visions in this series portrayed the three great enemies of the church, the devil and the two beasts. After this, John reassures the church of its final victory in the vision of the 144,000 before the throne. Now, in these verses, he in a symbolic way reminds the church of the Savior's promise that the gospel of the kingdom will be preached to the end of time (Mt 24:14). In spite of the efforts of the devil and the unbelieving world to silence the proclamation of the pure doctrine, the angel proclaiming the gospel will keep flying in midheaven.

It is perfectly proper, then, to see one fulfillment of that promise in the Lutheran Reformation which is history's most prominent illustration of the principle that God will not allow his word to be silenced. But we may also see an illustration of this truth in every other historical movement in which the gospel has been clearly and emphatically proclaimed. The vision simply assures us that false teachers will never silence the preaching of the gospel.

The basic lesson of this vision is further emphasized when the proclamation of the church is called the *everlasting* gospel. Just as the Savior promised that the gates of hell would never prevail against the church, so he also promised that his words would never pass away.

The promise that the gospel would be preached for a witness to all nations (Mt 24:14) is emphatically repeated here when we are told that the angel preached to "those who live on the earth, namely, to every nation and tribe and language and people." This again is one of the seven passages in Revelation in which four terms are used to describe the people of the earth (see 5:9). It is, however, the only passage in which the four terms are preceded by the phrase, "those who live on the earth." It is obvious that we are not dealing here with five groupings. The last four terms stand in apposition to the first phrase. The καὶ before "to every nation" is an explanatory καὶ and we may translate "namely," rather than "and."

Even though the KJV has translated "those who dwell [NIV: live] on the earth," this is not in the original Greek the same phrase that we find in other passages translated in this same or a similar way (see 3:10; 6:10; 8:13; 11:10; 13:8,12,14; 17:2,8). In all those passages the significant Greek word is the participle of κατοικέω (KJV: "those who dwell," "inhabiters"; NIV: "those who live," "inhabitants"). That phrase is always used to denote unbelievers. The common phrase is a reference to all those who make their home on the earth, those who cannot honestly sing, "Heaven is my home." In this passage the Greek phrase is the uncommon τοὺς καθημένους, literally, "those who sit on the earth," and it evidently does not, like τοὺς κατοικοῦντας (those who make their home on the earth), necessarily denote only unbelievers, for some of these people will surely heed the gospel message and be saved.

While the message which the angel proclaims to those who live on the earth is described as "the everlasting gospel" (v. 6), the words of the angel as they are quoted (v. 7) can hardly be viewed as a summary of that gospel message. The visions of the preceding chapter have made it crystal clear that this gospel is the good news of our redemption through the blood of the Lamb. The quoted words of the angel should be viewed rather as a summary of the purpose for which the gospel is proclaimed.

The angel says, "Fear God and give him praise, because the hour of his judgment has come, and worship him who made the sky and the earth and the sea and fountains of waters." The term, "the fear of God," covers a broad spectrum of meaning in the Holy Scriptures, ranging from abject terror before the wrath of God to childlike awe and respect before his ineffable grace. For the sinner the fear of God is "terror smiting the conscience through the knowledge of sin." That kind of fear is described by the Lord when he says, "Be afraid of (KJV: fear) the one who can destroy both body and soul in hell" (Mt 10:28). For the forgiven sinner the fear of God is holy awe which results from a contemplation of the undeserved pardon that has come to him from the just and holy God who is also the God of infinite grace. Of this latter kind of fear the psalmist spoke when he wrote, "With you there is forgiveness; therefore you are feared" (Ps 130:3). It is this trusting, loving fear that is primarily called for in the message of the angel, for only this fear is the concomitant of the preaching of the gospel.

This should not be understood to mean that the first kind of fear is never found in the heart of a believing child of God. Because of weakness of faith we are not always as sure as we ought to be of our forgiveness. Christians are sometimes also terrified at the thought of God's holy wrath. Such fear, however, is a characteristic of the old Adam rather than of the new man. The Lutheran confessions define the "childlike fear" of a Christian as a fear (*Erschrecken, pavor*, being afraid) which is relieved by faith, while the "slavish fear" of the unbeliever is the same kind of fear, but which is not relieved by faith (Apol. XII, 38).

Those who dwell on the earth are also summoned to give praise to God. Such praise also is a fruit of the gospel. Only those who through the preaching of the gospel have come to know the Lord as the God of forgiving grace in Christ can truly praise him. For apart from Christ the true God is a consuming fire (He 12:29) before whom no sinner can stand (Ps 130:3).

Nevertheless, here it would not be proper to restrict the meaning of the fear of God to trusting awe. The message is, after all, addressed to "every nation and tribe and language and people." Many of those who hear the message of God's forgiveness will not believe it. When they hear the angel say, "The hour of his judgment has come," their fear will be the abject terror that must grip the heart of the sinner who has rejected God's forgiveness through unbelief.

Finally, the angel calls upon men to worship the Creator of all things. "Worship" (προσκυνήσατε) means "kneel before." When the hour of judgment comes all people will bow the knee before the Creator (Php 2:10) — the believers, in joyful awe; the unbelievers, in abject terror.

While the message of the first angel is the life-saving gospel, the two other angels lay their emphasis on the law. The second angel proclaims God's judgment against Babylon. This is the first of the six passages in Revelation that mention Babylon. The first words of this angel are a quotation from the Old Testament. The Prophet Isaiah wrote, "Babylon has fallen, has fallen" (Is 21:9).

It is against this Old Testament background that we must interpret the Revelation passages that speak of Babylon. In Isaiah's time Babylon was threatening God's people with destruction. In John's time Babylon became a name for Rome, which was intent on destroying the church. Here its meaning cannot be restricted to Rome since the context ties it in with the final judgment on the last day. Therefore "Babylon" signifies all the enemies of the church for all time.

By proclaiming the fall of Babylon the angel assures the church of final victory. In the Old Testament the fall of Babylon was a signal of the imminent release of the chosen people from captivity and their return to the promised land. So the vision of the fall of the New Testament Babylon is a promise that the great tribulation which this wicked city has inflicted on the New Testament church will also come to an end and that the church will join the Lamb on Mt. Zion in the new Jerusalem (v. 1-5).

Babylon is described as "the great (city) which made all the nations drink of the wine of her adulterous desire." The KJV translation, "of the wine of the wrath of her fornication," though possible, does not seem to be correct. While θυμός sometimes means "wrath," the original meaning of the word is "deep desire or feeling." The NIV translation, "the wine of her maddening adulteries" also does not correspond to the original, which reads literally, "the wine of the desire of her fornication." This is a typical Hebraistic construction which would normally be translated in the way we have suggested, "the wine of her adulterous desire."

The significance of the phrase is not difficult to discover. The godless world and the apostate church, represented here by "Babylon," are always intent on leading men away from the worship of the true God. In biblical terminology, spiritual fornication is unfaithfulness to the God who has revealed himself in the Word. Adulterous Babylon seeks to persuade men to join her in spiritual adultery by proclaiming a false religion.

The message of the third angel is likewise one of doom and judgment. Those who drink the wine offered by Babylon and worship the beast and his image rather than the God who made heaven and earth will also "drink the wine of God's wrath which is poured unmixed into the cup of his anger." In this case we have translated θυμός with "wrath," because the context informs us that the "deep feeling" that is poured into the cup is God's anger (ὀργή). To drink the cup of God's anger is a common biblical figure of speech signifying an experience of God's punishment.

The wine of God's wrath is poured "unmixed" into this cup. It was customary in ancient times to mix wine with water. But nothing will dilute the bitterness of this drink. The full force of God's wrath will strike them. It will no longer be tempered with mercy.

This same thought is then expressed in more literal terms. The worshipers of the beast, who wear his brand, will be tormented in burning sulphur (literally, "in fire and sulphur") in the presence of the holy angels and the Lamb. The smoke of their torment will rise up through all eternity. Neither by day nor by night will they find rest. Those words describe the suffering of the damned. The Savior himself spoke in similar terms when he consigned those at his left to everlasting fire prepared for the devil and his angels (Mt 25:41).

There is an important lesson in the assertion that the lost are tormented in the presence of the holy angels and in the presence of the Lamb. The sinful human heart rebels against the idea of an eternal punishment in which the damned will never find rest. Men protest again and again that such punishment is incompatible with the love and mercy of God. Even true Christians sometimes find it difficult to accept this truth. But the Lamb, who bore the sins of the world, the loving Savior who gave his life for our salvation, is also the stern judge who sends those who reject his grace into eternal punishment. John evidently sees no inconsistency in this, and the holy angels who see all this utter no word of protest. It happens in their presence, and John's words imply that they concur wholeheartedly in the Lord's judgment. It is therefore fitting that God's saints (ἅγιοι) should adopt the attitude of the holy angels (ἀγγέλων ἁγίων) and confess that also in this, "he has done all things well" (Mk 7:37). In that confidence the people of God silence the objections of their own rebellious hearts.

In fact, John expects God's people to find encouragement in this scene. He writes, "Here is the patient endurance of the saints." Patient endurance (ὑπομονή) is a willingness "to remain under" and to bear patiently the burden which the Lord places upon us. In the days of fierce persecution in which John shared these visions with a suffering church, there must have been many Christians who were tempted to avoid persecution by acceding to the demands of the government and to renounce, or at least to hide, their faith in Jesus. But the message of the gospel (v. 6,7), the predicted defeat of the enemy (v. 8), and the sad end of those who bowed down before the beast (v. 9-11), all this was to be a source of encouragement, to help them suffer patiently all that a wicked government might do to them. The NIV again adds the words "calls for" to the original text (see the comments on 13:10).

These patient saints are described as "those who keep the commandments of God." Through the forgiveness that Jesus has earned for them they have become saints, holy people. As trees that have become good, they also bear good fruit (Mt 7:17). They have not become holy by keeping the commandments. That would be a clear denial of everything that John teaches about the holiness of God's people. They have been redeemed by the blood of the Lamb (5:9). Their garments have been washed in that same blood (7:14). In another letter John had written that we are cleansed from all sin by the blood of God's Son (1 Jn 1:7). Their holiness, therefore, is not a result of their obedience to the commandments. Rather, because they are saints, because they are forgiven sinners who have been sanctified and cleansed by holy baptism (Eph 5:26), they love the Lord who first loved them (1 Jn 4:19), and that love is the first step toward perfect obedience to all the other commandments of God's law. In his first epistle John had written, "This is the love of God, that we keep his commandments" (1 Jn 5:3). While their love and their obedience will never become perfect in this life, yet they have made a beginning and therefore they can rightly be described as those who keep the commandments of God. Of them it can no longer be said that their attitude is one of hatred and enmity against God, nor that they are unable to be subject to the law of God (Ro 8:7). All Christians are therefore properly described as "those who obey the commandments of God."

They are also described as those who keep "their faith in Jesus." There is no possessive pronoun in the original, which reads, literally, the "faith of Jesus," as the KJV translates. But the Greek definite article sometimes is the equivalent of a possessive pronoun. Moreover, "the faith of Jesus" is not the faith that Jesus has. "Of Jesus" is an objective genitive. Just as in English "the love of God" can mean the love which we have for God (*e.g.*, "That man has no love of God in his heart"), so in Greek "the faith of Jesus" means the faith we have in Jesus. Many commentators understand "faith" (πίστις) here to mean "faithfulness" to Jesus. Such an interpretation is remotely possible, since the Greek word has both meanings. However, it is difficult to see how Christians could keep (τηρεῖν) the faithfulness of Jesus. Besides, John in all of his writings uses this word only four times, and it would be difficult to show from the context that he ever uses it to denote "faithfulness." He does, however, use the verb (believe) very often, always in the sense of believing something or having confidence in someone. So it is most likely that in his usage πίστις means "faith" or "confidence." This confidence in Jesus makes patient endurance possible. This confidence also has made them saints, for through faith we appropriate to ourselves the forgiveness that God proclaims to us in the gospel.

The vision of the three angels closes with a final word of comfort. A voice from heaven commands John to write: "Blessed are the dead who die in the Lord from now on. Yes, says the Spirit, that they may rest from their labors, for their works accompany them."

Those who die in the Lord are those who die with their connection with Christ unbroken. Since that bond consists in faith, to "die in the Lord" means to die as a believing child of God. Such people are "blessed" (μακάριοι), that is, happy. This promise must have had special meaning for Christians who were in danger of being put to death for their faith. The unbelieving world may have looked upon them as miserable and wretched fools who did not know what was good for them. But just as Paul had written to the Christians in Rome that persecution and the sword could not separate them from the love of Christ (Ro 8:35), so John assured the members of the seven churches in Asia Minor that those who died as believing children of God would experience happiness from the moment of their death. They would not need to wait until a manifest victory over their enemies had been won in this world.

For those who had received the mark of the beast the hour of God's judgment would bring unending torment, even though in this present world they had appeared to be on the winning side. But for those who die in the Lord, death will be a release from labor and toil. The word we have translated "labors" (κόπων) also means "troubles" or "difficulties." The basic meaning remains the same. For God's people death brings relief from all the unpleasant experiences which we must endure in this world of sin.

The significance of the final words in this message of comfort is not clear from the immediate context. The Spirit says, "Their works accompany them." This certainly cannot mean that their works will earn the reward of salvation, for this would contradict the central message of the gospel which says that we are saved by grace without works. In light of the Savior's teaching concerning the last judgment (Mt 25:34-40), however, we may say with confidence that their works accompany them as evidences of the faith by which they were justified.

THE SIXTH VISION: THE HARVEST (14:14-20)

14) Καὶ εἶδον, καὶ ἰδοὺ νεφέλη λευκή, καὶ ἐπὶ τὴν νεφέλην καθήμενον ὅμοιον υἱὸν ἀνθρώπου, ἔχων ἐπὶ τῆς κεφαλῆς αὐτοῦ στέφανον χρυσοῦν καὶ ἐν τῇ χειρὶ αὐτοῦ δρέπανον ὀξύ. 15) Καὶ ἄλλος ἄγγελος ἐξῆλθεν ἐκ τοῦ ναοῦ, κράζων ἐν φωνῇ μεγάλῃ τῷ καθημένῳ ἐπὶ τῆς νεφέλης, Πέμψον τὸ δρέπανόν σου καὶ θέρισον, ὅτι ἦλθεν ἡ ὥρα θερίσαι, ὅτι ἐξηράνθη ὁ θερισμὸς τῆς γῆς. 16) καὶ ἔβαλεν ὁ καθήμενος ἐπὶ τῆς νεφέλης τὸ δρέπανον αὐτοῦ ἐπὶ τὴν γῆν καὶ ἐθερίσθη ἡ γῆ. 17) Καὶ ἄλλος ἄγγελος ἐξῆλθεν ἐκ τοῦ ναοῦ τοῦ ἐν τῷ οὐρανῷ, ἔχων καὶ αὐτὸς δρέπανον ὀξύ. 18) καὶ ἄλλος

ἄγγελος ἐξῆλθεν ἐκ τοῦ θυσιαστηρίου, ὁ ἔχων ἐξουσίαν ἐπὶ τοῦ πυρός, καὶ ἐφώνησεν φωνῇ μεγάλῃ τῷ ἔχοντι τὸ δρέπανον τὸ ὀξὺ λέγων, Πέμψον σου τὸ δρέπανον τὸ ὀξὺ καὶ τρύγησον τοὺς βότρυας τῆς ἀμπέλου τῆς γῆς, ὅτι ἤκμασαν αἱ σταφυλαὶ αὐτῆς. 19) καὶ ἔβαλεν ὁ ἄγγελος τὸ δρέπανον αὐτοῦ εἰς τὴν γῆν, καὶ ἐτρύγησεν τὴν ἄμπελον τῆς γῆς καὶ ἔβαλεν εἰς τὴν ληνὸν τοῦ θυμοῦ τοῦ Θεοῦ τὸν μέγαν. 20) καὶ ἐπατήθη ἡ ληνὸς ἔξωθεν τῆς πόλεως, καὶ ἐξῆλθεν αἷμα ἐκ τῆς ληνοῦ ἄχρι τῶν χαλινῶν τῶν ἵππων, ἀπὸ σταδίων χιλίων ἑξακοσίων.

14) *And I saw a white cloud, and sitting on the cloud one like a human being, who had on his head a gold crown and in his hand a sharp sickle.* 15) *And another angel came out of the temple, crying with a loud voice to the one who was sitting on the cloud, "Send your sickle and reap, for the hour to reap has come, because the harvest of the earth is dead ripe."* 16) *And the one sitting on the cloud swung his sickle on the earth, and the earth was harvested.*

17) *And another angel came out of the temple which is in heaven. He also had a sharp sickle.* 18) *And another angel, who was in charge of the fire, came out from the altar and cried with a loud voice to the one who had the sharp sickle, "Send your sharp sickle and gather the grape clusters of the vine of the earth, for her grapes are ripe.* 19) *And the angel threw his sickle on the earth, and he harvested the vine of the earth and threw it into the great winepress of the wrath of God.* 20) *And the winepress was trampled outside the city, and blood flowed from the winepress, reaching the horses' bridles for a distance of 1,600 stadia.*

The is the sixth in this series of visions. It is beyond question a representation of the day of judgment. In one of his parables the Lord had described the last judgment in similar terms (Mt 13:24-30,36-43), and in the Old Testament the Prophet Joel had described the last judgment in the words:

> Swing the sickle, for the harvest is ripe.
> Come trample the grapes, for the winepress is full
> and the vats overflow —
> so great is their wickedness (Jl 3:13).

The person sitting on the white cloud, while he is not identified by name, is certainly the Lord Jesus. He is described as one like "a human being," literally, "a son of man" (υἱὸς ἀνθρώπου). The comments on chapter 1 give the reasons why the KJV is incorrect in translating this phrase as a proper name. John here calls our attention to the fact that the supreme judge on the last day will be a human being. He made the same point in his

Gospel when he wrote, "The Father . . . has given him authority to judge because he is the Son of Man," (υἱὸς ἀνθρώπου) (Jn 5:27). At first glance it may appear that this passage demonstrates that our translation of υἱὸς ἀνθρώπου as "a human being" or "a son of man" is incorrect. But, as we pointed out (1:13), the name "the Son of Man" is used almost eighty times in the four Gospels, and in every passage except one both nouns have the article in the original Greek (ὁ υἱὸς τοῦ ἀνθρώπου). The absence of the article in John 5:27 is in accord with Greek usage, for when the predicate precedes the copula, as it does in this passage, the noun is definite even without the article (cp Jn 1:49 in the Greek text). Paul also told the people of Athens that God would some day judge the world by a man (Ac 17:31). To know that we will be judged by one who is a man like us should also be a source of comfort.

The judge sitting on the cloud wore a crown (στέφανος) of gold, a symbol of his royal authority. In his hand he held a sharp sickle, an instrument that a farmer in biblical times used to harvest his grain field.

An angel then came out of the temple to announce to the judge that the earth was ready for harvesting. This detail once more reminds us that the judge who presides over this trial is a man whose commission to carry out the judgment comes from God "out of the temple" in heaven. The angel also gives the reason why the harvest should now proceed. "The harvest of the earth is dead ripe," literally, "dried." The words make it plain that this is a grain harvest. When the harvest is ripe and the stems and kernels of the grain are dried, nothing can be gained by waiting longer. All that the farmer can realize from that field is there for the taking. In fact, any delay beyond that point only runs the risk of loss. So at just the right moment and at the command of the angel, "the one sitting on the cloud swung his sickle, and the earth was harvested."

In chapter 7 the four angels were commanded to hold the winds of destruction in check until all the servants of God were sealed, that is, until all the elect had been safely brought into the kingdom by the preaching of the gospel and the administration of the sacrament of baptism. Here that same truth is taught from another point of view. The harvest is "dead ripe," all the elect have been won, and the earth is no longer to be a place where men have the opportunity to come to faith. The time has come for the "wheat" to be gathered "into his barn" (Mt 13:12). This was the moment of fulfillment for the sowers who had gone out to sow the seed (Mt 13:1-9).

When John the Baptist (Mt 3:12) spoke in terms of wheat being gathered into the Lord's barn (NIV), or garner (KJV), he also spoke of the chaff that would be burned in unquenchable fire — a symbolic description of the fate of unbelievers in hell. But in the second part of John's vision the unbelievers are not compared to chaff in the grain harvest. Instead, the judgment of the wicked is compared to a harvest of grapes. It is striking that this grape harvest is not conducted directly by the man sitting on the cloud. Rather, "another angel" is sent out of the temple for that purpose. Like the man on the cloud, he also carries a sharp sickle. Just as the man on the cloud was commanded by an angel from the temple to begin the grain harvest, so a third angel, who "came out of the altar of incense" ordered this angel with the sharp sickle to commence the grape harvest.

We say that this is striking, for in other passages that speak of the last judgment, both in Revelation and in other parts of Scripture, the condemnation of the wicked is an act ascribed to the Lord Jesus (*e.g.,* Re 6:16; Mt 25:41). We are not told why in this vision the harvest of the wicked is carried out by an angel. It may be that the Holy Spirit wanted to remind us that God has "no pleasure in the death of the wicked" (Eze 3:11), and that "the Son of Man did not come to destroy men's lives but to save them" (Lk 9:55). At the same time it should be noted that the angel who harvests the wicked comes "out of the temple." He is obviously a messenger of God. John's way of presenting the last judgment here alerts us once more to the difficulty that human reason has in understanding the great truth that the God of justice who decrees the damnation of the wicked (Dt 27:26) is also the God of grace who wants all men to be saved (2 Tm 2:4).

The angel who came "out of the altar" is further described as the one who was "in charge of the fire." The significance of that description is very difficult to determine. Not every detail of the Savior's parables can be pressed to portray a spiritual truth. The same thing can be said of the visions of Revelation. Instead of using guesswork to find some spiritual meaning in this description of the angel, it is better to see it as a dramatic embellishment.

At the command of this angel who was in charge of the fire used at the altar, the angel who had come out of the temple harvested the grapes of the earth with his sickle. The bunches of grapes (the whole vine?) are cast into the great wine-press of the wrath of God. The word "great" stands in a very emphatic position here. Translated word for word, the original reads, "into the wine press of the wrath of God, the great one" (cp the Greek in 6:17, where the normal word order is found). By this emphatic position of the word "great" at the end of the sentence, we are alerted to the fact that this day of judgment is different from every other "day of the Lord" that had preceded it. The fact that John's words can be understood to mean that the whole vine is cast into the wine press is another indication that this is the last "day of the Lord," the last judgment.

The wine press was trampled outside the city. Throughout Revelation "the city" is usually a name for the church. Earlier, in chapter 11, we saw the Gentiles, the unbelievers, "trampling" (πατήσουσιν) the holy city underfoot for forty-two months. Now the grapes that symbolize these same unbelievers are "trampled" (ἐπατήθη) outside the city. The separation of believers from unbelievers, which the Savior had spoken of in the parable of the tares (Mt 13:24-30, 36-43) and of the net (Mt 13:47-50) has now taken place.

The finality and the severity of this judgment on the unbelieving world is graphically portrayed when we are told that "the blood" that came out of this great wine press covered the earth for a distance of 1,600 stadia. A stadion [our Engish word stadium] is about 600 feet. In depth it reached to the bridles of the horses. The blood that the priests carried into the temple was evidence that the death of the animal offered as a sacrifice for sin had taken place. John was well acquainted with the Old Testament declaration that the "life is in the blood" (Lv 17:11). This blood flowing out of the great wine press of God's wrath is a grim reminder that the lot of all unbelievers is eternal death outside of and away from the city of God.

This whole vision is so obviously a portrayal of the final judgment that only blind dispensationalists or rabid millennialists can fail to see it. The text makes it clear that this is the judgment of the whole earth (v. 16,19). We have already noted that the number four in Revelation is almost always in some way associated with the earth, while ten is the number of completeness. The multiplied squares of four and ten produce the number 1600. We may confidently say therefore that the number 1600 at the end of this verse, like the emphatic "great" at the end of the previous verse, is another reminder that this is the *final* judgment of the *whole* earth.

We would expect that this vision of the last judgment would bring this series of visions to a close. But we note here exactly the same pattern that we have already observed in the vision of the seven seals. The opening of this sixth seal brings John the first vision of the day of judgment (6:12-17). Then, after an interlude in which John has a vision of the church on earth and in heaven (7:1-17), the opening of the seventh seal introduces the vision of the seven trumpets. Here the sixth vision in the series brings John another vision of the last judgment (14:14-20). This vision of judgment day is then followed by a seventh vision in which John sees the church triumphant in heaven and is alerted to the vision of the seven bowls (NIV), or vials (KJV). (See the charts on pages 22-23.)

THE SEVENTH VISION: THE ANGELS WITH THE SEVEN LAST PLAGUES (15:1-8)

1) Καὶ εἶδον ἄλλο σημεῖον ἐν τῷ οὐρανῷ μέγα καὶ θαυμαστόν, ἀγγέλους ἑπτὰ ἔχοντας πληγὰς ἑπτὰ τὰς ἐσχάτας, ὅτι ἐν αὐταῖς ἐτελέσθη ὁ θυμὸς τοῦ Θεοῦ. 2) Καὶ εἶδον ὡς θάλασσαν ὑαλίνην μεμιγμένην πυρί, καὶ τοὺς νικῶντας ἐκ τοῦ θηρίου καὶ ἐκ τῆς εἰκόνος αὐτοῦ καὶ ἐκ τοῦ ἀριθμοῦ τοῦ ὀνόματος αὐτοῦ ἑστῶτας ἐπὶ τὴν θάλασσαν τὴν ὑαλίνην, ἔχοντας κιθάρας τοῦ Θεοῦ. 3) Καὶ ᾄδουσιν τὴν ᾠδὴν Μωϋσέως τοῦ δούλου τοῦ Θεοῦ καὶ τὴν ᾠδὴν τοῦ Ἀρνίου, λέγοντες,

> **Μεγάλα καὶ θαυμαστὰ τὰ ἔργα σου, Κύριε ὁ Θεὸς ὁ Παντοκράτωρ· δίκαιαι καὶ ἀληθιναὶ αἱ ὁδοί σου, 4) ὁ Βασιλεὺς τῶν ἐθνῶν· τίς οὐ μὴ φοβηθῇ, Κύριε, καὶ δοξάσει τὸ ὄνομά σου· ὅτι μόνος ὅσιος, ὅτι πάντα τὰ ἔθνη ἥξουσιν καὶ προσκυνήσουσιν ἐνώπιόν σου, ὅτι τὰ δικαιώματά σου ἐφανερώθησαν.**

5) Καὶ μετὰ ταῦτα εἶδον, καὶ ἠνοίγη ὁ ναὸς τῆς σκηνῆς τοῦ μαρτυρίου ἐν τῷ οὐρανῷ, 6) καὶ ἐξῆλθον οἱ ἑπτὰ ἄγγελοι οἱ ἔχοντες τὰς ἑπτὰ πληγὰς ἐκ τοῦ ναοῦ, ἐνδεδυμένοι λίνον καθαρὸν λαμπρὸν καὶ περιεζωσμένοι περὶ τὰ στήθη ζώνας χρυσᾶς. 7) καὶ ἓν ἐκ τῶν τεσσάρων ζώων ἔδωκεν τοῖς ἑπτὰ ἀγγέλοις ἑπτὰ φιάλας χρυσᾶς γεμούσας τοῦ θυμοῦ τοῦ Θεοῦ τοῦ ζῶντος εἰς τοὺς αἰῶνας τῶν αἰώνων. 8) καὶ ἐγεμίσθη ὁ ναὸς καπνοῦ ἐκ τῆς δόξης τοῦ Θεοῦ καὶ ἐκ τῆς δυνάμεως αὐτοῦ, καὶ οὐδεὶς ἐδύνατο εἰσελθεῖν εἰς τὸν ναὸν ἄχρι τελεσθῶσιν αἱ ἑπτὰ πληγαὶ τῶν ἑπτὰ ἀγγέλων.

1) *And I saw another sign in the sky, great and marvelous: seven angels with seven plagues, the last ones, because in them the wrath of God came to completion.*

2) *And I saw what looked like a sea of glass mixed with fire, and on the sea of glass stood those who had won the victory over the beast and his image and the number of his name.* 3) *They held the harps of God, and they sang the song of Moses, the servant of God, and the song of the Lamb, saying,*

Great and marvelous are your works,
O Lord God Almighty;
Just and true are your ways,
4) *O King of the nations;*
Who will not fear you, O Lord,
and praise your name?
For you alone are holy;
for all the nations will come
and will bow down before you;
For your righteous judgments
have become manifest.

5) *And after these things I saw the sanctuary of the tabernacle of the testimony opened in heaven,* 6) *and the seven angels who hold the seven plagues came out of the sanctuary. They were clothed with clean bright linen, and around their chests they wore golden belts.* 7) *And one of the four living creatures gave to the seven angels seven golden bowls full of the wrath of God, who lives forever and ever.* 8) *And the sanctuary was filled with smoke from the glory of God and from his power. And no one was able to enter the sanctuary until the seven plagues of the seven angels had run their course.*

The first verse is a summary of the whole chapter. Although John says here that he saw the seven angels, they do not actually put in their appearance until the middle of the chapter (v. 6). The seven plagues also come into prominence at that point in the vision. At first we are only told that the seven angels hold seven plagues, but these plagues are immediately identified as "the last ones," and then John explains why they are called the last plagues. They are called last, because in them the wrath of God comes to completion. Thus we are told from the very beginning that these plagues will culminate in the final destruction of the world. The four angels who held the four winds in check (7:1ff) will no longer be called upon to preserve the earth from total ruin.

The vision begins with a view of "what looked like a sea of glass" (ὡς θάλασσαν ὑαλίνην). While John does not say so, this is apparently the same glassy sea which he had seen at the beginning of his vision of the future (4:6). There the sea had been compared to crystal. Here John tells us that it was "mixed with fire." Since we were told in that earlier vision that the sea of glass was "before the throne," we may assume that the fiery appearance was a reflection either of the glory of the Lord (4:3) or of the seven lamps burning before the throne (4:5). In any case, the reference to fire hints at the presence of the Lord.

On the glassy sea John saw those who had won the victory (τοὺς νικῶντας) over the beast and his image and the number of his name. The beast spoken of here must be the beast from the sea (13:1-10), for this was the beast whose image was worshiped by the unbelieving world (13:14,15). The fact that "his image" is coordinated with "the number of his name" would lend some support for the conclusion that the number 666, mentioned at the end of chapter 13, is the number of the beast from the sea, the secular antichrist.

The saints in glory in this vision are described as τοὺς νικῶντας, those who won the victory, or overcame. This word echoes the seven promises of the seven letters, each one of which makes a promise to the one who overcomes (ὁ νικῶν, τῷ νικῶντι). In the vision of the beast from the sea it was said that the beast was able to overcome (νικῆσαι — 13:7) the saints. He had been able to persecute and to kill them. But here it becomes evident that in spite of their seeming defeat at the hands of the antichristian forces in the world, the Christians were nevertheless victors. John's words here again must have been of special significance to the persecuted church of his time. Like Paul, he taught those early Christians and us that in tribulation or distress or persecution or famine or nakedness or peril or sword "we are more than conquerors (ὑπερνικῶμεν) through him who loved us" (Ro 8:37).

Those who won the victory over the beast are not those who defeated or killed him, but those who refused to worship him (13:12) and to receive his mark or his number on their hands or foreheads (13:16). The word which we have translated "over" is actually the Greek preposition ἐκ, which means "out of." The sinful world from which these victors came was a world which was under the domination of the enemies of Christ. It was from that world that they had escaped by their victory over the beast, by refusing to pay him homage and in that way remaining faithful to the Savior and his word. Thus their victory is described as one that freed them "out of" the power of the beast.

The sea of glass on which the victors stand is a symbol of the perfect calm and peace of heaven, where no ill wind causes the least ripple of disturbance in the lives of the saints. The harps which they hold and with which they accompany their singing are symbols of the joy that will be the lot of those who remain faithful unto death.

The song they sing is called "the song of Moses, the servant of God." There are two well-known songs of Moses recorded in the Pentateuch (Ex 15:1-18 and Dt 32:1-43). The first of these was sung by Moses and the children of Israel to celebrate the victory over Pharaoh's army after the crossing of the Red Sea. The second was spoken by Moses to the children of Israel shortly before his death. It is possible to find echoes of both of those songs in the hymn recorded here by John. The words in the final song of Moses, for example, ". . . his works are perfect, and all his ways are just," express thoughts similar to the song of the saints, who are quoted as saying, "Great and marvelous are your works, . . . just and true are your ways." Nevertheless, it is more likely that John had in mind the song of Moses at the Red Sea, when he celebrated the victory of God's people over their enemies. The saints who have overcome in the battle with the beast are here also celebrating such a victory. The Prophet Hosea had foretold that some day the church "will sing as in the days of her youth, as in the day she came up out of Egypt" (Ho 2:15).

Even though these singing saints had won the victory over the beast, yet in their song there is not the slightest hint that they deserve any credit for the victory. Instead, they speak only of the marvelous greatness of the works of God and of the truth and justice of his ways.

God is addressed as "Lord, God Almighty" (κύριε ὁ θεὸς ὁ παντοκράτωρ). We have already noted that this is the standard Septuagint translation of the Old Testament formula, "Lord (Jahweh) God of hosts." The word κύριος, Lord, is also the standard New Testament name for Jesus. Undoubtedly in these facts we see the reason why this "song of Moses" is also called "the song of the Lamb." "Of the Lamb" (τοῦ ἀρνίου) certainly cannot be a subjective genitive, which would mean that this was a song sung by the Lamb. It is an objective genitive. The song is directed to the Lamb. While the words of the song could be understood as being directed to the Trinity, yet the Lamb here again certainly occupies the center of attention.

His works are described as "great and marvelous." The first three visions in this series had portrayed the awful power of the three great enemies of God's people, the dragon and the two beasts. It was made very clear there that the church was not able in her own strength to stand against those foes. All she could do was flee into the desert. Nevertheless the people of God were victorious. The only explanation for that victory is the marvelous greatness of the works of God. This victory was his work.

The victory of the church is an occasion for praising the truth and justice of God's government of the world. The saints confess, "Just and true are your ways" (v. 3). Jesus had promised that the gates of hell, that is, the power of the dragon and his two allies, the beasts from the earth and the sea, would never prevail against the church. When the devil was pursuing the woman in the wilderness (12:15) and believers were being overcome by the one beast (13:7) and killed by the other (13:15) it often must have seemed that the word of God was not true. The justice of God demands that sinners be punished. When the enemies of the church in the days of persecution seem to triumph and those who have washed their robes in the blood of the Lamb are being sent to exile and death, it seems that the government of the world is being conducted by the forces of injustice. But, as Luther said, we must not judge by isolated fragments of experience. Here, standing on the glassy sea, the saints could look back to that world from which they had come and know that all the ways of the Lord were justice and truth, and that he was truly "the king of the nations" (v. 3), who ruled "all the nations with an iron rod" (12:5), even though the eyes of the men on this earth had seen him only as a weak child (12:5).

In the song at the Red Sea Moses said to God,

> Who is like unto thee, O Lord, among the gods?
> Who is like thee
>   glorious in holiness
>   fearful in praises,
>   doing wonders? (Ex 15:11 KJV)

Those sentiments are echoed in the song of the saints on the sea of glass. They sing,

> Who will not fear you, O Lord,
>   and praise your name?
> For you alone are holy.

This rhetorical question asserts that no one can be found who will not fear the Lord and praise his name. The double negative (οὐ μή) is not an interrogative particle here, but it belongs to the verb and indicates that all men will *surely* fear the Lord. The first and basic meaning of φοβέομαι is to be frightened, or terrified. This will be true of the enemies of God when they come to know from experience what these victorious saints in glory know. But the word also means to reverence or to respect. In that sense the question also applies to the believing children of God. They already have overcome the terrors of conscience by faith in the forgiveness of sins. Thus all men will finally "fear" God, either with the fear of a terrified conscience or with the awe and respect of a believing heart.

They will all also praise his name. The "name" of God is what people know about God. Those who believe the gospel and know the grace of God by faith glorify and praise his name already in this world. Those who reject his grace will nevertheless be forced to praise him on the day when every knee shall bow to him and every tongue shall confess "that Jesus Christ is Lord to the glory of God the Father" (Php 2:11).

Three reasons are then given why all men will finally fear God and glorify his name. The first reason is given in the words, "You alone are holy." The Greek word ὅσιος, holy, is a rather rare word in the New Testament and is used of God only in Revelation. It has reference to the holiness of God especially as it manifests itself in punishing the wicked and rewarding the good. The saints in heaven know that their suffering in persecution and the "seeming triumph" of their enemies were not a result of God's indifference to the demands of his own justice and holiness.

All men without exception will finally fear the Lord and praise his name. "All nations will come and bow down" before him. The saints in heaven have in mind the day of final judgment. On that day all nations will be summoned before the throne of God to see him in his awesome holiness. This will bring about the response described in the rhetorical question.

Finally, this response will come because his "righteous judgments were made manifest." In this clause the past tense is used instead of the future. It is true that the past tense is often used in prophecies because the prophet in his vision sees the future as already having happened. Yet these are not the words of John but of the saints. So the past tense here speaks of a manifestation that has already become clear to them. Their experience has demonstrated that the judgments of God are always right, even though they often in this world appear unjust to us. These last words of their song repeat their earlier expression, "Just and true are your ways."

The scene now shifts away from the singing saints to the seven angels with the seven bowls. John saw "the sanctuary of the tabernacle of the testimony opened in heaven [or, in the sky]." The "tabernacle of the testimony" was a name given to the Old Testament tabernacle which Moses set up in the wilderness as the children of Israel journeyed to the promised land. This tabernacle was the place where sacrifices and prayers were offered to God by the priests in behalf of the people. It was viewed as the special dwelling place of God.

Out of the sanctuary came the seven angels who had been mentioned in verse 1. They are holy angels, clothed in bright clean linen to symbolize their purity. Even though they had been identified as holding the seven plagues, yet they did not bring the plagues with them out of the temple. Rather, they received seven bowls from one of the four living creatures whom we already met in chapter 4. The bowls were "full of the wrath of God, who lives forever and ever." It is clear from the beginning that the seven bowls symbolize punishments that will come on the earth because men have deserved the awful wrath of the ever-living God.

The temple was filled with "smoke from the glory of God and from his power." This is an obvious reference to the Old Testament vision in which the Prophet Isaiah was called into the public ministry (Is 6:1-13). In that vision Isaiah saw the temple filled with smoke (6:4). The smoke here came from the glory of God. The "glory" of God or "the glory of the Lord" was the bright light in which God made his presence visible to the children of Israel. Sometimes in the Old Testament that glory is compared to a fiery cloudy pillar. So it is not surprising to read that smoke issued from it to fill the temple.

Finally we are told that no one was allowed to enter the sanctuary until the seven plagues had run their course. Since the priests entered the sanctuary to intercede for the people, this part of the vision marks the end of all intercession, the end of the time of grace and repentance. Nothing is left for men now "but a certain fearful looking for of judgment" (He 10:27 KJV). In the days of Jeremiah, when the Israelites had hardened their hearts to God's call of repentance, the prophet was commanded to stop praying for his people (Jr 7:16; 11:14; 14:11). Here, in a symbolic way, the same judgment is pronounced on an impenitent world.

The pouring out of God's judgment on this impenitent world is then portrayed in the vision of the seven bowls.

The Fifth Vision: The Seven Last Plagues (16:1-21)

THE FIRST FIVE BOWLS (16:1-11)

1) Καὶ ἤκουσα μεγάλης φωνῆς ἐκ τοῦ ναοῦ λεγούσης τοῖς ἑπτὰ ἀγγέλοις, Ὑπάγετε καὶ ἐκχέετε τὰς ἑπτὰ φιάλας τοῦ θυμοῦ τοῦ Θεοῦ εἰς τὴν γῆν. 2) Καὶ ἀπῆλθεν ὁ πρῶτος καὶ ἐξέχεεν τὴν φιάλην αὐτοῦ εἰς τὴν γῆν· καὶ ἐγένετο ἕλκος κακὸν καὶ πονηρὸν ἐπὶ τοὺς ἀνθρώπους τοὺς ἔχοντας τὸ χάραγμα τοῦ θηρίου καὶ τοὺς προσκυνοῦντας τῇ εἰκόνι αὐτοῦ. 3) Καὶ ὁ δεύτερος ἐξέχεεν τὴν φιάλην αὐτοῦ εἰς τὴν θάλασσαν· καὶ ἐγένετο αἷμα ὡς νεκροῦ, καὶ πᾶσα ψυχὴ ζωῆς ἀπέθανεν, τὰ ἐν τῇ θαλάσσῃ. 4) Καὶ ὁ τρίτος ἐξέχεεν τὴν φιάλην αὐτοῦ εἰς τοὺς ποταμοὺς καὶ τὰς πηγὰς τῶν ὑδάτων· καὶ ἐγένετο αἷμα. 5) Καὶ ἤκουσα τοῦ ἀγγέλου τῶν ὑδάτων λέγοντος, Δίκαιος εἶ, ὁ ὢν καὶ ὁ ἦν, ὁ Ὅσιος, ὅτι ταῦτα ἔκρινας, 6) ὅτι αἷμα ἁγίων καὶ προφητῶν ἐξέχεαν, καὶ αἷμα αὐτοῖς δέδωκας πεῖν· ἄξιοί εἰσιν. 7) Καὶ ἤκουσα τοῦ θυσιαστηρίου λέγοντος, Ναί, Κύριε ὁ Θεὸς ὁ Παντοκράτωρ, ἀληθιναὶ καὶ δίκαιαι αἱ κρίσεις σου. 8) Καὶ ὁ τέταρτος ἐξέχεεν τὴν φιάλην αὐτοῦ ἐπὶ τὸν ἥλιον· καὶ ἐδόθη αὐτῷ καυματίσαι τοὺς ἀνθρώπους ἐν πυρί. 9) καὶ ἐκαυματίσθησαν οἱ ἄνθρωποι καῦμα μέγα, καὶ ἐβλασφήμησαν τὸ ὄνομα τοῦ Θεοῦ τοῦ ἔχοντος τὴν ἐξουσίαν ἐπὶ τὰς πληγὰς ταύτας, καὶ οὐ μετενόησαν δοῦναι αὐτῷ δόξαν. 10) Καὶ ὁ πέμπτος ἐξέχεεν τὴν φιάλην αὐτοῦ ἐπὶ τὸν θρόνον τοῦ θηρίου· καὶ ἐγένετο ἡ βασιλεία αὐτοῦ ἐσκοτωμένη, καὶ ἐμασῶντο τὰς γλώσσας αὐτῶν ἐκ τοῦ πόνου, 11) καὶ ἐβλασφήμησαν τὸν Θεὸν τοῦ οὐρανοῦ ἐκ τῶν πόνων αὐτῶν καὶ ἐκ τῶν ἑλκῶν αὐτῶν, καὶ οὐ μετενόησαν ἐκ τῶν ἔργων αὐτῶν.

1) *And I heard a loud voice out of the temple saying to the seven angels, "Come and pour out the seven bowls of the wrath of God on the earth."*

2) *And the first came away and poured out his bowl on the earth. And there came a bad and evil ulcer on the men who had the mark of the beast and who worshiped his image.*

3) *And the second poured out his bowl on the sea. And there came*
blood, like that of a corpse, and every living creature, the ones in
the sea, died.

4) *And the third poured out his bowl on the rivers and the springs*
of water. And there came blood. 5) *And I heard the angel of the*
waters saying,

Just are you, the one who is
and the one who was, the holy one,
in that you have pronounced these judgments,
6) *because they poured out the blood of saints and prophets,*
and you have given them blood to drink.
They deserve it.

7) *And I heard the incense altar say,*

Yes, Lord God Almighty,
true and just are your judgments.

8) *And the fourth poured out his bowl on the sun, and it was given*
power to burn men with fire. 9) *And men were burned with a*
great fire, and they blasphemed the name of the God who has
authority over these plagues, and they did not repent to give him
praise.

10) *And the fifth poured out his bowl on the throne of the beast,*
and his kingdom became darkened and men kept on biting their
tongues in their torment, 11) *and they blasphemed the God of*
heaven because of their torments and their ulcers, but they did
not repent of their deeds.

Perhaps the best clue to the significance of this vision is the close parallelism between it and the vision of the seven trumpets. First of all, both visions are introduced in the same way. The vision of the trumpets follows the opening of the seventh seal and the introduction to the seven bowls is actually the seventh in the series of visions that begins with chapter 12. Both visions follow a vision of judgment day and end with a vision of the same event. But even more striking are some of the details in the individual visions.

THE VISION OF THE SEVEN TRUMPETS	THE VISION OF THE SEVEN BOWLS
1st trumpet: A plague of hail and fire mixed with blood falls on the earth. A third of the earth is burned.	1st bowl, poured out on the earth: A bad and evil ulcer afflicts the men who have the mark of the beast.

Trumpet	Bowl
2nd trumpet: A mountain of fire cast in the sea. A third of the sea becomes blood, and a third of the creatures in the sea die.	2nd bowl, poured out on the sea: The sea turns into blood. Every living creature in the sea dies.
3rd trumpet: A great star falls on the rivers and fountains of water. A third of the waters becomes bitter and many men die.	3rd bowl, poured out on the rivers and fountains of water: They turn into blood.
4th trumpet: A third of the sun, moon, and stars is darkened.	4th bowl, poured out on the sun: Men are burned by the resulting heat.
5th trumpet: A star fallen from heaven opens the bottomless pit to release smoke to darken the sun. Men who do not have the seal of God suffer great torments from a locust plague.	5th bowl, poured out on the throne of the beast: His kingdom is darkened and men in his kingdom gnaw their tongues in pain.
6th trumpet: A great army comes from the region of the Euphrates.	6th bowl, poured out on the Euphrates: The way is prepared for a great army that comes to fight against God.
7th trumpet: The kingdom of the world becomes the kingdom of Christ amidst lightnings and crashes and thunders and an earthquake and hail.	7th bowl, poured out on the air: The earth passes away in crashes and thunders and lightning and an earthquake and great hail.

The similarity between John's vision of the seventh seal and the seventh in this series of visions is not an isolated coincidence. In prophetic dreams and visions, it is not unusual that the same prophetic message is repeated in succeeding visions. Such visions are at times strikingly similar to one another. Joseph had two dreams. In the first he saw his brothers' shocks of grain bowing down to his shock and in the second the sun, moon and stars bowing down before him (Gn 37:5-10). Both pointed to the same event, namely Joseph's exaltation in Egypt. The Pharaoh had two similar dreams, in which the seven cows and the seven ears of grain both denoted seven years (Gn 41:1-32). The message of Nebuchadnezzar's dream in which he saw the great image, which symbolized four great successive world empires (Dn 2:1-45), is repeated in different symbolism in Daniel's own night vision of the four great beasts (Dn 7:1-28). These examples convince us that it is possible that the message of John's two similar visions may well be one and the same.

The fact of the repetition itself is significant. In the case of Pharaoh's dream we are specifically told that the repetition signified that the dream would *surely* and *shortly* come to pass (Gn 41:32). While no reason is given for the repetition of John's vision, it is possible to conclude that in this case the Holy Spirit wanted to call attention to the special importance of the lesson taught by these two visions. That conclusion is reinforced by the fact that these two visions, the vision of the seven trumpets and that of the seven last plagues, are both the seventh in the previous series of seven visions. And it is in complete harmony with the many passages of Scripture which demonstrate that by far the greatest danger threatening the church is the danger posed by false doctrine.

The remarkable parallelism leads to the conclusion that the vision of the bowls deals with the same type of plagues that had been symbolized in the vision of the trumpets. In our comments on the seven trumpets we concluded the vision for the most part portrayed the false doctrines that would lead men astray. It must never be forgotten that the great battle fought between God and the devil is a battle for the minds and hearts of men. On the side of the church the prime weapon in that warfare is the sword of the Spirit, the Word of God. The devil's chief weapons are the lies that contradict the truth of God's Word. On that ground the battle was fought in the garden of Eden, and on that same ground it will be fought until the very end. We may therefore see in the seven last plagues for the most part a symbolic representation of the flood of false doctrine that will overwhelm the earth in the last days. The Apostle Paul had predicted that in the last days

> men will not put up with sound doctrine. Instead, to suit their own desires, they will gather around them a great number of teachers to say what their itching ears want to hear. They will turn their ears away from the truth and turn aside to myths (2 Tm 4:3f).

The damage done by this "great number of teachers" is well portrayed in the vision of the seven bowls.

By "false doctrines" we do have in mind not only the perversion of biblical teaching, but also every corrupted philosophy of life, every heathen religion and every other lie by which men are deceived — from the promises of prosperity and ease made by materialistic atheism to the unspoken conception that men can find rest and enjoyment in the stupefaction of mind and spirit produced by hours of watching the immoral antics of depraved television stars.

The first four bowls turn the earth, the sea, the rivers and fountains of water, and the sun into areas of disaster. The seventh bowl is poured on the air. The elements mentioned here are the basic building blocks of creation. Originally they were the basic source of all the blessings God wanted man to enjoy in this world.

On the spiritual level we may therefore see the earth, the sea, the waters, the sun and the air as symbols of spiritual blessings for men. The chief of these spiritual blessings is a proper understanding of law and gospel, which points the way to happiness and fulfillment both in this world and in the world to come. Yet among these blessings might be reckoned all the truths man can discover by the proper use of reason — truths which help man to exercise at least in some measure the kind of dominion over the birds of the air and the fish of the sea and the beasts of the earth that God intended man to have from the beginning.

One more thing should be said as background for the understanding of this chapter. The Bible in many places speaks of the loss of God's word, of the entrance of heresies and heathenish ideas, and of spiritual blindness and moral decay as punishments that are poured out on men as a reward for their stubborn unbelief and rejection of that word.

The vision begins with a loud voice speaking from the temple in heaven out of which the seven angels had come. The voice is not identified, but there can be no doubt the order given to the angel is the will of God. The seven angels are told to pour out on the earth the bowls filled with God's wrath.

When the first bowl is poured out on the earth the men who have the mark of the beast (13:16) and who worship his image (13:15) are afflicted with a bad and evil ulcer. In the judgment of God the worship of a false god always ends in pain. Such false gods are always worshiped when the revelation of the true God is distorted by false doctrine. In the Scriptures false doctrine is portrayed as a judgment of God visited on men as a punishment for their rejection of the truth. Paul says, for example,

> They perish because they refused to love the truth and so be saved. For this reason God sends them a powerful delusion so that they will believe the lie, and so that all will be condemned who have not believed the truth (2 Th 2:10,11).

"The bad and evil ulcer" may therefore very well be the spiritual disease which consists in false notions and ideas that bring suffering and grief to men and then can never give them rest from the torments of a raging conscience — something which even a heathen writer once described as the greatest torment that men can know.

These plagues do not afflict the worshipers of the true God, but only those who worship the beast and his image. If these plagues were material plagues that literally turn the whole sea and all the waters of the earth into blood, God's children would share in the suffering. It will not do here to compare the experience of the children of Israel in Egypt, because they were not spared in the first three plagues sent to punish Pharaoh. Only when the plague of flies was announced did God say that he would make a distinction between the land of Goshen and the rest of Egypt (Ex 8:22). Nor are we told in this chapter that there are specific localities in the world that are spared. Those who cling to the gospel with its promise of forgiveness and grace, however, are always safe from false religions and false philosophies, which always lead to pain and despair. That is not to say that this pain and despair will always be evident to us. Revelation, like the rest of the Bible, is a book of faith, and we will believe that men are miserable even when they deny it (cp. 3:17).

When the second bowl is poured out on the sea the sea turns to blood and all the living creatures in the sea are killed. The blood is described as that of a dead man, a particularly repulsive sight. We have already pointed out the similarity between this plague and the plague which followed the blowing of the second trumpet. There is, however, one striking difference. There one-third of the sea creatures died. Here they all perish. Thus the long-suffering patience of God that so often spares a remnant now comes to an end. And so false doctrine deprives the unbelieving world of the gospel, the source of all real life.

A similar calamity comes upon all the sources of fresh water on the earth, the rivers and fountains of water, when the third bowl is poured out. As we already pointed out in our discussion of the vision of the third trumpet, the message of salvation is often in Scripture compared to water by which the soul of man is refreshed. The message of the Savior's love is the water of life that quenches the thirst of man forever. But when the truth of the gospel is obscured and destroyed by false doctrine, the wells of salvation no longer bring refreshment to the souls of men. Instead they must drink blood. The imagery of Revelation is that of the Old Testament, and the thought of drinking blood was particularly repulsive to an Old Testament believer.

At this point John heard "the angel of the waters" speak. We are not directly told who this "angel of the waters" is, but very likely it is the angel who poured his bowl on these waters. The angel addresses God as "the one who is and the one who was, the holy one." Instead of "the holy one" a few manuscripts have the phrase "the one who will be" (cp 1:4,8; 4:8). The words of the angel speak of the justice of this punishment visited on the persecutors of the church. The men who are forced to drink blood are worthy of this judgment because they had shed the blood of saints and prophets. This was another way in which God assured the persecuted saints of John's time that their sufferings would not go unavenged by the holy God. John then tells us that the incense altar itself declares these judgments of the Lord God Almighty to be true and just. They are true because God's Word repeatedly tells us that God will punish those who bring pain and suffering to his people. They are just because in true justice no sin remains unpunished.

The fourth angel pours out his bowl on the sun. The sun is the source of light. As such, it is a symbol of God's Word and of all truth in every area of life. When the plague of false doctrine and false philosophies of life is poured out on this source of light, it becomes a curse that inflicts incredible spiritual suffering on men. It becomes, as Paul says, "a savor of death unto death" (2 Cor 2:16). And even though corrupt religions and philosophies have deprived men of the means of grace, they refuse to recognize their own fault in causing this calamity. Instead, they blaspheme the name of God and say wicked things about him as the source of these plagues.

With the pouring out of the fifth bowl comes a change of emphasis. This bowl is poured out on the throne of the beast. There can be no doubt that this is the beast from the sea (13:1-10), which, as we have seen, is a symbol of civil government in its antichristian aspect.

Civil government is also a source of great blessing for men. It is instituted by God to promote a quiet and peaceful life (1 Tm 4:2). But when false and devilish delusions turn governments into promoters and defenders of institutionalized robbery, militant atheism, atheistic evolution, murder of the unborn, pornography and countless other evils, what was intended to be a blessing becomes a curse and a source of pain and suffering. The intensity of that suffering is brought out especially by the imperfect tense of the Greek verb in the words "men kept on biting their tongues in their torment." But the time of grace has ended for them. We are told again that they blaspheme the God of heaven because of their pains and the ulcers, blaming him for these sufferings, rather than repenting of their sins, the real cause of their torment.

THE SIXTH BOWL: THE BATTLE OF ARMAGEDDON (16:12-16)

12) Καὶ ὁ ἕκτος ἐξέχεεν τὴν φιάλην αὐτοῦ ἐπὶ τὸν ποταμὸν τὸν μέγαν Εὐφράτην· καὶ ἐξηράνθη τὸ ὕδωρ αὐτοῦ, ἵνα ἑτοιμασθῇ ἡ ὁδὸς τῶν βασιλέων τῶν ἀπὸ ἀνατολῆς ἡλίου. 13) Καὶ εἶδον ἐκ τοῦ στόματος τοῦ δράκοντος καὶ ἐκ τοῦ στόματος τοῦ θηρίου καὶ ἐκ τοῦ στόματος τοῦ ψευδοπροφήτου πνεύματα τρία ἀκάθαρτα ὡς βάτραχοι· 14) εἰσὶν γὰρ πνεύματα δαιμονίων ποιοῦντα σημεῖα, ἃ ἐκπορεύεται ἐπὶ τοὺς βασιλεῖς τῆς οἰκουμένης ὅλης συναγαγεῖν αὐτοὺς εἰς τὸν πόλεμον τῆς ἡμέρας τῆς μεγάλης τοῦ Θεοῦ τοῦ Παντοκράτορος. 15) Ἰδοὺ ἔρχομαι ὡς κλέπτης· μακάριος ὁ γρηγορῶν καὶ τηρῶν τὰ ἱμάτια αὐτοῦ, ἵνα μὴ γυμνὸς περιπατῇ καὶ βλέπωσιν τὴν ἀσχημοσύνην αὐτοῦ. 16) καὶ συνήγαγεν αὐτοὺς εἰς τὸν τόπον τὸν καλούμενον Ἑβραϊστὶ Ἁρμαγεδών.

12) *And the sixth poured out his bowl on the great river, the Euphrates. And its water was dried up to prepare the way for the kings coming from the east.* 13) *And out of the mouth of the dragon, and the mouth of the beast, and the mouth of the false prophet I saw three unclean spirits, like frogs.* 14) *For they are miracle-working, demonic spirits, who go out to the kings of the whole earth to bring them together for the battle of the great day of God Almighty.*

15) *Behold, I am coming like a thief.*
Blessed is the one who stays awake
and keeps his garments,
That he may not walk naked
and that his shame may not be seen.

16) *And they brought them together to the place called "Armageddon" in Hebrew.*

After the sixth trumpet was blown John saw a great army coming from the region of the Euphrates River. That army killed a third of the human race. In the vision of the sixth bowl the river Euphrates again has a prominent place. When the sixth angel pours his bowl on the river it dries up to make a clear road for the "kings from the east." These kings are not identified more exactly. All that we can say is that during the days of the Old Testament prophets the greatest threats against the people of God came from the region of the Euphrates. Assyria, Babylonia and Persia were the enemies who oppressed the chosen people for hundreds of years.

The kings from the east, as well as the kings "of the whole world" are summoned to do battle against the people of God by demonic spirits who come out of the mouths of the dragon, the beast (from the sea), and the false prophet (the beast from the earth). These three great enemies of the church had been described in the first three of the seven visions (chapters 12 and 13).

The war to which these kings of the whole earth are summoned is called "the battle of the great day of Almighty God." The great day spoken of here is certainly the day of judgment. Any doubt about this is removed by the parenthetical remark that is obviously spoken by the divine judge, namely,

> Behold, I am coming like a thief.
> Blessed is the one who stays awake
>   and keeps his garments,
> That he may not walk naked,
>   and that his shame may not be seen.

Those words sound several themes which in the Gospels and Epistles are closely associated with the second coming of Christ. Several passages in the New Testament compare the second coming to the unexpected coming of a thief (Mt 24:43; Lk 12:39; 1 Th 5:2; 2 Pe 3:10), and the Savior as well as the apostles often call upon believers to remain wide awake in expectation of the second coming (Mt 24:42; Mk 13:35; Lk 12:36; Ro 13:1; 1 Th 5:6).

The demonic spirits issuing from the mouths of the dragon, the beast, and the false prophet will thus summon the kings of the earth to come together to do battle against the church, but they do not know that the day which they have chosen for the fight is the day which God had long before appointed as the day on which he would come to bring final redemption to his people (Lk 21:28). It is not their day, as they imagine, but it is the day of the Lord God Almighty. Thus the theme of the sure victory of the church is once more clearly emphasized. When the lies and heresies that threaten to deceive the very elect become so prevalent and dominant that the defeat of the gospel seems imminent, the Lord will intervene to bring an end to the rule and strategy of evil men and spirits. This vision reflects the words in which the Savior spoke of these last days. He said,

> "For false Christs and false prophets (cp v. 13, ψευδοπροφήτου) will appear and perform great signs (cp v. 14, σημεῖα) and miracles to deceive even the elect — if that were possible" (Mt 24:24).

After this parenthetical remark, in which the Savior announces his sudden coming and speaks an admonition to watchfulness and preparation, the account of the battle to be fought on the last day continues. John writes, "They (that is, the evil spirits) gathered them (the kings of the earth) in the place that is called in Hebrew, 'Armageddon.' " This word is found only here in the New Testament, and even though it is said to be Hebrew, it does not occur at all in the Old Testament. The most common explanation is that it reproduces two Hebrew words, *Har*, mountain, and *Megiddo*, a city in the plain of Esdraelon. The most famous mountain near Megiddo was Mt. Carmel, a small mountain range stretching from the sea to within a few miles of the city of Megiddo. Somewhere on that mountain Elijah met and defeated the prophets of Baal. At that mountain a great battle was fought. The forces of truth were outnumbered 400 to 1 by prophets of Baal. Yet the Lord's lonely prophet was vindicated and all the prophets of Baal were destroyed. That contest could well serve as a pattern for the last great battle between the truth of God and the lie of Satan and Antichrist. As we have already seen, that lie is in essence the promise that man will find happiness and fulfillment in what he can do for himself rather than in the blessings that come to him as a free gift of grace. In our time that lie finds expression on the secular level in hundreds of ways, from the false promises of an atheistic communism to the depraved notions that underlie the drug culture and, on the religious level, in the multiplied doctrines of salvation by works, from the warped promises of Eastern mysticism to the work righteousness of

Romanism and apostate Protestantism. In that multiplicity of falsehood we may see the kings of the earth gathering for a final contest on Mt. Carmel, the mountain of Megiddo.

Our only defense in that day is found in the garments that have been cleaned for us in the blood of Christ (7:14). If we keep them by faith, the shame of our own nakedness will not be seen when the Almighty Judge comes as a thief (v. 14).

THE SEVENTH BOWL: THE END OF THE WORLD (16:17-21)

17) Καὶ ὁ ἕβδομος ἐξέχεεν τὴν φιάλην αὐτοῦ ἐπὶ τὸν ἀέρα· καὶ ἐξῆλθεν φωνὴ μεγάλη ἐκ τοῦ ναοῦ ἀπὸ τοῦ θρόνου λέγουσα, Γέγονεν. 18) καὶ ἐγένοντο ἀστραπαὶ καὶ φωναὶ καὶ βρονταί, καὶ σεισμὸς ἐγένετο μέγας, οἷος οὐκ ἐγένετο ἀφ' οὗ ἄνθρωπος ἐγένετο ἐπὶ τῆς γῆς, τηλικοῦτος σεισμὸς οὕτω μέγας. 19) καὶ ἐγένετο ἡ πόλις ἡ μεγάλη εἰς τρία μέρη, καὶ αἱ πόλες τῶν ἐθνῶν ἔπεσαν. καὶ Βαβυλὼν ἡ μεγάλη ἐμνήσθη ἐνώπιον τοῦ Θεοῦ δοῦναι αὐτῇ τὸ ποτήριον τοῦ οἴνου τοῦ θυμοῦ τῆς ὀργῆς αὐτοῦ. 20) καὶ πᾶσα νῆσος ἔφυγεν, καὶ ὄρη οὐχ εὑρέθησαν. 21) καὶ χάλαζα μεγάλη ὡς ταλαντιαία καταβαίνει ἐκ τοῦ οὐρανοῦ ἐπὶ τοὺς ἀνθρώπους· καὶ ἐβλασφήμησαν οἱ ἄνθρωποι τὸν Θεὸν ἐκ τῆς πληγῆς τῆς χαλάζης, ὅτι μεγάλη ἐστὶν ἡ πληγὴ αὐτῆς σφόδρα.

17) *And the seventh poured out his bowl on the air. And a loud voice came out of the temple from the throne, saying, "It is done."* 18) *And there came flashes of lightning, crashes and thunders, and a great earthquake took place, such a great earthquake as has not happened on the earth since man was made.* 19) *And the great city split into three parts, and the cities of the nations fell. And Babylon the Great was remembered by God. He gave her the wine cup of his angry wrath.* 20) *And every island fled away, and the mountains were no more.* 21) *And great hail, with the hailstones weighing a hundred pounds each, fell from the sky on men, and men blasphemed God because of the plague of hail, because the plague it brought was very great.*

The pouring out of the seventh bowl is a representation of the last judgment — from the viewpoint of what that "great day of God Almighty" (v. 14) will mean for the enemies of the church. Many commentators have failed to understand this and have seen it only as a description of conditions shortly before the end of the world. But the conditions preceding the end had been the subject of the six preceding plagues. This is the end.

The seventh angel poured his bowl on the "air," the last great source of blessing for men. And John heard a great voice speak from the throne in the temple. It spoke one word: "γέγονεν" ("it is done," or "it has happened"). The Greek word is the perfect tense of the verb which in the past tense is often translated, "It came to pass" (KJV). There is a note of finality in that perfect tense, consistent only with the interpretation that this is indeed a vision of the last day. There are other reasons, too, for coming to this conclusion. But this one word is convincing in itself.

Since the voice comes "from the throne," it is the voice of God. Sometimes when the Bible refers to "God's word" it portrays the power by which he governs the universe. He upholds "all things by the word of his power," says the writer of Hebrews (1:3). When in the beginning he said, "Let there be light," there was light. When he says, "It is done," the course of history comes to its conclusion.

The word itself does not expressly indicate what has been done. That is spelled out by the words, "Babylon the Great was remembered by God. He gave her the wine cup of his angry wrath." These words echo a note which had been sounded at the very beginning of this series of visions (15:1) where we learned that in these seven last plagues "the wrath of God came to completion (ἐτελέσθη)." That verb also indicates to us that this is a vision of the τέλος, the end, and we see in it a foreshadowing of the γέγονεν on which we have commented above.

In the vision of the three angels (14:6-12) God had threatened Babylon with the cup of his anger out of which that proud city would drink the undiluted wine of God's wrath. It was this that had now come to pass with finality. This symbolism of the "wine of God's wrath" is regularly associated with judgment day. In the vision of the final harvest of the earth (14:14-20), John had spoken of "the great wine press of the wrath of God" (14:19), and in a later description of the final judgment we have the identical phrase that is used here (19:15: τοῦ οἴνου τοῦ θύμου τῆς ὀργῆς τοῦ θεοῦ, "the wine of the wrath of the anger of God").

When God said, "It is done," there were "lightning flashes and rumblings, and thunders, and a great earthquake." While a number of passages in Revelation speak of an earthquake, only two passages use the term "a great earthquake." The first of these occurs in the vision of the sixth seal (6:12), which is a clear prophecy concerning "the great day of his wrath" (6:17), the day of judgment (cp 16:14). Here special emphasis is laid on the greatness of the earthquake. It is not only called a σεισμὸς μέγας, a great earthquake, but John says that the like of it had never occurred since the time of the creation of man, in other words, in all history. Then in the emphatic position at the end of the sentence John repeats this thought twice more by saying, "so great an earthquake, so great" (τηλικοῦτος σεισμὸς οὕτω μέγας). These words and the whole context point to the fact that this is the final shaking that brings about the total destruction of the present world (cp He 12:26f).

The combination of an earthquake with "lightning flashes and rumblings and thunders" is found in three passages in Revelation (8:5; 11:19; 16:18). All four phenomena occur together for the first time when the angel throws the burning censer to the earth. There is nothing in that context that would associate these phenomena with the final judgment. However, in the vision of the seventh trumpet, which is clearly a prophecy concerning the consummation of history (11:15), these four phenomena together with "a great hail" (11:19) are portrayed as concomitants of the end of the world.

In the great earthquake "the great city split into three parts, and the cities of the nations fell." The next sentence shows that this "great city" is "Babylon the Great." This is the second of the six passages in Revelation that mention Babylon (see the comments on 14:8). The language here points to the total destruction of Babylon, the seat of antichristian power, together with all the cities of the earth. The language indicates that this is indeed a vision of the end.

The following words are an even stronger indication of the correctness of this interpretation. "Every island fled away, and the mountains were not found," that is, they disappeared from sight. The same kind of language had been used in an earlier description of the end of history. In the vision of the sixth seal John saw every mountain and island moved out of its place (6:14). We see in the disappearance of the mountains and islands not just a removal of places of refuge, but an indication of the destruction of the whole world in the last judgment.

The central truth in this vision was a message of comfort for the persecuted church of John's time. On the day of judgment the enemies of the church will receive their just reward. There will then be an end to all the antichristian heresies portrayed in the preceding six visions in this series. The collapse of Babylon and the cities of the nations signals an end to their power and their ability to harm the church.

The last scene of this vision underscores that truth. "A great hail, with the hailstones weighing a hundred pounds each, fell from the sky on men, and men blasphemed God because of the plague of hail, for the plague it brought was very great." Anyone who has seen the terrible destruction caused by a great hailstorm, in which the hailstones weigh but a few ounces, can imagine the destruction caused by these hailstones. In the great plague of hail that afflicted Egypt in the days of Moses, the hailstones killed every man and animal in the open field (Ex 9:19). When the cities of the nations and Babylon fell before the onset of this hailstorm, there was no protection left for the men who were caught in the open by these hundred-pound hailstones. The abrupt ending of the vision indicates that this is the end for an unbelieving world. Blasphemy was the last sound they made before their final destruction and judgment. And the church is now forever safe from their attacks. This hailstorm leaves no survivors.

Up to this point there is a clear division of the book into five divisions, each of which consists of seven distinct and clearly defined parts: the seven letters, the seven seals, the seven trumpets, the seven visions, and the seven bowls. This pattern now comes to an end. It is possible, however, to see in the remaining chapters of the book two distinct series of visions, the first of which portrays the victory of Christ over Antichrist and the second, his victory over Satan.

The Sixth Vision:
Christ and Antichrist (17:1 — 19:21)

THE VISION OF THE GREAT HARLOT (17:1-18)

1) Καὶ ἦλθεν εἷς ἐκ τῶν ἑπτὰ ἀγγέλων τῶν ἐχόντων τὰς ἑπτὰ φιάλας, καὶ ἐλάλησεν μετ' ἐμοῦ λέγων, Δεῦρο, δείξω σοι τὸ κρίμα τῆς πόρνης τῆς μεγάλης τῆς καθημένης ἐπὶ ὑδάτων πολλῶν,
2) μεθ' ἧς ἐπόρνευσαν οἱ βασιλεῖς τῆς γῆς, καὶ ἐμεθύσθησαν οἱ κατοικοῦντες τὴν γῆν ἐκ τοῦ οἴνου τῆς πορνείας αὐτῆς. 3) καὶ ἀπήνεγκέν με εἰς ἔρημον ἐν Πνεύματι. καὶ εἶδον γυναῖκα καθημένην ἐπὶ θηρίον κόκκινον, γέμοντα ὀνόματα βλασφημίας, ἔχοντα κεφαλὰς ἑπτὰ καὶ κέρατα δέκα. 4) καὶ ἡ γυνὴ ἦν περιβεβλημένη πορφυροῦν καὶ κόκκινον, καὶ κεχρυσωμένη χρυσίῳ καὶ λίθῳ τιμίῳ καὶ μαργαρίταις, ἔχουσα ποτήριον χρυσοῦν ἐν τῇ χειρὶ αὐτῆς γέμον βδελυγμάτων καὶ τὰ ἀκάθαρτα τῆς πορνείας αὐτῆς,
5) καὶ ἐπὶ τὸ μέτωπον αὐτῆς ὄνομα γεγραμμένον, μυστήριον, ΒΑΒΥΛΩΝ Η ΜΕΓΑΛΗ, Η ΜΗΤΗΡ ΤΩΝ ΠΟΡΝΩΝ ΚΑΙ ΤΩΝ ΒΔΕΛΥΓΜΑΤΩΝ ΤΗΣ ΓΗΣ. 6) καὶ εἶδον τὴν γυναῖκα μεθύουσαν ἐκ τοῦ αἵματος τῶν ἁγίων καὶ ἐκ τοῦ αἵματος τῶν μαρτύρων Ἰησοῦ. Καὶ ἐθαύμασα ἰδὼν αὐτὴν θαῦμα μέγα. 7) καὶ εἶπέν μοι ὁ ἄγγελος, Διὰ τί ἐθαύμασας; ἐγὼ ἐρῶ σοι τὸ μυστήριον τῆς γυναικὸς καὶ τοῦ θηρίου τοῦ βαστάζοντος αὐτὴν τοῦ ἔχοντος τὰς ἑπτὰ κεφαλὰς καὶ τὰ δέκα κέρατα. 8) τὸ θηρίον ὃ εἶδες ἦν καὶ οὐκ ἔστιν, καὶ μέλλει ἀναβαίνειν ἐκ τῆς ἀβύσσου καὶ εἰς ἀπώλειαν ὑπάγει· καὶ θαυμασθήσονται οἱ κατοικοῦντες ἐπὶ τῆς γῆς, ὧν οὐ γέγραπται τὸ ὄνομα ἐπὶ τὸ βιβλίον τῆς ζωῆς ἀπὸ καταβολῆς κόσμου, βλεπόντων τὸ θηρίον ὅτι ἦν καὶ οὐκ ἔστιν καὶ παρέσται.
9) ὧδε ὁνοῦς ὁ ἔχων σοφίαν. αἱ ἑπτὰ κεφαλαὶ ἑπτὰ ὄρη εἰσίν, ὅπου ἡ γυνὴ κάθηται ἐπ' αὐτῶν. καὶ βασιλεῖς ἑπτά εἰσιν· 10) οἱ πέντε ἔπεσαν, ὁ εἷς ἔστιν, ὁ ἄλλος οὔπω ἦλθεν, καὶ ὅταν ἔλθῃ ὀλίγον αὐτὸν δεῖ μεῖναι. 11) καὶ τὸ θηρίον ὃ ἦν καὶ οὐκ ἔστιν, καὶ αὐτὸς ὄγδοός ἐστιν, καὶ ἐκ τῶν ἑπτά ἐστιν, καὶ εἰς ἀπώλειαν ὑπάγει. 12) καὶ τὰ δέκα κέρατα ἃ εἶδες δέκα βασιλεῖς εἰσιν, οἵτινες βασιλείαν οὔπω ἔλαβον, ἀλλὰ ἐξουσίαν ὡς βασιλεῖς μίαν ὥραν λαμβάνουσιν μετὰ τοῦ θηρίου. 13) οὗτοι μίαν γνώμην ἔχου-

σιν, καὶ τὴν δύναμιν καὶ ἐξουσίαν αὐτῶν τῷ θηρίῳ διδόασιν. 14)
οὗτοι μετὰ τοῦ Ἀρνίου πολεμήσουσιν καὶ τὸ Ἀρνίον νικήσει
αὐτούς, ὅτι Κύριος κυρίων ἐστὶν καὶ Βασιλεὺς βασιλέων, καὶ οἱ
μετ' αὐτοῦ κλητοὶ καὶ ἐκλεκτοὶ καὶ πιστοί. 15) Καὶ λέγει μοι, Τὰ
ὕδατα ἃ εἶδες, οὗ ἡπόρνη κάθηται, λαοὶ καὶ ὄχλοι εἰσὶν καὶ ἔθνη
καὶ γλῶσσαι. 16) καὶ τὰ δέκα κέρατα ἃ εἶδες καὶ τὸ θηρίον, οὗτοι
μισήσουσιν τὴν πόρνην, καὶ ἠρημωμένην ποιήσουσιν αὐτὴν καὶ
γυμνήν, καὶ τὰς σάρκας αὐτῆς φάγονται, καὶ αὐτὴν κατακαύσου-
σιν ἐν πυρί· 17) ὁ γὰρ Θεὸς ἔδωκεν εἰς τὰς καρδίας αὐτῶν ποιῆ-
σαι τὴν γνώμην αὐτοῦ, καὶ ποιῆσαι μίαν γνώμην καὶ δοῦναι τὴν
βασιλείαν αὐτῶν τῷ θηρίῳ, ἄχρι τελεσθήσονται οἱ λόγοι τοῦ
Θεοῦ. 18) καὶ ἡ γυνὴ ἣν εἶδες ἔστιν ἡ πόλις ἡ μεγάλη ἡ ἔχουσα
βασιλείαν ἐπὶ τῶν βασιλέων τῆς γῆς.

1) *And one of the seven angels that had the seven bowls came,*
and he spoke to me and said, "Come, I will show you the judg-
ment of the great harlot who sits on many waters, 2) *with whom*
the kings of the earth have committed fornication, and those
who dwell on the earth have become drunk on the wine of her
fornication. 3) *And in spirit he brought me into a wilderness.*

4) *And I saw a woman sitting on a scarlet beast, full of blas-*
phemous names, with seven heads and ten horns. And the wom-
an was clothed with purple and scarlet, adorned with gold and
precious stone and pearls, with a golden cup in her hand full of
abominations and the filth of her fornication. 5) *And on her*
forehead was written a name, "Mystery, Babylon the Great, the
Mother of the World's Harlots and Abominations." 6) *And I saw*
the woman drunk from the blood of the saints and from the blood
of the martyrs of Jesus.

And when I saw her I was greatly amazed. 7) *And the angel said*
to me, "Why are you amazed? I will tell you the mystery of the
woman and of the beast that carries her, the one that has the
seven heads and the ten horns. 8) *The beast which you saw was*
and is not and will come out of the abyss and goes into destruc-
tion. And those who dwell on the earth, whose names from the
creation of the world have not been written in the book of life, will
be amazed when they see the beast because he was and is not and
shall be.

9) *Here is the mind that has wisdom: the seven heads are seven*
mountains on which the woman sits. They are also seven kings.
10) *Five have fallen, one is, the other has not yet come, and when*
he comes, he must remain for a short time. 11) *And the beast*
which was and is not, even he is the eighth and belongs to the
seven and goes into destruction. 12) *And the ten horns which you*
saw are ten kings, who have not yet received a kingdom, but with

the beast they receive authority (to rule) as kings for one hour. 13) *They share one opinion and they give their power and authority to the beast.* 14) *These will make war against the Lamb, and the Lamb will conquer them, because he is Lord of Lords and King of Kings; and those who are with him are called and elect and believing.*

15) *And he said to me, "The waters which you saw, where the harlot sits, are peoples and multitudes and nations and languages.* 16) *And the ten horns and the beast which you saw, these will hate the harlot and will cause her to be forsaken and naked and they will eat her flesh and will burn her in fire.* 17) *For God has put it into their hearts to carry out what he has in mind, to carry out a common design, namely, to give their royal authority to the beast until the words of God will be fulfilled.* 18) *And the woman whom you saw is the great city which rules over the kings of the earth.*

The preceding series of visions had ended with a preview of God's final judgment against Babylon, the great oppressor of the church. This judgment is now set forth in greater detail in a new vision. We are still dealing with the same general subject, since the vision is introduced by one of the seven angels who had the seven bowls.

The angel promises to show John "the judgment of the great harlot who sits upon many waters." John is further told that the kings of earth have committed adultery with the harlot and that "those who dwell on the earth have become drunk with the wine of her fornication." After the angel made this announcement, he carried John "in spirit" into the wilderness. (See the comments on 1:10 and 4:2 as to why ἐν πνεύματι should be translated "in spirit" and not, as the NIV translates, "in the Spirit.") The phrase describes the spiritual state in which John was able to see and hear things that normally are not accessible to the human senses.

The "wilderness" is mentioned in Revelation only here and in the vision of the dragon (12:6,14). Many commentators see no significance in this. They either ignore the fact or insist that the woman pictured here has no connection with the woman persecuted by the dragon. The fact that the word "wilderness" has the definite article in the earlier vision and has no article here might seem to indicate that John is speaking of two distinct wildernesses. However, the apostate Old Testament church is often described by the prophets as a faithful wife who has become a harlot. In the same way apostasy from the true worship of God is regularly described as whoredom. Isaiah, for example, wrote of Jerusalem, "See how the faithful city has become a harlot" (Is 1:21; cp Jr 2:2,20; Eze 16 and 23). Thus it would be in keeping with biblical imagery to see a close connection between the woman in the dragon vision and the woman who is portrayed here. There is no real reason why we cannot say that the harlot of this chapter is the apostate church — an identification in harmony with the rest of Scripture.

The apostate church is a "great harlot who sits upon many waters." The significance of this symbolism is explained later in this chapter, where we read, "The waters which you saw, where the harlot sits, are peoples and multitudes and nations and languages." One might be inclined to expect that if the church became apostate she would lose her supporters. The Savior had commanded his followers to beware of false prophets (Mt 7:15), and the apostles urged Christians to have no fellowship with those who are not faithful to the gospel (Ro 16:17; 2 Jn 10; 2 Cor 6:14-18). Already the Old Testament prophets had warned against false teachers (Dt 13:1ff; Jr 23:9-32).

If those who claim to be followers of Christ and who call him "Lord" would do what he and his called apostles and prophets say, an apostate church would find little success. But this reference to the "many waters" on which the woman sits is a reminder that the apostate church may greatly outnumber the "little flock" to which the heavenly Father is pleased to give the kingdom (Lk 12:32). Christians are thus admonished not to judge the faithfulness or the orthodoxy of the church by its size or success in this world. This mistake is made by the Roman Catholic theologian Bellarmin, who lists the large size of the Roman Church as one of the marks demonstrating that it is the true church of Christ on earth. But, in fact, this very assertion, the claim to catholicity, or universality, on the part of a church may be an indication that we are confronted by a manifestation of this harlot who sits on many waters and exercises authority over multitudes of nations. The world will love a church which proclaims doctrines that conform to the conclusions of human reason (Jn 15:19). Since religions of work righteousness are most acceptable to human reason, we can expect them to have catholic, or universal, appeal.

The angel tells John that the kings of the earth committed fornication with the harlot. Thus the secular rulers and leaders of the world join forces with the unfaithful church and support her in her apostasy. The history of the church in the Middle Ages furnishes countless examples of such kings who supported the false doctrine of the church and its departure from the true worship of God. In our own time we often see secular governments supporting apostate churches in their errors, as well as apostate churches encouraging governments in their antichristian endeavors. For example, when an attempt was made in 1982 to blunt the influence of evolutionary philosophy in the public schools of Arkansas, liberal churchmen joined in the effort to keep the concept of a Creator God from being recognized as a reasonable option to be considered by public school pupils even though the Declaration of Independence had spoken of inalienable rights with which men had been endowed by their "Creator." Countless other examples could be cited to demonstrate how an apostate church and governmental authorities work together to the detriment of the gospel and its free proclamation among all nations.

The proclamation of false doctrines by an apostate church has the result that "those who dwell on the earth . . . become drunk with the wine of her fornication." Just as a drunkard's mind becomes befuddled and clouded, so the unbelieving world, the people whose home is on this earth and whose citizenship is not in heaven (Php 3:20), cannot think clearly and correctly about those things that matter most. Their minds are blinded by the false views promulgated by a church that has become unfaithful.

When John was brought in spirit into the wilderness he saw the woman whom the angel had described earlier. She was seated on a scarlet beast, full of blasphemous names, with seven heads and ten horns. This scarlet beast is the beast from the sea, which had been described as having seven heads and ten horns and blasphemous names (13:1). The only new feature is the color of the beast, which is κόκκινος, scarlet. The woman's robe is described as being πορφυροῦν καὶ κόκκινον (v. 4), purple and scarlet.

This word-picture of the woman dressed in scarlet sitting on the scarlet beast recalls how the kings of the earth had committed adultery with the woman. The beast from the sea, described in chapter 13, now reappearing here, is a symbol of the secular antichrist, or civil government in its antichristian aspects. The woman wears garments of the same color as the beast. The apostate church has taken on the color of the world. She has forgotten the admonition of Paul, "Be not conformed to this world, but be ye transformed by the renewing of your mind" (Ro 12:2). When we see the woman sitting on the beast, we see an alliance between the antichristian forces in the secular governments and the apostate church. In the widespread state-church system, so common in European countries since the time of Constantine, we find a concrete fulfillment of this vision. This is especially deadly where the church is the dominating force in that antichristian combination. Whoever sits on the animal exercises control over it.

The apostate church is described not only as wearing the color of the beast. She is also dressed in purple, an expensive cloth, and gilded with gold and precious stone and pearls. In her hand she holds a golden cup. The alliance with the secular government speaks of the power of the apostate church. These words portray her wealth.

More often than not, great wealth has an evil influence on the church and the leaders of the church. The literature of the Reformation period contains many protests against the luxurious living of the clergy, and St. Paul spoke of religious professionals who "think religion is a way to make money" (1 Tm 6:5, Beck's translation). Already the Old Testament prophets denounced the luxurious living of those who claimed to be God's people (*e.g.*, Am 6:1-6). Church history records countless examples of wealth and the desire for wealth exerting a corrupting influence on churches and churchmen. The world hates those who are not of the world (Jn 15:19). But that hatred diminishes as interests coincide. The desire for wealth contributes to the process by which the church more and more takes on the scarlet color of the world.

In fact, the temptations of wealth and worldly prestige have had such debilitating effects on the visible church that some orthodox scholars have suggested that this vision of the harlot Babylon represents the cares, the riches and the pleasures of this world which often lead Christians astray (cp Mt 13:22; Lk 8:14). This interpretation is not out of harmony with the doctrinal content of the rest of Scripture. Nor is it radically out of harmony with the interpretation which we have adopted as preferable. It views the desire for wealth and prestige as a cause of the church's apostasy rather than as a part of her defection from the purity of biblical doctrine.

The result is that instead of offering the world the treasures of the gospel in earthen vessels (2 Cor 4:7) the church holds out to the world a golden cup filled "with abominations and the filth of her fornication" (v. 4). Instead of nourishing men with the wine and milk of the gospel, which is to be offered to men "without money and without price" (Is 55:1), the church has prostituted her message for gain and makes men drunk with the wine of her fornications (v. 2). The wine in the cup is the false doctrine by which she leads men away from the truth of salvation by faith alone and grace alone. In our time we see that spiritual fornication not only in the Church of Rome, but also in much of modern Protestantism.

It is therefore not surprising that John saw written on her forehead the words, "Mystery, Babylon the Great, the Mother of the World's Harlots and Abominations" (v. 5). When the Apostle Paul spoke of the great man of sin who would claim supreme authority in the religious and secular realm, he called him the "mystery of iniquity" (2 Th 2:6). The word μυστήριον (mystery) denotes a secret. From Paul's description it is easy to see why this name is given to the great Antichrist. Paul says that he sits in the temple of God. He holds a highly visible position in the church, from which he tries to establish his rule in God's temple, that is, in the church. But at the same time he is the embodiment of iniquity, or lawlessness (ἀνομία). Paul's description helps us to understand this vision and strengthens the conviction that we are here dealing with the apostate visible church. Christ knows those who are his (2 Tm 2:19). He sees the invisible church. It is a glorious church, without spot or wrinkle or blemish, because it has been sanctified by the washing of holy baptism (Eph 5:26) and has not denied its baptismal faith. The church apostate, as she appears to the world, is also a glorious church. But her glory consists not in the forgiveness of sins, but in worldly power, pomp, and prestige.

One of the great mysteries with which we must deal in the doctrine of the church is indicated by the next name on the harlot's forehead: "Babylon the Great." As we have already noted in the previous chapter, Babylon is the great enemy of God's people. The apostate church deserves this name. By her spiritual adultery, her unfaithfulness to God's Word, she does more damage to the work of the true church than a secular Babylon ever could do. This concept of the visible church had already been symbolized in chapter 11, where it was said that our Lord was crucified in the city where God's temple stood. Therefore the city deserves no longer to be called Jerusalem, but "Sodom" and "Egypt."

The apostate church is also called the "Mother of the World's Harlots and Abominations." The real church is the mother of all Christians (Ga 4:26). The outwardly wealthy and powerful but spiritually bankrupt church is the very opposite. By her false doctrines she encourages spiritual fornication and idolatrous religion, unfaithfulness to the true God and a form of worship that has the characteristics of idolatry. The word "abominations" was a word often used in the Old Testament to denote idols and idol worship. Because God has revealed himself in the words and teachings of Scripture, men fall away from the worship and knowledge of the true God when they depart from the teachings of the Bible. And when such a departure reaches the point where Jesus is no longer proclaimed as God or where salvation is no longer through faith in Christ alone but depends on man's works, a false god is being proclaimed, even if many of the outward trappings of Christianity remain. The God of the Bible does not give eternal life to men because they have merited such life by their imperfect good deeds. Such a god exists only in the depraved imagination of men.

Not only has the so-called "church" become spiritually adulterous. John sees the apostate church as an active persecutor of the true children of God. This is one of the great mysteries revealed to John in this vision. The saints who in his day were being martyred by the secular Roman government would at some time in the future be put to death by an apostate church. Many people undoubtedly saw the conversion of Constantine and the origin of the state church system as a great victory for Christianity. We would expect that if the church is able to sit on the back of the seven-headed beast she would use the power and authority of the government to further the cause of the gospel. Instead, when the woman in John's vision became seated on the scarlet beast, she became "drunk with the blood of the saints and the blood of the martyrs of Jesus." The church history of the Middle Ages and even of our own time gives us countless examples of how the church used the authority of the government for the persecution and sometimes even the slaughter of men and women who wanted to be faithful to God's Word and who sought to give the gospel its proper place in the life of the church.

The next verses again seem very difficult, but most of the difficulty comes from our natural inclination to try to fit what is said here into the Roman history of John's day. If we treat the numbers here as symbolic, as they should be in keeping with the nature of the book, much of the difficulty disappears.

There can be no doubt that the vision speaks of the city of Rome. This is already indicated rather clearly when it is said that the seven heads of the beast on which the woman is seated are "the seven mountains on which the woman sits" (v. 9). While it is true that other cities were built on seven hills, as some commentators point out, it is also true that when men spoke about "the city of seven hills" they meant Rome. Any doubt about this identification is completely removed by the last sentence in the chapter: "The woman whom you saw is the great city which rules over the kings of the earth." At John's time this was the capital of the Roman empire. What Babylon was to the chosen people of the Old Testament, Rome was to the elect of God in the New Testament. And just as the symbolic significance of Babylon still was meaningful long after that city had fallen into ruins, so the symbolic significance of Rome is still meaningful for us today. In this chapter we are dealing with another great threat to the church's existence.

That this threat should come from within the church itself seems strange. When John saw the woman he was greatly amazed (v. 6b). At that point the angel promised to tell him more about the woman and the beast with seven heads and ten horns. Of the beast the angel said, "He was, and is not, and is about to come up out of the abyss, and he goes into destruction." This is evidently a statement of some significance, since it is echoed and reechoed in the further description of the beast. Later in the same verse we are told, "He was, and is not, and shall be." The KJV has "yet is" instead of "shall be." This is the reading in a few manuscripts, but most of them have "shall be." This latter reading is corroborated by the parallel thought in the previous sentence, "he is about to come up." A part of the description of the beast is repeated in verse 11, which says that he "was, and is not, . . . and goes into destruction." This thought is also reflected in verse 10, "The one is, the other has not yet come, and when he comes he must remain for a short time."

This is evidently an important feature of this vision, but it is at the same time rather mysterious. The pattern followed here seems to be a caricature echoing the description of God found earlier in the book. In three passages God was described as "the one who is and who was and who is to come" (1:4,8; 4:8) and in two additional passages as "the one who is and who was" (11:17; 16:5). In our comments on 1:4 we have already pointed out that in this description of God there is undoubtedly an allusion to the name which God gave himself at the burning bush, namely, "I AM," which is closely related to the name Jehovah, or Jahweh, that is, "HE IS." That name expresses the eternal immutability of God. What he was, he still is, and always will be.

The beast seeks to rival God. The Apostle Paul, in speaking of the great Antichrist to the Thessalonians (2 Th 2:4), said that he sits in the temple of God and claims to be God. The association of the beast with the number "seven" seems to point to this claim also. Everywhere in Revelation, except in connection with this beast, the number seven always has some connection with God and his covenant with men. The beast arrogates the divine number to himself and thus lays claim to divinity. But while God was and is and is to be, the beast "was and is not," and even if he appears on the scene again he remains only "a short time" and always "goes into destruction." We may interpret the present tense of the verb ὑπάγει (he goes) as an iterative present describing what happens again and again.

To a church undergoing persecution this must have been a source of great comfort. Times of suffering and pain always seem long to those who are afflicted. But John assures his people that the enemies who seek to destroy them "last but a little hour." Behind the scenes of history the true God, who always is and always has been and always will be, still exercises his governing power. At the same time, however, John warns his people that the enmity of the beast will never die out. He will appear on the scene again and again, but always as one destined for destructon.

The great power and prestige of the beast comes to our attention again when we read that "those who dwell on the earth, whose names from the creation of the world have not been written in the book of life, will be amazed when they see the beast, because [or, that] he was and is not and shall be." We have already commented on all the significant phrases here in an earlier chapter (13:8).

The first words of verse 9, "Here is the mind that has wisdom," are reminiscent of a similar sentence in an earlier vision of the beast, "Here is wisdom" (13:18). By this, John seems to indicate that he is about to give us some clues to the understanding of the vision.

The seven heads of the scarlet beast, he says, are seven mountains on which the woman sits. This is an obvious reference to Rome, "the city of seven hills." The embodiment of the apostate church is to be looked for especially in Rome. This verse lends another piece of biblical evidence to support the assertion of the Lutheran confessions that the pope in Rome is the great Antichrist.

The seven heads have yet another significance. "They are seven kings; five have fallen, one is, and the other has not yet come." Many attempts have been made to fit these words into the pattern of Roman history, but all such attempts end in failure. It soon becomes obvious that the seven kings spoken of here cannot be seven specific emperors of the Roman empire.

It is much more tempting to see in "the one who is" a symbolic figure representing all the emperors of Rome, especially those who manifested their antichristian character by active persecution of the church. If this is the significance of the king that "is," then it would follow that the five that "have fallen" are symbols of the five great world empires which in Old Testament times threatened to wipe out the people of God.

The first of these five was Egypt, whose Pharaoh at the time of Moses set out to destroy the children of Israel. But God miraculously intervened with the ten plagues and the drowning of the Egyptian army in the sea. The second great empire to threaten the existence of the Old Testament church was Assyria, which destroyed the northern kingdom of Israel and gladly would have destroyed the tribe of Judah, from which the Savior was to come, if God had not intervened to destroy the army of Sennacherib instead. After Assyria came Babylonia, which led Judah and Jerusalem into captivity. Again, they strove to end all hope for a Messiah to be born in Bethlehem. But God intervened to bring the tribe of Judah back to the promised land. The fourth great empire was that of Persia, which at first seemed to favor the church by not only permitting but actually supporting the rebuilding of the temple. But that empire came close to destroying the Messianic line when Xerxes gave the order to exterminate all Jews (Est 3:13). The fifth and last great enemy of the church of the Old Testament was the empire of Alexander, which in the person of Antiochus Epiphanes came close to wiping out the worship of the true God among the Jews. The pattern followed in the history of the secular antichrist is always: "He was, he is not, he will be, and he will go into destruction."

So the secular antichrist in John's day, the persecuting Roman empire, would suffer the same fate. This was the assurance with which God's people could keep hope from dying out in their hearts. And yet they were never to set their hope on an earthly millennial reign which would follow the destruction of this antichrist. There is always another such king in the church's future, but he, too, is limited and will remain for only a short time.

But in the background of history, behind the overt manifestations of hatred against Christinity, stands the beast from the sea, the devil's instrument in his war against the true church. He is the eighth great enemy operating in and through the seven kings. Whenever one of the seven kings is destroyed, the beast appears to have suffered a deadly wound (13:3). When that happens, there are those who proclaim that the millennial dawn has broken across the eastern skies of ecclesiastical history. But the deadly wound is always healed, and the beast again rises out of the abyss of hell, but only to be sent back to destruction in God's good time. This is the pattern of the history of the enemies of the church.

The seven heads of the beast do not portray the full history of the beast's activity. John had also seen ten horns growing out of the seven heads. The angel tells him that these ten horns are ten more kings (v. 12). The reign of all these kings lies in the future. "They have not yet received a kingdom." But they will receive authority to rule as kings and will be allied with the beast. Yet like all the enemies of the church that preceded them, their reign will be of limited duration. It will last only for "one hour." Since ten is the number of completeness, this part of the vision summarizes the whole future history of the secular antichrist. The ten kings are a symbolic representation of all the future secular enemies of the church.

All of them have the same attitude toward the church. "They share one opinion and they give their power and authority to the beast" (v. 13). They use their power and their authority in the service of the beast, whose aim is to destroy the church. But as they battle against the church they are really waging war against the Lamb (v. 14). Yet the Lamb will always be victorious because he is Lord of lords and King of kings. His victory is also the victory of his people, for "those who are with him are called and elect and believing." They have been called by the gospel in time as they were elected from all eternity. Because of this election and through the call they have become believers. Because this passage represents the clear relationship between the call, election and faith, the translation "believing" is better than "faithful" for πιστοὶ in this context.

Someone may be able to improve upon the details of the above intepretation, but concerning one thing there can be no doubt. This vision of the beast and the woman is another portrayal of the calamities that the church will suffer at the hands of her enemies and of the assurance of the final victory for those who put their trust in the Lord. The vision is a symbolic representation of the promise of Christ that "the gates of hell shall not prevail" against the church (Mt 16:18).

The angel, having spoken of the beast and its heads and horns, now turns his attention once more to the woman. In our preliminary remarks on the first verse of this chapter we commented on the angel's explanation of the waters on which the woman was sitting. The angel also tells John that the ten kings and the beast will hate the harlot. The angel's words remind us of God's words to the city of Jerusalem in Ezekiel 16. There Jerusalem is accused of having committed fornication with the Egyptians, the Assyrians and the Babylonians. God threatens the city with punishment on that account. He says through Ezekiel, "I will hand you over to your lovers. . . . They will . . . leave you naked and bare" (Eze 16:39). The fate decreed through Ezekiel for apostate Israel is the fate decreed through John for the apostate New Testament church. The secular governments with whom she makes an unholy alliance will turn against the apostate church. They will make her destitute and naked, eat her flesh, and burn her with fire. Just as God used the king of Assyria as the "rod of his anger" (Is 10:5) to punish Israel, even though the king of Assyria was following his own evil inclinations in doing so (Is 10:7), so God takes governments into his service to act as agents of his wrath against an unfaithful people. What he has in mind (τὴν γνώμην αὐτοῦ) and what they have in mind (μίαν γνώμην) is not the same goal. Yet, in a sense, it is the same. God puts into the hearts of men to carry out what he has in mind, namely, to punish the church for her spiritual adultery. They, of course, do not intend to serve the Lord but to place their resources into the service of the beast. Nevertheless the outcome of the whole process is that "the words of God will be fulfilled" (v. 17). Even the wicked plans of the church's enemies must help to carry out God's plan and to fulfill his promises.

The final words of the angel once more identify the woman as the city of Rome. The first city that John's readers would have thought of as the "great city which rules over the kings of the earth" (v. 18) was the capital of the Roman empire. As at that time Rome was the center from which the persecution of the church was directed, so in the time of the ten kings, whose coming still lay in the future (v. 12), Rome would remain the center of enmity against the true church of God. In the church of Rome, which officially damned the doctrine of salvation by grace through faith at the Council of Trent, the apostasy of the church reached its fullest development. The Lutheran confessions unequivocally identify the papacy of Rome as the great Antichrist. This is at least a partial fulfillment of the prophecies of chapter 17.

THE DEFEAT OF BABYLON (18:1-24)

1) Μετὰ ταῦτα εἶδον ἄλλον ἄγγελον καταβαίνοντα ἐκ τοῦ οὐρανοῦ, ἔχοντα ἐξουσίαν μεγάλην, καὶ ἡ γῆ ἐφωτίσθη ἐκ τῆς δόξης αὐτοῦ. 2) καὶ ἔκραξεν ἐν ἰσχυρᾷ φωνῇ λέγων, Ἔπεσεν ἔπεσεν Βαβυλὼν ἡ μεγάλη, καὶ ἐγένετο κατοικητήριον δαιμονίων καὶ φυλακὴ παντὸς πνεύματος ἀκαθάρτου καὶ φυλακὴ παντὸς ὀρνέου ἀκαθάρτου καὶ μεμισημένου, 3) ὅτι ἐκ τοῦ οἴνου τοῦ θυμοῦ τῆς πορνείας αὐτῆς πέπωκαν πάντα τὰ ἔθνη, καὶ οἱ βασιλεῖς τῆ γῆς μετ' αὐτῆς ἐπόρνευσαν, καὶ οἱ ἔμποροι τῆς γῆς ἐκ τῆς δυνάμεως τοῦ στρήνους αὐτῆς ἐπλούτησαν. 4) Καὶ ἤκουσα ἄλλην φωνὴν ἐκ τοῦ οὐρανοῦ λέγουσαν, Ἐξέλθατε ὁ λαός μου ἐξ αὐτῆς, ἵνα μὴ συνκοινωνήσητε ταῖς ἁμαρτίαις αὐτῆς, καὶ ἐκ τῶν πληγῶν αὐτῆς ἵνα μὴ λάβητε· 5) ὅτι ἐκολλήθησαν αὐτῆς αἱ ἁμαρτίαι ἄχρι τοῦ οὐρανοῦ, καὶ ἐμνημόνευσεν ὁ Θεὸς τὰ ἀδικήματα αὐτῆς. 6) ἀπόδοτε αὐτῇ ὡς καὶ αὐτὴ ἀπέδωκεν, καὶ διπλώσατε τὰ διπλᾶ κατὰ τὰ ἔργα αὐτῆς· ἐν τῷ ποτηρίῳ ᾧ ἐκέρασεν κεράσατε αὐτῇ διπλοῦν· 7) ὅσα ἐδόξασεν αὐτὴν καὶ ἐστρηνίασεν, τοσοῦτον δότε αὐτῇ βασανισμὸν καὶ πένθος. ὅτι ἐν τῇ καρδίᾳ αὐτῆς λέγει ὅτι Κάθημαι βασίλισσα καὶ χήρα οὐκ εἰμὶ καὶ πένθος οὐ μὴ ἴδω· 8) διὰ τοῦτο ἐν μιᾷ ἡμέρᾳ ἥξουσιν αἱ πληγαὶ αὐτῆς, θάνατος καὶ πένθος καὶ λιμός, καὶ ἐν πυρὶ κατακαυθήσεται· ὅτι ἰσχυρὸς Κύριος ὁ Θεὸς ὁ κρίνας αὐτήν. 9) Καὶ σλαύσουσιν καὶ κόψονται ἐπ' αὐτὴν οἱ βασιλεῖς τῆς γῆς οἱ μετ αὐτῆς πορνεύσαντες καὶ στρηνιάσαντες, ὅταν βλέπωσιν τὸν καπνὸν τῆς πυρώσεως αὐτῆς, 10) ἀπὸ μακρόθεν ἑστηκότες διὰ τὸν φόβον τοῦ βασανισμοῦ αὐτῆς, λέγοντες, Οὐαὶ οὐαί, ἡ πόλις ἡ μεγάλη, Βαβυλῶν ἡ πόλις ἡ ἰσχυρά, ὅτι μιᾷ ὥρᾳ ἦλθεν ἡ κρίσις σου. 11) Καὶ οἱ ἔμποροι τῆς γῆς κλαίουσιν καὶ πενθοῦσιν ἐπ' αὐτήν, ὅτι τὸν γόμον αὐτῶν οὐδεὶς ἀγοράζει οὐκέτι, 12) γόμον χρυσοῦ καὶ ἀργύρου καὶ λίθου τιμίου καὶ μαργαριτῶν καὶ βυσσίνου καὶ πορφύρας καὶ σιρικοῦ καὶ κοκκίνου, καὶ πᾶν ξύλον θύϊνον καὶ πᾶν σκεῦος ἐλεφάντινον καὶ πᾶν σκεῦος

**ἐκ ξύλου τιμιωτάτου καὶ χαλκοῦ καὶ σιδήρου καὶ μαρμάρου,
13) καὶ κιννάμωμον καὶ ἄμωμον καὶ θυμιάματα καὶ μύρον καὶ
λίβανον καὶ οἶνον καὶ ἔλαιον καὶ σεμίδαλιν καὶ σῖτον καὶ κτήνη
καὶ πρόβατα, καὶ ἵππων καὶ ῥεδῶν καὶ σωμάτων, καὶ ψυχὰς
ἀνθρώπων. 14) καὶ ἡ ὀπώρα σου τῆς ἐπιθυμίας τῆς ψυχῆς ἀπῆλθεν
ἀπὸ σοῦ, καὶ πάντα τὰ λιπαρὰ καὶ τὰ λαμπρὰ ἀπώλετο ἀπὸ σοῦ,
καὶ οὐκέτι οὐ μὴ αὐτὰ εὑρήσουσιν. 15) οἱ ἔμποροι τούτων, οἱ
πλουτήσαντες ἀπ' αὐτῆς, ἀπὸ μακρόθεν στήσονται διὰ τὸν φόβον
τοῦ βασανισμοῦ αὐτῆς κλαίοντες καὶ πενθοῦντες, 16) λέγοντες,
Οὐαὶ οὐαί, ἡ πόλις ἡ μεγάλη, ἡ περιβεβλημένη βύσσινον καὶ
πορφυροῦν καὶ κόκκινον, καὶ κεχρυσωμένη ἐν χρυσίῳ καὶ λίθῳ
τιμίῳ καὶ μαργαρίτῃ, 17) ὅτι μιᾷ ὥρᾳ ἠρημώθη ὁ τοσοῦτος πλοῦ-
τος. Καὶ πᾶς κυβερνήτης καὶ πᾶς ὁ ἐπὶ τόπον πλέων καὶ ναῦται καὶ
ὅσοι τὴν θάλασσαν ἐργάζονται, ἀπὸ μακρόθεν ἔστησαν 18) καὶ
ἔκραζον βλέποντες τὸν καπνὸν τῆς πυρώσεως αὐτῆς λέγοντες, Τίς
ὁμοία τῇ πόλει τῇ μεγάλῃ; 19) καὶ ἔβαλον χοῦν ἐπὶ τὰς κεφαλὰς
αὐτῶν καὶ ἔκραζον κλαίοντες καὶ πενθοῦντες, λέγοντες, Οὐαὶ
οὐαί, ἡ πόλις ἡ μεγάλη, ἐν ᾗ ἐπλούτησαν πάντες οἱ ἔχοντες τὰ
πλοῖα ἐν τῇ θαλάσσῃ ἐκ τῆς τιμιότητος αὐτῆς, ὅτι μιᾷ ὥρᾳ
ἠρημώθη. 20) Εὐφραίνου ἐπ' αὐτῇ, οὐρανὲ καὶ οἱ ἅγιοι καὶ οἱ
ἀπόστολοι καὶ οἱ προφῆται, ὅτι ἔκρινεν ὁ Θεὸς τὸ κρίμα ὑμῶν ἐξ
αὐτῆς. 21) Καὶ ἦρεν εἷς ἄγγελος ἰσχυρὸς λίθον ὡς μύλινον μέγαν,
καὶ ἔβαλεν εἰς τὴν θάλασσαν λέγων, Οὕτως ὁρμήματι βληθήσεται
Βαβυλὼν ἡ μεγάλη πόλις, καὶ οὐ μὴ εὑρεθῇ ἔτι. 22) καὶ φωνὴ
κιθαρῳδῶν καὶ μουσικῶν καὶ αὐλητῶν καὶ σαλπιστῶν οὐ μὴ
ἀκουσθῇ ἐν σοὶ ἔτι, καὶ πᾶς τεχνίτης πάσης τέχνης οὐ μὴ εὑρεθῇ
ἐν σοὶ ἔτι, καὶ φωνὴ μύλου οὐ μὴ ἀκουσθῇ ἐν σοὶ ἔτι, 23) καὶ φῶς
λύχνου οὐ μὴ φάνῃ ἐν σοὶ ἔτι, καὶ φωνὴ νουμφίου καὶ νύμφης οὐ
μὴ ἀκουσθῇ ἐν σοὶ ἔτι· ὅτι οἱ ἔμποροί σου ἦσαν οἱ μεγιστᾶνες τῆς
γῆς, ὅτι ἐν τῇ φαρμακείᾳ σου ἐπλανήθησαν πάντα τὰ ἔθνη, 24) καὶ
ἐν αὐτῇ αἷμα προφητῶν καὶ ἁγίων εὑρέθη καὶ πάντων τῶν ἐσφαγ-
μένων ἐπὶ τῆς γῆς.**

1) *After these things I saw another angel coming down out of the
sky. He had great authority, and the earth was illumined by his
glory.* 2) *He cried with a loud voice, saying,*

Fallen, fallen, is Babylon the great.
She has become a dwelling-place of demons,
and a prison for every unclean spirit,
and a prison for every unclean bird,
and a prison for every unclean and hated beast,
3) *because all the nations have drunk of the wine of*
her adulterous desire,
and the kings of the earth have committed adultery with her,

and the merchants of the earth have become rich from the
abundance of her luxury.

4) *And I heard another voice from the sky which said,*

Come out of her, my people,
in order that you may not share in her sins,
and that you may not receive some of her plagues;
5) *because her sins have touched the sky*
and God has remembered her unrighteous deeds.
6) *Repay her as she also repaid,*
pay her back double for what she has done;
in the cup in which she mixed, mix her a double portion.
7) *As much glory and luxury as she gave herself,*
so much torture and grief give to her,
because in her heart she says,
I sit as a queen,
and I am not a widow,
and sorrow I shall never see.
8) *Therefore her plagues will come on one day,*
death, and sorrow, and famine,
and she shall be burned in fire;
for powerful is the Lord God who judges her.

9) *And the kings of the earth who have fornicated and lived in*
luxury with her will weep and mourn for her when they see the
smoke of her burning, 10) *as they stand far away because they*
are terrified by her punishment, and say,

Woe, woe, O great city!
Woe, woe, O strong city!
because in one hour your judgment came.

11) *And the merchants of the earth weep and mourn over her,*
because no one buys their cargo any longer, 12) *a cargo of gold*
and silver and precious stone and pearls, of the finest linen, and
purple and silk and scarlet, and every kind of aromatic wood,
and every kind of ivory objects, and every kind of objects made of
precious wood and brass and iron and marble, 13) *cinnamon and*
spice and incense and myrrh and frankincense and wine and
olive oil and fine flour and grain and cattle and sheep and a
cargo of horses and chariots and bodies and souls of men.

14) *The fruit your soul desired has deserted you,*
all the costly, splendid luxuries have been
lost to you;
they will never ever find them again.

15) *The merchants who sold these things who were made rich by*
her, will stand far off because they are terrified by her punish-
ment, weeping and mourning, 16) *saying,*

Woe, woe, O great city,
who was clothed in fine linen and purple
and scarlet,
gilded with gold and precious stone
and pearl,
17) *because in one hour such great wealth*
was made a wasteland.

And every ship captain and all ocean travelers and sailors and
those who make their living on the sea stood far away 18) *and*
cried out when they saw the smoke of her burning, saying, "Who
is like the great city?" 19) *They threw dust on their heads and*
cried out as they wept and mourned, saying,

Woe, woe, O great city,
by whom all who have ships on the sea
were made rich out of her treasures,
because in one hour she was made a wasteland.
20) *Rejoice over her, O heaven,*
and saints and apostles and prophets,
because God has judged her for her judgment
over you.

21) *And a mighty angel picked up a stone, like a large millstone*
and cast it into the sea, saying,

In this way Babylon, the great city will be overthrown with
violence and will nevermore be found.
22) *And the sound of harpists and musicians,*
flutists and trumpeters
will never be heard in you again.
No craftsman of any trade
will ever be found in you again,
and the sound of a millstone
will never be heard in you again,
23) *and the light of a lamp*
will never shine in you again,
and the voice of bridegroom and bride
will never be heard in you again,
because your merchants were the great ones of the earth,
because by your witchcraft all the nations were led astray,
24) *and in her was found the blood of prophets and saints,*
even of all those who were slain on the earth.

Many of the comments that might be made on this chapter have already been made in connection with the proclamation of the fall of Babylon (14:8). The whole of this chapter is a dramatic portrayal of the fall of the enemies of the church, or the end of all the pleasures, cares and riches by which Satan had led believers to abandon Christ.

At the beginning of this vision John saw an angel who had great authority. The brightness of his glory illumined the earth as he repeated the message of the angel in chapter 14, "Babylon the great has fallen." The word "has fallen" (ἔπεσεν) is repeated twice as an assurance that this will certainly come to pass. Once Babylon was a center of civilization and culture and wealth, but now she had become the dwelling place of evil spirits and unclean birds and wild animals. Not all manuscripts have the words "a prison for every unclean beast," and the words are omitted in both the NIV and the KJV.

The NIV again translates (cp 14:8) the words, τοῦ οἴνου τοῦ θυμοῦ τῆς πορνείας, with "the maddening wine of her adulteries." While θυμός can mean "anger," one is hardly justified in treating τοῦ θυμοῦ as a descriptive genitive and translating it as "maddening." When θυμός is joined with πορνεία in a genitival relationship it undoubtedly must have its basic meaning of "passion" or "desire." We have understood τοῦ θυμοῦ as an epexegetical genitive and τῆς πορνείας as a descriptive genitive and therefore have translated, "the wine of her adulterous desire" (see the comments on 14:8). The adulterous relationship between Babylon and the kings of the earth was treated in detail in the previous chapter.

The only new note in verse 2 is the reference to the merchants of the earth who have become rich through the abundance (literally, the power) of Babylon's luxury. This is one of the dominant themes of the rest of the chapter.

Before describing Babylon's fall in detail, John first speaks of a voice which summoned God's people to separate themselves from Babylon, the apostate church and the seat of Antichrist. The angel reminds John and us that to remain in an apostate church is to be a partaker of her sins, and that those who share in her sins will also share at least in some of the plagues that will come upon her (v. 4). The call to separate from the apostate church is very similar to the command of Moses addressed to the children of Israel at the time of the rebellion of Korah, Dathan and Abiram (Nu 16:23-27). Those who refuse to separate run the risk of perishing with Babylon.

The previous chapter had spoken of the great prosperity of the antichristian element in the visible church. The following verses will describe its show of wealth. One of the great problems in the Christian's life, dealt with many times in the Bible, especially in the book of Job, is the prosperity of the wicked and the suffering of the righteous. When wickedness is clothed in purple and scarlet and adorned with gold and precious gems and pearls, it sometimes seems that God has surrendered the government of the universe to the devil. But when the angel tells John that the sins of Babylon, the apostate church, have touched the sky, he reminds us of the truth which Paul teaches when he says that in their prosperity the impenitent are piling up sins for the day of judgment (Ro 2:15). The sins of the wicked, even though they seem to go unpunished, are not forgotten by God. He will "remember" them (v. 5). This is, of course, an anthropomorphism, an ascribing of human actions to God by way of analogy. God in his omniscience does not "forget" or "remember" things. But when the prophet wants to impress on us that God forgives our sins, he tells us that God will not remember them (Jr 31:34). Likewise, when the angel here wants to underscore the certain punishment of Babylon, he says that God will remember her unjust deeds.

The justice of Babylon's punishment is then portrayed in the words,

> Repay her as she also repaid,
> pay her back double for what she has done;
> in the cup in which she mixed, mix her a double portion.
> As much glory and luxury as she gave herself,
> so much torture and grief give to her,
> because in her heart she says,
> I sit as a queen,
> and I am not a widow,
> and sorrow I shall never see.
> Therefore her plagues will come on one day,
> death, and sorrow, and famine,
> and she shall be burned in fire;
> for powerful is the Lord God who judges her.

The basic principle of justice is expressed concretely in the words "an eye for an eye, and a tooth for a tooth." Justice will be done to the church's enemies. The voice from heaven says, "Repay her as she also repaid." This same concept of a perfect balance between guilt and punishment is expressed also in the words, "As much glory and luxury as she gave herself, so much torture and grief give to her." In those words the church is assured again that the prosperity and power of her enemies will end in pain and sorrow. On the night before the crucifixion John had heard Jesus say to his disciples, "You will weep and mourn while the world rejoices. You will grieve, but your grief will turn to joy" (Jn 16:20). Here John hears the corollary of the promise proclaimed in the message, "The joy of the world will be turned into sorrow."

It is a little more difficult to see why the voice should say that Babylon will be paid back "double" for what she has done. That thought is repeated in the next words, which call for a double portion for Babylon in the cup in which she had mixed a drink for others. The figure of a cup is often used as symbol of suffering. The apostate church has inflicted much spiritual anguish on men by obscuring the gospel, which is the only source of real joy and comfort for men. By her persecutions she has become responsible for much physical pain and mental sorrow. The apostate church will receive twice the suffering that she has inflicted. At first glance that appears to be a violation of the principle, "An eye for an eye," for it seems to call for "two eyes for an eye." This concept of double punishment is rarely found in Scripture. In one of the few passages in which it is found, God, through the Prophet Jeremiah, threatened to punish apostate Israel with a double recompense (Jr 16:18). Yet we see in this a reflection of the principle enunciated by Jesus when he said that the disobedient servant who knew the master's will shall be beaten with many stripes (Lk 12:47). This threat, then, is another indication that the Babylon with which we are dealing here is not a heathen entity but the apostate church which had the revelation of God but rejected it in unbelief.

Thus the proud boast of the apostate church that she will abide forever as a queen and never be widowed (v. 7) is a delusion. The apostate church claims for herself Christ's promise that the gates of hell will not prevail against his church. She also claims for herself the title "the bride of Christ." But God calls her an unfaithful wife, an adulteress. According to the Old Testament Levitical law a priest's daughter who was guilty of fornication was to be executed by burning with fire (Lv 2:19). The context of this statute gives as a reason for such harsh punishment in this case the fact that the priests were "holy unto the Lord." Because the priest's daughter belonged to a family whose head stood in a very special relationship to God, therefore the punishment for her sins was also especially severe.

This same punishment of being burned with fire is decreed also for Babylon. Thus we have here another indication that Babylon is the ecclesiastical Antichrist since the punishment decreed for her fornication is that which was reserved for women who belonged to the priestly class in Israel. The apostate church also once stood in a special relationship to God.

That this punishment is sure is emphasized once more by the words, "Powerful is the Lord God who judges her." The words "the Lord God" are a translation of the Greek κύριος ὁ θεός, which is the equivalent of the Hebrew *JHVH Elohim*. We have already commented on this name (1:8). The church is in this way once more assured in the dark days of her persecution that the Lord has not forgotten her. Thereby she is encouraged to hope and to wait patiently for the day of her deliverance and to remain faithful to the true God. The God who watches over her and has promised that the gates of hell will not prevail is a powerful God who can keep that promise.

On the other hand, the kings of the earth who had joined the apostate church in her fornication and luxury will be powerless to help her on the day when her judgment is carried out. And she will be powerless to help them on their day of judgment. When they see "the smoke of her burning" (v. 9) they can only weep and wail from a distance because they are filled with fear at the sight of the terrible punishment that has so suddenly come upon her. Yet they remember that she was once a great and powerful (μεγάλη καὶ ἰσχυρά) city. It is significant that the same word (ἰσχυρός) is used to describe both the Lord God and Babylon. In times of persecution God's people are often distressed by the power of Babylon, which seems to threaten the very existence of the church and tempts them to lose hope. But the sight of Babylon burning before the kings of the earth leaves no doubt as to whom the kingdom and the power really belong.

As the kings of the earth who had supported Babylon with their power were helpless and unable to prevent the city's fall, so the merchants who had supplied her with luxuries and the ship captains who had transported those items of luxurious living likewise could only weep and mourn (v. 11-19). The detailed listing of the things which contributed to the wealth and luxury of Babylon (v. 11-13) sets before us in a very concrete way the great prosperity of the apostate church. We see in this long list of trade items another reminder that, like the temple of God in Jerusalem at the time of Christ, also the New Testament apostate church would be changed from a house of prayer into a place of merchandise. Church history furnishes us with a particularly powerful illustration of that degenerative process in the sale of indulgences. Here even the forgiveness of sins became an article of commerce, which brought untold wealth into the coffers of the church. We are reminded that wealth, as well as power, is no indication that a church is faithful to God.

The words of verse 14 are evidently addressed to Babylon: "The fruit your soul desired [literally, the fruit of the desire of your soul] has deserted you, all the costly , splendid luxuries [literally, all the costly things and the shining things] have been lost to you; they will never ever find them again." The text does not tell us who spoke these words, but since everything else in this context is spoken by the voice from heaven (v. 4), the NIV is probably not justifed in adding the words, "They will say" to the text.

The word ὀπώρα, fruit, is an unusual word found in the New Testament only here. It originally denoted the season of late summer/early autumn, when fruits were ready to harvest. It later became a name for the fruit that was gathered at that time of the year. Perhaps John used this particular word rather than the more common word for fruit since Babylon's end was near. The late fruit was now ripe. The words of this verse emphasize that the future hope Babylon had expressed earlier (v. 7b) will not be fulfilled. The certainty and permanence of her disappointment is emphasized by the triple negative at the end of the verse (οὐκέτι οὐ μή). The fact that the church prefers the treasures of this world over the spiritual and heavenly treasures offered in the gospel is another indication of her apostasy.

Just as the kings stood far off and bewailed the punishment of Babylon (v. 9,10) so the merchants are now portrayed in almost the same terms. They, too, express their sorrow and say,

> Woe, woe, O great city,
> who was clothed in fine linen and purple and scarlet,
> gilded with gold and precious stone and pearl,
> because in one hour such great wealth was made
> a wasteland.

The description of Babylon here echoes the description of the harlot in the previous chapter (17:4), except that in that place there is no mention of fine linen.

The merchants who had supplied Babylon with these luxuries are joined by the ship captains and the sailors who had delivered this cargo to the city. They, too, speak their woes over the sudden destruction of the city (v. 17-19).

After the angel describes the sorrow of Babylon's supporters, he calls upon the persecuted church to rejoice over the fallen city. The first exhortation to rejoice is addressed to heaven. Here heaven is either personified and addressed — as when the Old Testament psalms call upon inanimate creation to praise the Lord — or it is a figurative term for its inhabitants, the angels and departed saints. If the latter is intended we may view the first καὶ as an explanatory conjunction and translate, "Rejoice, O heaven, even you saints and apostles and prophets." The reason for their joy then follows in the words, "Because God has judged her for her judgment over you" (literally, "God has judged your judgment from her"). From the statement, "I saw the woman drunk with the blood of the saints and with the blood of the martyrs (or witnesses) of Jesus" (17:6), we conclude that Babylon had pronounced the death sentence over the saints. In the last verse of this chapter we read that Babylon was totally destroyed because "in her was found the blood of prophets and saints, even of all those who were slain on the earth." The words of the angel here clearly proclaim that Babylon is being punished for her persecution of the church. Thus the church in her time of suffering is assured that God has not abdicated his rule over the universe. In the end God will pronounce and carry out his judgment against the enemies of his true church, his believing children, and thus manifest his righteous judgments (15:4).

The Babylon spoken of here will be called to account for her killing of the apostles and prophets. Babylon, then, is a name not only for the antichristian forces at work in the visible church of the New Testament, but also of the Old Testament. Most of the prophets who were killed during the course of Old Testament history were not slain by heathen nations but by men who outwardly called themselves God's people and yet had apostasized from the true God. For that reason Jesus told the Jewish leaders of his time that the blood of all the slain prophets would be required of them (Lk 11:50). So also in New Testament times it was the Jews, the "chosen people," who called for the slaying of Jesus and the apostles (*e.g.*, Ac 12:1-3; 22:22). When they urged secular rulers to carry out the death penalty on faithful Christians, this was a concrete illustration of how the harlot sits on the beast, the secular antichrist, and uses him to serve her purposes. And when the apostate church of the Middle Ages called upon the secular government to burn those whom she adjudged to be heretics, we see a repetition of that historical theme.

The final verses of this chapter once more portray the total destruction of Babylon. The description of the city's complete devastation is introduced by a prophetic symbolic action on the part of an angel who now appeared to John. Just as the Old Testament prophets often were commanded to perform some action that would serve as a symbolic representation of their message, so this angel threw a large millstone into the sea. As that millstone disappeared in the depths of the ocean, so Babylon would be overthrown with violence. No musical instruments would ever be heard there again. No workman would ever again ply his trade there. No flour would ever be ground nor any lamp lighted there. No wedding celebration would ever take place there again. The Prophet Jeremiah had pictured the desolation of Jerusalem in the same terms when he wrote, "I will take from them the voice of mirth, and the voice of gladness, the voice of the bridegroom, and the voice of the bride, the sound of millstones, and the light of the candle" (Jr 25:10). Jeremiah had predicted that this situation would last only for seventy years. But the sixfold repetition of "never again" (οὐ μὴ ἔτι) in this curse speaks with a finality that assures perpetual victory to the church over all her enemies.

One cannot but wonder whether the angel's accusation that all the nations (πάντα τὰ ἔθνη) were led astray by the witchcraft of Babylon did not remind John of the commission which John had heard the risen Savior give to his church when he commanded his disciples to make disciples of all nations (πάντα τὰ ἔθνη). The disciples were sent out into all the world to gather the sheep of the Good Shepherd into the sheepfold of the holy Christian church. The apostate church sent out her merchants to gather in the material treasures the world has to offer. The true church was through her proclamation of the gospel to lead men on the path of righteousness and to turn them from the error of their way. The apostate church by her witchcraft led men astray from the truth (v. 23). The word for witchcraft, φαρμακεία, from which our word "pharmacy" is derived, reminds us that ancient witches used all sorts of drugs and magic potions. The false doctrines of Antichrist are such a devil's brew that brings spiritual stupor to the minds of men and makes doubly certain of this by silencing the voice of the prophets and of the saints (v. 24). For this she is to be utterly destroyed.

THE CHURCH'S VICTORY (19:1-21)

The Marriage Supper of the Lamb (19:1-10)

1) Μετὰ ταῦτα ἤκουσα ὡς φωνὴν μεγάλην ὄχλου πολλοῦ ἐν τῷ οὐρανῷ λεγόντων,

> **Ἁλληλουϊά· ἡ σωτηρία καὶ ἡ δόξα καὶ ἡ δύναμις τοῦ θεοῦ ἡμῶν, 2) ὅτι ἀληθιναὶ καὶ δίκαιαι αἱ κρίσεις αὐτοῦ· ὅτι ἔκρινεν τὴν πόρνην τὴ μεγάλην ἥτις ἔφθειρεν τὴν γῆν ἐν τῇ πορνείᾳ αὐτῆς, καὶ ἐξεδίκησεν τὸ αἷμα τῶν δούλων αὐτοῦ ἐκ χειρὸς αὐτῆς.**

3) καὶ δεύτερον εἴρηκαν, Ἁλληλουϊά· καὶ ὁ καπνὸς αὐτῆς ἀναβαίνει εἰς τοὺς αἰῶνας τῶν αἰώνων. 4) καὶ ἔπεσαν οἱ πρεσβύτεροι οἱ εἴκοσι τέσσαρες καὶ τὰ τέσσερα ζῶα, καὶ προσεκύνησαν τῷ Θεῷ τῷ καθημένῳ ἐπὶ τῷ θρόνῳ λέγοντες, Ἀμὴν Ἁλληλουϊά. 5) καὶ φωνὴ ἀπὸ τοῦ θρόνου ἐξῆλθεν λέγουσα,

> **Αἰνεῖτε τῷ Θεῷ ἡμῶν, πάντες οἱ δοῦλοι αὐτοῦ, οἱ φοβούμενοι αὐτόν, οἱ μικροὶ καὶ οἱ μεγάλοι.**

6) Καὶ ἤκουσα ὡς φωνὴν ὄχλου πολλοῦ καὶ ὡς φωνὴν ὑδάτων πολλῶν καὶ ὡς φωνὴν βροντῶν ἰσχυρῶν, λεγόντων,

> **Ἁλληλουϊά, ὅτι ἐβασίλευσεν Κύριος ὁ Θεὸς ἡμῶν ὁ Παντοκράτωρ. 7) χαίρωμεν καὶ ἀγαλλιῶμεν, καὶ δώσομεν τὴν δόξαν αὐτῷ, ὅτι ἦλθεν ὁ γάμος τοῦ Ἀρνίου, καὶ ἡ γυνὴ αὐτοῦ ἡτοίμασεν ἑαυτήν, 8) καὶ ἐδόθη αὐτῇ ἵνα περιβάληται βύσσινον λαμπρὸν καθαρόν·**

τὸ γὰρ βύσσινον τὰ δικαιώματα τῶν ἁγίων ἐστίν. 9) Καὶ λέγει μοι, Γράψον, Μακάριοι οἱ εἰς τὸ δεῖπνον τοῦ γάμου τοῦ Ἀρνίου κεκλημένοι. καὶ λέγει μοι, Οὗτοι οἱ λόγοι ἀληθινοὶ τοῦ Θεοῦ εἰσιν. 10) καὶ ἔπεσα ἔμπροσθεν τῶν ποδῶν αὐτοῦ προσκυνῆσαι αὐτῷ. καὶ λέγει μοι, Ὅρα μή· σύνδουλός σού εἰμι καὶ τῶν ἀδελφῶν σου τῶν ἐχόντων τὴν μαρτυρίαν Ἰησοῦ· τῷ Θεῷ προσκύνησον. ἡ γὰρ μαρτυρία Ἰησοῦ ἐστιν τὸ πνεῦμα τῆς προφητείας.

1) *After these things I heard what seemed to be the loud sound of a great crowd in heaven, saying,*

> *"Alleluia!*
> *Salvation and glory and power belong to our God,*
> 2) *for true and just are his judgments;*

for he has judged the great harlot
who corrupted the earth with her harlotry
and he has exacted vengeance for
the blood of his servants from her."

3) *And a second time they said,*

"Alleluia!
for her smoke arises forever and ever."

4) *And the twenty-four elders and the four living creatures fell down and worshiped the God who sits on the throne, saying,*

"Amen. Alleluia!"

5) *And a voice came from the throne, saying,*

"Praise our God,
all you servants of his,
you who fear him,
small and great."

6) *And I heard what seemed to be the sound of a great crowd, and what seemed to be the sound of many waters and what seemed to be the sound of loud thunderings, saying,*

"Alleluia!
for the Lord, our God, the Almighty One reigns.
7) *Let us be glad and rejoice*
and let us give praise to him,
for the wedding of the Lamb has come
8) *and his wife has made herself ready,*
and she was given clean, bright fine linen to wear,
for the fine linen is the "not guilty" verdicts pronounced
on the saints."

9) *And he said to me, "Write. Blessed are those who are invited to*
the wedding supper of the Lamb." And he said to me, "These are
the true words of God." 10) *And I fell down before his feet to*
worship him. And he said to me, "Don't do that! I am a fellow-
servant of yours and of your brothers who have the testimony
about Jesus. Worship God. For the testimony of Jesus is the spirit
of prophecy."

Two scenes now close the vision that portrays for us the victory of Christ and his church over both the secular and ecclesiastical Antichrist. The alliance between the two was portrayed in chapter 17. The next chapter depicts the fall of the ecclesiastical Antichrist. The first part of this chapter still belongs to the story of the collapse of the apostate church. And it sets before us, by way of contrast, the victory of the true church.

In the previous chapter the church was summoned to rejoice over God's judgment against Babylon. In this section we hear the church's response to that call. Three times John hears a loud "Alleluia" from the victorious church. This is the only passage in the New Testament where this common Old Testament Hebrew word, which means "Praise the Lord," occurs. The twenty-four elders, whom we first met in the introduction to John's vision (4:4; 5:8) and again in the vision of the end of the world in chapter 11 (v. 16), respond to the church's "Alleluias" with an "Amen" and an "Alleluia" of their own (v. 4).

Earlier, in the vision of the fifth seal (6:9-11) John had heard the souls of the martyrs asking how long the Lord would delay the punishment of their murderous persecutors. They had asked, "Until when, O Lord, will you put off your judging (κρίνεις) and your avenging (ἐκδικεῖς) of our blood?" Now in the complete destruction of Babylon they see the answer to that prayer, for God has judged (ἔκρινεν) the great harlot and avenged (ἐξεδίκησεν) the blood of her servants.

After the angel had described the utter devastation of Babylon, John heard what seemed to be the sound of a large crowd of people in heaven who said, "Praise the Lord." While this "great crowd" is not identified, the whole context shows clearly that these are the members of the church triumphant. They first of all ascribe salvation, glory and power to God. The power of the enemies of the church loomed large in the preceding context. In spite of their great power, the beast and the great harlot could not rob the church of salvation. God's power is too great for them. Thus the church recognizes that salvation does not come through her own strength and wisdom. The power to save belongs to God alone, and the praise and glory for that salvation belong to God alone.

Praise belongs to him because "his judgments are true and right." They are true not only because he makes no mistakes when he judges, but also because he had often promised that the servants of the devil would never prevail against his church. Now that Babylon has been totally destroyed and his redeemed children are safe in the glories of heaven, it is manifestly demonstrated that he always keeps his threats and promises and that his word is always true.

His judgments are also just. In the days of persecution when the wicked prosper, live long and become mighty in power (Job 21:7), while the righteous are pursued and persecuted and slain, it often seems to men that God's decisions are not right and just.

But in the end, when the scales are balanced, the unbelieving rich man is tormented while the believing Lazarus is comforted. The psalmist tells us that he was troubled by the seeming injustice of this world until he went to the sanctuary of God and understood the "final destiny" of the wicked (Ps 73). The redeemed saints in the sanctuary of heaven now recognize God's justice beyond all possibility of doubt since they no longer walk by faith but by sight. In this way God demonstrated his glorious saving power.

The redeemed church knows that God's judgments are true and right "because he has judged the great harlot." Throughout the Bible God had made it clear in many ways that he would not tolerate the falsification of his Word. Babylon, the great harlot, the apostate church, had done that by her witchcraft, through which she led all nations astray (18:23). Her great fall demonstrated the truthfulness of God's threats. By her spiritual fornication and unfaithfulness to the heavenly bridegroom she had corrupted the earth (v. 2) and according to the divine principles of justice it was right that she should be overthrown.

In that way God would avenge the blood of his servants (v. 2). There are many who have concluded from the Sermon on the Mount that vengeance is not compatible with Christianity. Yet here the saints rejoice over God's vengeance and praise him for it. It is true that in the Sermon on the Mount as well as in the Garden of Gethsemane, where he told Peter to sheathe his sword, the Savior forbids his church to use force as a weapon against the force used by her enemies. Paul also says that the weapons of our warfare are not carnal (2 Cor 10:4) and that we are not to avenge ourselves (Ro 12:19). But this does not in any way imply that vengeance is wrong. Rather, when God through the apostle forbids Christians to avenge themselves, he also promises that he will repay. The exaction of vengeance is a right that belongs to him (Ro 12:19). On earth God begins to carry out vengeance through those whom he ordains to act as his agents in this matter, namely, the secular authorities (Ro 13:1-4). On the day of judgment he will carry it out directly and finally balance all the books. Therefore vengeance exacted by God for the persecution and murder of his Christians is recognized as something perfectly just and right. For this the church can also rightly rejoice and properly thank and praise the Lord and sing her Alleluias.

So for the second time the shout goes up, "Alleluia!" In Hebrew a coordinate conjunction often introduces a subordinate idea. John's use of the Greek language often shows the influence of Hebrew grammar. The next phrase, introduced by καὶ, in reality gives the reason for the second Alleluia, and the καὶ of this verse is equivalent to the ὅτι (because) of the preceding sentence. The victorious church praises God because "her (Babylon's) smoke goes up forever and ever." The kings of the earth, the merchants and the sailors could only mourn and stand far off because of their fear at the sight of the "smoke of her burning" (18:9,15,18), because they must sense that the same punishment is reserved for them. The fact that this smoke will rise "forever and ever" teaches us that the fall of Babylon is not just a temporal setback from which she will rise again. It also teaches that her punishment does not consist in annihilation. It is an eternal punishment. It will never end. By the same token, the church's victory is not just a temporary victory. It is an eternal victory. It will never end.

For the third time in the book we read that the twenty-four elders fall down and worship God (cp 4:10; 11:16). With an "Amen" they express their approval of the church's joy over the destruction of her great enemy. Those who say that the writers of the imprecatory psalms, which ask God to punish the enemies of his people, are "sub-Christian" should see in this "Amen" a divine approval of such prayers. The twenty-four elders also speak an "Alleluia" of praise to God for his judgment against Babylon.

If the "Alleluia" of the elders is not sufficient to convince men that such praises are pleasing to the Lord, the next words of the chapter should remove all doubt. John heard a voice coming from the throne on which God was sitting. That voice again calls upon the servants of God, all who fear him, both small and great, to praise our God — the sign of God's own approval for these "Alleluias" of the saints.

Once more John heard the sound of the great crowd, but this time the sound of their voices had evidently reached a crescendo. He compares it to the sound of a rushing waterfall and loud thunder. For the third time the saints shout an "Alleluia." This time they give as the reason for their praise the fact that "the Lord God (κύριος ὁ θεός), the Almighty One, reigns." The Greek verb ἐβασίλευσεν we could treat either as a gnomic aorist, which we would translate in the present tense, or as an ingressive aorist, which we would translate, "The Lord God, the Almighty, has begun to reign." In the latter case it would state the situation as the church viewed it after the long period of persecution during which she saw little outward evidence of God's ruling power.

The saints then encourage each other to sing Alleluias as they say, "Let us be glad and rejoice and give him praise." This call goes out "because the marriage of the Lamb has come, and his wife has made herself ready" (v. 7). The Lamb's wife is the holy Christian church. In the Old Testament the chosen people are often spoken of as the wife of Jahweh, their God. The same figure of speech is taken over by the New Testament. Christ is often called the Bridegroom and the church his wife. In one of his parables the Savior spoke of the day of judgment as the day when the heavenly Bridegroom would come to claim his bride and to take her to his eternal home (Mt 25:1ff). When the saints see that this day has arrived it is a new occasion for their rejoicing and gladness.

The bride of the Lamb has prepared herself for this occasion. She is ready to greet the Bridegroom. The Apostle Paul helps us understand what is meant by the church's preparation for the day of judgment, the day of the Lamb's marriage. He writes (Eph 5:25-27),

> Husbands, love your wives, even as Christ loved the church and gave himself for it, that he might sanctify and cleanse it with the washing of water by the word, that he might present it unto himself as a glorious church, not having spot or wrinkle or any such thing, but that it should be holy and without blemish.

These words help us interpret John's vision.

The καὶ at the beginning of verse 8 again introduces a subordinate thought and explains in what the preparation of the bride consists. We are told that she is given clean, bright fine linen to wear. The wedding dress she wears is not one she brought to the wedding. It was a gift, freely bestowed to make her fit for this occasion. The word "given" reflects the doctrine of salvation by grace alone. The symbolism of this dress of fine linen is explained in the words, "The fine linen is the righteousnesses [δικαιώματα] of the saints."

There is some dispute about the translation of δικαιώματα τῶν ἁγίων, which we have rendered "the 'not guilty' verdicts pronounced on the saints." The word δικαίωμα is derived from δικαιόω, which means "to declare right, or righteous." The ending — μα in Greek indicates the product of a process. The most natural meaning of δικαίωμα would be a declaration of righteousness, a verdict of "not guilty." The word is sometimes used for any judgment, adverse or favorable, because in rendering any verdict, a judge utters his declaration about what is right (Re 15:4).

In biblical usage δικαὶωμα most often means a regulation or an ordinance. At first glance it may seem that this is far removed from the basic meaning of the word, but an ordinance is merely a formal declaration that a certain action is right.

The NIV has translated δικαιώματα with "righteous acts." There is really only one passage in the New Testament where δικαίωμα seems to mean a righteous act, and even this is not entirely certain (Ro 5:18). It is entirely possible to translate δικαίωμα in Romans 5:18 with "a verdict of 'not guilty' " and make prefectly good sense in the context. In fact, it probably makes better sense than the NIV's "one act of righteousness." Though the NIV translation of τὰ δικαίωματα τῶν ἁγίων, "the righteous acts of the saints," does not necessarily support the idea of justification by works, it does seem to imply it. We know from other passages of Scripture that our own good works are in themselves imperfect, but that they are acceptable to God through Jesus Christ. His blood washes away all the stains of sin that mar all the good deeds of the Christian (1 Pe 2:5). If we view the works of the believer as righteous in that sense, we may accept the NIV rendering.

From all this we conclude that when John says the bride is clothed in fine linen which consists of the δικαιώματα τῶν ἁγίων he has in mind that righteousness which God gives the sinner when he declares him to be righteous for the sake of Christ's vicarious obedience and which the sinner makes his own by faith. The only difficulty that confronts us in this interpretation is the plural form of the word, which evidently prompted the NIV translators to hit on the plural "righteous acts." However, the plural form could be a reference to the many individual acquittals which are pronounced in the preaching of the gospel and the absolution. Through that proclaimed forgiveness accepted by faith, the individual believers, who collectively form the bride of Christ, are adorned with the only garment that makes it possible for them to stand beside the holy Bridegroom in the presence of the righteous God.

The "fine linen, clean and bright" is the equivalent of the robes which were worn by the saints in chapter 7 and which were washed and made white in the blood of the Lamb. This interpretation would also be in harmony with those passages of the Bible that speak of the forgiveness of sins as clean garments worn by believers. A close parallel to the symbolism of our text is found in the words of Isaiah (61:10),

> I will greatly rejoice in the Lord,
> my soul shall be joyful in my God;
> for he hath clothed me with the garments of salvation,
> he hath covered me with the robe of righteousness,
> as a bridegroom decketh himself with ornaments,
> and as a bride adorneth herself with her jewels. (KJV)

The book of Zechariah also uses such symbolism to portray the forgiveness of sins. Zechariah saw a vision in which the high priest was stripped of his filthy garments and clothed with clean, fresh raiment (Zch 3:4).

Only the forgiveness of sins makes us fit for heaven. Paul says that the washing of holy baptism causes the church to be without "spot, or wrinkle, or any such thing" (Eph 5:27). This fact compels us to question the NIV translation of this verse. Luther was right to translate the phrase τὰ δικαιώματα τῆν ἁγίων, "*die Gerechtigkeit der Heiligen*" (the righteousness of the saints).

This picture of the wedding supper of the Lamb shows the persecuted church that a time will come when the abused children of God will escape forever from their enemies and the woes those enemies brought on them. As such, it is a renewed assurance that our sorrow will be turned into joy.

The angel commanded John to write, "Blessed [or, happy] are those who are invited to the marriage supper of the Lamb." In all the sorrows of this life, the anticipation of the happiness which awaits us helps us bear all adversity with patience and trust in God. He will surely do what he has promised. The angel emphasizes this truth when he tells John that the words he has just written are "the true words of God." These remarks of the angel remind us that the purpose of the doctrine of verbal inspiration, *i.e.*, that all the words of the Bible are "the true words of God," is to make us sure of the happiness that lies before us because of the atoning work of the Savior.

Through the words of the angel John was moved to fall down at his feet to worship him. The angel, however, cautioned John not to do this because he also, like John, was a servant, a co-worker with John and his brothers "who have the testimony of Jesus [or, concerning Jesus]," that is, of all those who preach the gospel of Christ. John is instead commanded to worship God.

This vision then closes with the words, "For the testimony about Jesus is the spirit of prophecy." The word "spirit" (πνεῦμα) is sometimes a synonym for "soul." James, for example, says, "As the body without the spirit is dead, so also faith without works is dead" (Jas 2:26). We would therefore be justified in translating, "The testimony about Jesus is the soul of prophecy," or perhaps even, "The testimony about Jesus is the very heart and soul of prophecy." Preaching which does not keep Christ and his atoning work in the center of the message is not the prophetic work that God has given his church. What is said in the pulpit may not be false, it may even in form be biblical, but if Christ and his atoning work are not there, that preaching will be just as lifeless as faith without works, even though men may consider it lively and interesting. Only when Christ is held before an audience as Savior and Redeemer are the hearers being invited to the wedding dinner of the Lamb. Only then are they offered the fine linen, bright and clean, that will serve as their wedding garment and qualify them to remain at that celebration (see also Mt 22:11-13).

The Rider on the White Horse (19:11-21)

**11) Καὶ εἶδον τὸν οὐρανὸν ἠνεῳγμένον, καὶ ἰδοὺ ἵππος λευκός, καὶ
ὁ καθήμενος ἐπ' αὐτὸν Πιστὸς καλούμενος καὶ Ἀληθινός, καὶ ἐν
δικαιοσύνῃ κρίνει καὶ πολεμεῖ. 12) οἱ δὲ ὀφθαλμοὶ αὐτοῦ φλὸξ
πυρός, καὶ ἐπὶ τὴν κεφαλὴν αὐτοῦ διαδήματα πολλά, ἔχων ὄνομα
γεγραμμένον ὃ οὐδεὶς οἶδεν εἰ μὴ αὐτός, 13) καὶ περιβεβλημένος
ἱμάτιον βεβαμμένον αἵματι, καὶ κέκληται τὸ ὄνομα αὐτοῦ Ὁ
Λόγος τοῦ Θεοῦ. 14) καὶ τὰ στρατεύματα τὰ ἐν τῷ οὐρανῷ ἠκολούθει αὐτῷ ἐφ' ἵπποις λευκοῖς, ἐνδεδυμένοι βύσσινον λευκὸν καθαρόν. 15) καὶ ἐκ τοῦ στόματος αὐτοῦ ἐκπορεύεται ῥομφαία ὀξεῖα,
ἵνα ἐν αὐτῇ πατάξῃ τὰ ἔθνη· καὶ αὐτὸς ποιμανεῖ αὐτοὺς ἐν ῥάβδῳ
σιδηρᾷ· καὶ αὐτὸς πατεῖ τὴν ληνὸν τοῦ οἴνου τοῦ θυμοῦ τῆς ὀργῆς
τοῦ Θεοῦ τοῦ Παντοκράτορος. 16) καὶ ἔχει ἐπὶ τὸ ἱμάτιον καὶ ἐπὶ
τὸν μηρὸν αὐτοῦ ὄνομα γεγραμμένον ΒΑΣΙΛΕΥΣ ΒΑΣΙΛΕΩΝ
ΚΑΙ ΚΥΡΙΟΣ ΚΥΡΙΩΝ.**

**17) Καὶ εἶδον ἕνα ἄλλεγον ἑστῶτα ἐν τῷ ἡλίῳ, καὶ ἔκραξεν ἐν
φωνῇ μεγάλῃ λέγων πᾶσιν τοῖς ὀρνέοις τοῖς πετομένοις ἐν μεσουρανήματι, Δεῦτε συνάχθητε εἰς τὸ δεῖπνον τὸ μέγα τοῦ Θεοῦ,
18) ἵνα φάγητε σάρκας βασιλέων καὶ σάρκας χιλιάρχων καὶ
σάρκας ἰσχυρῶν καὶ σάρκας ἵππων καὶ τῶν καθημένων ἐπ' αὐτῶν,**

καὶ σάρκας πάντων ἐλευθέρων τε καὶ δούλων καὶ μικρῶν καὶ μεγάλων. 19) Καὶ εἶδον τὸ θηρίον καὶ τοὺς βασιλεῖς τῆς γῆς καὶ τὰ στρατεύματα αὐτῶν συνηγμένα ποιῆσαι τὸν πόλεμον μετὰ τοὺ καθημένου ἐπὶ τοῦ ἵππου καὶ μετὰ τοῦ στρατεύματος αὐτοῦ. 20) καὶ ἐπιάσθη τὸ θηρίον καὶ μετ' αὐτοῦ ὁ ψευδοπροφήτης ὁ ποιήσας τὰ σημεῖα ἐνώπιον αὐτοῦ, ἐν οἷς ἐπλάνησεν τοὺς λαβόντας τὸ χάραγμα τοῦ θηρίου καὶ τοὺς προσκυνοῦντας τῇ εἰκόνι αὐτοῦ· ζῶντες ἐβλήθησαν οἱ δύο εἰ τὴν λίμνην τοῦ πυρὸς τῆς καιομένης ἐν θείῳ. 21) καὶ οἱ λοιποὶ ἀπεκτάνθησαν ἐν τῇ ῥομφαίᾳ τοῦ καθημένου ἐπὶ τοῦ ἵππου τῇ ἐξελθούσῃ ἐκ τοῦ στόματος αὐτοῦ, καὶ πάντα τὰ ὄρνεα ἐχορτάσθησαν ἐκ τῶν σαρκῶν αὐτῶν.

11) *And I saw heaven standing open, and, behold, a white horse, and the one who sat on him is called Faithful and True, and he judges and makes war in a righteous way.* 12) *His eyes seemed like fiery flames, and on his head were many crowns. He had a name written which no one but he himself knows.* 13) *And he was clothed in a garment that had been dipped in blood, and his name was called The Word of God.* 14) *And the armies that are in heaven were following him on white horses, clothed with clean, white fine linen.* 15) *And out of his mouth comes a sharp sword in order that with it he may strike down the nations, and he will rule them with an iron rod. And he will tread the wine press of the fury of the anger of God the Almighty.* 16) *And on his garment and on his thigh he has written a name: "King of kings and Lord of lords."*

17) *And I saw an angel standing in the sun, and he cried with a loud voice to all the birds flying in mid-heaven, "Come, gather together for the great supper of God* 18) *in order that you may eat the flesh of kings, and the flesh of generals, and the flesh of strong men, and the flesh of horses and of those who sit on them, and the flesh of all, freemen and slaves, and small and great."*

19) *And I saw the beast and the kings of the earth and their armies gathered together to make war with him who sat on the horse and his army,* 20) *and the beast was captured and with him the false prophet, who did miracles before him, with which he deceived those who had received the mark of the beast and had worshiped his image. These two were thrown alive into the lake of fire which burns with sulphur.* 21) *The rest were killed with the sword that comes out of the mouth of him who sits on the horse, and all the birds were filled with their flesh.*

There can be no question about the identity of the rider on the white horse in this chapter. Not all commentators are agreed in the identification of the rider on the white horse in chapter 6, but no such disagreement is possible here. He is first of all "faithful and true." These same two adjectives were used to describe the Savior in the letter to Laodicea (3:14), and in the first chapter of Revelation he was called "the faithful witness" (1:5). In the vision of the souls under the altar he was described as "holy and true" (6:10).

Later in this vision it is said that the rider on the white horse has the name "The Word of God." Even though this is the only place in the whole Bible where the Lord Jesus is given that name, yet in the first chapter of John's Gospel he is called "the Word," and in the first chapter of John's first epistle "the Word of life."

In his comments on the first chapter of John's Gospel, Luther says that when Jesus is called the "Word" this is a rare and unusual use of that term which is unclear in every language. Ordinarily when the Bible speaks of the Word, or the Word of God, or the Word of the Lord, it has the biblical message in view. That is the primary meaning of the term. Why this name is given to Jesus is not the easiest question to answer. But the Greeks had a proverb that says, Λόγος ἄγαλμα τῆς ψυχῆς, (a word is an image of the soul). By this they meant that when we listen to the words a man speaks we can gain some insight into his thoughts, feelings and attitudes. The Lord Jesus expressed a similar thought when he said, "Out of the fullness of the heart the mouth speaks" (Mt 12:34). Just as a man can best let us know what is in his heart by speaking words to us, so God gave us the best insight into his heart by sending his Son into this world. Thus Jesus serves his heavenly Father as our words serve us. It seems that this is the chief reason why in this vision he is given the name "Word of God."

John begins his description of this vision by saying, "I saw heaven standing open." In this open heaven he saw the rider on the white horse. That he is called "faithful and true" has particular significance in view of the name he later receives in this vision. Because he is God's Word, because through his words and deeds God has spoken to us, it is important to know that what he says is true and that what he promises will surely come to pass. Just those thoughts are emphasized by these words "faithful and true."

"He judges and makes war in a righteous way" (v. 11). Earlier in this chapter the church had exulted over the judgment the Lord pronounced against Babylon (v. 2), and in the first series of visions the martyred saints had prayed for such judgment against the enemies of the church (6:10). This judgment is a righteous judgment. It is important to emphasize this, for the human mind always wrestles with the problem of evil. Even children in Sunday school ask, "Why doesn't God kill the devil?" This problem is always intensified in times of persecution, when the suffering church is tempted to ask, "Why does God permit his enemies, the enemies of his gospel and of his church, such destructive freedom?" In view of that question the psalmist Asaph (Ps 73:17) can only point to "their end" (KJV) or to "their final destiny" (NIV). The eyes of faith always see what John sees here in his vision. Though "the mills of God grind slowly" and truth is "forever on the scaffold, wrong forever on the throne" in this evil world, yet the judge of all will finally "judge the world in righteousness" (Ac 17:31) and the day of judgment will be the day "when his righteous judgment will be revealed" (Ro 2:5) and all men will see that God's judgment is always right and just. But for the present this, like every other doctrine of Scripture, remains an article of faith.

The rider on the white horse also wages war in righteousness. The purpose of a just war is always to punish those who have done wrong. Deplorable as such fighting may be, it is still required by a just God who decrees that all sin should be punished. Unfortunately even those human governments which make an effort to wage war only under justified conditions on justified grounds in a justifiable way fall far short of the divine ideal. But the battle that Christ fights against the forces of evil is always just in every way. This, too, brings comfort to a church suffering under an unjust government, which punishes those who do well and encourages the evildoers (1 Pe 2:13).

The fact that the rider is faithful and true and that he judges and makes war in righteousness is closely related to the piercing quality of his eyes, which are "like a flame of fire" (v. 12). That phrase had formed a part of the description of the Savior in the first vision in John's book (1:14). In connection with 1:14 we pointed out that the "eyes of God" refers to his omniscience. Because Christ knows what is in man (Jn 2:24), he sees all the secrets of men (Ro 2:16), and because he is faithful and true, all his judgments must be true and right. In that confidence God's people can wait patiently for their vindication.

"And on his head there were many crowns." These words, as we have already noted in connection with the first verses of chapter 6, have been used as evidence to prove that the rider on the white horse in that chapter cannot be the Savior, since the rider described there wears only one crown. But in the first verses of chapter 6 we saw the Savior when his victorious gospel began its march through history. But after that the Savior is portrayed as winning one victory after another so that now he is King of kings and Lord of lords (v. 16). Those kings and lords who acknowledge him freely in faith as their Lord who has redeemed them by his blood will gladly cast their crowns before his feet (Re 4:10). Those who are his enemies will be forced to surrender their crowns to him. It is therefore not at all surprising to read that he now wears many crowns.

The word for crown here is διάδημα, diadem. The crown ascribed to him in chapter 6 was a στέφανος. The diadem was originally the crown worn by the kings of Persia and later also by Alexander the Great and Hellenistic kings. We noted earlier that when the Revelation was written, the wearing of the diadem symbolized a claim to divine honor. The στέφανος was, among the Greeks, the crown received as a prize in the athletic games. The στέφανος in chapter 6 is a symbol of victory while the many διαδήματα he wears here are a symbol of divine and universal rule over all the kings of the earth.

We are told also that the rider on the white horse has a written name which no one knows but the rider himself. A similar statement had been made in the letter to Pergamos (2:17) about the Christian who remains faithful unto death. To give someone a name means to describe what he is. A description of what Christ really is will always go far beyond all human understanding. The mystery of the personal union of the two natures in Christ is one which no man except Christ can really grasp (cp 1 Tm 3:16). When Luther said that "Word of God" is a rare and unusual name for Christ, a use of a term which is unclear in every language, he was saying essentially the same thing that John says here. How it is possible for God to become man is something that human reason will never be able to fathom. The incarnation is a miracle of such magnitude that every other miracle becomes child's play next to it.

Yet, in spite of his inexpressible greatness, Christ is "clothed in a garment that had been dipped in blood" (v. 13). This is an obvious reference to a Messianic prophecy in Isaiah in which that prophet saw the Savior as a victorious warrior returning from a battle against the enemies of Israel. There are many well-known and much-quoted passages that speak of the great power of the cleansing blood of Christ; therefore many are tempted to consider the blood on the garments of the rider as the holy precious blood of the Savior shed for our salvation. Such an interpretation, of course, would not be out of harmony with Scripture. However, the prophecy of Isaiah is clear and sheds light on the words of John here. Isaiah wrote (Is 63:1-6),

> Who is this coming from Edom,
> from Bozrah, with his garments stained crimson?
> Who is this, robed in splendor,
> striding forward in the greatness of his strength?
> "It is I, speaking in righteousness,
> mighty to save."
> Why are your garments red,
> like those of one treading the wine press?
> "I have trodden the wine press alone,
> from the nations no one was with me.
> I trampled them in my anger
> and trod them down in my wrath;
> their blood spattered my garments,
> and I stained all my clothing.
> For the day of vengeance was in my heart,
> and the year of my redemption has come.
> I looked, but there was no one to help,
> I was appalled that no one gave support;
> so my own arm worked salvation for me,
> and my own wrath sustained me.
> I trampled the nations in my anger;
> in my wrath I made them drunk
> and poured their blood on the ground."

These words of the Old Testament prophet tell us that the blood with which the garment of the rider is spattered is the blood of his enemies, or rather, the blood of the enemies of God's people. Edom was one of the great enemies of Israel in Old Testament times. Therefore we have here in John's vision another assurance given to the suffering and persecuted church that the Savior sitting at the right hand of God and ruling over all the nations of the earth will not allow his church to go down in defeat.

Behind the rider on the white horse rode the armies of heaven seated "on white horses, clothed with clean, white fine linen" (v. 14). Their garments were not stained with blood, thus symbolizing the truth which Isaiah expressed when he said that the Messiah would tread the wine press "alone," and would win the victory without anyone's help. The white horses and the fine clean white linen symbolize the sinless purity of this angelic army. The perfect participle, ἐνδεδυμένοι, clothed, indicates that their purity is a permanent condition. The angels are now confirmed in their holiness and can never fall away from God. It is also to be noted that the description of the clothing of the angels is very similar to that ascribed to the bride of the Lamb (v. 8). She was clothed with βύσσινον λαμπρὸν καθαρόν, fine linen, shining and clean. They are clothed in βύσσινον λευκὸν καθαρόν, fine linen, white and clean. Are we justified in saying that when John says that the clothing of the saints is λαμπρόν, shining, while that of the angels is merely λευκόν, white, he was pointing out that the righteousness of Christ worn by believers outshines even that of the holy angels? It might be instructive to remember that Matthew tells us that in the transfiguration the garments of Jesus became λευκὰ ὡς τὸ φῶς, "as white as the light," and Luke says that it became λευκὸς ἐξαστράπτων, "as white (NIV: bright) as a flash of lightning." The words added to describe the shining quality of that whiteness form phrases which are synonymous with λαμπρόν, "shining." John, who was there, may well have remembered that scene as he saw these things in his vision.

Out of the rider's mouth came "a sharp sword, with which he is to strike down the nations." Again we have a flashback to the very first vision in Revelation, in which John also saw a sharp sword coming out of the mouth of the glorified Savior (1:16), only there it is also called a two-edged sword. The basic significance of this metaphor is clear. Usually, when the word sword is used in a figurative sense in the Bible, it is a metaphor for war, or bloodshed. At times it symbolizes the Lord's judgment (or the instrument by which that judgment is carried out, *e.g.*, Jr 12:12; Is 66:16; Eze 38:21). But there are several passages where it clearly is a symbol for the Word of God (Is 49:2; Eph 6:17), which is also compared to a two-edged sword (Hb 4:12). This latter symbolism is repeated here.

The context contains a rather complex metaphor. We are dealing with the Savior's judgment over his enemies. Thus the sword here is certainly not a representation of the preaching of the gospel, although some find justification for such an interpretation in the word ποιμανεῖ (he will shepherd), used also in this verse. The sword that comes out of the Savior's mouth is his word of judgment which is expressed in God's law. The threats of the law are the instrument by which he punishes those who oppose him. Those threats are not just predictive, that is, they not only foretell what will happen to the enemies of Christ, but they are creative and governing words which produce that which they say. The enemies must fall because "the Scriptures must be fulfilled." Thus the Word is both the message of judgment and the instrument of judgment.

The sword represents judgment. This is evident from the purpose clause. The sword proceeds out of his mouth "in order that with it he may strike down the nations" (v. 15). The judgment, defeat and destruction of the unbelieving world is set forth here.

This same concept is expressed when we are told that "he will rule [or, shepherd] them with an iron rod." This is another of the several references in Revelation to Psalm 2, where the Hebrew text is translated, "You will rule them with an iron scepter." What the psalmist meant to convey to his readers with those words is clarified by what follows, namely, "You will dash them to pieces like pottery" (Ps 2:9). The verb ποιμανεῖ (he will rule, or shepherd) in this context must refer to what the shepherd does with recalcitrant sheep. That the shepherd's rod, or staff, here is an instrument of punishment is also implied by the fact that it is made of iron.

All this is then summed up in a common biblical metaphor, "He will tread the wine press of the furious anger of God, the Almighty" (v. 15). John had used the wine press as a symbol of God's judgment on the unbelieving world in an earlier vision (14:19,20). As in ancient times the juice was pressed from the grapes by walking on them in a winepress, so the Savior will crush the enemies of the church under his feet. The same Savior, whose first coming manifested the gracious and ineffable love of God, is also the final judge of men who will carry out the furious anger of God for the punishment of those who reject his gracious rule as the Good Shepherd. The fury which he will manifest is the wrath of an Almighty God against which even his most powerful enemies will not be able to stand.

While the punishment is anticipated in the first part of this vision, the second part portrays the execution of the judgment. In this part of the vision John sees an angel standing in the sun issuing an invitation to "all the birds flying in mid-heaven." These are undoubtedly the high-flying birds, especially the eagles, hawks and vultures. These birds of prey are invited to "the great supper of God." This great supper consists of the flesh of the enemies of God, who are designated by ten terms: 1) kings, 2) generals (*chiliarchs*, literally, "rulers of a thousand"), 3) strong men, 4) horses, 5) those who ride on them, 6) all, 7) freemen, 8) slaves, 9) small, and 10) great. Since ten is the number of completeness we may be justified in seeing in this an indication of the total victory of the Savior over all his enemies. In the Old Testament the disobedient heard the threat that their flesh would be eaten by vultures and ravens (Pr 30:7). The Prophet Ezekiel spoke that same threat against Gog, who is portrayed as one of God's powerful enemies (Eze 39:4).

After he heard the angel deliver this threat, John saw the armies of the beast and the kings of the earth gathered to wage war against the rider on the white horse and his army of angels. No great battle appears to take place. John simply says that the beast was captured and with the beast also the false prophet. This beast is the beast from the sea, the secular Antichrist. The false prophet is identified as the one who did miracles before the beast and thereby deceived those who had received the mark of the beast and worshiped his image. This is obviously a reference to 13:13-16, and it identifies the false prophet as the beast from the earth — a symbol of the ecclesiastical Antichrist.

Both beasts are quickly cast alive into "the lake of fire which burns with sulphur." This is a symbol of the eternal punishment of hell. Eternal suffering in hell is the final lot of those who seek, as servants of Satan, to destroy the church. A similar end awaits all those who serve the two beasts. They are killed with the sword of the rider on the white horse (v. 21).

This brings the sixth series of visions to a close. Like all the other series it ends with a portrayal of the last judgment, in this case as it applies to the antichristian forces in the world. This series of visions which began with chapter 17 might well be titled, "The Victory of the Church over Antichrist."

Now that the beast and the false prophet have been finally disposed of in the fires of hell, only one more enemy remains to be dealt with, Satan himself. His defeat is described in the next chapter.

The Seventh Vision: The Church's Final Victory (20:1 — 22:5)

CHRIST AND SATAN (20:1-3)

1) Καὶ εἶδον ἄγγελον καταβαίνοντα ἐκ τοῦ οὐρανοῦ, ἔχοντα τὴν
κλεῖν τῆς ἀβύσσου καὶ ἅλυσιν μεγάλην ἐπὶ τὴν χεῖρα αὐτοῦ.
2) καὶ ἐκράτησεν τὸν δράκοντα, ὁ ὄφις ὁ ἀρχαῖος, ὅς ἐστιν Διά-
βολος καὶ Ὁ Σατανᾶς, καὶ ἔδησεν αὐτὸν χίλια ἔτη, 3) καὶ ἔβαλεν
αὐτὸν εἰς τὴν ἄβυσσον, καὶ ἔκλεισεν καὶ ἐσφράγισεν ἐπάνω αὐ-
τοῦ, ἵνα μὴ πλανήσῃ ἔτι τὰ ἔθνη, ἄχρι τελεσθῇ τὰ χίλια ἔτη· μετὰ
ταῦτα δεῖ λυθῆναι αὐτὸν μικρὸν χρόνον.

1) *And I saw an angel coming down out of heaven, having the*
key to the abyss and a great chain in his hand. 2) *He laid hold of*
the dragon, the old serpent, who is the Devil and Satan, and he
bound him for a thousand years, 3) *and cast him into the abyss,*
and locked it and set a seal on it, in order that he might no longer
deceive the Gentiles until the thousand years come to an end;
after this he must be released for a short time.

Commentators on Revelation are often misled by the notion that every vision in Revelation portrays some future event. That this is not the case is demonstrated beyond all doubt by the vision of the woman's child and the dragon in chapter 12. No one can deny that that vision portrays the birth and ascension of Christ and all the attempts of the devil to destroy the woman's Son between his birth and ascension, after which he is forever beyond the devil's reach.

In 20:1-3 we have a portrayal of Christ's victory over the devil. The "angel coming down out of heaven" is Christ. We have already discussed the possibility of such an interpretation in connection with chapter 10. We will only repeat here that the word angel means, literally, a messenger, and in its basic meaning it certainly can be applied to Jesus, who was sent as God's spokesman to the world (He 1:1) and who in the Old Testament is often called "the angel of the Lord."

Everything that is said about this angel fits the Lord Jesus better than it fits any created angel. We are told that this angel has "the key of the abyss." "Abyss" is most certainly a name for hell and in chapter 1 Jesus is quoted as saying, "I have the keys of death and of Hades [hell]."

This angel also lays hold of Satan and binds him with a great chain and locks him up in the abyss. Jesus had spoken of his dealings with the devil in just such terms. Once, when the Pharisees and the teachers of the law accused Jesus of being in league with the devil because he cast out demons, Jesus overcame that accusation by pointing out that then Satan would be fighting against his own interests. To illustrate what was really happening, Jesus told them, "No one can enter a strong man's house and carry off his possessions unless he first ties up the strong man. Then he can rob his house" (Mk 3:27; Mt 12:29). Jesus is thus saying that by delivering the man from devil possession he proved that he had tied up the devil and was therefore free to carry off the devil's possessions.

No serious commentator maintains that the "great chain" with which the devil is bound is a chain of steel. Such chains cannot hinder a spirit's freedom of movement. The chains with which the devil is bound must be something that hinders his efforts and keeps him from doing what he would like to do if he had complete freedom to act. We must also be careful not to construct a mental picture of the chaining of the devil and then draw conclusions from that subjective idea rather than from the words that evoked the concept.

It is not necessary to view the chaining of Satan as a binding with a set of handcuffs and leg irons, or as something that leaves no more freedom of movement than a straitjacket. It is possible, as has been suggested, to think of it as a chain similar to one which prevents a vicious wild animal from harming those who stay beyond its reach. That this latter picture is more in keeping with the wider context of Scripture becomes evident when we hear Jude (v. 6) saying,

> The angels who did not keep their positions of authority but abandoned their own home — these he has kept in darkness, bound with everlasting chains for judgment on the great Day.

According to Jude's inspired and inerrant words, the evil angels are all bound with *everlasting* chains, and yet they are still free to roam about to the degree that God permits. The story of

Job illustrates that Satan can go only as far as God's will permits him to go. This, too, argues in favor of a binding such as we have described.

Some have argued that since John says the devil is bound and cast into hell with a seal on his prison door, this must mean that the presence of the devil has been removed from the earth. But this argument is also not biblically tenable. It is related to the rationalistic conclusion that since Jesus is in heaven his body and blood cannot be present in the Lord's Supper. Heaven and hell are not the kind of places that can be shown on a map. The Bible tells us, for example, that the angels are always in heaven (Mt 18:10), and yet we know that they are with us here on earth. In the same way, the angels who sinned (and that also includes Satan, the leader of the evil angels) were "sent to hell . . . into gloomy dungeons to be held for judgment" (2 Pe 2:4), yet we also know that the devil is free to prowl "around like a roaring lion looking for someone to devour" (1 Pe 5:8).

Likewise the millennialistic conclusion that for a thousand years the presence of the devil will be removed from the earth is by no means justified by John's words in these verses. There is not a single passage anywhere in Scripture that tells us that the devil will be removed from the earth for any length of time prior to the day of judgment. Those who find that concept here have read it into the text.

We return to the "great chain." If this is not a chain of steel or other material, as is granted by all serious commentators, then what kind of chain is it? The context tells us that it is a chain which prevents the devil from deceiving the nations any longer, that is, it prevents, or hinders, the devil in his attempts to lead men astray into eternal damnation. From the Bible we know of only one thing that can do this. It is the preaching of the gospel, the "Good News" that the Son of God was manifested to destroy the works of the devil (1 Jn 3:8). This is to be proclaimed to "every creature" (Mk 16:15) and to "all nations" (Mt 28:19). What John said in his description of the sequel to the "war in heaven" (cp 12:7-12) is surely apropos here, namely, "They won the victory over him because of the blood of the Lamb and because of the word of their testimony" (12:11). So long as the gospel is preached to the nations, the devil will be hindered in his attempt to deceive the nations. The more widely and the more purely the gospel is proclaimed, the shorter Satan's chain becomes.

It is for this reason also that in our translation of this passage we have rendered the Greek words, ἵνα μὴ πλανήσῃ ἔτι τὰ ἔθνη, "in order that he might no longer deceive the Gentiles," rather than the more common rendering, "in order that he might no longer deceive the nations." The Greek word ἔθνη, while it is often translated in English with "nations," usually refers only to the non-Jewish nations. The only widely used modern English version of the Bible which bears this distinction in mind is the Smith-Goodspeed version, which reads, "to keep him from leading the heathen astray any longer."

The translation, "that he might no longer deceive the nations," is confusing for some people. Under the influence of millennial thought they see in those words an indication of the complete political subjugation of the nations of the world to Christ as the millennial king. But when they see the nations of the world in more or less open rebellion against God and the widespread immorality and godlessness of our time, they find it difficult to envision the New Testament era as a time when the devil is bound so that he can no longer deceive the nations.

However, when we read the Revelation of John against the background of the rest of the Bible, the translation, "in order that he might no longer deceive the Gentiles," reflects a rather common biblical theme. In spite of the many Old Testament passages that urged the Israelites to share their faith with the Gentiles, the fact remains that any large-scale conversion of the Gentile world had to wait for the great commission the Lord gave to his disciples after his resurrection.

During his public ministry the Lord Jesus at times dealt with Gentiles, such as the centurion at Capernaum (Mt 8:5ff) and the Canaanite woman, whose daughter he healed of demon possession (Mt 15:21ff). But in the latter case, when his disciples urged him to help the woman, he made the pointed remark, "I was sent only to the lost sheep of Israel." When he sent his apostles out on their first mission, he told them specifically, "Do not go among the Gentiles (εἰς ὁδὸν ἐθνῶν) or enter any town of the Samaritans" (Mt 10:5).

The conversion of the Gentile, or heathen, world on a larger scale was being left as a post-ascension assignment for the followers of Christ. That was surely what Jesus had in mind when at his farewell gathering on Maundy Thursday he told his disciples, "I tell you the truth, anyone who has faith in me will do what I am doing. He will do even greater things than these, because I am going to the Father" (Jn 14:12).

In keeping with that prophetic statement and in harmony

with the historical development of Gentile Christianity, Luke in his gospel (21:24) speaks of New Testament times as the "times of the Gentiles" (καιροὶ ἐθνῶν). Especially in the letters of Paul we find the thought expressed that in the New Testament age the Gentiles would have special and greater opportunities to enjoy the fruits of the gospel. In that enjoyment they escaped from the deception and control of the devil. In the closing words of his letter to the Romans (16:25-27) Paul wrote,

> Now to him who is able to establish you by my gospel and the proclamation of Jesus Christ, according to the revelation of the mystery hidden for long ages past, but now revealed and made known through the prophetic writings by the command of the eternal God, so that all nations (πάντα τὰ ἔθνη) might believe and obey him — to the only wise God be glory forever through Jesus Christ.

From other letters of Paul, as well as other passages in Romans, it becomes clear that when Paul mentions "all nations" he has in mind especally the heathen nations which had received very little of the gospel in earlier times. In his letter to the Ephesians Paul describes his own ministry and, by implication, the whole New Testament ministry as a service by which the Gentiles in a very special way will come to participate in the blessings which God first gave to Israel. He writes (Eph 3:4-6),

> In reading this, then, you will understand my insight into the mystery of Christ, which was not made known to men in other generations as it has now been revealed by the Spirit to God's apostles and prophets. This mystery is that through the gospel the Gentiles (τὰ ἔθνη) are heirs together with Israel, members together of one body, and sharers together with the promise in Christ Jesus.

Earlier in the same context (2:11-13) he had written,

> You who are Gentiles by birth (τὰ ἔθνη ἐν σαρκὶ) . . . were separate from Christ, excluded from citizenship in Israel and foreigners to the covenants of the promise, without hope and without God in the world. But now in Christ Jesus you who once were far away have been brought near through the blood of Christ.

The same theme is prominent in the book of Acts. There it is made clear again and again that when Israel refused to accept the gospel proclaimed by Paul the result of their rejection was that the Gentiles received the gospel in fuller measure. In the synagogue of Pisidian Antioch (Ac 13:46) Paul told the Jews, "We had to speak the word of God to you first. Since you reject it and do not consider yourselves worthy of eternal life, we now turn to the Gentiles (εἰς τὰ ἔθνη)." It was very likely on the basis of this experience in Antioch and others like it that Paul told the Romans (11:11) that through the fall and rejection of the Jews "salvation has come to the Gentiles" (τοῖς ἔθνεσιν).

Paul emphasized this theme in his preaching to the heathen. At Lystra and in Athens he called upon the heathen who worshiped the idols of the Greek world to repent of their idolatrous worship. In both cities he clearly indicated that a new age had dawned for the Gentiles. At Lystra (Ac 14:16) he told the people, "In the past he let all the nations (πάντα τὰ ἔθνη) go their own way," and at Athens (Ac 17:30) he said, "In the past God overlooked such ignorance [the ignorance displayed in idol worship], but now he commands all people everywhere to repent."

Paul's success in his missionary efforts among the heathen was the clear evidence that the time of the Gentiles had come. When he and Barnabas returned from the first missionary journey (Ac 14:27) they reported to the church in Syrian Antioch how God "had opened the door of faith to the Gentiles [τοῖς ἔθνεσιν]."

This concept of a special time of salvation for the Gentile world is by no means limited to the New Testament. It is surprising that the Jewish believers found it so hard to recognize the dawning of that new age and found fault with Peter for preaching in the home of the Gentile Cornelius (Ac 10,11; see also Ac 15). The Psalms and the writings of the prophets are filled with predictions that speak about masses of Gentile converts worshiping the God of Israel. They were only echoing the promise to Abraham that in his seed all the nations (πάντα τὰ ἔθνη, Ga 3:8) of the earth would be blessed (Gn 12:3).

All this will help us understand what John has in mind when he says here that Christ bound the devil with a great chain "in order that he might no longer deceive the nations," *i.e.*, "the Gentiles." The evangelization of the heathen world, which began with Christ's great commission and especially the missionary journeys of Paul, put countless heathen beyond the reach of the devil. We are among them.

That will also explain how the devil is loosed "for a short time" (v. 3). The Bible speaks of widespread apostasy during the last days of the world's history. Where the message of the gospel is no longer to be heard or where it is so obscured by false teaching that the light of salvation shines very dimly, the devil is free to continue to deceive men and to lead them astray to the eternal destruction of their souls. The devil is loosed whenever large segments of the visible church become apostate and non-evangelical cults and sects proliferate.

This interpretation is in perfect harmony with the Savior's own description of the last times. He says (Mt 24:21-25),

> For then there will be great distress, unequaled from the beginning of the world until now — never to be equaled again. If those days had not been cut short, no one would survive, but for the sake of the elect those days will be shortened. At that time if anyone says to you, "Look, here is the Christ!" or, "There he is!" do not believe it. For false Christs and false prophets will appear and perform great signs and wonders to deceive [πλανῆσαι, cp. πλανήσῃ in Re 20:3] even the elect — if that were possible.

In those words the Savior speaks of a time that will be shortened. That theme is echoed here in the "short time" spoken of by John. The Lord also speaks of a proliferation of false prophets and false Christs who will deceive man. John's words imply that during that short time the devil will once more be able to deceive the nations. The whole tenor of Jesus' words implies that the gospel message, which alone can keep men out of the clutches of the devil, will during those shortened days be obscured.

Once we have clearly understood what is meant by the chain with which the devil is bound, the interpretation of the thousand years also becomes relatively simple. We have noted before that the numbers of Revelation are symbolic. There is nothing in this context to show that the number 1000 here is to be interpreted otherwise than all the other numbers in the book. Ten is the number of completeness. Therefore all that we can say with confidence is that the thousand years represent a complete period of time whose length is firmly fixed by the eternal decrees of God.

We can say also that the thousand years during which the devil is bound began when Christ redeemed us from the devil's power by his vicarious atonement and commanded his church to carry the message of forgiveness to the ends of the earth. The thousand years will come to an end when the preaching of the gospel becomes muted and false teachers and false Christs multiply as the devil's instrument to lead the nations astray.

The thousand years, therefore, can confidently be viewed as a representation of the whole New Testament period.

The only question concerning which some doubt might remain is whether the "short time" of which John speaks here is a part of the thousand years or lies outside of that framework. It should be pointed out that the original Greek says that the devil will be bound ἄχρι τελεσθῇ τὰ χίλια ἔτη, which we have translated, "until the thousand years come to an end." The verb form is an aorist subjunctive and not a perfect tense, as both the KJV and NIV translations would seem to imply. While we cannot say that the NIV translation, "until the thousand years were ended," is impossible, it is by no means certain. The most natural interpretation is that Satan will remain bound until shortly before the end of the world, or shortly before the thousand years come to an end with the final day of judgment.

The only real argument against this view is found in the μετὰ ταῦτα (after this, literally, "after these") phrase, which introduces the final clause of verse 3, "he must be released for a short time." The pronoun ταῦτα (these) could be understood as referring back to the word "years." In that case we would be forced to understand John as saying, "After these thousand years he must be released for a short time." But this, too, is by no means required. The phrase μετὰ ταῦτα is used a number of times in Revelation (*e.g.*, 4:1; 7:9; 9:12; 15:5; 18:1; 19:1; cp. μετὰ τοῦτο, 7:1), and in every case the pronoun refers to the preceding events. That may very well be the case here. This particular point is not of great significance and changes the whole picture very little. If the antecedent of the pronoun ταῦτα is "years," then we will have to say that the thousand years do not include the "short time." On the other hand, if the phrase μετὰ ταῦτα refers to the binding and imprisonment of Satan, the "short time" is almost certainly to be viewed as the closing period of the thousand years. While it is neither possible nor necessary to make any dogmatic assertion on this point, the second view would seem to fit better with what is said about the thousand years in the next part of the vision.

THE THOUSAND YEAR REIGN (20:4-6)

In his description of the next part of the vision John writes,

4) Καὶ εἶδον θρόνους, καὶ ἐκάθισαν ἐπ' αὐτούς, καὶ κρίμα ἐδόθη αὐτοῖς, καὶ τὰς ψυχὰς τῶν πεπελεκισμένων διὰ τὴν μαρτυρίαν Ἰησοῦ καὶ διὰ τὸν λόγον τοῦ Θεοῦ, καὶ οἵτινες οὐ προσεκύνησαν

**τὸ θηρίον οὐδὲ τὴν εἰκόνα αὐτοῦ καὶ οὐκ ἔλαβον τὸ χάραγμα ἐπὶ τὸ
μέτωπον καὶ ἐπὶ τὴν χεῖρα αὐτῶν· καὶ ἔζησαν καὶ ἐβασίλευσαν
μετὰ τοῦ Χριστοῦ χίλια ἔτη. 5) οἱ λοιποὶ τῶν νεκρῶν οὐκ ἔζησαν
ἄχρι τελεσθῇ τὰ χίλια ἔτη. Αὕτη ἡ ἀνάστασις ἡ πρωτη. 6) μακάριος καὶ ἅγιος ὁ ἔχων μέρος ἐν τῇ ἀναστάσει τῇ πρώτῃ· ἐπὶ τούτων
ὁ δεύτερος θάνατος οὐκ ἔχει ἐξουσίαν, ἀλλ' ἔσονται ἱερεῖς τοῦ
Θεοῦ καὶ τοῦ Χριστοῦ, καὶ βασιλεύσουσιν μετ' αὐτοῦ τὰ χίλια ἔτη.**

4) *And I saw thrones, and they sat upon them, and judgment was
given to them, and (I saw) the souls of those who were beheaded
because of their witness about Jesus and because of the Word of
God, namely, those who did not worship the beast and his image
and did not receive his mark on their forehead and on their hand;
and they lived and reigned with Christ a thousand years.* 5) *The
rest of the dead did not live until the thousand years come to an
end. This is the first resurrection.*

6) *Blessed and holy is he that has a part in the first resurrection. Over them the second death has no power, but they will continue to be priests of God and of Christ, and they will rule with him for the thousand years.*

This passage is used by millennialists as proof for their doctrine that prior to the day of judgment Christ will return and set up an earthly, visible kingdom in Palestine which will last for a thousand years. According to this view the "first resurrection" is the physical resurrection of the believing children of God, whose bodies will be raised so that they might rule with Christ in this visible kingdom. This doctrine teaches that the unbelievers will not be raised until the thousand years, the so-called millenium, come to an end.

As evidence for a "double" resurrection, many millennialists cite Paul's words concerning the second coming in 1 Thessalonians. There the Apostle says, "The dead in Christ will rise first" (4:16). This is viewed as proof positive that the unbelieving dead will not rise at that time. Yet there is not a scintilla of proof for a double resurrection, separated by a thousand years, in that passage. Not one word is said about believers rising a thousand years before unbelievers. Rather, what Paul says is that the living believers will be taken to heaven only after the dead believers have been raised first. The contrast here is not between the believing dead and the unbelieving dead but between living believers and dead believers. Paul asserts that living believers will have no advantage over dead believers when Christ comes again. In fact, the dead believers will rise first.

Before we proceed to a study of John's words we should also note that here we have the only passage in the Bible that speaks of anyone reigning for a thousand years. Apart from Revelation 20, the phrase, "a thousand years," is used only in two other passages of the Bible (Ps 90:4; 2 Pe 3:8), and those passages deal only with the timelessness of God. What the thousand years represents must therefore be determined from the context alone.

Even people who reject the whole doctrine of the millennium are in the habit of speaking of "the thousand-year reign of Christ" in connection with this chapter. Those who deny the millennium are often accused of not believing the words of John here. In answer we often say that the words must be understood figuratively. But this is not the correct defense against that accusation. The fact is that John says not one word about a thousand-year reign of *Christ*, either literally or figuratively.

He writes, "I saw thrones and they sat on them." It is not Christ whom he sees here. These words do not yet identify the people sitting on the thrones. We can conclude from the word "thrones" that these people are very likely in a ruling position of some kind, even though the word "throne" (θρόνος) is not necessarily a king's chair.

John continues by saying, "Judgment was given to them." Here it is clearly stated that they occupy positions of authority. Rendering judgment is a function of governors and kings. This is in accord with many other passages of Scripture that tell us plainly that on the last day the believers will participate with Christ in the final judgment (*e.g.*, Mt 19:28; 1 Cor 6:3).

At the end of this verse we are told that those whom John saw sitting on the thrones "reigned with Christ for a thousand years." Thus it is clear that the thrones do symbolize royal authority. The reigning that is in the foreground here is not the ruling activity of Christ, but rather of those seated on the thrones.

A careful reading of the text will show clearly that this is the case. If a man says, for example, "I lived on a farm with my parents for fourteen years before I left home to go away to school," that does not give us one iota of information about how long his parents lived on that farm. When John says that those sitting on the thrones reigned with Christ a thousand years, it ought to be obvious to any fair-minded interpreter that this passage cannot be used as proof to demonstrate that Christ will set up a special reign "for a thousand years" anywhere. The book of Revelation tells us instead that he will reign "forever and ever" (11:15). There are dozens of passages that speak of Christ's eternal kingdom, but not one single passage that speaks of or even hints at a kingdom of Christ that will last a thousand years.

Moreover, the passage does not say one word about a millennial kingdom of Christ which will have as its capital the city of Jerusalem. Millennialists insist that the reigning spoken of here will take place on this earth after Christ will return visibly a thousand years before the day of judgment. To such people we say, "Pay attention to the words." And we also direct them to the words our Lord Jesus told Pontius Pilate, "My kingdom is not of this world" (Jn 18:36).

Millennialists generally appeal to Old Testament passages that describe the reign of the Messiah in terms of an earthly kingdom, where perfect peace will exist between natural enemies, where the lion will lie down with the lamb and nation will not lift up sword against nation. Not one of those passages, however, says that this has to do with a temporal and earthly kingdom. Millennialists who hold that after the millennium there will be a great military engagement in which the unbelieving world will rebel against the Messiah who has kept their wickedness in check ought to bear in mind what Isaiah says. For example, in his description of the "peaceable kingdom" Isaiah says that when that kingdom is established, "the nations" will not "train for war anymore" (Is 2:4). Millennialists evidently do not pay attention to these words. They teach that at the end of the millennium the nations will once more train for war.

These Old Testament passages speak, not of a temporal and physical peace, but of the spiritual peace and rest that the Messiah will bring to his people. The New Testament teaches us very clearly that this kingdom was firmly established before the apostles died (*e.g.*, Mk 9:1). In the forgiveness of sins earned by Christ and proclaimed to the world by the apostles we find the peace that passes all understanding (Php 4:7). These passages also portray for us God's perfect kingdom, which will endure forever and will be visibly and tangibly realized when the whole creation "will be liberated from its bondage to decay and brought into the glorious freedom of the children of God" (Ro 8:21). But that world will not endure for a mere thousand years. There those that are Christ's will rule with him forever and ever (22:5).

Now John identifies those who are sitting on the thrones. They are "the souls of those who had been beheaded because of their witness about Jesus and because of the Word of God." The accusative, τὰς ψυχάς (the souls), must be the object of the verb "I saw." If there is still any doubt that John is not speaking here of an earthly reign, these words leave no more room for such uncertainty. John did not see resurrected bodies. He saw souls, disembodied souls of beheaded people who had died for their faith.

John is here not really saying anything that will surprise those who know their Bibles well. The Scriptures tell us that when believing children of God die they go to live with Christ in the glories of heaven. In the symbolism of this passage John teaches us the same truth. Paul had proclaimed that truth when he wrote in Romans (8:35,37),

> Who shall separate us from the love of Christ? Shall trouble or hardship or persecution or famine or nakedness or famine or sword? . . . No, in all these things we are more than conquerors through him that loved us.

When the heathen in Rome during the Neronian persecution saw the head of Paul rolling in the sand of the arena, they undoubtedly believed that Paul had been defeated and destroyed by the emperor. But the persecution in which he died and the sword that cut off his head had not separated Paul from Christ's love. He could even in the moment of utter outward defeat say, "In all these things we are more than conquerors through him that loved us." When Paul contemplated that moment in the closing days of his life he spoke of the "crown of righteousness" which the righteous Judge would award to him on the day of his departure (2 Tm 4:6-8). He evidently looked forward to living and reigning with Christ even in death.

Now in the days of Domitian, when John wrote, Christians were again being beheaded for their witnessing. The genitive in the phrase, τὴν μαρτυρίαν 'Ιησοῦ (the witness of Jesus), is an objective genitive, which we have translated, "their witnessing about Jesus." While there is no possessive pronoun in the original Greek text, the definite article in Greek, as in German, often has the force of a possessive pronoun.

As the believers in John's time saw their friends and relatives arrested and martyred it often must have seemed to those whose faith was being severely tried that the scarlet beast, the secular Antichrist, was winning the battle and that the church was in danger of going down in defeat. As they mourned over the slain and beheaded bodies of their dead fellow believers they were in need of encouragement and comfort.

John's vision spoke to that need. When John says that he saw the souls of those who had been beheaded, it was just as though he were saying to a sorrowing church, "The government of the empire has beheaded our brothers and sisters in Christ. It seems that the enemies of the church have triumphed and the church is going down in defeat. Our friends are dead. But the government has only killed their bodies. And that is all we, too, see with these mortal eyes. But God granted me a vision in which I saw their souls. Those souls were not lying there on the bloody sand. They were sitting on thrones in heaven. They were not dead. They were living and reigning with Christ." What a message of encouragement and hope!

Millennialists sometimes hold that here the word "soul" must be a figure of speech for "person" as it is in the sentence, "Let every soul be subject unto the higher powers" (Ro 13:1 KJV). It is, of course, true that the word can be used in that way. But John does not say, "I saw the souls that were beheaded." Had he used such language, the word "soul" would obviously mean "person." But he says, "I saw the souls of those [persons] who were beheaded," which can only mean that those souls had been separated from their beheaded bodies.

Another argument sometimes heard is that the bodies must have been there because John could see these people and souls are invisible. But that very argument shows how untenable the chiliastic position is. This was a "vision" in which John saw many things that are ordinarily invisible. To say, "I saw souls," is really no more surprising than to say, "I saw an angel." Angels are just as invisible as souls.

When the martyrs are described as "those who did not worship the beast or his image and did not receive his mark," some commentators see this as a reference to the demand of the government that the Christians burn incense before the statue of the emperor. While that may be correct, it is more in keeping with the context to see this simply as a description of those who remained faithful and loyal to Christ and persevered in their Christian faith.

John says of these souls that "they lived and reigned with Christ." Many translators render ἔζησαν in English with "they came to life" or "they lived again." "Lived again" would be ἀνέζησαν in Greek. Even though the Bauer-Arndt-Gingrich *Lex-*

icon says that the *textus receptus* has that reading here, neither the UBS Greek New Testament nor Nestle's text gives that variant, which would obviously be wrong even if it were found in a few manuscripts.

It is obviously wrong because the subject of this verb is "souls." Of souls, especially the souls of the believers, it cannot be said that they came to life. The souls John saw here had never died. In his Gospel John helps us to understand what he means here. There he wrote that at the grave of Lazarus the Lord told Martha, "Whoever lives and believes in me will never die" (Jn 11:26). Paul spoke of the time of his death as the moment when he would leave his body and go to be with the Lord (Php 1:28). Peter described his own death as a matter of laying aside the tent of his body (2 Pe 1:13f). When the body dies, the spirit returns to God who gave it (Ec 12:7). For children of God that continued existence is described as a living with Christ. Their souls do not come to life. They just keep on living.

Grammatically speaking, it is possible to treat ἔζησαν as an ingressive aorist. The NIV has done that with its rendering, "They came to life." But the context does not allow this, mainly because of the above argument. In addition, the aorist ἔζησαν is followed by another aorist ἐβασίλευσαν, and this, in turn, is followed by an accusative denoting duration of time. If, under those conditions, John had wanted to express the idea of a resumption of life, he would have been forced to use the word ἀνέζησαν. As it is, ἔζησαν must be treated as the same kind of aorist as ἐβασίλευσαν. They are both constative aorists. What John says is that during the whole period of the thousand years, the souls, without interruption, lived and reigned with Christ.

Of the unbelieving dead John says that "they did not live until the thousand years came to an end." Here the NIV again translates ἔζησαν with "come to life." The translators seem to have been misled by the "until" which introduces the dependent clause in this verse. Their rendering implies that the dead unbelievers came to life at the end of the thousand years. But while unbelievers continue to exist after death their continued existence is never called ζωή or life.

A definition of life derived from the Bible will help us to understand what John is really saying here. Life in the biblical sense might be defined as "the enjoyment of or participation in the blessings of God." This definition does not need to be essentially changed when we speak of the three kinds of life which we usually distinguish. Temporal or physical life is the enjoyment of or participation in the temporal or physical blessings of God. Spiritual life is the enjoyment of the spiritual blessings of God and eternal life the enjoyment of the eternal blessings of God. Already in this world unbelievers are by their very unbelief unable to participate in any of the spiritual blessings of God. Therefore the Bible says that they are dead in trespasses and sins (Eph 2:1), and if they die in their sins they remain spiritually dead. Their "souls" do not live. They do not become alive in the biblical sense when they are raised out of the grave, for they are raised to condemnation. What this means becomes clear from the context in which that is said. John writes of the resurrection, "Those who have done good will rise to live, and those who have done evil will rise to be condemned" (Jn 5:29). We are told also to what they are condemned. They will be thrown into the lake of fire which is "the second death." Just as life is more than existence, just as it is the enjoyment of God's blessings, so death is not non-existence. Rather it is an existence in which men are cut off from the blessings of God, whether they are physical, spiritual or eternal. The unbelieving dead will be conscious of their pain and torment, but their continued existence, while it might be called βίος, life in a purely physical sense, cannot be called ζωή, life on a far higher level.

The clause, "until the thousand years are finished," does not imply that they will begin to live when the thousand years come to an end. When the Bible tells us that Michal had no children *until* the day of her death (2 Sm 6:23) this does not mean that she had children after she died. An "until" clause or phrase does not of itself tell us what happened when the designated point was reached. That always depends on the context. And the context here tells us that when the thousand years end the unbelievers will be raised to eternal death, to eternal separation from the blessings of God. Thus John is saying that while the believing dead will live during the thousand years, that is, enjoy the blessings of God which apply to them in their disembodied state, so the unbelieving dead will not live during that time, will exist in a state of separation from all the blessings of God.

The living and reigning with Christ on the part of the martyred believers is called "the first resurrection." These words have been the object of much unnecessary speculation. Some Lutherans have on the basis of these words taught that before the end of the world there will be a separate physical resurrection of the martyrs. Often this is coupled with some mild form of millennialism. It seems that here John is speaking only of martyrs because their fate was of special concern during the persecutions. The Bible elsewhere adds that all believers will continue to live on even if they suffer bodily death (Jn 11:23). Moreover, what was said above in regard to the "souls" that John saw forbids any millennialistic reference to a bodily resurrection.

Committed millennialists see in this "first resurrection" an allusion to two resurrections, one at the beginning and the other at the end of the millennium, the first a resurrection of believers, and the second a resurrection of the rest of the dead. It is held that Paul's words to the Thessalonians, "The dead in Christ shall rise first" (1 Th 4:16), refer to the first of these two resurrections. This teaching of two resurrections is clearly contradicted by the words of Jesus in John 6:39,40:

> This is the will of him who sent me, that I shall lose none of all that he has given me, but raise them up *at the last day*. For my Father's will is that everyone who looks to the Son and believes in him shall have eternal life, and I will raise him up *at the last day*.

If these words represent two resurrections of the kind assumed by millennialists, a day a thousand years before the end would have to be called "the last day," an interpretation that violates all the laws of logic. If the believers are raised a thousand years before the end of the world, they will not be raised on "the last day."

There is no other passage that speaks of "two resurrections" in those terms. There is, however, a passage in John's Gospel that speaks of two resurrections in another sense. That passage is of special importance because it helps to establish the view of the author of Revelation. In his Gospel (5:25,28,29) John records these words of Jesus:

> I tell you the truth, a time is coming and has now come when the dead will hear the voice of the Son of God and those who hear will live. . . . Do not be amazed at this, for a time is coming when all those who are in their graves will hear his voice and come out — those who have done good will rise to live, and those who have done evil will rise to be condemned.

Jesus in these words speaks of two distinct resurrections that are separated in time. But when he speaks of two resurrections, Jesus makes no distinction between one resurrection of believers and another of unbelievers. In the second of these resurrections "all that are in their graves" evidently come out of them in the same hour. The language hardly lends itself to two such widely separated resurrections as are envisioned by millennialists.

The first resurrection of which Jesus speaks is a spiritual resurrection. It was taking place while Jesus was living on this earth and would continue to take place also in the future ("the hour is coming and *has now come*"). This is the resurrection that takes place when those who are spiritually dead listen to the voice of the Son of God as it comes to them in the preaching of the gospel, whether that preaching is done by Christ himself or by those to whom Christ said, "He that heareth you, heareth me" (Lk 10:16 KJV).

The conversion of the sinner, by which he comes to faith, is spoken of in the Bible as a resurrection. Paul, for example, speaks of a resurrection which we experienced when we were raised to newness of life through baptism (Ro 6:1-11). He speaks of Christians as people who were "raised with Christ" (Col 3:1; cp. 2:12). In Ephesians he quotes what may have been part of an early Christian hymn, "Wake up, O sleeper, rise from the dead, and Christ will shine on you" (Eph 5:14). Earlier in the same letter he wrote that God "made us alive with Christ" and "raised us up with Christ" (2:4,6). Men who are dead in transgressions and sin (Eph 2:1) become alive spiritually when they come to faith in the Savior. This is the "first resurrection" which Christians experience.

The second resurrection of which Jesus speaks in John 5 is one that lies in the future. In that resurrection all those who are "in their graves" will hear the voice of the Son of God. This is the bodily resurrection which will take place on "the last day." It is a resurrection of both believers and unbelievers since for some it will be a "resurrection of life" and for others a "resurrection of damnation" (KJV). Since in this damnation unbelievers will be sentenced to eternal separation from God we might call it a "resurrection of death."

The "first resurrection" of Revelation 20, therefore, is the conversion of the sinners. On the day of his conversion the sinner comes to spiritual life. He is born again. And the life that begins on that day is eternal life, which will not be interrupted by the death of the body. The soul continues to enjoy that new life even while it is separated from the body. That is the simple biblical explanation of what John means when he says that the souls of the martyrs lived and reigned with Christ "a thousand years."

From this context it is now a very simple matter to determine what is meant by the thousand years. For each individual believer his real life begins on the day of his conversion, and when he dies his soul will continue to live and reign with Christ until the day when his body will be raised to join his soul in the enjoyment of all the eternal blessings of God. Of the martyrs of John's day we can likewise say that their true life began on the day they became believers. When they were beheaded John saw their souls living and reigning with Christ for a thousand years. At the end of the thousand years, as John tells us in the verses to follow, their dead bodies will be raised to be reunited with their living souls. The thousand years, therefore, are a symbolic term for the whole time between the early days of the church and the day of resurrection. As in the previous vision, the thousand years are the whole New Testament period. This is so clear from the context that we can use this passage as evidence that in the language of Revelation ten and its multiples are symbolic numbers for the concept of completeness.

John concludes this vision with the fifth of the seven beatitudes of Revelation (20:6).

> Blessed and holy is he that has a part in the first resurrection. Over them the second death has no power, but they will continue to be priests of God and of Christ, and they will rule with him for the thousand years.

The word translated "blessed" is again the word μακάριος, happy. The word points to the assured bliss of those who had been tortured and killed for their faith. The word is therefore another reaffirmation of Paul's assertion that even if we are troubled and persecuted and killed for Christ's sake we are more than conquerors through him (Ro 8:37).

Those who have a part in the first resurrection are here said to be not only happy but also holy. That assertion is additional evidence that our above interpretation of the first resurrection is correct.Through that first resurrection we enjoy and participate in the blessings of the vicarious atonement and of the gospel promise of forgiveness. We believe that promise, and our faith puts us outside the reach of the devil's power. Through that forgiveness we are made holy and free from all guilt.

Because God's people are holy the second death has no power over them. The first death is undoubtedly the death they suffered at the hands of a persecuting government. That death had not been able to rob them of real life, the eternal life which had become theirs when they were born again. Because they have part in the first resurrection, by which they were raised to everlasting life, the second death, eternal damnation in hell, cannot touch them. Thus they are forever beyond the reach of the chain of the devil, to whom is ascribed the power of death (He 2:14) and who is called "a murderer from the beginning" (Jn 8:44).

We have translated ἔσονται ἱερεῖς with "they will continue to be priests," because they were priests already from the day of their conversion. Peter says that all Christians are a "royal priesthood" (1 Pe 2:9) and at the very beginning of Revelation John had told his readers that Jesus made us priests to God (1:6). In the light of that it would seem as though their priesthood will continue even during the thousand years. In what that priesthood consists during the thousand years we are not told. One of the major functions of a priest is to offer sacrifices. It can be said on the basis of the songs which we hear the redeemed sing in Revelation that these priests are most assuredly bringing their sacrifices of thanksgiving and praise before the throne. Since intercessory prayer is also one of the chief functions of the priestly office we might conceivably find in these words some justification for the statement in the Apology of the Augsburg Confession that the Lutheran Church concedes that the saints in heaven may pray for us (Apol. xxi [ix], 8).

Once more, then, we are told that the beheaded saints will rule with Christ during the thousand years. Some manuscripts do not have a definite article with the "thousand years" of this verse. The evidence for this reading is about evenly divided, but it would seem that the context does call for an article of previous reference.

The ruling of the saints in heaven must have been of great comfort to a suffering church. The authorities who oppose the church and who are agents of the beast from the sea appear to have ruling power over God's people. This is how it looks especially in times of active persecution. For that reason John (and the Holy Spirit who inspired him to write these words) evidently considered it worthwhile to remind the church a second time that their dead fellow believers who had suffered such an ignominious outward defeat at the hands of those who had ruled over them on earth are in reality ruling the universe with Christ. The Scriptures do not explain for us what this ruling with Christ entails, but perhaps we can say on the basis of what John tells us here that these heavenly priests in the church triumphant with their prayers for the church help to bring about the final victory of the church militant.

THE DEFEAT OF SATAN (20:7-10)

7) Καὶ ὅταν τελεσθῇ τὰ χίλια ἔτη, λυθήσεται ὁ Σατανᾶς ἐκ τῆς φυλακῆς αὐτοῦ, 8) καὶ ἐξελεύσεται πλανῆσαι τὰ ἔθνη τὰ ἐν ταῖς τέσσαρσιν γωνίαις τῆς γῆς, τὸν Γὼγ καὶ Μαγώγ, συναγαγεῖν αὐτοὺς εἰς τὸν πόλεμον, ὧν ὁ ἀριθμὸς αὐτῶν ὡς ἡ ἄμμος τῆς θαλάσσης. 9) καὶ ἀνέβησαν ἐπὶ τὸ πλάτος τῆς γῆς, καὶ ἐκύκλευσαν τὴν παρεμβολὴν τῶν ἁγίων καὶ τὴν πόλιν τὴν ἠγαπημένην· καὶ κατέβη οὗρ ἐκ τοῦ οὐρανοῦ καὶ κατέφαγεν αὐτούς· 10) καὶ ὁ διάβολος ὁ πλανῶν αὐτοὺς ἐβλήθη εἰς τὴν λίμνην τοῦ πυρὸς καὶ θείου, ὅπου καὶ τὸ θηρίον καὶ ὁ ψευδοπροφήτης, καὶ βασανισθήσονται ἡμέρας καὶ νυκτὸς εἰς τοὺς αἰῶνας τῶς αἰώνων.

7) *And when the thousand years come to an end, Satan will be released from his prison,* 8) *and he will go out to deceive the nations which are in the four corners of the earth, Gog and Magog, to bring them to the battle. Their number is as the sand of the sea.* 9) *And they came up over the broad expanse of the earth and they surrounded the camp of the saints and the beloved city. But fire came down from heaven and devoured them.* 10) *And the devil who deceived them was thrown into the lake of fire and sulphur, where the beast and the false prophet are, and they will be tormented day and night forever and ever.*

In his eschatological discourses in the Synoptic Gospels (Mt 24; Mk 13; Lk 21) the Lord Jesus had spoken of the great tribulation that would come shortly before the end of the world and of the many false Christs and false prophets who would deceive men and even threaten the salvation of the elect. This vision presents that same prophecy in vivid imagery.

Toward the close of the New Testament period, when the thousand years are coming to an end, Satan, who had been bound at the beginning of the thousand years, will once more be set free. We have seen that the devil is free to deceive men when the message of the gospel is muted and obscured by the proliferation of false Christs and false ways of salvation. As we survey our modern world it would surely appear that we are living in this last period of world history. Never before has the world seen the development of so many antichristian cults. Never before has the gospel been so wickedly denied by an apostate church. Even theologians speak of our times as the "post-Christian era." Satan appears to have been released from his prison.

Having been released, the devil will go out to marshal the antichristian forces of this world for a final battle against the church. He gathers his forces from the four corners of the earth to bring them to the battle. The nations whom he misleads into an open attack on the church are called Gog and Magog. Nothing certain can be said about Gog and Magog except that in the prophecies of Ezekiel these are great enemies of God's people. There Gog is described as the prince of Meshech and Tubal. The millennialist identification of Meshech and Tubal as the Russian cites of Moscow and Tobolsk is pure fantasy and guesswork. Magog is the land from which Gog comes. Its identification with Russia and Russian communism is also guesswork pure and simple. Yet we may still say that the forces of atheistic communism are a part of this Satanic army that the devil marshals to bring about the destruction of the church.

The battle that is described here is undoubtedly the same battle as the battle of Armageddon in chapter 16 and the battle fought by the beast and the false prophet against the rider on the white horse in chapter 19. In his prophecy Ezekiel depicts the defeat of these antichristian forces in the same terms as those in which John describes it in chapter 19, namely, as a great sacrificial feast in which the birds and the wild animals will eat the flesh of the defeated armies (Eze 39:17-20). By these visionary scenes the church is reminded that till the end of time the world will remain her enemy and that the devil will use all the world's resources in a final attempt to destroy the church.

These resources are formidable. The soldiers in Satan's army are as the sand of the sea in multitude. John sees how they march across the broad expanse of the earth to surround the camp of the saints and the beloved city. The camp of the saints and the beloved city is the church. The word "beloved" here in Greek is a perfect participle portraying the unfailing and enduring love of God for his people. The armies described here are not primarily a military force but a symbolic representation of all the spiritual and moral evil with which the church must contend. The civil and political forces inimical to the church are only a small part of the army arrayed against the elect of God.

As Paul says, our enemies are not flesh and blood but spiritual wickedness in high places (Eph 6:11).

But even though the situation appears hopeless and though the beloved city is surrounded on every side, there is no need for the church to rely on her own strength and might. "For us fights the valiant one." In Ezekiel's vision concerning Gog and Magog God said, "I will pour down torrents of rain, hailstones, and burning sulfur on him and on his troops and on the many nations with him . . . I will send fire on Magog" (Eze 38:22; 39:6). In similar fashion John sees fire coming down from heaven to destroy the armies of Satan. The account of the victory, as in the previous battle against the beast and the false prophet, is again very short. Just one line sums up the divine judgment on the church's enemies. Fire comes down from heaven and devours them. One is left with an impression of the ease with which God can put an end to all threats to his people when and where it pleases him.

With his supporting forces destroyed, the devil who deceived them is thrown into the lake of fire. With that event the church's enemies are all put out of action. Her victory is now complete. The two beasts of chapter 13 and the great red dragon whom we first met in chapter 12 have all been conquered and cast into the lake of fire, so that they will no longer be able to threaten the church.

John is assuring his readers that Christ's promise that the gates of hell will not prevail against his church will most assuredly finally be fulfilled. Those who tormented and tortured God's people in temporary periods of persecution will themselves be punished forever and ever (εἰς τοὺς αἰῶνας τῶν αἰώνων, "to the ages of the ages").

Human reason finds the concept of eternal punishment offensive, and the question is often asked, "How can a finite period of sinning call for an infinite period of suffering?" Such an argument cannot even be defended before the bar of human reason. The length of time it takes to commit a sin has no bearing on the length of the punishment which that sin has merited. Many a man has been sentenced to life imprisonment for a crime it took seconds to commit. Jehovah's Witnesses often argue that since the devil and wicked men are cast into a lake of fire the punishment cannot be eternal. They ask, "How can a fire burn forever?" According to them, there is not enough fuel in the universe to keep that fire going. But when God says, "Let there be," the created world comes into existence out of nothing. And just as God needed no material from which to make the world so he needs no fuel to make this fire burn, if indeed it is a material fire. The fire that causes torments for Satan and other evil spirits may not be the kind of fire with which we are acquainted, but it is a real and tormenting fire, nevertheless.

All such arguments, however, only display an unwillingness to believe the plain words of Scripture, which says that the devil will be tormented εἰς τοὺς αἰῶνας τῶν αἰώνων, forever and ever. A more plausible argument holds that the punishment of the devil is not eternal because the word αἰὼν does not necessarily mean eternity. This is true. It can also mean "a very long time." However, this is not true of the phrase εἰς τοὺς αἰῶνας τῶν αἰώνων. Those words can only mean "to all eternity." Even the abbreviated phrase εἰς τοὺς αἰῶνας can only have that meaning. These words, εἰς τοὺς αἰῶνας τῶν αἰώνων, used here to describe the torment of the devil, are used eight times in other books of the New Testament (Ro 16:27; Ga 1:5; Php 4:20; 1 Tm 1:17; 2 Tm 4:18; He 13:21; 1 Pe 4:11; 5:11). Every one of those passages is a doxology which says that glory is to be given to God εἰς τοὺς αἰῶνας τῶν αἰώνων, and surely no one would say that glory should be given to him only for a long time.

In Revelation itself this phrase is used twelve times. Three of them occur in doxologies similar to the passages cited above (Re 1:6; 5:13; 7:12). In four of them either Jesus or God are described as living εἰς τοὺς αἰῶνας τῶν αἰώνων. Surely no one could reconcile with the teaching of the Bible the idea that Jesus and God will live only for a very long time. One of the passages says that Jesus will rule εἰς τοὺς αἰῶνας τῶν αἰώνων (11:15), which again must mean "to all eternity." Note that every one of the passages cited above is used in connection with some statement made about God.

Three of these passages speak of punishment that lasts εἰς τοὺς αἰῶνας τῶν αἰώνων. The first speaks of the punishment of those who worship the beast (14:11), the second of the punishment of Babylon (19:3), and the third of the eternal punishment of the devil (20:10). The remaining passage says that the saints will reign εἰς τοὺς αἰῶνας τῶν αἰώνων, obviously again, "forever and ever."

Even the shortened phrase, εἰς τοὺς αἰῶνας, is used in contexts which force us to conclude that the writer has eternity in mind and not just a long period of time. Like the longer phrase, it is used in doxologies (Mt 6:13; Ro 1:25; 11:36; Jd 25). The last of these is especially significant for it ascribes glory and majesty and power and authority to God πρὸ παντὸς τοῦ αἰῶνος καὶ νῦν καὶ εἰς πάντας τοὺς αἰῶνας, "before all ages, now, and forevermore." Once it describes the duration of the Savior's kingdom (Lk 1:33). The remaining passage in which it is used also clearly shows that the word denotes eternity and not just a long period of time. It says that Jesus is the same yesterday and today and εἰς τοὺς αἰῶνας, which in the context can only mean forever (He 13:8; cp. He 2:10-12).

There is no doubt, then, that this passage teaches the eternal punishment of the devil. Only those who refuse to believe what the Bible says but do not want to reveal their unbelief are tempted to read anything else into these words.

THE FINAL JUDGMENT (20:11-15)

11) Καὶ εἶδον θρόνον μέγαν λευκὸν καὶ τὸν καθήμενον ἐπ' αὐτὸν οὗ ἀπὸ τοῦ προσώπου ἔφυγεν ἡ γῆ καὶ ὁ οὐρανός, καὶ τόπος οὐχ εὑρέθη αὐτοῖς. 12) καὶ εἶδον τοὺς νεκρούς, τοὺς μεγάλους καὶ τοὺς μικρούς, ἑστῶτας ἐνώπιον τοῦ θρόνου, καὶ βιβλία ἠνοίχθησαν· καὶ ἄλλο βιβλίον ἠνοίχθη, ὅ ἐστιν τῆς ζωῆς· καὶ ἐκρίθησαν οἱ νεκροὶ ἐκ τῶν γεγραμμένων ἐν τοῖς βιβλίοις κατὰ τὰ ἔργα αὐτῶν. 13) καὶ ἔδωκεν ἡ θάλασσα τοὺς νεκροὺς τοὺς ἐν αὐτῇ, καὶ ὁ θάνατος καὶ ὁ Ἅιδης ἔδωκαν τοὺς νεκροὺς τοὺς ἐν αὐτοῖς, καὶ ἐκρίθησαν ἕκαστος κατὰ τὰ ἔργα αὐτῶν. 14) καὶ ὁ θάνατος καὶ ὁ Ἅιδης ἐβλήθησαν εἰς τὴν λίμνην τοῦ πυρός. οὗτος ὁ θάνατος ὁ δεύτερός ἐστιν, ἡ λίμνη τοῦ πυρός. 15) καὶ εἴ τις οὐχ εὑρέθη ἐν τῇ βίβλῳ τῆς ζωῆς γεγραμμένος, ἐβλήθη εἰς τὴν λίμνην τοῦ πυρός.

11) *And I saw a great white throne and him who sat on it, before whose face the earth and the sky fled, and no place was found for them.* 12) *And I saw the dead, great and small, standing before the throne, and books were opened. And another book was opened, which is the book of life. And the dead were judged out of the things written in the books according to what they had done.* 13) *And the sea gave up the dead that were in it, and death and Hades gave up the dead that were in them, and they were judged, each one according to what he had done.* 14) *And death and Hades were cast into the lake of fire. The lake of fire is the second death.* 15) *If anyone was not found written in the book of life he was thrown into the lake of fire.*

When the Lord Jesus spoke of the day of judgment he said that he would sit on his throne in heavenly glory (Mt 25:31). He who sits on the great white throne spoken of here is undoubtedly the Savior, although he is not identified by name. The many

Bible passages that speak of the Son of God as the final judge of the world make the identification certain.

This is the last and the clearest of John's six visions of the last judgment (cp 6:12-17; 11:15-19; 14:14-20; 16:17-21; 19:17-21). In the first of those visions John saw men trying to escape from "the wrath of the Lamb." In this vision the earth and the sky themselves flee from the face of the one who sits on the throne. The awesome majesty of the Judge is impressed on us by these words.

Many have seen in the words, "No place was found for them [the earth and the sky]," an assertion that the earth and the sky will be annihilated at the last judgment, that they will no longer be found in any place. This is hardly the normal way to understand these words in the context. John saw that when the earth and the sky fled, no place was found for them. That does not say that they will no longer be found anywhere. If those words are read without preconceived notions about annihilation, they would simply be understood to mean that no place was found where they could hide. They had to stay "to face the music." In the first vision of judgment we were told only that frightened men sought to escape the judgment by calling upon the mountains to fall on them and the rocks to cover them (6:16). On that note the vision ended, and we were left to assume that they were unable to escape. They found no place in the caves and the rocks where they could hide. Here we are told that even the earth and sky will seek a place of refuge from the Judge's wrath, but there will be no place where they can hide from the wrath of the Lamb.

There are many other passages as well that are difficult to reconcile with the concept of annihilation. One of the clearest of those passages is found in Romans, where Paul says that this created world "will be liberated from its bondage to decay and brought into the glorious freedom of the children of God" (8:21). The "glorious freedom of the children of God" certainly is not annihilation. We will deal with another similar passage in the next chapter.

The passages that are adduced as evidence for annihilationism either do not clearly support that view or, on closer scrutiny, actually speak against it. It is often claimed that since the Bible says the world will be "burned up in the fire" of the last judgment it will be annihilated. But burning, as such, annihilates nothing. When a block of wood is burned its form is destroyed, but every single atom of that piece of wood is still in existence, though most in the form of invisible gas.

But how should we answer when we are told that the heaven and the earth will be destroyed (He 2:10,11)? Jehovah's Witnesses insist that to be destroyed, or to perish, means to be annihilated. Their denial of the doctrine of hell and eternal punishment is to a great extent built on Scripture passages which say that unbelievers will "perish." But as we have clearly seen in the previous vision, the Bible definitely does teach eternal damnation, which is in itself an argument against the annihilationist definition of "perish." Moreover, the Apostle Peter says that the world "perished" in the waters of the flood (2 Pe 3:6), and it certainly was not annihilated in the flood. Just as the created world survived the waters of the flood, so we also may expect that this same world will in some form survive the fire of the last judgment. We know it will have a different form because Paul says that "this world in its present form is passing away" (1 Cor 7:31). What its future form will be we do not know. We only know that heaven and earth will be renewed in such a way that no evil of any kind will be found there. It will be a world where everything is right (2 Pe 3:13). The next chapter will give us a picture of that world.

The earth and the sky, however, do not occupy the center of attention in this vision. John's attention is focused on the dead who were standing before the throne. They had evidently been resurrected, a process which is described in verse 12. The dead are described as "the great ones and the small ones." Whether this means "adults and children" or "the leaders and the common people" makes no difference. The phrase evidently indicates the universality of the judgment. No one is so great and powerful that he can evade the judgment, and no one so insignificant as to escape the notice of the one who sits on the throne.

The statement, "Books were opened," is awesome in its simplicity. According to the psalmist the wicked man says that God has forgotten his evil deeds and that he will never call them to account (Ps 10:11,13). While wicked men may not always verbalize such thoughts, these words do express the secret hope of every guilty heart. But on the day of judgment, books will be opened. What is written in those opened books is indicated by the context. When the books are opened men are judged out of what is written there, "according to what they have done." The record is complete.

Besides the books in which the deeds of men are recorded, another book is opened. This is a different kind of book. It is the book of life. This book is mentioned seven times in Revelation (3:5; 13:8; 17:8; 20:12,15; 21:27; 22:19). This is another example of the sevenfold structure of the book. An examination of these passages will show that this book contains the names of the elect, the ones who will share in the glories of heaven. Their names were written in that book from the creation of the world (13:8; 17:8; cp Eph 1:3-6). Paul also refers to this book of life (Php 4:3). Moses spoke of a book in which were written all the names of those who are saved (Ex 32:32). This same book is alluded to also by David (Ps 69:28), Daniel (11:1) and Malachi (3:16).

It is significant that there are two sets of books, one containing a record of all the deeds of men and the other containing no record of deeds but only names. The reason for this is clear to everyone who knows what the Bible says about salvation and damnation. Those who are saved and blessed with all spiritual blessings are those whom God has chosen and predestined from eternity (Eph 1:3-6). Their salvation is caused by God's gracious election. Those who are lost are not lost because their names are written in what might have been called the book of death, not because they were predestined to damnation, but solely because of their deeds recorded and remembered before the throne on judgment day.

Nevertheless it must be noted that each one (ἕκαστος, v. 13) of the dead is judged out of the book in which the deeds of men are written. How is this to be reconciled with the reference to the book of life? The same question arises in connection with the statement of Paul that each one of us must appear before the judgment seat of Christ to be rewarded according to what we have done (2 Cor 5:10). How is it possible for the apostle, who laid such emphasis on salvation by grace without works, to write in this way? Are we here dealing with an insoluble contradiction?

The answer is found in many passages of Scripture. One of the clearest of these is Christ's statement that he had not come to destroy the law but to fulfill it (Mt 5:17). The law demands that a person, in order to be saved, must keep all the commandments. Jesus did not come to set aside this requirement. He kept the commandments as our Substitute, and by faith we make his obedience our own, so that we can say that in him we have fulfilled all the requirements of the law. In God's book all of the Savior's righteousness is credited to our account. If God would ask us on the day of judgment whether we have done everything the law requires, we can say, "Yes, through him who knew no sin but was made to be sin for us that we might be made the righteousness of God in him" (2 Cor 5:21). Through the forgiveness of sins all the wrong deeds that might have been recorded in the books have been erased and blotted out (Is 43:25). While God says that he will remember the sins of Babylon (Re 18:5), he also promises to forget the sins of his people (Jr 31:34; Is 43:25). The only works of the believers that will be remembered are the good deeds that they have done in faith (Mt 25:35f; Re 14:13) and which are acceptable to God through the forgiveness we have in Christ (1 Pe 2:5). In that sense also believers will be judged according to their works.

Millennialists generally hold that the judgment described in these verses will concern only unbelievers, since the believing saints already had been raised from the dead a thousand years earlier, at the beginning of the millennium. We need not repeat here the arguments against such a double resurrection. But it should be pointed out that there is nothing in this text which says that these are the unbelieving dead who stand before the throne for judgment. The very fact that the book of life is also opened at this judgment is proof positive that the believing dead are also there. It is sometimes argued that since Jesus said that those who believe will not come εἰς κρίσιν, "into judgment" (Jn 5:24), believers will not be judged. However, the words of Paul in 2 Corinthians 5:21 (cited above) clearly show that the words are properly translated "will not be condemned" (NIV; cp also KJV). The context of the passage in John also calls for that translation.

The resurrection described in these words is a general resurrection of all the dead. In his Gospel John had said that all who are in the graves will come forth on the day of judgment (5:29). But here he says that even the sea will give up the dead that were in it. The bodies that were irretrievably lost in the waters of the ocean and never recovered for burial will be there.

John continues, "Death and Hades gave up the dead that were in them." These words give us some difficulty, especially in the light of what is said in the next verse, "Death and Hades were cast into the lake of fire." The word "Hades," or "hell," is used three times in Revelation, each time in conjunction with the word "death" (see 1:18; 6:8). Elsewhere in the New Testament it is used six times. In almost every case the translation "hell" fits the context. It is, however, also agreed by most reliable commentators that the "lake of fire" is hell, but then we have the rather strange concept of hell being cast into hell. We do not know enough about the next world to speak with great assurance about this difficulty. It has been suggested that perhaps Hades is "hell" as the abode of the souls of the unbelievers while they exist separated from the body and that the lake of fire is "hell" as the place of eternal torment for body and soul. That explanation is as good as any.

We are not accustomed to speaking about the souls of unbelievers as dead. Such language is confusing to modern ears because of the almost universal acceptance of the term "immortality of the soul." It is perhaps more in keeping with biblical terminology to speak of the continued existence of the soul. The souls of unbelievers exist in a state of death, that is, of separation from the blessings of God; and the souls of believers continue to exist in a state of life, that is, of enjoyment of the blessings of God. The dead who are given up by death would then refer to the bodies of all the dead and the dead who are given up by Hades are the souls of unbelievers.

The lake of fire is defined as the second death. "Death" means separation. The first death is the physical, or bodily, death — the separation from the physical and temporal blessings of God that normally comes to all men, believers and unbelievers alike. The second death is eternal separation from God in the torment of hell. There has been much discussion among Christian theologians about whether the fire of hell is literal fire, or whether it is a symbolic term used to convey the thought of the excruciating pain to be suffered by the damned. Perhaps the best advice was given by the theologians who said that we should not argue about what kind of fire it will be but zealously seek to make sure that we will never find out from experience. This is one of the "open questions" about which Christian theologians ought not to quarrel.

Earlier we had been told that the beast and the false prophet (10:20) and Satan (20:10) were cast into the lake of fire. In the closing verse of this chapter we are told that all those whose names were not written in the book of life were also cast into the lake of fire. All unbelievers share the fate of the devil and all the forces of evil.

Just as in the first series of visions, that of the seven seals, the vision of the last judgment was followed by a vision of the saints in glory, so the vision of the final judgment in this series is followed by two visions of heaven and its glories. The first of these is the vision of the new heaven and the new earth.

THE NEW HEAVEN AND THE NEW EARTH (21:1-8)

1) Καὶ εἶδον οὐρανὸν καινὸν καὶ γῆν καινήν· ὁ γὰρ πρῶτος οὐρανὸς καὶ ἡ πρώτη γῆ ἀπῆλθαν, καὶ ἡ θάλασσα οὐκ ἔστιν ἔτι. 2) καὶ τὴν πόλιν τὴν ἁγίαν Ἰερουσαλὴμ καινὴν εἶδον καταβαίνουσαν ἐκ τοῦ οὐρανοῦ ἀπὸ τοῦ Θεοῦ, ἡτοιμασμένην ὡς νύμφην κεκοσμημένην τῷ ἀνδρὶ αὐτῆς. 3) καὶ ἤκουσα φωνῆς μεγάλης ἐκ τοῦ θρόνου λεγούσης, Ἰδοὺ ἡ σκηνὴ τοῦ Θεοῦ μετὰ τῶν ἀνθρώπων, καὶ σκηνώσει μετ᾽ αὐτῶν, καὶ αὐτοὶ λαοὶ αὐτοῦ ἔσονται, καὶ αὐτὸς ὁ Θεὸς μετ᾽ αὐτῶν ἔσται, 4) καὶ ἐξαλείψει πᾶν δάκρυον ἐκ τῶν ὀφθαλμῶν αὐτῶν, καὶ ὁ θάνατος οὐκ ἔσται ἔτι, οὔτε πένθος οὔτε κραυγὴ οὔτε πόνος οὐκ ἔσται ἔτι· ὅτι τὰ πρῶτα ἀπῆλθαν. 5) Καὶ εἶπεν ὁ καθήμενος ἐπὶ τῷ θρόνῳ, Ἰδοὺ καινὰ ποιῶ πάντα. καὶ λέγει, Γράψον, ὅτι οὗτοι οἱ λόγοι πιστοὶ καὶ ἀληθινοί εἰσιν. 6) καὶ εἶπέν μοι, Γέγοναν. ἐγὼ τὸ Ἄλφα καὶ τὸ Ὦ, ἡ ἀρχὴ καὶ τὸ τέλος. ἐγὼ τῷ διψῶντι δώσω ἐκ τῆς πηγῆς τοῦ ὕδατος τῆς ζωῆς δωρεάν. 7) ὁ νικῶν κληρονομήσει ταῦτα, καὶ ἔσομαι αὐτῷ Θεὸς καὶ αὐτὸς ἔσται μοι υἱός. 8) τοῖς δὲ δειλοῖς καὶ ἀπίστοις καὶ ἐβδελυγμένοις καὶ φονεῦσιν καὶ πόρνοις καὶ φαρμακοῖς καὶ εἰδωλολάτραις καὶ πᾶσιν τοῖς ψευδέσιν τὸ μέρος αὐτῶν ἐν τῇ καιομένῃ πυρὶ καὶ θείῳ, ὅ ἐστιν ὁ θάνατος ὁ δεύτερος.

1) *And I saw a new heaven and a new earth; for the first heaven and the first earth had gone away, and the sea no longer existed.* 2) *And I saw the holy city, New Jerusalem, coming down out of the sky from God, prepared as a bride adorned for her husband.*

3) *And I heard a loud voice from the throne which said, "Behold the dwelling of God is with men and he will dwell with them, and they will be his people, and God himself will be with them. He will be their God,* 4) *and he will wipe away every tear out of their eyes, and death will no longer exist, nor will there be any more sorrow, or crying, or pain, because the former things have passed away.*

5) *And he that sat on the throne said, "Look, I am making all things new." And he said, "Write, for these words are trustworthy and true."* 6) *And he said to me, "It is done. I am the Alpha and the Omega, the Beginning and the End. Anyone who is thirsty I will allow to drink without charge from the spring of the water of life.* 7) *He that is victorious will inherit these things, and I will be his God and he will be my son.* 8) *But those who are cowardly and unbelieving and abominable and murderers and adulterers and sorcerers and idolaters and all the liars will have*

their lot in the lake burning with fire and sulphur, which is the second death."

The concept of a new heaven and a new earth is already found in the Prophet Isaiah (66:22), and new heavens and a new earth are also spoken of by the Apostle Peter in the New Testament (2 Pe 3:13). Much speculation has been carried on in regard to the origin of this new heaven and earth. Many of the later Lutheran dogmaticians were of the opinion that this new universe would be created out of nothing, just as the first universe came into being *ex nihilo.* They held that the present universe would be annihilated. Luther, however, believed that after the present form of the world is destroyed in the fire of the last judgment God would fashion this new heaven and earth out of the remains. The word heaven in this context undoubtedly means "sky," as it does in Genesis 1.

While we may not be able to settle this question of annihilationism or restorationism in a dogmatic way, yet one argument that is often heard must be rejected. It is sometimes said that this material world must be destroyed because matter is evil. This concept of the inherent evil of matter is not a biblical concept. It is either a remnant of the Gnostic heresy which did so much damage to the early church or of Neoplatonism, which had a strong influence on the church of the Middle Ages.

The biblical world view does not hold that matter, as such, is evil. Matter was created by God out of nothing and was called good by God himself at the creation. The incarnation also testifies against the view that matter is evil in itself. The Son of God became flesh, and yet he was wholly without sin. Moreover, if matter had to be destroyed there could be no resurrection of the body.

It should also be borne in mind that there is no passage in Scripture that tells us in so many words that the created world will once more be reduced to the nothingness out of which it came. There is likewise no passage which says that the second sky and earth, like the first, will again be made out of nothing.

When God said through Isaiah that he would "make" a new heaven and a new earth he does not use the same Hebrew word that was used to describe the creating of the world in the beginning. This would seem to indicate that the second world will not be made out of nothing. The Apostle Paul undoubtedly had this new earth in mind when he said that the present world will be delivered from its bondage to decay and share in the glorious liberty of God's people (Ro 8:21). While we might be able to say that an annihilated earth will have been delivered from decay, it would be difficult to think of such a non-existent earth as sharing in the glorious freedom of God's people. We are therefore inclined to agree with Luther's simple view. Beyond that, speculation about the exact form of the new heaven and earth should be avoided. In our present state we are poorly equipped even to think in terms appropriate for that world.

How different this new world will be is indicated in two ways. First, the original heaven and earth will be gone. The fire which will destroy the original world will melt down everything as in a blast furnace (2 Pe 3:10). Secondly, there will be no sea in this new earth. That must have been of special significance for John when he wrote this book. He tells us in the very first chapter that he had been exiled to the island of Patmos. Patmos was only a short distance from Ephesus, where John had been living. The fellow Christians with whom he was most intimately acquainted and whom he referred to as his "little children" (1 Jn 2:1) were still living there. He was separated from them by the sea. But he saw that in the new earth there would no longer be any sea. There would no longer be anything to separate us from those we love or to hinder the free fellowship of God's children with each other.

Out of the new sky John saw what he calls "the holy city" coming down from God. This city will be described in detail in the next vision. Here we are told only that its name is "New Jerusalem" and that it resembles a bride beautifully dressed (NIV) for her husband.

The concept of a spiritual, heavenly city called Jerusalem is not new or unique. John had used that symbolism already in chapter 11. It also is used elsewhere in the New Testament. The writer of Hebrews told the Jews who had accepted Jesus of Nazareth as the promised Messiah,

> You have come to Mount Zion, to the heavenly Jerusalem, the city of the living God. You have come to thousands upon thousands of angels in joyful assembly, to the church of the firstborn whose names are written in heaven (He 12:22).

The Apostle Paul also used the same kind of language when he drew a comparison between "the present city of Jerusalem" and "the Jerusalem that is above" (Ga 4:25,26). This second Jerusalem, he says, is the mother of all those who are justified by faith.

There can be no doubt that those passages speak of the holy Christian church. On the basis of this context we cannot decide with dogmatic certainty whether John here is speaking of a literal city to be built by God on the new earth or whether the language is wholly symbolic. Earlier the church had been described as the Lamb's wife dressed in bright fine linen (19:7,8). When the city is in this chapter described in similar terms it would appear that we are dealing with purely figurative language. When John therefore says that he saw the city coming down out of heaven, or the sky, he very likely is saying in figurative terms what Paul said in a more literal way when he wrote concerning the second coming, "God will bring with Jesus those who have fallen asleep in him" (1 Th 4:14). The following vision makes such a figurative interpretation of the language employed here by John necessary.

The description of the city as "a bride adorned for her husband" is reminiscent of the description of the church in the previous chapter, where the beginning of the church's glorification on the last day is called the marriage of the Lamb. It also reminds us of that great multitude standing before the throne who had washed their robes and made them white in the blood of the Lamb (7:14). We cannot doubt that the adornment of the New Jerusalem consists of the robes of righteousness and the garments of salvation with which God himself has clothed his people (Is 61:10).

When John says that he heard a loud voice speaking from the throne, he must mean the throne which he had seen at the beginning of this long series of visions (4:2) and to which he had referred many times. The message comes directly from God and must therefore be a reliable promise on which a suffering and persecuted church can build her hopes for a better time to come.

The voice from the throne said, "Behold, the dwelling of God is with men, and he will dwell with them." The "dwelling of God" is our translation of ἡ σκηνὴ τοῦ θεοῦ, literally, "the tent of God." Ordinarily a tent is a temporary dwelling, easily moved from place to place and used by people who do not intend to remain in one place for very long. At first glance it seems strange that this word should be used in this context, which introduces us to a vision in which John will see the saints dwelling in God's presence forever.

But John and his readers, who were acquainted with the Old Testament, knew that during Israel's wilderness wanderings the special place where God gave his people visible evidence of his gracious presence with them was a tent, a tabernacle. In the Old Testament that tent was never called "the tent of God." It was occasionally called "the tent of the Lord" (ἡ σκηνὴ τοῦ κυρίου), but more commonly it was simply called "the tent" or "the tent of witness," "the tabernacle of testimony" (ἡ σκηνὴ τοῦ μαρτυρίου). In chapter 15 John had used this very phrase to describe the temple of God in heaven (ὁ ναὸς τῆς σκηνὴ τοῦ μαρτυρίου ἐν τῷ οὐρανῷ). Once that tabernacle was in heaven. Now it has come down to the earth.

It is thus clear that the word "tent," or "tabernacle," is not used here to emphasize the temporary nature of the dwelling but rather to point out that in the new heaven and the new earth God would be living in the midst of his people in a very special way. This presence of God with his people is in some way comparable to the special way in which God manifested his presence to the children of Israel when they traveled through the wilderness. On their way to the promised land they saw the pillar of cloud and fire hovering over the tabernacle. God's presence is indicated by the use of the word "tent" or "tabernacle." In this case "tent" represents an eternal dwelling. We find a parallel in the parable of the unjust steward, where the final dwelling-places of God's people are called "eternal tents" (αἰωνίους σκηνάς).

To underscore that truth the voice went on to say that God will "dwell," literally "tent" (σκηνώσει), with them. Like the noun, here the verb "to tent" does not imply anything less than an eternal action of God. The redeemed at that time will no longer walk by faith, but by sight. They will have clear, tangible, visible evidence that God is dwelling with them, just as Israel had such evidence of God's nearness in the tabernacle. Because of the sufferings inflicted on them by their enemies, John's contemporaries may have thought at times that God had forsaken them and that the government of the world had been taken over by Satan and the two beasts. This promise was to assure them that God was still controlling the course of history in order that someday they would see the truth of what they now could only believe.

But what of the words, "They *will* be his people, and God himself *will* be with them. He *will* be their God"? They were already his people when John wrote those words. John helps us understand these words by a statement he makes in his First Epistle, "Now we are children of God, and what we will be has not yet been made known" (3:2). At that time it will be manifest to all that believers are indeed members of God's family. Paul expresses that same hope when he speaks of the day of judgment as the time when the sons of God will be revealed, when it will become manifest who and what the children of God really are (Ro 8:19).

The voice said, "God himself will be with them." This, too, may seem surprising, for God was with them also in those days of persecution. But often he seemed to be far away, and they had no tangible evidence of his presence and providential care. Rather, it seemed that he had abandoned them to their enemies. But on the day when the heavenly Jerusalem will come down from the sky, they will have the tangible visible evidence for which they must often have longed. God will be with them in such a way that his presence will be manifest. In his First Epistle John had written, "We shall see him as he is" (3:2).

The voice continues, "He will be their God, and he will wipe away every tear out of their eyes, and death will no longer exist, nor will there be any more sorrow, or crying, or pain, because the former things have passed away." That God is really their God, that he loves them and is concerned about them, that he had in all those former times desired and planned their salvation, was now evident. There is no longer any reason to weep, for death has been conquered, as Paul had predicted it would be when he wrote, "The last enemy to be destroyed is death" (1 Cor 15:26). The story of man's redemption began when man fell into sin and brought the curse of death into the world. It will be complete when death itself will go out of existence, at least for the children of God.

In his Gospel John had preserved the promise that Jesus gave to his disciples on the night of his betrayal, "You will grieve, but your grief will turn to joy" (Jn 16:20). Now in this vision John sees the final and complete fulfillment of that promise. Sorrow, crying and pain, all these have vanished from the church in its hour of final triumph. The old order of things has passed away (NIV).

John continues, "And he that sat on the throne said, 'Look, I am making all things new.'" In those words God reminds John and us that the conquest of death and pain and sorrow is his work. When modern scientists and theologians speak of the renewal of society and the building of a perfect social order as the task to which science and government and the church should devote themselves they forget that such a perfect world can come only when the present order of things is destroyed and a new heaven and a new earth are brought into being by God himself. The present world labors under the curse of sin and must perish to make room for the new order of things, which will be brought into being not by human effort and ingenuity but only by the almighty power of God. The task of the church, therefore, is not to build a perfect social order, but to proclaim the gospel promises through which men will come to share in the new order of things which God will make.

We are reminded of this when God speaks to John again. John writes, "And he said, 'Write for these words are trustworthy and true.' " Although we have translated, "he said," John actually uses a present tense, καὶ λέγει, "and he says." The New Testament writers often use what is called the historical present when they speak of past events. This use of the present tense usually indicates that the event described is still very vivid in the mind of the narrator. There is a similar use of the present tense in colloquial English.

When God spoke to John a second time, he told him to write. One of the very first words John heard when his vision of the future began was the command to "write" (1:11). It was repeated a number of times (1:19; 2:1,8,12,18; 3:1,7,14; 14:13; 19:9). In all those other instances John was told what to write. Here, however, he is told why he should write, namely, "because these words are trustworthy and true."

What John had seen and heard was not meant for his eyes and ears alone. He was to share the message with others. What he produced in this book was to be a part of the writings which had come into being by the inspiration of God; it was to become a part of the Holy Writings, the Holy Scriptures, all of which were written for our learning, to teach us, "so that through endurance and the encouragement of the Scriptures we might have hope" (Ro 15:4).

John is assured that there is no danger that he will ever be shamed or embarrassed by what he was to write. The words he had heard from God are "trustworthy and true." The prophecies which he made when he described his visions in writing were not guesses that might or might not come true. Because they are "trustworthy and true" the church can safely find in them a firm hope in times of great tribulation. The tears of God's people will surely be wiped away and death and pain and sorrow will surely come to an end. God was through John putting his promises down in writing, just as a human contractor is willing to put into writing what he intends to carry out.

These written divine promises are therefore trustworthy and dependable, "worthy of all acceptation."

God now spoke to John a third time. He said, "It is done" (γέγοναν). The Greek word is actually an unusual third person plural form and should really be translated, "They are done." The only possible subject of the verb is "these words" in the previous sentence, and the meaning must be that the things which those words have foretold have come true. Whatever God promises is as good as done, because he is the eternal one for whom there is no past or future but only one eternal timeless today.

To this he alludes when he continues, "I am the Alpha and the Omega, the Beginning and the End." At the beginning of the book (1:18), before the vision of John began, God has described himself in the same terms, although many manuscripts at that place have only the first part of the sentence. The meaning remains the same since "Alpha" and "Omega," the first and last letters of the Greek alphabet, are figurative synonyms for "beginning" and "end." Before the earth and the world were formed God was (Ps 90:2), and when the present sky and earth have passed away he still will be. In the new order of things he will be the God in charge, just as he is the God who rules and governs the present world in which evil governments and apostate churches often seem to prosper. But these words help to reassure us that the enemies of God's people endure only for a time. When they and the world in which they often seem to be in control come to an end, God still will be.

Whether the next words refer to an action of God in the present world or to something he will do in the new heaven and the new earth is difficult to determine. God says, "Anyone who is thirsty I will allow to drink without charge from the spring of the water of life." We have felt justified in translating τῷ διψῶντι with "anyone who is thirsty" because the article evidently is a generic article denoting all thirsty people as a class. It goes without saying that these are people who are spiritually thirsty, the contrite who sense their great spiritual need of forgiveness and salvation.

Both the Old and New Testaments speak of the gospel offer of forgiveness and salvation in those terms. Isaiah introduced one of his most eloquent promises concerning eternal life and the unfailing kindness of God with the following words (Is 55:1):

Come, all you who are thirsty,
come to the waters;
and you who have no money,
come, buy and eat!
Come, buy wine and milk
without money and without cost (Is 55:1).

In his Gospel John himself had recorded the conversation of Jesus with the Samaritan woman at Jacob's well. To that woman Jesus said, "Whoever drinks the water I give him will never thirst. Indeed, the water I give him will become in him a spring of water welling up to eternal life" (Jn 4:14). Earlier in that conversation the Savior had called the water of which he was speaking "living water," which seems to be a synonym of the "water of life" spoken of here. The exact term "water of life," however, occurs only in Revelation. From this we correctly conclude that God's words to John describe the gospel offer that God will continue to make to men so long as this present world stands. The future verb δώσω, "I will allow," is a durative future, denoting a present act that will continue indefinitely.

At the beginning of the next chapter John speaks of the river of the water of life, which flows down the middle of the main street in the heavenly Jerusalem. Nothing is said about anyone drinking from that river, yet the language is strikingly similar to that which is used here. So it is possible to conclude that here we are dealing with a symbol of the joy that will be ours in eternity.

Nevertheless, in that same chapter (22:17), that symbol obviously portrays the preaching of the gospel. The offer of the water of life to those who are thirsty most likely refers to the preaching of the gospel, which will continue to be efficacious thoughout the course of this world's history in spite of the efforts of Satan and the two beasts to suppress it. Here, then, is a promise that God will continue to build and preserve his church by satisfying the spiritually thirsty with his free and gracious offer of forgiveness, by which he will bring them into the heavenly Jerusalem.

The Lord says, "He that is victorious will inherit these things, and I will be his God and he will be my son." Every one of the seven letters in chapters 2 and 3 contained a promise for "the one who is victorious." In those passages the enemies over whom the victory is won are never specifically identified, but in the intervening visions God's people are twice identified as people who have won a victory over named enemies. In chapter 12 they are described as having overcome the devil because of the blood of the Lamb and because of the word of their testimony (12:11) and in chapter 15 as having won the victory over the beast and his image. It is therefore clear that the one who is victorious is the Christian who has successfully resisted all the efforts of the devil and the anti-Christian world to rob him of his faith.

The victorious believer has the promise that he will inherit "these things." "These things" refers back to all the blessings that had been enumerated in the previous verses, including the heavenly Jerusalem, freedom from death and pain, from tears and crying and grief. But two blessings that had been mentioned previously are mentioned again, as if to emphasize that these are the greatest of them all, namely, "I will be his God, and he will be my son." This echoes an earlier promise (v. 3) in slightly different words. Release from sorrow and pain could come to men through annihilation, such as is promised in the Hindu nirvana. A heaven filled merely with material blessings and treasures could not bring lasting happiness. Only the infinite majesty of God will be able to satisfy and to keep us occupied through the endless ages of eternity. For that reason the church fathers often spoke of the "beatific vision" as the greatest of all the eternal blessings that will be ours in heaven.

God's final words to John in this vision remind us that not all men will share in the glories of the new Jerusalem. He says, "But those who are cowardly and unbelieving and abominable and murderers and adulterers and sorcerers and idolaters and all the liars will have their lot in the lake which burns with fire and sulphur, which is the second death." It is rather remarkable that in this roster which describes some of the vilest crimes known to men, the "cowardly" and the "unbelieving" should lead the list. But this is a reminder of the historical context in which this book was written. Uppermost in the minds of the people for whom John wrote, when they heard those words, must have been those apostate Christians who under the threat of persecution had renounced their faith in Christ. Unlike the Lord's faithful martyr Antipas (2:13) and the faithful Christians in Pergamos (2:13) and Philadelphia (3:8), they had denied the name of Christ because of the fear of death, and thus were rightly branded as cowards and unbelievers. Like the beast and the false prophet (19:20) and Satan (20:10) they will be cast into the lake of fire. This will be their allotted portion (μέρος), their share in eternity. Side by side with the most glorious gospel promises, God also proclaims the most severe threats of the law, so that the new man may be encouraged by the promises and the old man terrified by the threats.

THE NEW JERUSALEM (21:9-27)

The General Description of the City (21:9-21)

**9) Καὶ ἦλθεν εἷς ἐκ τῶν ἑπτὰ ἀγγέλων τῶν ἐχόντων τὰς ἑπτὰ
φιάλας τῶν γεμόντων τῶν ἑπτὰ πληγῶν τῶν ἐσχάτων, καὶ
ἐλάλησεν μετ' ἐμοῦ λέγων, Δεῦρο, δείξω σοι τὴν νύμφην τὴν
γυναῖκα τοῦ Ἀρνίου. 10) καὶ ἀπήνεγκέν με ἐν πνεύματι ἐπὶ ὄρος
μέγα καὶ ὑψηλόν, καὶ ἔδειξέν μοι τὴν πόλιν τὴν ἁγίαν Ἱερουσαλὴμ καταβαίνουσαν ἐκ τοῦ οὐρανοῦ ἀπὸ Θεοῦ, 11) ἔχουσαν τὴν
δόξαν τοῦ Θεοῦ· ὁ φωστὴρ αὐτῆς ὅμοιος λίθῳ τιμιωτάτῳ, ὡς λίθῳ
ἰάσπιδι κρυσταλλίζοντι· 12) ἔχουσα τεῖχος μέγα καὶ ὑψηλόν,
ἔχουσα πυλῶνας δώδεκα, καὶ ἐπὶ τοῖς πυλῶσιν ἀγγέλους δώδεκα,
καὶ ὀνόματα ἐπιγεγραμμένα, ἅ ἐστιν τῶν δώδεκα φυλῶν υἱῶν
Ἰσραήλ. 13) ἀπὸ ἀνατολῆς πυλῶνες τρεῖς, καὶ ἀπὸ βορρᾶ πυλῶνες τρεῖς, καὶ ἀπὸ νότου πυλῶνες τρεῖς, καὶ ἀπὸ δυσμῶν πυλῶνες
τρεῖς. 14) καὶ τὸ τεῖχος τῆς πόλεως ἔχων θεμελίους δώδεκα, καὶ
ἐπ' αὐτῶν δώδεκα ὀνόματα τῶν δώδεκα ἀποστόλων τοῦ Ἀρνίου.
15) Καὶ ὁ λαλῶν μετ' ἐμοῦ εἶχεν μέτρον κάλαμον χρυσοῦν, ἵνα
μετρήσῃ τὴν πόλιν καὶ τοὺς πυλῶνας αὐτῆς καὶ τὸ τεῖχος αὐτῆς.
16) καὶ ἡ πόλις τετράγωνος κεῖται, καὶ τὸ μῆκος αὐτῆς ὅσον τὸ
πλάτος. καὶ ἐμέτρησεν τὴν πόλιν τῷ καλάμῳ ἐπὶ σταδίων δώδεκα
χιλιάδων· τὸ μῆκος καὶ τὸ πλάτος καὶ τὸ ὕψος αὐτῆς ἴσα ἐστίν.
17) καὶ ἐμέτρησεν τὸ τεῖχος αὐτῆς ἑκατὸν τεσσεράκοντα τεσσάρων πηχῶν, μέτρον ἀνθρώπου, ὅ ἐστιν ἀγγέλου. 18) καὶ ἡ
ἐνδώμησις τοῦ τείχους αὐτῆς ἴασπις, καὶ ἡ πόλις χρυσίον καθαρὸν ὅμοιον ὑάλῳ καθαρῷ. 19) οἱ θεμέλιοι τοῦ τείχους τῆς πόλεως
παντὶ λίθῳ τιμίῳ κεκοσμημένοι· ὁ θεμέλιος ὁ πρῶτος ἴασπις, ὁ
δεύτερος σάπφειρος, ὁ τρίτος χαλκηδών, ὁ τέταρτος σμάραγδος,
20) ὁ πέμπτος σαρδόνυξ, ὁ ἕκτος σάρδιον, ὁ ἕβδομος χρυσόλιθος,
ὁ ὄγδοος βήρυλλος, ὁ ἔνατος τοπάζιον, ὁ δέκατος χρυσόπρασος,
ὁ ἑνδέκατος ὑάκινθος, ὁ δωδέκατος ἀμέθυστος. 21) καὶ οἱ δώδεκα
πυλῶνες δώδεκα μαργαρῖται· ἀνὰ εἷς ἕκαστος τῶν πυλώνων ἦν ἐξ
ἑνὸς μαργαρίτου. καὶ ἡ πλατεῖα τῆς πόλεως χρυσίον καθαρὸν ὡς
ὕαλος διαυγής.**

9) *And one of the seven angels who have the seven bowls, who carry the seven last plagues, came, and he spoke with me, saying, "Come, I will show you the bride, the wife of the Lamb."*

10) *And in spirit he carried me away to the top of a great and high mountain and he showed me the holy city Jerusalem coming down out of heaven from God,* 11) *having the glory of God. The source of her light was like a very precious stone, like a jasper stone, shining like crystal.* 12) *It had a wall, great and high. It had twelve gates, and at the gates twelve angels, and twelve names engraved, which are the names of the twelve tribes of the children of Israel,* 13) *on the east three gates, on the north three, on the south three, and on the west three.* 14) *And the wall of the city had twelve foundations, and on them the twelve names of the twelve apostles of the Lamb.*

15) *And he who spoke with me had a golden measuring rod, that he might measure the city and her gates and her wall.* 16) *And the city was laid out with four corners. Her length and breadth were equal. And he measured the city with the rod at 12,000 stadia. The length and the breadth and the height of it are the same.* 17) *And he measured its wall, (which was) 144 cubits, a human measurement, which is also angelic.* 18) *The substructure of the wall was jasper, and the city was pure gold, like pure glass.* 19) *The foundations of the city's wall were adorned with every precious stone. The first foundation was jasper; the second sapphire; the third, chalcedony; the fourth, emerald;* 20) *the fifth, sardonyx; the sixth, carnelian; the seventh, chrysolite; the eighth, beryl; the ninth, topaz; the tenth, chrysoprase; the eleventh, jacinth; the twelfth, amethyst.* 21) *And the twelve gates are twelve pearls, each of the gates was (made) out of one pearl. And the street of the city was pure gold, like transparent glass.*

We are here dealing with a symbolic representation of the church triumphant. The new Jerusalem apparently is not to be thought of as a literal city. Perhaps the clearest indication of this is the reference to the names of the twelve apostles on the twelve foundations (v. 14). A name written on something may indicate ownership or identification. There is nothing in the New Testament that would in any way lead to the conclusion that the foundations of the new Jerusalem belong to the twelve apostles, but there is a clear statement that the twelve apostles are the foundation of the church. Paul says that the Christian church is "built on the foundations of the apostles and prophets" (Eph 2:20). That, of course, does not mean that the apostles and prophets in their persons are the foundation of the church, but rather that the Word of God, which was proclaimed by the apostles and prophets, is the foundation of the faith which makes us members of the church. That thought is borne out also by the statement of Jesus that the confession of Peter would be the foundation on which he would build his church (Mt 16:16).

Another indication pointing to the conclusion that we are here dealing with a symbolic representation of the church is the shape of the city. It is a perfect cube, as high as it is broad and long. This was also the shape of the holy of holies in the tabernacle and, later, in Solomon's temple. The holy of holies was considered the special dwelling place of God, where the Lord spoke with Moses face to face and where the high priest appeared before the Lord with the atoning sacrificial blood. In the previous vision, the new Jerusalem was the place where God lives with his people in a special intimate communion. The heavenly Jerusalem is thus the new holy of holies in which God will dwell with his own forever.

Another factor that enters into this picture is the fact that the twelve gates bear the names of the twelve tribes of Israel. The fact that there are three gates in each of four sides seems to be another allusion to the tabernacle in the wilderness. God commanded that on each of the four sides of the tabernacle three tribes were to set up their camps (Nu 2). In New Testament terminology the true Israel of God is the invisible church, which consists of all those who by faith are the children of Abraham. The names of the twelve tribes which are written on the twelve gates are not given here, but we may be safe in assuming that they are the same twelve names that had been used in the description of the church militant in an earlier chapter (7:4-8). The names on the gates imply that only those who by faith claim membership in God's chosen people, the elect, the spiritual Israel, are allowed to enter the city. This description of the heavenly Jerusalem is a symbolic portrayal of the church after the passing away of the old order of things.

This conclusion is verified by the text itself in so many words when the heavenly Jerusalem is identified as "the bride, the wife of the Lamb." The bride of Christ is the Christian church (19:5-9).

Another general remark that might be made before we look at the vision in detail is that all the figures used in describing the city are twelves or multiples of twelve. The city has twelve gates, presided over by twelve angels, engraved with twelve names, and made of twelve pearls. The wall of the city has twelve foundations bearing the twelve names of the twelve apostles. The city measures 12,000 stadia in length, breadth, and height. The city wall is 144 cubits thick. All of this verifies the conclusion that twelve is the number that symbolizes the church, as we noted in the discussion on chapter 7.

After those general remarks on this vision, we proceed to look at some of its details. John is introduced to this vision by one of the seven angels who had the seven bowls and who carried the seven last plagues. These seven angels had first appeared to John in chapter 15. If we follow the strict rules of Greek grammar we have to conclude that John here says that the seven angels were loaded with, or carried, the seven last plagues, since the participle, γεμόνεων (full of, or, loaded with), being in the genitive, cannot grammatically modify the noun φιάλας (bowls), which is in the accusative case.

Most translators, however, assume that John made a mistake in grammar and construe the genitive participle as modifying the accusative noun which it follows and translate, "seven bowls full of the seven last plagues," although the NASB has a marginal note which takes notice of what it evidently considers to be clumsy Greek. On the other hand, John knew very well that a participle modifying a noun should be in the same case as the noun. In an earlier verse he says that the seven bowls were full of the wrath of God, and there the case of the participle indicates very clearly that it modifies the noun, "bowls" (15:7). Moreover, in that context he twice describes these angels as having the seven last plagues before he mentions that the seven bowls were given to them (15:1,6). So it is possible, although not necessary, to think of the angels as carrying the seven plagues even before they have the bowls in their hands. The Greek word γέμω, which is usually translated "to be full of," can also be used of an animal that carries a load on its back, in which case it is to be translated "loaded with." Besides, John nowhere says that the plagues were in the bowls but he speaks of the bowls as being filled with the wrath of God. For those reasons we have chosen to translate in a way that indicates that the seven last plagues were carried in some way by the angels.

That raises once more the question of the grammatical "mistakes" in John's Greek, and we repeat our earlier observation that irregularities in grammar are not on the same level as mistakes in facts. It is perfectly possible to express the truth in poor grammar. When the Holy Ghost inspired the holy men of God to write down the truth of God in the Bible he used the holy writers as he found them and employed the literary style to which they were accustomed. Yet the perfectly logical explanation of what at first glance appears to be poor Greek here reminds us again that while it is true that not all his seeming grammatical irregularities are easily explained, yet John's Greek is not so "bad" as is sometimes suggested.

The angel who appeared to John promised to show John "the bride, the wife of the Lamb." There is no doubt that this is a promise to show John the church in her heavenly glory, in contrast to the suffering church militant which he was addressing in this book.

Immediately after giving John this promise the angel carried him away "in spirit to the top of a great and high mountain." John says, literally, "he carried me away on a mountain (ἐπὶ ὄρος)" but this is an example of ellipsis in which the reader is expected to supply another verb, the thought being, "he carried me away and set me down on a mountain." The phrase, "in spirit," which John uses a number of times in this book (1:10; 4:2; 17:3), is again not a reference to the Holy Spirit but rather to the spiritual state of heightened awareness to spiritual things in which John was able to see the things shown to him in these visions. See the comments on the earlier uses of this phrase (1:10; 4:2; 17:3).

Just as Moses had seen the whole promised land from the top of Mt. Nebo (Dt 34), so John from the top of this mountain was able to see the holy city Jerusalem coming down from God out of heaven. In the first vision of the heavenly Jerusalem which he had described in the opening verses of this chapter John evidently had not been granted a clear vision of the city. He only says that she was adorned like a bride for her husband.

Now, however, he is able to describe the city in detail. He says, first, that she has the glory of God. This seems to be another allusion to the wilderness tabernacle. The "glory of the Lord" is the bright light in which God manifested his presence to his people in the wilderness and also in later times. When the tabernacle was set up and dedicated we are told that "the glory of the Lord filled the tabernacle" (Ex 40:34,35). The same thing happened again when Solomon's temple was consecrated to the Lord's service (1 Kgs 8:11). While this bright light is usually called "the glory of the Lord," yet in Romans (9:4) it is simply called "the glory" and Ezekiel clearly calls it "the glory of the God of Israel" (Eze 8:4; 9:3; 10:19; 11:22,23; 43:2,4). This phrase, "the glory of God," was used once before by John (15:8), perhaps also in this specialized sense, to indicate the gracious presence of the Lord with his people in the new Jerusalem. This understanding of "the glory of God" is indicated also in the later statement that the glory of God gives light to the heavenly city (v. 23).

John goes on to say, "The source of her light was like a very precious stone, like a jasper stone, shining like crystal." Most modern versions translate φωστήρ (the source of her light) with "radiance" or "brilliance." However, the word means "a light-giver, a luminary," and it certainly has that meaning in the only other place in the New Testament where the word is used (Php 2:15). Moreover, the definition "radiance," or "brilliance," does not seem to be well-founded.

Besides, the definition "the source of her light" makes perfectly good sense, both in the narrower and wider context. When the φωστήρ is said to be like a very precious stone, like a jasper stone, shining like crystal, this seems to echo the description of God in the vision of the throne in 4:3 where he that sat on the throne is described as being "in appearance like a stone, a jasper and a carnelian." In the vision of the throne in the next chapter (22:4) God is said to give light to the saints in glory, and in an earlier verse (21:23) John says that the city has no need of the sun or moon; it has no need of sources of light, because the glory of the Lord gives light to the city and the Lamb is its lamp. For those reasons we understand the φωστήρ, the source of the city's light, to be God himself. Thus we see in this statement another indication of God's gracious presence with his people in the New Jerusalem.

The New Jerusalem is described as having a great and high wall. Walls around ancient cities served only one purpose. They protected the inhabitants from enemy assaults. All the enemies of the church will be cast into the lake of fire and therefore no longer threaten the church. The wall symbolizes this security which the people of God will enjoy in the new heaven and the new earth.

The names of the twelve tribes on the twelve gates leading into the city indicate that these gates are to be used only by Israelites. All true Israelites, and only true Israelites, have access to this holy place. No uncircumcised person was allowed to eat of the passover (Ex 12:48), and the Jews permitted no uncircumcised person to enter the immediate temple area in the earthly Jerusalem. Likewise, no unbeliever will be allowed to enter the heavenly city. We need not repeat here what has already been said about the New Testament significance of the word Israel. See, for example the comments on the letter to Smyrna (2:9).

We are not specifically told why there are twelve angels stationed at the twelve gates. Because angels are so often portrayed as the protectors of the children of God many assume that they are stationed at the gates to defend the city against its enemies. Such an interpretation is not impossible. However, the reference to the tree of life and other parallels to the garden of Eden in the following context suggest that the angels standing at the gates of the holy city serve a purpose similar to that carried out by the cherubim that were placed at the entrance to the garden of Eden. They are there to see to it that no unbeliever enters these gates to partake of the tree of life. The presence of the angels thus reinforces the lesson taught by the names of the Israelite tribes inscribed on the gates.

The measuring of the city is reminiscent of the scene described in chapter 11, where John was commanded to measure the temple but to leave the outer court and the city unmeasured because those areas were occupied by the Gentiles, that is, unbelievers. Here, however, the entire city is measured, for this city has no one in it that does not belong there. The church triumphant, unlike the visible church as we find it in this world, is not a mixed multitude. The tares will be separated from the wheat (Mt 13:37-43) and the good fish from the bad (Mt 13:47-50).

We have already taken note of the fact that the city is a perfect cube, measuring 12,000 stadia in each direction. Some modern translators (e.g. AAT, NASB) give the modern equivalent of this figure, which is actually a little less than 1,400 miles. This figure to a certain extent explains why some commentators find difficulties in this survey of the city. It is hard to imagine a wall more than a thousand miles high which is only a little more than two hundred feet wide. But to give the measurements in modern equivalents really destroys the symbolism since all the measurements are in multiples of twelve. The figures are not geographical but symbolical. They help us determine the significance of twelve as a symbolic number.

The perfect cubic shape of the city, besides being similar to the contours of the holy of holies, also implies that God's design in sending out his apostles to gather in the elect has been successfully completed. Paul had spoken of the holy temple of the Lord, the Christian church, as growing (Eph 2:21) as more and more of those who are afar off are brought near (Eph 2:17); Peter had described individual Christians as living stones being incorporated into the church (1 Pe 2:15); but John sees the church as a completed whole in which there is no more room for additions, for the building of the city is obviously finished. The shape of the city therefore once more reminds us that the present world will stand until all the elect of God are gathered in. Since the city measures 12,000 stadia in each direction, which is 12 x 10 x 10 x 10 stadia, and since twelve is the number of the church, the identification of the number ten as the symbol of completeness or perfection must be correct.

The wall is 144 cubits wide. Since the city is a perfect cube, the wall is apparently as wide at the top as at the bottom, which is another indication that the picture set before our eyes is not to be understood literally. That impression is reinforced by John's statement that the measurement is that "of a man, that is, of an angel." The exact significance of that remark is not easy to determine. It may mean nothing more than that the angel who spoke to him and who measured the wall appeared to him in the form of a man. Just as the human form of this spiritual being was not an exact representation of what an angel is in actual fact, so this material form of the holy city is intended to set before us a representation of something that is basically a spiritual reality.

The inexpressible beauty of the heavenly city is described in terms of gold and precious jewels. The substructure of the wall was "jasper." Neither the commentators nor the dictionaries are agreed on exactly what kind of stone this was, although there is general agreement that in ancient times the word "jasper" (ἴασπις) was not restricted to the semi-precious stone now called by that name. Many commentators believe that the word here means "diamond" while others suggest "opal." Just because we are not able to understand and to identify clearly everything that is said in this description of the city, we are left with an impression of indescribable beauty.

To conclude that the wall was of jasper, however, seems to conflict with John's statement that the city was pure gold and that the first foundation was jasper. We are here once more faced with a difficulty in vocabulary. The word ἐνδώμησις, "material," is a rare word, derived from the word δωμέω, which means "build." Our translation "substructure" is a guess at what John wanted to say and is probably no better than "material."

Each of the twelve foundations is made of a single, or one kind of, precious stone, and each gate is carved out of one pearl. Nothing like such a structure can be imagined in the world in which we live, and we are thus reminded that this present world no longer exists and that it will be replaced by a world of incomparable excellence and beauty. Many of the stones mentioned as forming the foundations cannot be positively identified. We know only that the twelve foundations represent the twelve apostles, and the fact that they are represented by precious stones reminds us of what a great treasure and blessing the apostles and their message have been to the church.

The description of the street of the city as pure gold, as transparent as glass, again reminds us that we are here dealing with realities which transcend all our present experience. Nevertheless, it creates the impression of surpassing value and excellence. The unquestioned beauty of that blessed place should create in us all a longing to see what that world is really like. The ancient poet has perhaps written the ideal comment on this description when he wrote the words which have been translated,

> I know not, oh, I know not,
> What joys await us there,
> What radiancy of glory,
> What bliss beyond compare. (TLH, 613).

The City Itself and Its Inhabitants (21:22-27)

22) Καὶ ναὸν οὐκ εἶδον ἐν αὐτῇ· ὁ γὰρ Κύριος ὁ Θεὸς ὁ Παντοκράτωρ ναὸς αὐτῆς ἐστιν, καὶ τὸ Ἀρνίον. 23) καὶ ἡ πόλις οὐ χρείαν ἔχει τοῦ ἡλίου οὐδὲ τῆς σελήνης, ἵνα φαίνωσιν αὐτῇ· ἡ γὰρ δόξα τοῦ Θεοῦ ἐφώτισεν αὐτήν, καὶ ὁ λύχνος αὐτῆς τὸ Ἀρνίον. 24) καὶ περιπατήσουσιν τὰ ἔθνη διὰ τοῦ φωτὸς αὐτῆς, καὶ οἱ βασιλεῖς τῆς γῆς φέρουσιν τὴν δόξαν αὐτῶν εἰς αὐτήν· 25) καὶ οἱ πυλῶνες αὐτῆς οὐ μὴ κλεισθῶσιν ἡμέρας, νὺξ γὰρ οὐκ ἔσται ἐκεῖ· 26) καὶ οἴσουσιν τὴν δόξαν καὶ τὴν τιμὴν τῶν ἐθνῶν εἰς αὐτήν. 27) καὶ οὐ μὴ εἰσέλθῃ εἰς εὐτὴν πᾶν κοινὸν καὶ ὁ ποιῶν βδέλυγμα καὶ ψεῦδος, εἰ μὴ οἱ γεγραμμένοι ἐν τῷ βιβλίῳ τῆς ζωῆς τοῦ Ἀρνίου.

22) *And I saw no temple in it, for the Lord God Almighty and the Lamb are its temple.* 23) *And the city has no need of the sun nor of the moon to shine for it; for the glory of God gave it light, and the Lamb was its lamp.* 24) *And the nations will walk by its light and the kings of the earth will bring their glory into it.* 25) *And its gates will never be shut by day, for there will be no night there.* 26) *And they will bring the glory and the treasure of the nations into it.* 27) *And nothing that is unclean and no one who does*

what is abominable or who tells lies will ever enter it, except those who are written in the Lamb's book of life.

Having described the appearance of the New Jerusalem with its walls and foundations, its street and its gates, John calls attention to the city itself. He writes, "A temple I did not see in it." The word "temple" stands in an emphatic position in the sentence. John was surprised by the lack of a special place of worship. The temple was the place where the Israelites appeared in the presence of the Lord. It was the place where they enjoyed their closest communion with God. There the means of grace through which God bestowed his favor and forgiveness were dispensed.

But in the New Jerusalem there is no more need for any institution through which God deals with his people. Rather, here they live in direct communion with God. John says, "The Lord God Almighty and the Lamb are its temple." At first glance it may seem strange that God and the Lamb are called a temple. This certainly does not mean that there is a special place in the city where the people can come into his presence as they did in the earthly tabernacle. The omnipresence of God assures us that when God dwells with his people in the New Jerusalem, he will dwell with them everywhere. His special and intimate presence turns the whole place into a temple. The Prophet Zechariah (14:20f) had foretold,

> On that day HOLY TO THE LORD will be inscribed on the bells of the horses, and the cooking pots in the Lord's house will be like the sacred bowls in front of the altar. Every pot in Jerusalem and in Judah will be holy to the Lord Almighty, and all who come to sacrifice will take some of the pots and cook in them. And on that day there will no longer be a Canaanite in the house of the Lord Almighty.

In the Levitical temple worship regulations, God had ordained that the words "HOLY TO THE LORD" should be inscribed on the miter worn by the high priest, but Zechariah predicted that the time would come when everything in Jerusalem would be holy and totally dedicated to the Lord's service. While those words are to a certain extent fulfilled in the New Testament church through the forgiveness of sins, yet we shall see their complete fulfillment only in the new heaven and new earth, when God's visible presence will make the whole city a place of worship.

No sun or moon will be needed in the New Jerusalem, for the glory of God will give light to the city. "The glory of God" is another name for "the glory of the Lord," the Shekinah, the bright light in which God made his presence visible to ancient Israel and which shone around the shepherds when the angels came to announce the birth of the Savior. That glory will no longer appear just for a short time only to disappear again for centuries and millennia, but it will be a constant illumination for God's people.

Not only will they see the glory of the Lord without interruption, but the Lamb will likewise be the lamp of the city. This is the only passage in the Bible in which the Lord Jesus is called a λύχνος, an oil-burning lamp, although there are many passages both in the Old and New Testaments that speak of him as a light. The term λύχνος here is in some ways parallel to the word φωστήρ (luminary) in verse 11 of this chapter. Both the λύχνος and the φωστήρ are sources of light. We may also view the two coordinate clauses, "the glory of the Lord will give light to it" and "the Lamb is its lamp," as a poetic synonymous parallelism. Some Lutheran scholars believe that the appearance of the glory of the Lord in the Old Testament is a special manifestation of the second person of the Holy Trinity. If this is true, as it may well be, then "the glory of the Lord" and "the Lamb" in this verse would be synonymous terms, and the glory of the Lord gives light to the city through the God-man, whose face on the Mount of Transfiguration shone with the brightness of the sun, and who will shine in that way for God's people through all eternity.

The Prophet Isaiah had foretold that the Messiah would be a light for the Gentiles, for the nations of the earth (42:6). John also sees that prophecy fulfilled in the New Jerusalem. He says, "The nations will walk by its light." Some commentators have deduced from this verse that only Jewish believers will live inside the city while Gentile believers will live in the surrounding suburbs where the light of the city will still reach them. It is true that the word ἔθνη sometimes means "Gentiles" or "non-Jewish peoples," but at other times it simply means "nations." In light of what is said in verses 14 and 15 of the next chapter and of all the passages that teach clearly that there is no distinction between Jewish and non-Jewish believers (*e.g.*, Ga 3:28; Eph 2:14f) such a separation of Jewish and Gentile believers is unacceptable here. "The nations" spoken of here must be the people of "all nations and tribes and peoples and tongues"

(7:9) who will stand before the throne in the white robes that have been washed in the blood of the Lamb (7:14). These are the nations of the redeemed who live within the walls of the holy city. Outside those walls we find only unbelievers. They are far away in hell and will never be allowed to enter.

The same must be said of the kings who "bring their glory into it" (v. 24). Like the twenty-four elders who cast their crowns before the throne and said that the Lord their God was worthy to receive glory and honor and power (4:10f), so the kings of the earth who accept the message of the gospel will bring "their glory" into the city. "Their glory" is not necessarily that which made them glorious. The Greek word δόξα often means praise. Therefore, "their glory" could be the praise which they bring to God and the Lamb. The basic thought is the same. At the time when John wrote this book the rulers of the earth were enemies of the church and of the gospel, but before the history of the church militant would come to an end even kings and emperors would join the multitude that would eventually dwell in the New Jerusalem.

The complete safety and security of those who live in the holy city is set before us in the statement, "Its gates will never be shut by day, for there will be no night there." City gates were closed as the light began to fade so that the inhabitants might sleep in peace knowing that every enemy would find it difficult, if not impossible, to mount a surprise attack under cover of darkness. Modern translators have often found it difficult to translate the γάρ (for) in the second half of this sentence. While ἡμέρας ("by day") could be a plural accusative form, it is doubtful whether in this context John would speak of "days" since, according to the context, the succession of days and nights has come to an end. We therefore have understood the form of the word as a genitive singular. The genitive does not indicate duration of time. That would require the accusative form. The genitive indicates that at no time during the day will the gates ever be shut. Since it is the approach of darkness that calls for the closing of the gates, they will never be closed. This is a city with neither sun nor sunset, where the inhabitants walk in the unchanging glory of the unchangeable God.

The fact that the gates are never closed also symbolizes the non-existence of any enemies, of any threat, to the safety of those who live here. Their salvation is final and complete. The devil, the beast, and the false prophet who sought their destruction have, after all, been cast into the lake of fire in total defeat.

For that reason, too, the gates do not need to be shut at any time during the day. No watchmen on the walls of that city will ever need to sound an alarm to warn of an approaching army of enemies. Gog and Magog are no more. This city offers full and eternal security to all who are granted the privilege of living there. What a glorious future John held out to the persecuted Christians of his time who were not safe anywhere from the threat of the Roman government.

During those persecutions the believers often suffered the loss of their earthly possessions, but John had a word of comfort for that situation too. He wrote, "They will bring the glory and the treasure of the nations into it." Under the influence of the Aramaic language, the New Testament writers often use an impersonal third person plural where classical Greek would use a passive verb. It would be better perhaps to translate, "The glory and the treasure of the nations will be brought into it." Unlike the kings mentioned earlier, the nations evidently do not bring in their treasures willingly. These people who had persecuted the church and robbed the believers of their possessions would finally have to restore what they had taken from the saints.

The word which we have translated "treasure" is translated by most versions with "honor." While "honor," or "value," is the primary meaning of the Greek word τιμή, yet the word can also mean "that which is valued highly." Since the construction of the sentence implies, as we have noted, that the nations do not bring these gifts themselves, it will hardly do to understand "the glory of the nations" as "the praise which the nations give" but rather as "that which made the nations glorious," that is, their treasured possessions that made them great. In that context then it would seem that τιμή is best translated as "treasures."

When the Old Testament prophets spoke of the coming and the kingdom of the Messiah they often said that the treasures of the nations would be brought to him. Solomon spoke the following words regarding the kingdom of the Messiah in Psalm 72:10,15:

> The kings of Tarshish and of distant shores
> will bring tribute to him;
> The kings of Sheba and Seba
> will present him gifts . . . .
> May gold from Sheba be given him.

Isaiah (60:5) expressed a similar hope for the New Testament church when he said,

> The wealth of the seas will be brought to you,
> to you the riches of the nations will come.

In a prophecy which the writer of the letter to the Hebrews understood as a prediction concerning the end of the world (He 12:26; cp Hab 2:6) the Prophet Haggai (2:7,8) had written,

> The treasures of all nations will come,
> and I will fill this temple with glory, . . .
> The silver is mine,
> and the gold is mine.

While the KJV renders the first line of this passage with "The desire of all nations shall come," a literal translation of the Hebrew text would be, "The desirable things of all nations shall come." Most modern versions have therefore used the word "treasure" or "wealth" instead of "desire," which has often been misunderstood as a name for the Messiah. That interpretation became common, thanks to a line in a popular hymn, "Come, desire of nations, come."

The correct understanding of "desirable things" is bolstered by the reference to silver and gold in the next verse (Hg 2:8). John's statement here seems to echo the words of Haggai and similar prophecies if we understand τιμή in the sense of "treasure."

While the Messianic prophecies cited above have been partially fulfilled in the New Testament church, yet the use that Hebrews makes of the Haggai prophecy suggests that a complete fulfillment will come in the new heaven and the new earth in which all desirable things will be the possession of the children of God. Just what form these treasures will take when creation is reconstituted out of the melted down ruins of the present heaven and earth we do not know. But what John says here is in keeping with Paul's words to the Corinthians, "All things are yours, whether Paul or Apollos or Cephas or the world or life or death or the present or the future — all are yours, and you are of Christ, and Christ is of God" (1 Cor 3:21-23). Now we walk by faith so far as that truth is concerned, but in the new world that, too, is something we will see.

Having revealed what we will find in the New Jerusalem, John goes on to tell us what will not be found there. He writes, "Nothing that is unclean and no one who does what is abominable or who tells lies will ever enter it, except those who are written in the Lamb's book of life." The original Greek actually says that "everything that is unclean surely shall not enter it," a Hebraistic construction that is rather common in the New Testament.

When John says that nothing unclean shall enter the city he is using the language of the Old Testament Levitical law. Jews who were ceremonially unclean were not allowed to participate in the worship services in the temple, nor were they permitted to offer anything unclean to the Lord. We have here another indication that the whole city is to be treated as the temple or the special dwelling place of God. The Prophet Isaiah had made a similar prediction concerning Jerusalem. He prophesied (Is 52:1),

> Put on your garments of splendor,
> O Jerusalem, the holy city,
> The uncircumcised and defiled [KJV: unclean]
> will not enter you again.

John's words here help us to understand that Isaiah was not speaking of the earthly city of Jerusalem but of Jerusalem as the New Testament church, and especially as the church triumphant in eternity.

The ceremonial laws concerning uncleanness were a pedagogic and symbolic way of making clear to the children of Israel that there is something that makes man, as he is, unfit to approach the holy God. The Bible teaches us that this is sin, and that the only way sin can be removed is through the forgiveness earned for us by Christ. But since forgiveness is received only through faith, John is in these words expressing in a symbolic way the truth which he had proclaimed in his Gospel, "He that believeth not the Son shall not see life, but the wrath of God abideth on him" (Jn 3:36, KJV).

John also says, "No one who does what is abominable or who tells lies will ever enter it." Literally, the Greek reads either "he who does an abomination and a lie" or "he who makes an abomination and a lie." The words "abomination" and "lie" were commonly used in the Old Testament as a designation for an idol, and if we would translate "he who makes an abomination, that is, an idol," we would have in these words a denunciation of idolatry as a sin that excludes men from heaven. The word "does" (ποιῶν) can be, and often is, translated with "make." In Hebrews, for example, we read that God "made" (ἐποίησεν) the world. Paul in his denunciation of the idolatrous worship of the heathen says that by making images they "change the truth of God into a lie" (Ro 1:25).

The phrase ὁ ποιῶν . . . ψεῦδος (he who does, or makes, . . . a lie) is a most unusual one and is used only by John. It is found only here and in 22:15. In that place it could also refer to idolatry since it would be possible to translate the last phrases in that sentence, "the idolaters, even everyone who loves and makes a lie," that is, a false god. If we translate in this way, we do well to remember that false gods are not made only out of wood or stone or gold or silver. A false god is made also when the truth about God is obscured by false doctrine. A god, for example, who saves men who earn heaven from him by a relatively decent life is not the God of the Bible, but an idol. In reality every false doctrine is a step toward creating a god out of the imagination of the sinful human heart. Even if we do not interpret the "lie" in these two passages as "idol," we ought not to forget that the most damaging lies are those that rob men of the assurance which only the truth of the gospel can bring to human hearts.

It might be possible to find some help for the understanding of John's language here in several other passages in which he speaks of "doing" the truth. He uses that expression in his First Epistle, where he writes, "If we say that we have fellowship with him and walk in darkness we are lying and not doing the truth" (1:16). While John may mean more than "telling the truth" by this expression the context clearly indicates that this is at least part of what he wants to say. "Doing the truth" stands in clear contrast to "lying," and John is pronouncing a judgment on people who are saying something false.

In his Gospel John also uses this expresion (3:11). But there "doing the truth" (ποιῶν τὴν ἀλήθειαν) is contrasted to "doing evil things" (φαῦλα πράσσων). In that context the translation "telling the truth" would hardly fit. So while we have translated "he who does what is abominable and who tells lies" (literally, "a lie") the fact remains that in this case the English language does not offer an expression that does full justice to John's concept.

Translators have also found some difficulty in translating the conjunction, εἰ μή, with which the closing clause in this chapter begins. Many of them translate it with "but only." The particles εἰ μή sometimes mean "but." However, the most common meaning is "except." Apparently most translators hesitate to translate in that way because such a rendering would imply that even those who are written in the book of life are unclean and guilty of serious sins. Yet if such a translation is understood in the light of the law-gospel antithesis, it would be possible to make good sense out of the translation "except." It would actually be a way of indicating that salvation is by grace alone, since those who are elected to salvation are totally unworthy of the great honor bestowed on them, of having their names inscribed in the Lamb's book of life. We might therefore understand John as saying that no one out of the whole mass of sinful and unclean mankind will be saved except those who by God's grace have been elected to eternal life and who, as a result of their election, have been brought to faith through the preaching of the gospel.

This is the fourth and the last time John speaks of "the book of life" (cp 13:8; 17:8; 20:15). When he speaks of "those who are written in the book of life" he uses an obvious ellipsis. What he means is that their names are written there (cp 13:8; 17:8). When he calls it "the Lamb's book of life," he reminds us that men, who are by nature sinful and unclean, are fit to be inscribed in that book only through the merits of the Lamb of God, who takes away the sin of the world (Jn 1:29).

PARADISE RESTORED (22:1-5)

1) Καὶ ἔδειξέν μοι ποταμὸν ὕδατος ζωῆς λαμπρὸν ὡς κρύσταλλον, ἐκπορευόμενον ἐκ τοῦ θρόνου τοῦ Θεοῦ καὶ τοῦ Ἀρνίου. 2) ἐν μέσῳ τῆς πλατείας αὐτῆς καὶ τοῦ ποταμοῦ ἐντεῦθεν καὶ ἐκεῖθεν ξύλον ζωῆς ποιοῦν καρποὺς δώδεκα, κατὰ μῆνα ἕκαστον ἀποδιδοῦν τὸν καρπὸν αὐτοῦ, καὶ τὰ φύλλα τοῦ ξύλου εἰς θεραπείαν τῶν ἐθνῶν. 3) καὶ πᾶν κατάθεμα οὐκ ἔσται ἔτι. καὶ ὁ θρόνος τοῦ Θεοῦ καὶ τοῦ Ἀρνίου ἐν αὐτῇ ἔσται, καὶ οἱ δοῦλοι αὐτοῦ λατρεύσουσιν αὐτῷ, 4) καὶ ὄψονται τὸ πρόσωπον αὐτοῦ, καὶ τὸ ὄνομα ἐπὶ τῶν μετώπων αὐτῶν. 5) καὶ νὺξ οὐκ ἔσται ἔτι, καὶ οὐκ ἔχουσιν χρείαν φωτὸς λύχνου καὶ φωτὸς ἡλίου, ὅτι Κύριος ὁ Θεὸς φωτίσει ἐπ' αὐτούς, καὶ βασιλεύσουσιν εἰς τοὺς αἰῶνας τῶς αἰώνων.

1) *And he showed me a river of the water of life, clear as crystal, issuing from the throne of God and of the Lamb.* 2) *Between its street and the river, there was a tree of life (visible) from this side and from that, producing twelve (kinds of) fruit. The tree yields its fruit month by month, and the leaves of the tree are for the healing of the nations.* 3) *And there will no longer be any curse.*

> *And the throne of God and of the Lamb will be in it, and his servants will worship him,* 4) *and they will see his face, and his name will be on their foreheads.* 5) *And there will no longer be any night, and they need neither lamplight nor sunlight, for the Lord God will shine on them, and they will reign forever and ever.*

The reader of these verses cannot help thinking of the description of the garden of Eden in the second chapter of the Bible. In Eden a river went out to water the garden. In the New Jerusalem John sees a river flowing out of the throne of God with the water of life. The tree of life, whose fruit evidently had the power to bestow everlasting life, grew in the middle of the garden. Here John sees the tree of life growing once more along the banks of the river, and he says that its leaves serve to heal the nations. In the garden of Eden Adam and Eve had lived in intimate communion with God. Such communion the inhabitants of the New Jerusalem also enjoy. In the account of the Fall we are told of the curse that struck the earth and brought the punishment of death to the whole human race. In the New Jerusalem "there is no more curse." For this reason these verses are very properly titled "Paradise Restored."

Since the words that follow (22:6-21) really complete the account that began in chapter 1 and are part of the historical background of the book of Revelation, we can say that with this portrayal of paradise regained the vision of John comes to an end. It forms a very fitting conclusion to the whole record of what God has done for the salvation of man. The story of that redemption began with man's fall out of the state of bliss in which he had been created and in which he lived in the garden of Eden. Because of the Fall, man was driven out of the garden and the way to the tree of life was barred by the cherubim with the flaming sword. But God promised to send the seed of the woman and the seed of Abraham to destroy the serpent and to bring the blessing of life once more to dead and dying men (Gn 3:15; 12:3; Ps 133:3), to remove the curse brought by sin (Ro 5:12-19). That promise was kept when the woman's Son came into the world to destroy the power of the old dragon over men (Re 12). In the seven visions of Revelation God assured a persecuted church that the work of salvation would be carried to a successful conclusion in spite of all the efforts of the old serpent, the devil, to frustrate it. All of this history finds its culmination in this vision in which we find ourselves in spirit back once more in the place where that history began in a garden where the water of life flows freely from the throne of God and where the tree of life produced its leaves during every month of the year for the healing of the nations. We have come full circle from Genesis 2. For a believing child of God this is a powerful argument for the canonicity of Revelation. As we have noted in the introduction to this commentary, there were some people in the early church who did not believe that Revelation was part of the inspired Word of God. But the book forms such a consistent part of the whole of Scripture and rounds off the message of salvation in such a symmetrical way that it is really hard to imagine a complete Bible without this book of comfort for a suffering Christendom which in this world must always walk by faith and not by sight.

The details of the vision need not detain us long. We have already discussed what John meant by the water of life in connection with the previous chapter (21:6). In that passage the article is used with both "water" and "life" (τοῦ ὕδατος τῆς ζωῆς) while here neither word has the article. The absence of the article in Greek often lays stress on the quality of the thing named so that the anarthrous noun almost becomes an adjective. The sense of the Greek phrase might be expressed in English by translating, "He showed me a water-of-life river flowing from the throne of God."

The fact that the river flows, literally, "out of the throne of God and of the Lamb," reminds us that the source of our salvation is not to be found in anything we have done or merited. The sole source of our salvation is God, not just any God, but that God who has prepared his salvation for us through the Lamb, who now sits with him on his throne (3:21).

The river is as clear as crystal. There are no impurities in this water which gives life to those who drink it. Since it is sin that brings death into the world (Ro 5:12), only the forgiveness of sins can give life. Therefore we cannot go astray by identifying the water of life with the forgiveness of sins that has been won for us by the Lamb of God. This forgiveness is complete and flawless, so that nothing more is required of us to make us perfect, blameless and sinless before God. The grace of God, the forgiveness it provides for us, the righteousness with which it clothes us, the salvation which it promises us, all of these are so pure that we need nothing more to make us holy and without blemish or spot. It is possible, however, to look upon the genitive ζωῆς (of life) as an explanatory genitive or a genitive of apposition and thus to say that the water is life itself. Such an interpretation is not really radically different from the one we prefer.

The next verse is very difficult to translate. All the words are very simple, but on the basis of what John writes it is difficult to visualize the scene described. Some scholars do not place a period at the end of the first verse but rather after the phrase "in the center of its street," thus making the river flow down the middle of the street. Others translate the words, ἐν μέσῳ τῆς πλατείας αὐτῆς καὶ τοῦ ποταμοῦ, with "between its street and the river." The next phrase is also difficult. Since we do not know from which angle John was viewing the scene it is almost impossible to determine what he meant by ἐντεῦθεν καὶ ἐκεῖθεν, "from here and from there." The words could mean "at the nearer and farther end of the street," or "on this side and that side of the river." If the latter is correct we would expect that the words "of the river" would follow rather than precede the phrase. Either of these translations would require at least two trees of life in the scene being described. While in the garden of the Eden there was only one, that, of course, does not mean that in John's vision there could not have been many such trees growing along the banks of the river. The singular noun "tree" could be a collective. However, it is also possible in keeping with John's words, to visualize one large tree of life growing between the river and the street and equidistant from both ends of the street. As is the case with many of the scenes described in

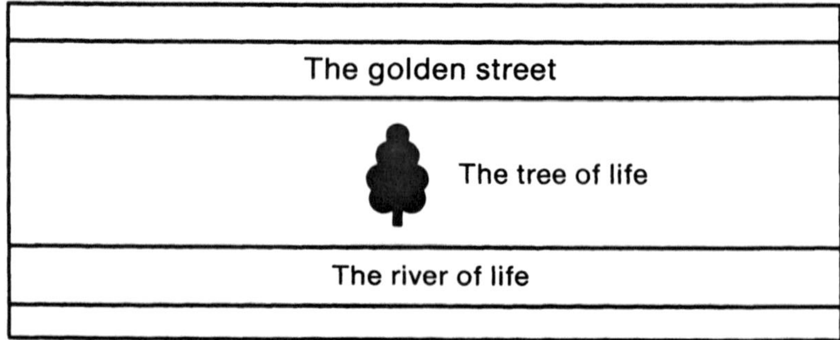

Revelation, the exact details of the vision are not of great significance. What is significant here is that in the new paradise men once more have access to the tree of life. In the Genesis account it is clear that the fruit of the tree of life had the power to bestow everlasting life on those who ate of it. This tree of life in the vision of John is therefore also a source of life for the inhabitants of the holy city. The tree is described as "bearing twelve fruits," which seems to mean twelve kinds of fruit, one kind for each month of the year. It is thus not only a source of everlasting life but also of abundant life (cp Jn 10:10). The imagery clearly proclaims again that there shall be no more death. Neither will there be any more disease or pain. The leaves of the tree of life are "for the healing of the nations." All the afflictions from which men suffered in the former world because of sin are now completely removed.

Thus "there shall be no more curse." The Hebraistic construction here is especially forceful. A literal translation of it reads, "Every curse shall be no more." All of the consequences of sin are forever gone. Instead, the redeemed will enjoy to the fullest the fulfillment of God's promise to Abraham, "In thee and in thy seed shall all the families of the earth be blessed" (Gn 12:3).

Once more, then, John emphasizes the presence of God with his people. He writes, "The throne of God and the Lamb will be in it [that is, in the holy city], and his servants will serve him." We can also translate, "His servants will worship him," since the word translated "serve" is used in the New Testament only of the performance of religious duties. The words of John indicate that joy and praise will characterize life in the New Jerusalem.

The greatest source of that joy is expressed with the words, "They shall see his face." John had enunciated a similar thought in his First Epistle, where he wrote, "We shall see him as he is" (3:2). We can have only a very poor understanding of the joy that this will bring. We catch a brief glimpse of it in the story of the transfiguration, when Peter and James and John saw the Savior's glorified face and said, "Lord, it is good to be here." Peter might well have had that sight in mind when he spoke of the time when Jesus would once more be revealed in his glory and in that connection spoke also of the inexpressible and glorious joy that believers have even though they "do not see him now" (1 Pt 1:8). It is not surprising that the ancient church fathers spoke of the bliss of heaven as the "beatific vision."

"His name will be on their foreheads," John continues. He repeats here what he had said earlier (14:1), namely, that they will be God's possession through all eternity. And once more he emphasizes the source of light in the new heaven and the new earth. "There will no longer be any night, and they need neither lamplight nor sunlight, for the Lord God will shine upon them." Those last words surely recall the words of the Aaronic benediction, "The Lord make his face shine upon thee, and be gracious unto thee." Whatever the sum total of the blessings are that are included in those words, they surely speak of the gracious love of God in which we shall bask through all eternity.

John's vision closes with the words, "And they shall reign forever and ever." In the very first of this long series of visions, John had heard the four living creatures and the twenty-four elders singing about the redeemed saints and saying that "they will reign on the earth" (5:9-11). They were kings and priests from the moment of their conversion, but their kingship and priesthood were hidden under the dark clouds of suffering and persecution. But now in the presence of God and the Lamb, with the face of the Lamb clearly visible to them, the glory of their royal priesthood is no longer secret or hidden, but visible and manifest.

And it will never come to an end. What had been said of Christ, namely, "He shall reign forever and ever" (11:15), is now also said of them: "They shall reign forever and ever." With such promises to give them hope, it is really not surprising that the early martyrs could face the lions in the arena and sing songs of praise to their God and Savior while they waited for the doom that had been decreed for them by emperors whose rule could last but a few years.

The Conclusion (22:6-21)

ANOTHER CLAIM TO INSPIRATION (22:6,7)

6) Καὶ εἶπέν μοι, Οὗτοι οἱ λόγοι πιστοὶ καὶ ἀληθινοί, καὶ ὁ Κύριος ὁ Θεὸς τῶν πνευμάτων τῶν προφητῶν ἀλπέστειλεν τὸν ἄγγελον αὐτοῦ δεῖξαι τοῖς δούλοις αὐτοῦ ἃ δεῖ γενέσθαι ἐν τάχει. 7) καὶ ἰδοὺ ἔρχομαι ταχύ. μακάριος ὁ τηρῶν τοὺς λόγους τῆς προφητείας τοῦ βιβλίου τούτου.

6) *And he said to me, "These words are faithful and true, and the Lord, the God of the spirits of the prophets, sent his angel to show his servants the things which must soon take place.* 7) *Behold, I am coming soon. Blessed is he who keeps the words of the prophecy of this book."*

The first verse of this section is really a transition sentence that could just as well be included as the closing verse of the vision. It echoes the first verse of Revelation and, as we have said, is really part of the historical record of how this book came to be written. The words, "to show his servants the things which must soon take place," are an exact reproduction of words in the first verse of the book. The words, "he sent his angel," are very similar to words in that verse also.

The speaker is evidently the angel who had shown John the holy city. This assumption creates somewhat of a difficulty, however. There is no indication in the text that there is a change in speakers between verses 6 and 7. At least the first half of verse 7, "Behold, I am coming soon," cannot be the direct words of the angel, who is one of the seven angels with the bowls, though the preceding context (21:9,15; 22:1) seems to imply this.

For the second time the angel says, "These words are faithful and true" (cp 21:5). The phrase, "faithful and true," is used four times in Revelation. Twice it is said of Christ that he is faithful and true (3:14; 19:11), and twice these attributes are ascribed to the words written in the book. This calls our attention to the close relationship between the words of the Bible and Christ, the incarnate Word of God (19:13). The words of the Bible, because they are the words of God, also share in the attributes of God. They are faithful because he is faithful and always keeps his promises (Ro 4:21). They are true because he is truthful and cannot lie (He 6:18). The legitimacy of deducing the inerrancy of Scripture from its divine inspiration and from the truthfulness and faithfulness of God is reflected in John's ascription of the attributes of faithfulness and truth to the words of this book. These attributes also emphasize the book's claim to inspiration. Because the words are faithful and true they can serve as a firm basis for the faith and hope of a persecuted and suffering church.

The inspiration of the Bible is also reflected in the description of the Lord as "the God of the spirits of the prophets." Although the Holy Spirit is spoken of as "the seven Spirits of God" in Revelation (1:4; 3:1; 4:5; 5:6), it is hardly possible to say that "the spirits of the prophets" are the Holy Ghost. That the apostles and prophets did their preaching and writing under the influence and guidance and control of the Holy Ghost is plainly taught in Scripture. David wrote, "The Spirit of the Lord spoke through me" (2 Sm 23:2). Zechariah spoke of the words which the Lord "had sent by his Spirit through the earlier prophets" (Zch 7:12). Paul claimed that the words he used were taught by the Holy Ghost (1 Cor 2:13). Peter spoke of the Spirit of Christ who was at work in the prophets of the Old Testament (1 Pe 1:11), and in his Second Epistle he said, "Men spoke from God as they were carried along by the Holy Spirit" (1:21). There are many similar passages.

However, while the Holy Ghost is said to "come upon" the prophet or to "be in" the prophets, and to "work through" the prophets, yet there is no other passage in the Bible where the Holy Spirit is called "the Spirit of the prophets." Moreover, even though Jesus speaks of God the Father as "my God" there is no warrant in Scripture for saying that the Father is "the God of the Holy Spirit." For those reasons it certainly is correct to understand "the spirits of the prophets" as the spirits belonging to prophets themselves, that is, the inner mental and spiritual nature of the prophets that moves them to be willing to be God's spokesmen. The word "spirit" is in the Bible often used of the new spiritual life that the Holy Ghost creates in men when he brings them to faith. We therefore can conclude that "the spirits of the prophets" is the new spiritual life that the Holy Ghost created within the prophets when he made them his servants.

The Lord is the God of the spirits of the prophets because he created the new spirit that makes the prophets ready and willing and able to serve as messengers of God. God took the spiritual life of the prophets into his service. More than that, he sustains and augments that spiritual life and guides the prophets in their actions and their speaking.

The inspiration of the book of Revelation is directly taught in the statement that the Lord sent his angel to show his servants the things that must soon take place. Only God really knows for certain what will take place in the future. He says that these future things will take place ἐν τάχει, "soon." This must be interpreted in the light of the whole preceding context, which demonstrates that this word refers to the whole of New Testament history up to and even beyond the day of judgment. There is no way that John could have known this future history, even in its rough outlines. From a human point of view, there was no way anyone could without divine revelation know in those times whether the church would survive in a powerful empire intent upon wiping out Christianity. The Prophet Isaiah emphatically teaches that no prophet can of himself have a clear knowledge of the future (Is 41:22,23,26; 42:9; 43:9; 44:7,8,25,26; 45:21; 48:3-5). And the Lord definitely forbids all efforts to predict the future without his commission and command (Dt 18:10-12). Against that biblical background, the statement of the angel here clearly assures John that he is to act as the Lord's messenger under divine inspiration.

Even though there is no break in the construction to indicate that a new speaker is being quoted in the next verse, the words, "Behold, I am coming soon," are not the words of the angel. These words are the keynote in this concluding section of the book. They are repeated twice in the following verses (12,20), and there can be no doubt that the speaker is the Lord Jesus (cp v. 16,20).

The promise of a quick return on the part of the Savior has been of special comfort to Christian believers, especially in the dark days of history when the church was threatened most directly by her enemies. That promise constantly assures the struggling and suffering children of God that "the strife will not be long" and that today's "noise of battle" will be turned into tomorrow's "victor's song."

Peter correctly predicted that the promise that the Savior would return quickly would become an occasion for mockery on the part of wicked men (2 Pe 3:3f). In that connection he discusses the meaning of the word "quickly." He reminds us that from God's point of view a thousand years is not a long time (2 Pe 3:8), just as Moses already said to the Lord, "A thousand years in your sight are like a day that has just gone by" (Ps 90:4).

The speaker of the next words is not identified. There is no reason why we should not assume that these are also words spoken to John by Jesus. He says, "Blessed is he who keeps the words of the prophecy of this book." This is the sixth of the seven beatitudes found in Revelation. The first of these beatitudes (1:3) had pronounced a blessing on "the one who reads" and on "those who hear the words of the prophecy and who keep the things that are written in it." Thus we have here another indication of the close connection between this section and the first verses of Revelation. The sixth of the Revelation beatitudes also echoes the words of Jesus, "Blessed are those who hear the word of God and keep it" (Lk 11:28). It is difficult to escape the conviction that with this beatitude Jesus is also designating the book of Revelation as part of the Word of God.

"To keep the words of this prophecy" surely means to accept the prophecies with a believing heart. The people who believe these words are indeed blessed. To believe the words and promises of God is a source of true happiness. The first readers of this book were, on the basis of a purely human judgment, unfortunate people who were in constant danger of suffering deprivation and death, shame and disgrace, and yet the Savior promises them happiness in the assurances of final victory and bliss held out to them as a present treasure to be received and enjoyed by faith.

JOHN AND THE ANGEL (22:8-11)

At the beginning of the book John had identified himself as the author of Revelation (1:9). He now identifies himself once more and writes,

> **8) Κἀγὼ Ἰωάννης ὁ ἀκούων καὶ βλέπων ταῦτα. καὶ ὅτε ἤκουσα καὶ ἔβλεψα, ἔπεσα προσκυνῆσαι ἔμπροσθεν τῶν ποδῶν τοῦ ἀγγέλου τοῦ δεικνύοντός μοι ταῦτα. 9) καὶ λέγει μοι, Ὅρα μή· σύνδουλός σού εἰμι καὶ τῶν ἀδελφῶν σου των̃ προφητῶν καὶ τῶς τηρούντων τοὺς λόγους τοῦ βιβλίου τούτου· τῷ Θεῷ προσκύνησον. 10) Καὶ λέγει μοι, Μὴ σφραγίσῃς τοὺς λόγους τῆς προφητείας τοῦ βιβλίου τούτου, ὁ καιρὸς γὰρ ἐγγύς ἐστιν. 11) ὁ ἀδικῶν ἀδικησάτω ἔτι, καὶ ὁ ῥυπαρὸς ῥυπανθήτω ἔτι, καὶ ὁ δίκαιος δικαιοσύνην ποιησάτω ἔτι, καὶ ὁ ἅγιος ἁγιασθήτω ἔτι.**

8) *I, John, am the one who heard and saw these things. And when I heard and saw, I fell to worship at the feet of the angel who was showing me these things.* 9) *And he said to me, "Don't do it. I am a fellow servant of yours and of your brothers the prophets and of those who keep the words of this book. Worship God!"*

10) *And he said to me, "Do not seal up the words of the prophecy of this book, for the time is near.* 11) *He who is unjust, let him be unjust still; he who is filthy, let him be filthy still; he who is just, let him still do what is just; and he who is holy, let him be holy still."*

John here not only identifies himself as the author but he also claims to have been an eyewitness and earwitness of the things recorded in the previous chapters. Even though modern scholars often describe the Apocalypse as imaginative literature produced by some unknown genius, John outrightly denies that this book is the product of his imaginative skill. His words make clear once more that these things were truly revealed to him by God.

The holy writers often lay stress on the fact that their writings are the testimony of men who were firsthand witnesses of the things that were said and done. In his First Epistle John had made a similar claim (1:1-4). Peter likewise makes this same claim for himself (2 Pe 1:16-18). Jesus also stressed the importance of this fact, when he promised the guidance of the Holy Spirit to his disciples and in that connection said, "You also must testify for you have been with me from the beginning" (Jn 15:26f; cp 14:26; 16:13-15). For that reason also the successor of Judas to the apostolic office had to be chosen from among those men who had been constant companions of the Savior during his public ministry (Ac 1:21f). And even though St. Luke was himself not an eyewitness he claims that what he wrote had been learned from eyewitnesses (Lk 1:1-4).

When John fell down to worship the angel who was showing him these things, the angel warned him not to do this but to direct his worship to God. The angel's warning to John is a strong protest against any kind of saint or angel worship. The exact meaning of the Greek phrase that we have translated, "Don't do it," (ὅρα μή), is perhaps better reflected in our warning cry, "Watch out," or "Be careful." It implies the presence of danger. The angel's words confirm that such worship is a sin which rouses the anger of the Lord who calls himself a jealous God and refuses to share his glory with anyone else (Ex 20:3-5;

Is 42:8). It also reminds us of the error of the modern view that any kind of worship is a good and noble practice.

The angel rejects John's attempts to worship him by saying, "I am a fellow servant of yours," literally a "fellow slave." In the first verse of the book John had called himself God's "servant," or "slave." Both angels and men have been created to serve God with unquestioning obedience and together to offer their worship and praise to God.

The angel also identifies himself as a fellow servant with John's "brothers," "the prophets." This designation is another hint that the writer of Revelation is the Apostle John. In our introduction we called attention to the belief of the early church father Eusebius who held that the author of Revelation was not the apostle but another man by the same name. While the designation of John as a brother of the prophets is not conclusive evidence against the opinion of Eusebius, yet the New Testament contains a number of passages that speak of the apostles and prophets as occupying a unique position in relation to the Lord and to the church (*e.g.* Eph 2:20; 3:5; Lk 11:49; 2 Pe 3:2; Re 18:20). It seems appropriate, therefore, to call an apostle a brother of the prophets.

This conclusion is supported by the reference to "those who keep the words of this book." This is certainly a description of all believers beside John and his brothers, the prophets, who had been mentioned separately. If we see the angel as a representative of the whole heavenly host and John as a representative of all the apostles, then we have in this verse the same classification of God's worshipers that we had met earlier in the vision of Babylon's fall (18:20). There John calls upon heaven (or the angels), the saints (here described as those who keep the words of this book), the apostles and prophets to rejoice over their defeated enemy.

Having warned John against worshiping him, the angel told him not to seal up the words of the prophecy of this book, because "the time is near." This was a command to publish the book for all to read. The message of this book is not to be kept as a secret from the church. Because of the abuse that Revelation has suffered at the hands of millennialistic interpreters, orthodox Christians often have neglected it and even have abandoned it to the false teachers, so that the book has for all practical purposes been sealed up, by non-use on the part of the orthodox and by misuse on the part of chiliasts. Some of the earlier anti-millennialistic church fathers went so far as to attempt to remove this book of supreme comfort from the canon. But the command to John shows that God wants this book to be read and studied. Those who do study it in the light of the clear passages of Scripture will soon discover that this book does not promise a thousand years of material bliss in an earthly paradise, but the endless joy of the heavenly Jerusalem, a joy in which we participate even now in a limited way because we have overcome the dragon by the blood of the Lamb and the promises of the gospel.

The message of these visions is to be openly proclaimed because "the time is near." These words are repeated from 1:3 in a slightly altered form. What John means by the time, the καιρός, must be determined from the context. This context speaks not only of the speedy return of Christ, but begins with a reference to "the things that must happen soon." This καιρός refers not only to the time of the second coming but also to the set time when all the prophecies of this book will be fulfilled. The people of John's time and of all times needed to be reminded that the church would continually struggle against outward enemies, who would seek to destroy her by force, and against "false sons within her pale," who would attempt to subvert the Christian faith by false doctrine. But God has set a καιρός, a very definite time limit for their power. The church needs that reminder so that it will neither despair nor develop false millennial dreams of earthly glory. This is an amillennial world where truth is forever on the scaffold and wrong forever on the throne — a world where God's people need the comfort that flows from the assurance of final victory and from the conviction that the moment of that victory will not be delayed beyond God's appointed hour. This victory is not so far away as it often seems to be. The time is near.

The next words, "He who is unjust," etc., evidently refer to the moment when the last prophecy will have been fulfilled. The great day of the wrath of the Lamb will have come (6:17). The present world will have perished in the lightning and the rumbling and the thunder and the great hail that will accompany the last judgment (11:15-19). The sickle will have been put to the harvest of the earth (14:14-20). The seventh bowl with the last of the seven last plagues, which bring the end of this world as we know it, will have been poured out (15:17-21). The beast and the false prophet will have been cast into the lake of fire (19:20) and Satan will have been forced to join them (20:10). The building of the church, God's holy temple (Eph 2:20), the New Jerusalem, will have been completed. The purpose for which the wicked world had been allowed to stand, namely, that the gospel might be preached for a witness to all nations (Mt 24:14) and that the rider on the white horse might win the victories for which God had sent him into the world (6:1,2; 11-16), will have been fulfilled.

That will be the end of man's time of grace. John is alerted to the fact by the next words of the angel, "He who is unjust, let him be unjust still; he who is filthy, let him be filthy still." The opportunity for repentance and forgiveness will have come to an end. These words are a solemn warning to the sinner not to delay his own repentance. If they will not say to God, "Thy will be done," the time will come when God will say to them, "Your will be done! Be as wicked and as filthy as you want to be, for from this moment on this is all that you ever will be." Many an impenitent sinner has already in this life experienced the disappointment and dissatisfaction and the horrible ennui that a life devoted to the service of sin often brings before it ends. To have nothing but that bitterness to look forward to in all eternity is already in itself a punishment too horrible to contemplate.

But for those who are faithful unto death, there is a bright prospect. The angel continues, "He who is righteous, let him still do what is right; he who is holy, let him be holy still." The danger of being tempted under the pressure of persecution to surrender the faith by which we become righteous before God will be past. The danger of being misled by the false prophet who looks like the Lamb but who speaks the lies of the dragon will no longer be a constant threat to the children of God. Like the holy angels they will be confirmed in their bliss, unable to sin anymore and therefore also unable to die anymore. They will be righteous and holy, fit inhabitants of the holy city forever, dwelling in the presence of the holy God with whom no evil is allowed to dwell. This is indeed "a consummation devoutly to be wished," and the prospect ought to encourage every child of God to be faithful unto death.

JESUS SPEAKS TO JOHN (22:12-19)

As an added encouragement the Savior again speaks to John and, through John, to the seven churches and to us:

12) Ἰδοὺ ἔρχομαι ταχύ, καὶ ὁ μισθός μου μετ᾽ ἐμοῦ, ἀποδοῦναι ἑκάστῳ ὡς τὸ ἔργον ἐστὶν αὐτοῦ. 13) ἐγὼ τὸ Ἄλφα καὶ τὸ Ὦ, ὁ πρῶτος καὶ ὁ ἔσχατος, ἡ ἀρχὴ καὶ τὸ τέλος. 14) μακάριοι οἱ

πλύνοντες τὰς στολὰς αὐτῶν, ἵνα ἔσται ἡ ἐξουσία αὐτῶν ἐπὶ τὸ ξύλον τῆς ζωῆς καὶ τοῖς πυλῶσιν εἰσέλθωσιν εἰς τὴν πόλιν. 15) ἔξω οἱ κύνες καὶ οἱ φαρμακοὶ καὶ οἱ πόρνοι καὶ οἱ φονεῖς καὶ οἱ εἰδωλολάτραι καὶ πᾶς φιλῶν καὶ ποιῶν ψεῦδος.

16) Ἐγὼ Ἰησοῦς ἔπεμψα τὸν ἄγγελόν μου μαρτυρῆσαι ὑμῖν ταῦτα ἐπὶ ταῖς ἐκκλησίαις. ἐγώ εἰμι ἡ ῥίζα καὶ τὸ γένος Δαυίδ, ὁ ἀστὴρ ὁ λαμπρὸς ὁ πρωϊνός.

17) Καὶ τὸ Πνεῦμα καὶ ἡ νύμφη λέγουσιν, Ἔρχου. καὶ ὁ ἀκούων εἰπάτω, Ἔρχου. καὶ ὁ διψῶν ἐρχέσθω, ὁ θέλων λαβέτω ὕδωρ ζωῆς δωρεάν.

18) Μαρτυρῶ ἐγὼ παντὶ τῷ ἀκούοντι τοὺς λόγους τῆς προφητείας τοῦ βιβλίου τούτου· ἐάν τις ἐπιθῇ ἐπ' αὐτά, ἐπιθήσει ὁ Θεὸς ἐπ' αὐτὸν τὰς πληγὰς τὰς γεγραμμένας ἐν τῷ βιβλίῳ τούτῳ· 19) καὶ ἐάν τις ἀφέλῃ ἀπὸ τῶν λόγων τοῦ βιβλίου τῆς προφητείας ταύτης, ἀφελεῖ ὁ θεὸς τὸ μέρος αὐτοῦ ἀπὸ τοῦ ξύλου τῆς ζωῆς καὶ ἐκ τῆς πόλεως τῆς ἁγίας, τῶν γεγραμμένων ἐν τῷ βιβλίῳ τούτῳ.

12) *"Behold, I am coming soon, and my reward is with me, to repay each one according to his work.* 13) *I am the Alpha and the Omega, the First and the Last, the Beginning and the End.* 14) *Blessed are those that wash their robes, in order that the right to the tree of life may be theirs and that they may enter by the gates into the city.* 15) *Outside are the dogs, namely, the sorcerers and the adulterers and the murderers and the idolaters, even everyone who loves and makes* [*or, tells*] *a lie.*

16) *"I, Jesus, have sent my angel to bear this testimony to you for the churches. I am the Root and the Offspring of David, the bright Star of the Morning.*

17) *"And the Spirit and the bride say, 'Come.' And let the one who hears say, 'Come.' And the one who is thirsty, let him come. He who wants it, let him take water of life as a free gift.* 18) *I testify to every one who hears the words of the prophecy of this book, if anyone adds to these things, God will add to him the plagues that are written in this book;* 19) *and if anyone takes away from the words of the book of this prophecy, God will take away his share in the tree of life and in the holy city, which are written in this book."*

Because the words spoken in verse 9 and those spoken in the next two verses are introduced in exactly the same way, with "And he said [literally, "says," a historical present] to me," we have assumed that those words were spoken by the angel. But with verse 12 we evidently again have a change of speakers, and the rest of the words in this section are spoken by the

Savior. Jesus identifies himself as the speaker by name in a later verse (16). Some commentators have concluded that all these words were spoken by the angel. This is not absolutely impossible, because in prophecies of the Old Testament the first person pronouns sometimes clearly denote God even when there is no expressed indication that anyone other than the prophet is speaking (cp, *e.g.*, Ps 22). The words of the prophet sometimes become so thoroughly identified with the words of God that the prophet's personality recedes into the background completely and God seems to speak directly to men with the mouth of the prophet. This is one of the phenomena that is of some interest for a clearer understanding of the process of inspiration.

For all practical purposes it really makes no difference whether Jesus here is speaking directly to John or through the agency of the angel, but for the second time he says, "Behold, I am coming soon," and he adds, "My reward is with me to repay each one according to his work." In one of his Messianic prophecies, the Prophet Isaiah had described the Messiah in similar terms. He wrote,

> "See, the Sovereign Lord comes with power,
> and his arm rules for him.
> See, his reward is with him,
> and his recompense accompanies him" (40:10).

The words of Jesus here indicate that he himself is indeed the Sovereign Lord who will come with power and great glory to reward every man according to his works. It is Jesus who will be sitting upon the throne (20:11-15) to judge all men according to their works.

The next words of the Savior again take us back to chapter 1. There the Lord God is quoted as saying, "I am the Alpha and the Omega" (1:8), and Jesus says, " I the First and the Last" (1:17). These words of Yahweh, or the LORD, are quoted from the book of Isaiah. The Lord Jesus identifies himself with Yahweh (or Jehovah) and thus confounds the error of the *Jehovah's Witnesses*, who insist that Jesus is not true God but merely the "servant" of Jehovah. With these words Jesus also claims eternality as one of his attributes, for if "there was a time when he was not," as all Arians claim, then he is not the first.

This description of Jesus is followed by the last of the seven beatitudes in Revelation. Not all the manuscript copies of Revelation have the same wording for this beatitude, and this is reflected in our English translations. The KJV reads, "Blessed are they that do his commandments," while the NIV has "Blessed are those who wash their robes." While these two versions appear to be radically different in our translations, in the original Greek the two sentences really look very much alike. The KJV version is based on the reading οἱ ποιοῦντας τὰς ἐντολὰς αὐτοῦ while the NIV is based on οἱ πλύνοντες τὰς στολὸς αὐτῶν. A blurred copy or poor handwriting could easily lead to confusion here. Either reading would fit into the context of Revelation. In chapter 7 the saints before the throne are described as people who have "washed their robes and made them white in the blood of the Lamb" (7:14), but in chapter 12 as "those who keep the commandments of God" (12:17). The manuscript evidence is rather evenly divided, and either reading could be adopted on the basis of the evidence. Both readings are in conformity with the teaching of the Bible, although the immediate context, which speaks of men being rewarded according to their work (v. 12) would seem to tip the scales in favor of the wording we have in the KJV. We would, however, in that case need to explain once more that the only men who can really be said to have kept the commandments of God are those who through faith have made the vicarious obedience of Christ their own. The KJV rendering lays the stress on the active obedience of Christ. The NIV translation emphasizes the passive obedience of Christ as the source of our blessedness, by reminding us of the blood in which our garments are washed (cp Re 7:14).

Through Christ's perfect obedience, whether the emphasis here is on its active or passive aspect, we have gained the right to eat of the tree of life and to enter by the gates into the city. For through that faith by which we have appropriated the merits of the Savior, we have become the children of Abraham (Ro 4:11; Ga 3:7), and therefore members of the twelve tribes whose names are inscribed on those gates.

Having spoken of the blessedness of the believers who will inhabit the holy city and have eternal life, the Savior once more reminds us that not all men will reach that blissful place. He says, "Outside are the dogs, namely, the sorcerers and the adulterers and the murderers and the idolaters, even everyone who loves and makes a lie." The Jews were accustomed to giving the Gentiles, who did not accept Yahweh as their God, the name "dogs." Even the Lord Jesus alluded to that custom when he spoke to the Syro-Phoenician woman (Mt 15:26). Paul used it of unbelievers, whether Jew or Gentile (Php 3:2). John, too, uses the word here as a designation for unbelievers.

That raises a question about the "and" (καὶ) which follows the word "dogs." The Greek word must sometimes be translated "even," or "namely." And if we say that "dogs" is a name for all unbelievers, then "the dogs and the sorcerers and the adulterers and the murderers and the idolaters" do not constitute five separate classes of men, but indicate four classes of unbelievers. Therefore we translate, "Outside are the dogs, namely, the sorcerers and the adulterers and the murderers and the idolaters." From the perspective of the Scriptures, these words denote sins of which *all* people are guilty. Sorcerers are those who try to usurp God's control over his creation and to compel the Almighty to do their will. Adulterers and murderers are people who have lust and hatred in their hearts. Idolaters are those who do not always give God the supreme place in their lives. To such sins all of us must plead guilty, and if we have not by faith washed our robes in the blood of the Lamb, or made the active obedience of Christ our own, then we still belong at least to one class of these unbelieving "dogs."

The question of whether the last "and" between "idolaters" and "everyone who loves and makes a lie" should also be understood as explanatory has already been discussed (cp 21:8). "Everyone who loves and makes a lie" is either an idolater, who makes "lying vanities," as idols are called by the psalmist (31:6) and the Prophet Jonah (2:8) in the KJV, or the phrase designates a fifth classification of unbelievers, namely, those who tell lies gladly.

In any case, damnation is certain for those who die in their sins. Such people will have no share in the tree of life or in the holy city, because they have not accepted the forgiveness that the Lamb of God earned also for them when he took away the sins of the world.

Having spoken this word of warning, Jesus identifies himself by name as the speaker and says, "I, Jesus, have sent my angel to bear this testimony to you for the churches." These words were not spoken to John alone, for the pronoun "you" is a plural in the original. We have here, first of all, a reference to the members of the seven churches that had been listed in chapter 1, but also to the members of all Christian congregations of all time. Jesus' remark regarding the sending of the angel is a repetition of what was said at the beginning of the book. The Lord Jesus made his Revelation known by sending his angel to the Apostle John (1:1).

Jesus then describes himself and says, "I am the Root and the Offspring of David." He is both David's Son and David's Lord. As the Root of David he is David's Creator, the source of David's being. Yet David was also his most outstanding ancestor. These words again set before us the two natures in Christ, the God-man. As God he is David's "Root." As man he is David's "Offspring." He also calls himself "the bright Morning Star." As the morning star in the east is the clear proclamation of the coming of a new day so the coming of Jesus into the world brings to those who know him as their Savior the sure promise of the great, new eternal day which will never again be followed by a dark night.

To the glories of that new day he then invites all men to come. He sent his Spirit to establish his church on earth, and through this Spirit and the church he established, Jesus issues his invitation to all. "The Spirit and the Bride say, 'Come.' " The bride is, of course, the church. There are no restrictions to this gracious call issued by the Spirit through the church. Men are just invited to come. The great mission task of the church, which she carries on under the guidance of the Holy Ghost, is here described in its simplest terms.

And those who hear the invitation are to pass it on to the others. "Let the one who hears say, 'Come.' " Everyone who has heard the invitation to the marriage supper of the Lamb is to extend the call to those who have not yet heard it. Thus the invitation has been handed down from generation to generation and from nation to nation. And the fact that we know that "the time is near" (v. 10) lends urgency to the task. The promise of blessing to those who are called to the marriage supper (19:9) encourages us to carry it on with all our might.

And no one is excluded from the salvation offered by the Spirit and the Bride except those who feel no need of it and do not want it. The Savior continues, "And the one who is thirsty, let him come. He who wants it, let him take water of life as a free gift." Those who thirst are those who have learned to see their great need for the water of life, the water that flows out of "the wells of salvation" (Is 12:3). They begin to feel that thirst as they hear and believe that all sinners will be kept outside the walls of the heavenly Jerusalem, that all sinners will be cast into the lake of fire unless they wash their robes in the cleansing flood that flows from the fountain opened on the cross. And if they are thirsty they are welcome to come. If they want it, they can have it without any further conditions. It is there as a free gift, theirs "without money and without cost," as Isaiah says (55:1).

Before the final announcement of his imminent return, the Savior once more stresses the divine authority with which this book speaks. In the last weeks of his life Moses repeated the commandments and the statutes which the Lord had given to the children of Israel. He commanded them neither to add nor to take away from these commandments (Dt 4:2). They were, after all, the commandments of the Lord God. Solomon tells us why we should not dare to add to the words of the Lord, when he writes, "Do not add to his words, or he will rebuke you and prove you a liar" (Pr 30:6). Unlike the words of men, the words of God are not in need of amendment or improvement, either by addition or subtraction.

The command Jesus gives in regard to the words of this book indicates once more that we are here dealing with the words of God himself. It is thus another testimony to the inspiration and authority of the Apocalypse. God will bring the plagues which are described here on anyone who makes any additions to this book. And if anyone rejects and removes anything that is written here, Jesus threatens that God will deprive that man of his share in the tree of life and in the holy city. It is evident that the Lord wants us to take this book seriously and to use it as a significant part of God's Word. For the neglect with which orthodox Lutherans have often treated it, we need God's gracious forgiveness — just as those who have added all sorts of unjustified millennialistic interpretations to this book need God's pardon.

These words have often been applied to the whole Bible. While they apply directly only to what John has written in Revelation, they nevertheless express a warning that is pertinent to the whole of Scripture. If we believe, as we ought, that "all Scripture is inspired by God" (2 Tm 3:16), and that everything in the Scriptures was written to teach us (Ro 15:4), we must also believe that God does not want us to add or to take away from what he inspired and caused to be written. Finally, God in his providential care did arrange it so that Revelation stands at the end of the New Testament canon. As a result, the ordinary reader will conclude that what is said here of the Apocalypse also applies to Genesis and every other book of the Bible.

JOHN'S FINAL WORD TO THE CHURCHES (22:20,21)

Twice in the previous context the Savior had announced his imminent return for the final salvation of his church. John now singles out that promise as being of special significance. He says,

20) Λέγει ὁ μαρτυρῶν ταῦτα, Ναί, ἔρχομαι ταχύ. Ἀμήν, ἔρχου, Κύριε Ἰησοῦ.

21) Ἡ χάρις τοῦ Κυρίου Ἰησοῦ μετὰ πάντων τῶν ἁγίων. Ἀμήν.

20) *The one who is giving this testimony says, "Yes, I am coming soon." Amen. Come, Lord Jesus!*

21) *The grace of the Lord Jesus be with all the saints. Amen.*

"These things" are the things written in the whole book (cp v. 18,19). The one who gives this testimony is the Lord Jesus, who sent his angel to bear witness to these things. John reminds his hearers that he who alone can undo the seals of the book of the future (5:5) will most assuredly come. He has given us that promise. And when he comes he will forever deliver his people from the sufferings of this present time (Ro 8:18) and from dangers that threaten them in this world, and he will bring them safely into the holy city.

In this "post-Christian age," in which the ecu-mania of prominent church men has led them to downgrade the importance of doctrine and to give almost any heresy a right to exist in the visible church, and in which godless governments are once more making it difficult to be faithful unto death, we ought to be able to understand why John responds to the Savior's promise of a quick return with the prayer, "Yes, indeed, come, Lord Jesus." May he come soon to defeat those who have attacked his church from within and without! May he come soon to bring us to "the heavenly country bright," "the sweet and blessed country" where "no clouds his glory hide"!

"The grace of the Lord Jesus be with all the saints. Amen." With this benediction John reminds us that all the glorious blessings promised to us in the visions of Revelation are ours not because of any merit on our part but solely through the free grace of God in Christ. To him be all praise and glory forever! Amen.

CPSIA information can be obtained at www.ICGtesting.com
Printed in the USA
LVOW13*1504060913

351220LV00003B/3/P

9 780810 001909